"Good Morning, Dancers!"

A Practical Guide to Teaching Elementary Dance Arts

Karen Hahne

ISBN | 979-8-218-07698-6

DEDICATION

With warmth and gratitude, I dedicate this book to my dear friends and colleagues, the LAUSD elementary dance teachers, and their courageous and inspiring leader, Shana Habel. Thank you for letting me be part of your universe for so many years. I give you all the following poem . . .

Our Universe Dances
March 2022

A collection of completely unique, finely crafted, and brilliant points of light exists in the massive universe, and many planets revolve around each of them.

Each brilliant light shares its gifts with the many others it encounters in the universe and, in so doing, intensifies and recreates them all.

The lights all move in a colorful swirl, revealing every imaginable shape and wondrous formation.

Together, they organize to form a galaxy—complex, powerful, resilient, and ever evolving.

Lights dart in and out of the galaxy, defining unique paths and leaving trails of visible stardust in their wake.

Time passes, and NOTHING stays the same for very long, but long enough to leave an impression.

An imprint forms and re-forms the colors, configurations, and breathing life, of which each point of light is an essential part.

This galaxy is an entity unto itself, clearly defined by its purpose and will, traveling among many others.

Often overlapping, the points of light come together to blend beauty and form yet never yield their uniqueness.

Our universe consists of countless brilliant galaxies, ever expanding and changing, each along its own journey.

As one tiny point of light veers off into a new direction, it is proud and blessed to have been given permission to fly among the stars and be a part of their brilliant galaxy for a moment in time.

Fly on, my dear stars. Burn brightly into the future and remember to occasionally take a look at the breathtaking thing of which we are all part.

With burning love,
Karen, 2022

CONTENTS

Part VI. EXPERIENCING AND RESPONDING – The impact of your own and others' work

Part VII. APPENDICES – Resources and further information

INTRODUCTION

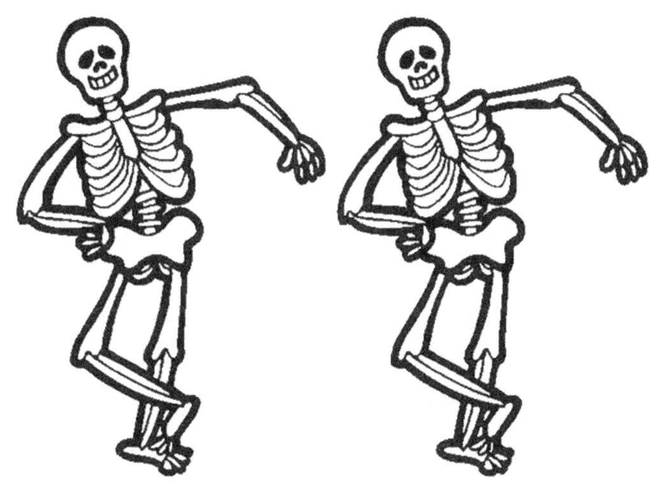

Dear reader,

I'm guessing you have picked up this book because your level of interest in the fine art of movement that is DANCE falls somewhere between marginally curious and deeply passionate. Wherever you are, it is my hope that this guide helps you in your quest to bring dance to young people, who will use the experience to grow into creative, confident, healthy, and loving beings.

First of all, the title. It's what I say to greet my students at the beginning of each class (unless it is afternoon, at which time I change the middle word). And I don't just say it with words—I move my arms and upper body in any way I feel moved at the moment, and they respond in kind. It's just a way of breaking the nonmovement ice.

As for the subtitle, this is a road map of sorts that I hope you will find useful in developing your own dance teaching practice. If you are already a practicing dance educator, you are probably often asked the question "What kind of dance do you teach?" People generally want a short answer to that question; and since what we do is so complex, I usually respond by saying, "I teach dance as an art form, so . . . a little bit of everything." That usually satisfies the casual inquirer. What I propose by the label *dance arts* is simply to include all aspects of this glorious art form in one two-word name, just as visual arts, theatre arts, media arts, martial arts, culinary arts, etc. do. In fact, dance includes so much that it makes good sense to refer to it in the plural, doesn't it?

And speaking of arts and since you have picked up this book, you probably have at least an interest in teaching kids. So you are aware of the fact that the arts enable them to open up and strengthen neural pathways in their brains, affecting all aspects of development, and are not simply a tool to be used to teach the "important stuff." The arts ARE the important stuff! Why learn language if you have nothing to talk or write about? The arts give meaning to our life experiences, document our history and culture, and encourage us to evolve as human beings. Put that together with the job of education, which is to give young people the tools and skills they need to be self-sufficient, resilient, and independent, and voilà! You have a gold mine of opportunity to offer in which young people can thrive!

In this book, I offer you what has helped me as a dance educator, which is an organizational framework that makes sense (well, it does to me anyway). Overthinking anything can make tasks unapproachable, and dance arts are so vast in scope and depth that to make sense of it all, an accessible structure is essential. Basically, that need is what germinated this book.

In the chapters that follow, I have attempted to organize and clarify a dance curriculum for children that can be used in the context of a school or community setting, where children are already brought together for the purpose of education, enrichment, or recreation. Private studio settings generally have a slightly different purpose—that being dance technique training. But certainly, the concepts outlined in this book can be included in any dance education setting.

The lesson examples in many chapters of this book have all been carefully constructed, practiced, revised, and practiced again and again. They could likely still be revised some more, but as teaching is a continually evolving thing, I will leave the next ideations to you.

You may find very conspicuous by its absence a whole chapter devoted to dance students with special needs or diverse learners. For me, it's simple: **all learners are diverse learners**, and **all students have special needs**. Dance arts (and many arts) tend to be great equalizers, and I have found that keeping differently abled students separated is counterintuitive, even in the context of a curriculum guide. On a side note: Many years ago, I had a conversation with a veteran advocate for special education students, and he proclaimed that "every student, with special needs or without, should have an IEP." And I could not agree more! Of course, the reality of life within our current educational system does not allow teachers to develop and carry out an individualized education plan for every student. But one can dream.

Anyway, in teaching (which is also an art form), adaptations and considerations for a multitude of learning differences can and should be made for every class we teach. Give yourself the creative freedom to do so since you are the one in the room who possesses the necessary wisdom and experience. And be forthcoming about asking for input from colleagues and other partners who might know your most diverse students well. I have found that they can be receptive to being included in the experience and usually have great insights.

Moving forward, it is my sincere belief that dance is an art form that is both liberating and informing; and here, I offer you some of my personal philosophies on that subject:

DEFINITIONS
The two words around which all of our work revolves . . .

***DANCE** IS THE ART OF MOVEMENT that involves the body, the mind, and the heart working in harmony with one another to create an experience that strengthens and expands the capabilities of all three.*

***CREATIVITY** is generating an original thought or idea influenced but not dictated by outside sources and personal experience and, by using skill and craft, transforming that idea into something that can be shared with others.*

GOALS
Areas where we should safely push our students' boundaries . . .

Goals for the body
- Healthy physical development
- Alignment of the spine, legs, arms, and neck
- Strength, stamina, and flexibility
- Coordination and precision
- Experiencing new ways of moving the *whole* body
- Injury prevention and safety

Goals for the mind
- Concentration, focus, and self-control
- Organization of sensory input (auditory, visual, kinesthetic, proprioceptive, and tactile)
- Awareness of time, counting, and rhythm
- Perception of space, distance, and shape
- Understanding of the laws of physics (motion, momentum, gravity, and force)

- Originality and craftsmanship in dance composition
- Making connections to prior knowledge

Goals for the heart

- Healthy social and emotional development
- Developing a feeling of belonging as part of a community
- Engagement and interest
- Making connections between inner feelings and self-expression
- Experiencing improvement and success (personal growth)
- Moving with confidence
- Discovering new abilities and talents

Thank you for your interest in dance education at any level. It is my sincere hope that this book is useful to you and helps you inspire a love of dance in others.

Moving on . . . and on . . . and on!

—KH

PART I
The Teaching Experience

Aspects of your role as
a dance educator

Chapter 1

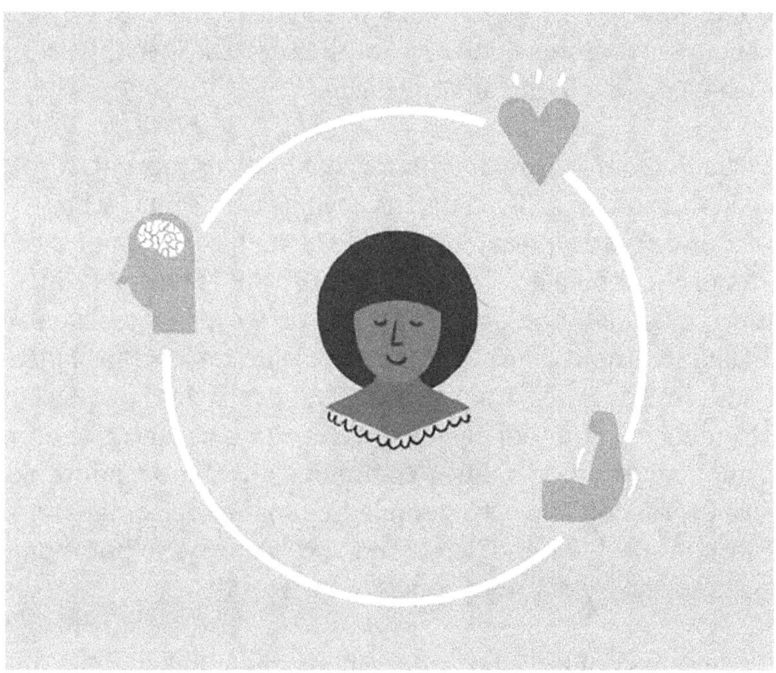

Self-Care
The dance teacher's physical, mental, and emotional well-being

If you are a dance teacher or would like to be, congratulations! You are part of an elite group of individuals who are creative, strong, flexible, determined, and full of life! It is not a job for those who prefer quiet and relaxation (especially if you are teaching kids). And it is not a job for those who like an easy paycheck without putting much thought or effort into their work. And it is not a job for those who don't wish to be inspired and uplifted while on the job. And of course, we are not in it for the money. Teaching dance is exhausting—on the body, the mind, and the heart. But it feeds and strengthens all of those parts of us as well. Since dance arts is such an intense field, self-care needs to be part of our job and not just relegated to our free time. You know what your body, mind, and heart need. But it helps to hear about what others do to care for themselves. So in this chapter, I offer what I do as a friend and colleague.

First, I would like to dispel the rumor that gives us teachers a gut punch in the area of self-worth. The saying goes **"Those who can, do; and those who can't, teach."** Ouch. But that is not the whole story. It should go on to say **"But DANCE TEACHERS can do both!"** We really don't have a choice, do we? Is it possible to teach dance without dancing? Maybe we didn't make the choice to have a professional performing career, but every class we teach is a performance, in front of an audience of students who give us an opportunity to share our gifts with them. It gives us a platform for creative expression and considerable freedom to do something with what inspires us. I, for one, am proud and fortunate to be among the most extraordinary of professionals in the world!

So the three legs of the stool are the body, the mind, and the heart; and below are some ways to keep the stool standing on all three:

Physical well-being. The best things for your body are the **absence** of the following: pain, injuries, stress, and fatigue. And for me, the first line of defense against these things is making an investment in comfortable and supportive SHOES. They can be costly but can mean the difference between looking forward to your next class and dreading it. As experts in body alignment, we know how every joint must be supported enough to handle whatever impact we apply to it. Our feet, being the first responders, absorb the initial impact, which continues through a rippling effect throughout the body. Shoes are the entry point.

The biggest problem I have found in teaching children is that their physical needs and mine are different. For example, children oftentimes need a frenetic release of energy and a higher level of impact to strengthen their growing bones and joints—both of which become dangerous as we get older. Have you ever noticed how children can't seem to help themselves when given the opportunity to stomp, run, leap, shake, and jump up and down really hard? As we often have a need to model certain movements at a certain level of intensity for our students, I have found it useful to identify students who exemplify the movement and ask them to demonstrate. In addition, it can be helpful to design choreography around commonalities between your needs and those of your students. Give yourself permission to both step out when you need to and bring them along for the ride at your pace.

Teaching dance requires stamina, and when class is over, the last thing we want to do is more exercise. I have found that changing little movement habits throughout my day to be a powerful preventative and therapeutic remedy. Regarding physiological function, a physical therapist once told me that "the strong get stronger, and the weak get weaker." This means that when there is a weakness, our bodies compensate by strengthening other areas. If you are able to detect certain weaknesses, either by experiencing pain or an inability to do certain movements, I highly recommend getting a consultation with a physical therapist or other body training professionals to determine what the need is and what adaptations need to be made to offset its effects. I know, we are considered body training professionals, and we are. However, it is difficult to look at ourselves in that way. Having another pair of eyes on us is necessary in some cases. Personally, I have found certain simple quadriceps stretches to be helpful in preventing some of my lower back pain. Also, pushing down on the floor with my feet while sitting in a chair and doing relevés while brushing my teeth have helped with core support and joint inflammation. Just some ideas.

Mental well-being. Our students, as well as we, need to experience a balance of challenge and success. Throughout our adult lives, we have likely accumulated many successes and overcome many challenges. That is just what we do to survive. A former colleague of mine used to define what she did periodically as "reinventing myself." This sounds overwhelming, but for me, it happens quite naturally and without any self-coercion. At a certain point, I just feel compelled to do something totally different, and I give myself permission to do so. This can mean approaching a concept in a new way, simplifying and going deeper into a concept, or even listening to and taking suggestions from students. These are challenges; and when we overcome them, our mental capacity is strengthened, and we feel empowered to take on the next one. One word of caution, however: don't try and change too many things at once. This can lead to confusion and a feeling of being overwhelmed. Pace yourself.

Making mistakes or even just having technical difficulties, such as a sound system malfunction, can also lead to new discoveries in what is really important in your teaching. Trust yourself to be able to flow with it. Keep notes on lessons and update them periodically, but don't throw away the old ones that worked. Sometimes bringing things back after not using them for a while can remind you of past success. I have found dance lessons to be in a constant state of evolution.

Emotional well-being. It would be really easy right here to offer suggestions such as taking a long walk on the beach, sipping wine with friends, or taking up a new hobby when you are feeling down or burnt-out. But hey, you know that already. Instead, when you reach a point where you are no longer inspired by the lessons or choreography you are teaching, there are several things you can do to regenerate as part of your job.

First of all, play music YOU LIKE! And change it up when you get tired of it. Your students will probably not mind, and doing this can breathe new life into your work. Create movements and dances that interest you, and make connections to the curriculum, which should not be too hard to find. If you find a quiet and private moment in your school or studio, put on an inspiring song and let yourself improvise. I don't do that very often, but when a moment inspires me, it helps to remember why I chose this profession in the first place—that feeling unlike any other. I have found that no matter how stressed I might be feeling going into a class, when the music starts, everything is suddenly OK; and I let it be.

And finally, don't disregard the love that children bring. They may hide it well, but occasionally, they let it spill. If you are lucky, some of it will land on you, so soak it in and let it grow. Peace.

Chapter 2

Notes on Child Development
Observations of where your students are at and what to expect of them

Knowing what to expect out of your young dancers at various stages of life is as essential as knowing the subject you are teaching. What we always want is for our students to walk the thin line between success and challenge in their learning; and knowing what we can, and cannot, expect of them will help us see more clearly where that line is. Whether we want to admit it or not, we are teaching the whole child, which includes their physical, emotional, mental, and social development. Yes, ALL of them!

Many years ago, a great music teacher that some of my children had in middle school proclaimed, "I don't teach music. I teach kids!" And are we not the same? We identify as dance teachers, but maybe we really are *dancing kid teachers*. Sounds pretty good to me!

Regarding Students with Special Needs

I have found that nearly any concept/lesson can be simplified, modified, scaffolded, or adapted and made appropriate for students at all ability levels. I give myself permission to do so with all of my dance lessons.

The best situation I have found is when students with special needs are included in classes of students without special needs (as if there is such a thing). That way, students can be "buddies" with one another, and lessons can be structured around partnering. Keep in mind that some students who may be chronologically in the fourth or fifth grade could be functioning at a first- or second-grade level. However, it would not always be appropriate to simply teach them a first- or second-grade lesson, which still might be too complex.

Also, the difference between a child's developmental age and their chronological age is most likely not the same across the board in all areas of development. For example, a child may be ten years old but may have an intellectual disability, which causes them to function in some areas at about a six-year-old level. However, this child is still a ten-year-old and has four more years of physical growth and life experience that has resulted in greater physical strength and taught them many things, such as popular cultural and community norms or practical skills, such as computer gaming and using tools and devices.

If you have the opportunity to get to know your students with special needs, I recommend focusing on an area of their development where they are functioning relatively high and designing your classes to accentuate and build upon their strengths. You may think this is counterproductive and that the most obvious approach would be to remediate the areas where the student is delayed. But think about it: how would you like it if everything in your learning life was focused on things you weren't good at? Might be discouraging. And maybe the saying "a high tide lifts all boats" could apply to student learning simply because confidence comes from success and builds the courage needed to face more challenging tasks.

Below are simply some brief observations I have made over the years of being both a dance teacher and a parent of what children at each grade level can and should be doing. I have also provided a **main theme** in a single word, plus its definition, for each grade level that I think sums up where they are in their development and a way in which they are able to learn.

Prekindergarten

EXPERIENCE: *"To make practical contact"*

Preschool students are both delightful and challenging. They have likely never been to school before, so it is really important that they have a strong and positive first impression. Our role as dance educators presents a great opportunity to give them just that!

Many of my dance lessons for students between the ages of three and five years include variations of familiar songs. Young children, who are easily distracted, can have their attention focused by using a multisensory approach. Getting the students singing, moving, touching, listening, and watching all at the same time leaves them little opportunity to do anything else, which may ease anxiety about being away from home, as well as build neuron connections in the brain to help organize sensory input. Avoid talking to them too much and explain things in clear and concise ways, including using demonstration and visual aids, such as pictures and objects.

The word *experience* reminds us that much of what we are bringing our youngest students is likely something they have never done or seen or, yes, experienced before. Right before our eyes, they are moving their bodies in brand-new ways and gaining awareness of their own abilities. Our job is to let them indulge in this process with the knowledge that they are figuring it out for possibly the first time, and hopefully, it will be a time that inspires them to continue along a healthy and creative path. We are leading these little colts to water, and they will most likely drink!

A word about teaching credentials: Most multiple-subject teaching credentials begin at kindergarten (with the exception of early childhood education), and single-subject teaching credentials span from kindergarten through grade 12. Both the California Arts Standards (CAS) and the National Core Arts Standards (NCAS) include pre-K in all art forms, so I feel it is justified to include standards-based lessons for this age-group.

Kindergarten

DISCOVER: *"To find in the course of a search"*

Most four- and five-year-olds are still highly motivated by multisensory experiences, and of course, dance is in that category. They are curious about everything they see and often will not hesitate to reach out and touch, ask, or change the subject toward what it is that's at the forefront of their mind at that moment. They are still developing language, so they tend to sometimes make grammatical errors and use unusual combinations of words, which are mostly adorable.

This group of students may or may not have been to school before, and you will probably be able to tell the difference by their level of receptiveness to following directions and working with others. The good news is, most young children learn quickly when surrounded by others who demonstrate certain listening and behaving skills. Two helpful concepts for students at this age are OPPOSITES and PATTERNS. They are learning about many aspects of the world, and these simple structures can help their young minds organize all the information they are taking in. It is fairly simple to apply dance concepts using both of these structures.

Regarding social and emotional learning for this age-group, they are primarily focused on themselves, which may seem egotistical; but it is where they need to be in their development. However, gently helping them look outside themselves while keeping the focus inward is beneficial, and activities that do that are built into dance learning.

To help our students *discover* new abilities with their bodies, we can guide them through the experience of moving in new ways AND expect them to remember and take notice of what they have done. We can also encourage them to use initiative to seek out and try new things. Look for the light bulbs going off in their heads and all over their bodies!

First Grade

EXPERIMENT: *"To undertake a procedure to make a discovery"*

I have found this age-group to be full of surprises! They are able to embody ideas that you think they would not understand, and they can explain them in simple and often-insightful terms. They seem eager to try new things with their bodies and are learning some limitations and safety practices. This is a great age to begin developing good movement habits, such as standing with straight legs, bending knees when jumping, and lifting and supporting the spine.

There seems to be a broad range of abilities and skill levels in this age-group. Most likely, they have been to school before and are at least familiar with how school works and what is expected of them. But of course, they are still learning a lot of that. At this age, students can combine concepts and are eager to explore new things they can do with their bodies. They are also emerging from focusing on themselves, are able to collaborate and work with others on simple projects, and can function as part of a group. Making friends comes easily to most and is of primary importance, and dancing can provide an easy way to help them do that.

At this age, children are ready to **experiment** using the abilities they have already developed in new ways. We can give them the opportunity to begin making creative choices within a clear and simple structure. They will enjoy the journey when they can see the destination and be able to find something new when they arrive.

<u>Second Grade</u>

PRODUCE: *"To make something from raw materials"*

Children at this age can do so much! They have been in school for two to three years and are usually quite proficient in how to function in school and are eager to learn many new and multilayered concepts. Dance elements of space and time are easily explored simultaneously and in several different ways. Working in partners is also an effective practice for students at this age and level of development since they are beginning to learn and practice social skills and empathy in one-to-one relationships.

Intellectually, second graders are exploding in their understanding of abstract concepts and humor. They are capable of participating in group activities and sharing their ideas. They respond to others' comments, both negative and positive; and of course, positive reinforcement goes a long way! They are extremely talkative at this age, which is important for their development of language. However, at times, the chatting can go too far and should be gently reined in. Providing them opportunities to talk one-on-one with each other can meet their needs and yours.

Physically, students at this age are developing quite a bit of strength and coordination and are ready to take some risks and be challenged. Movement habits and techniques for safe physical training, such as proper alignment of the body, can be emphasized and reinforced at this age.

We can certainly expect our second graders to use initiative to **produce** a wide variety of dance patterns and sequences following multistep processes. If we give them the ingredients, they can put them together and begin to discover their own creativity along the way. Of course, guidance is needed, and our job is to find a balance between structure and just the right allowance for independence.

<u>Third Grade</u>

INVENT: *"To make up something that has not existed before"*

This is a time of rapid growth in children, and it is obvious in the various physical sizes of students in a class of third graders. Some look much older, and some much younger. Kids at this age are high-energy and are very eager to learn and try new things. They have a lot of skills and want to do something with them, and they are able to work independently with minimal assistance.

Their social circles are starting to expand beyond gravitating to a single partner, which means they can work very well in small groups, communicating and interacting with multiple teammates toward a common goal. In fact, they seem to be focusing more toward friends and the media and are influenced slightly less by family. They also seem to be in a period of rapid emotional development and can become moody and easily set off by comments or actions of others. Often, our job as teachers includes counseling, doesn't it? Also, the tone and mood we set in our classes has a big influence on children of this age.

Creatively, students of this age are on fire! They are curious and ready to take risks—if they feel emotionally safe. They are ready to test their own abilities, **invent** new things, and really enjoy stepping back and looking at what they have done and take pride in their accomplishments. They can handle somewhat complex and multilayered activities, such as a process that has three steps or intentionally creating movements that include the elements of time, space, AND energy. They are also able to comprehend more sophisticated academic language and vocabulary.

<u>Fourth Grade</u>

DEVELOP: *"To grow and become more advanced or elaborate"*

At this stage of life, children seem to be beginning to define their own identity. For their whole lives, they have heard what others have to say about them; and now they are using that information—along with their own experiences, likes and dislikes, self-awareness, and, unfortunately, the media—as influences to begin to form their own unique personalities. They are quite independent at this stage and can take responsibility and make judgments and intelligent choices. They are friendly with adults rather than fearful, and they are not afraid to ask questions, which are usually good ones! They are very observant, and their attention can be focused in productive ways; however, they can also be hyperfocused on flaws and inconsistencies in themselves and in others. Fairness is important, so I have found that explaining the reasons for everything and being consistent and transparent are helpful policies, especially since they can listen to lengthy explanations better than younger students can.

Physically, they are growing at a rapid rate, as you will see in the wide range of sizes in a given group; and their bodies are starting to tighten up a bit due to bones growing faster than muscles and connective tissue. It is important to remind them to be gentle when they stretch but also to understand how important it is for them to do so for the sake of their lifelong flexibility and skeletal health. Emphasis on correct alignment of the knees, hips, and shoulders are extremely important.

Creatively, these minds are very active and often will attempt to do more than is necessary, which can lead to confusion and a sense of failure. This is because they are becoming aware of the connections that exist between so many of the various things they are learning, and they are trying to make sense of it all. They can pay attention to detail and use all the information they are taking in to **develop** and form complex dance studies. Just be sure you are there to guide them when needed and allow them some creative freedom. Their eagerness for an opportunity to do or create something of their own can potentially take them off on a tangent, which might also be an example of the beginnings of defiance of authority. If they are getting too far off, simple reminders of the purpose or point of the task at hand can help refocus their efforts. And the end result might have a very inventive and unexpected twist!

<u>Fifth Grade</u>

CONSTRUCT: *"To build or make something by organizing ideas"*

As a teacher, you can have high expectations of your students at this age! Their intelligence and creativity will not cease to surprise and inspire you. They are defining and elaborating on who they are and what they like and dislike; and those preferences are made very clear by their affect, choices, and even by what they wear and who they attempt to emulate. Their social connections are strong, and best friendships can begin, and bonds form over any activity. They desperately need opportunities to communicate with one another, share ideas, and collaborate; and they can do so within a complex multistep process.

Of course, their lives outside our dance classroom are the highest in importance to them, and it is helpful to remember that influences can range from healthy and nurturing to destructive and frightening. We have the opportunity to provide them with a healthy vehicle for self-expression if and when they need it. They may exhibit various behaviors, such as eye-rolling, whispering to each other, or even refusal to participate. I try not to take these gestures personally or allow them to escalate into real problems but rather see them as the individual's way of expressing their level of approval of what is being asked of them. Their image in the eyes of their peers is of such great importance to them that risking embarrassment can be overwhelming to some. Do everything you can to de-emphasize judgment between them and of them.

Maintaining good physical/technical habits is essential as they might be approaching adult size, and of course, puberty is looming large in all aspects of their lives. Emotionally, their passion for certain ideas or issues is apparent; and through our art form, they have an opportunity to explore, define, and, of course, express their own opinions.

A fifth grader's capacity to see and understand abstract ideas is so much fun to work with as well. Setting up creative assignments that require them to **construct** a work of art as individuals or in groups is the best way to keep their very busy minds engaged. If not too much time goes by between your dance lessons (say a week at the most), carrying projects over multiple classes can give them a sense of accomplishment and investment.

Sixth Grade

BLEND: *"To combine into an integrated whole producing a harmonious effect"*

When children get to be this age, they may have formed opinions about what dance is and whether or not it has any meaning to them. Also, they are practically consumed by the influence of their peers and will often define their own level of interest in something based on that of a close friend. They can be extremely judgmental of one another and of themselves, which can interfere with their creative learning, especially when it comes to anything to do with body image. Unfortunately, dance has a really bad reputation for placing high value on that. With students at this age, it is important to focus hard on the intent of the movements, the effort with which a movement is performed, and the craft used in constructing a dance study rather than the appearance of certain individuals.

By now, most of the students have grown to nearly their adult height, and reinforcing safe and healthy physical habits is essential. They commonly say "I can't do that" when asked to do something they think might make them look foolish, such as a deep plié, a high jump or leap, hip movements, or a tricky step pattern. Sadly, when they say things like that out loud, they are only convincing themselves that it's true. Their bodies, however, are still quite pliable; and as teachers, we can constantly remind them that practice and work can make dramatic change. I like to remind them that maybe they can't do something as well as they would like right now, but with practice, they most certainly can. Not trying is the only way to ensure that they can't!

Developing an aesthetic eye is possible for students at this age. Hopefully, they have had opportunities to practice various art forms and even dance in their lives previously, and creativity is part of the whole arts education package. At this age, students can flow through the creative process making choices along the way, using skills and craft to **blend** together just the right mixture of all of the elements of dance to complete and perform an end product of which they can feel proud and in which they become invested. Giving them ample opportunity to revise and improve their work is helpful, but if carried on too long, there is the risk of fatigue turning into disinterest in the project. Finding the right balance in that regard can make or break their enthusiasm for your classes, which is already hanging in the balance.

Chapter 3

Professional Team Participation

Being part of a greater learning community

As a dance educator, there are probably two, and possibly more, teams of which you are a valued member: (1) your dance colleagues, with whom you can share expertise, and (2) your school or community site partners, to whom you bring your unique perspective as an arts educator.

Whatever your relationship with your learning communities (e.g., as a colleague, an itinerant teacher, a classroom teacher, a parent, a volunteer, or an outside teaching artist), as a dance educator, you are in a unique position to bring something of great value to your community. You also have the responsibility of being an ambassador of the arts and being the best possible representative of dance that you can be simply because you might be the only one of your kind in your school community. Also, it is important that you become an asset to the school rather than a burden, which can require negotiation skills.

Your first responsibility is, of course, to the students, who will likely remember their early dance experience as a rich and lively aspect of their childhood. Your level of participation with other various teams will, of course, depend on their size, scope, and purpose. It may be true that 80 percent of the work in any group is done by 10 percent of its membership, which is a ratio that members of all teams need to work to improve.

AMONG ARTS COLLEAGUES

This relationship is vital! Your dance educator colleagues are the best resource you have when in need of inspirational ideas, continuing education opportunities, and—let's face it—emotional support because they are the only other people who know and can truly appreciate what you do. Arts educators of other disciplines are also a source of great inspiration and fellowship, and collaboration between art forms can open doors to new and exciting perspectives.

Keeping in regular touch with your dance community can be done fairly easily with the availability of Zoom, FaceTime, and other messaging platforms, plus telephone, email, and text messaging. Of course, the very best way to connect is in person, where the fullest and most lively connections can be made. Whenever possible, build regular standing meetings into your teaching schedule and keep open the possibility of connecting with colleagues one-on-one when needed. Also, setting up and working on projects together, such as lesson studies, can breathe new life into your practice.

AMONG SCHOOLS OR COMMUNITY PROGRAMS

In your role as a dance or arts ambassador at your site, call upon your ability to negotiate by seeking compromise without sacrificing your most basic needs. Resources are often stretched, and historically, the arts bear the brunt of budget cuts. Also, if you are a temporary or itinerant team member, you will likely not be the highest priority of the school or community setting simply because you are not there all the time. Unfortunately, out of sight, out of mind holds true. Remember, it is not because you are not important, but being a part of everyday life is different from being even a frequent visitor.

Considerations for successful participation as an outside specialist/educator:

- **Purpose** of your being there in the first place
- **Program scheduling** and frequency of lessons
- **Space**, where your classes will be held and what is needed
- **Length** of each dance class for optimal learning
- **Inclusion** of students with special needs
- **Classroom teacher participation** in a school setting
- **Classroom and student behavior management**

Putting the pieces of this puzzle together is an art in itself! Of course, the situation at each school or community setting is unique, but a few things remain consistent. First of all, student welfare and safety are the highest priorities. From there, boundaries may be defined with which you can customize your program. For example, if the only appropriate space on a school campus is available only certain days of the week or hours of the day, your program will need to be scheduled around that.

Purpose

Whether your reason for being at a school or community site is to provide studio dance instruction, be part of an after-school program or enrichment, provide a break for classroom teachers, enhance the advanced studies/pull-out curriculum, be part of an arts education cohort, or simply produce a show, you and everyone around you should be clear on why you are there. Your program should be developed with that overarching purpose in mind.

Program Scheduling

There are several ways to create a schedule for students to receive the most out of a dance program. Daily, twice-weekly, or weekly classes are the best options for students to learn and retain the skills you are there to help them develop. Dance classes less frequent than weekly are not recommended due to the amount of review that will need to be done, especially for the younger learners.

Daily classes are best for the purpose of putting together a performance. Short-term frequent instruction builds needed momentum that carries a group up to and through the performance process. Too much is forgotten if days go by between sessions, and more review must be done. The downside of this schedule is the high impact it would have on the school or community. This model reflects more of an artist-in-residence situation. Also, units of study in other content areas are usually taught daily, so why not dance? Reshaping and enhancing brain function occur most effectively with greater frequency.

Twice-weekly classes are ideal for a somewhat short-term session, such as twelve to sixteen lessons total over the course of six to eight weeks. This provides students with a fairly short time lapse between classes, which aids in their retention and reduces the need for lengthy review. It can also be effective if working toward a performance at the end.

Weekly classes seem to fit in well with existing school and community program schedules around which classroom teachers and families can plan. However, it is the least effective for student retention of concepts, vocabulary, and skills practice; and it is not practical if working toward a performance.

A personal story from when my children were young includes a swimming program that was part of their elementary education. The swimming teachers insisted that the students have class for thirty minutes DAILY for two weeks. They stressed that this was the best way for them to learn and retain aquatic skills. Without question, the school complied, and every student received swimming instruction on that schedule. For one of my sons, who experiences developmental delays, remarkable change was seen during the swim session. His first grade teacher at the time shared with me that she wished he could swim every day for the whole year due to his increased alertness and general higher functioning during that short period of time!

Another program in which this same son of mine once participated was called Lose the Training Wheels. It was designed to help older children and adults learn to ride a two-wheeled bicycle. It was very specific in scheduling: five consecutive days for seventy-five minutes each day, followed by fourteen days at fifteen minutes per day. Considerable research had been done to determine this schedule, and their claim was that was the best way in which the older brain could learn the skills needed to ride a bike. My son participated strictly on this schedule, and by the end, he was able to ride a bike! To this day and without having to relearn the skills, he still can ride whenever he tries, which is only occasionally.

My point in sharing these stories is that our young dancers are learning skills and developing movement habits that will remain with them throughout their lives, and dance is a healthy and powerful way of helping them do that. The more consistent and frequent, the better!

Space

Refer to chapter 4, "Your Teaching Space," for more details.

Your dance space MUST be as follows:
- **Available** when your classes are scheduled, and you should never be displaced without adequate notice (minimum of twenty-four hours)
- **Large enough** for all students in your class to stretch their arms out in all directions and not touch anyone else
- **Well ventilated** with functioning heat or air-conditioning and access to fresh air
- **Well lit** with both natural and artificial lighting
- **Clear** of all obstructions
- **Safe** and free of hazards, such as wires, unsecured items that might fall, and excessive amounts of boxes or furniture
- **Clean** enough for students to touch and move on the floor (teacher must have access to a broom, dustpan, and mop at all times)
- **Private** enough for students to maintain concentration and experience dance to the fullest extent (some distraction is unavoidable, but you may need to ask passersby not to draw attention to themselves, or you can put up a polite sign)
- **Equipped** with a chalk, dry-erase, or pin-up board and a sound system or access to electrical outlets to plug in your own

Class Length

The length of each individual dance class is a thing to be considered, and there are several factors at play in determining this aspect of your teaching schedule. Again, you must consider your purpose when deciding how many minutes your dance classes should be.

If elementary school students simply need a "dance break" for fifteen to thirty minutes, it is hardly worth making the transition to another space on campus and involving a highly trained and experienced dance educator in person. Many great videos are available for this purpose.

If a school or community program is committed to providing students with a standards-based dance program with an in-person professional educator at their site, the classes should be **between forty and sixty minutes** in length. The shorter time is better suited for pre-K and kindergarten students, and the longer length is better for older students simply because of both the high level of physical exertion and focus needed to participate in dance instruction.

Inclusion

Regardless of your setting, welcoming students with special needs to your dance classes is beneficial for everyone! The most important consideration is that they have the support they need, which will vary from individual to individual. If you are part of a school, there will be highly skilled professional educators and support staff as part of the community who will be the people to turn to when you need specific information on students' needs.

I have found the most effective way to include all learners in dance is by integrating those with special needs with those without. However, students with special needs have just that—special needs! They may require the support of someone who knows them better than you and who can inform you of what the best strategies for success might be or certain equipment or modifications that will allow them access to your curriculum.

I encourage you not to feel like you need to have access to every student's IEP—that is unrealistic. But communication with those who do can be helpful.

Classroom Teacher Participation

If you are teaching in an elementary school setting and don't see your students frequently enough to remember their names, you might not know them well enough to effectively manage every aspect of their moment-to-moment needs. In this case, the presence of a familiar and informed adult, such as their classroom teacher or teaching assistant, is essential. The level at which that person participates in dance instruction is broadly variable. First and foremost, it is the dance educator's job to provide instruction in the art of dance and address some of the basic needs of the students, such as tying shoelaces or tending to any basic health-related needs they may have (such as whether they should be allowed to leave class to use the bathroom). However, that line is blurry when it comes to children. Every adult they come in contact with should be there to provide needed support. When it comes to actual instruction, the classroom teacher has valuable information regarding the personality dynamics in the classroom and some of the routines they already know, which could aid in the smooth flow of dance instruction, so collaboration to some extent is highly recommended.

Classroom and Student Behavior Management

Students can and should know what is expected of them in any situation at their school or community program, and since dance instruction with a new and possibly unfamiliar teacher could confuse them, it is best to align your expectations for behavior with those of the school or community culture. Of course, there are some norms that are unique to dance, and those should be spelled out clearly to students and reinforced often or as needed.

For example, talking while dancing interferes with breathing, distracts others, and makes it impossible to hear directions or the music. So it should be kept to a minimum. A potential issue is what students wear, such as hoods, sweaters tied around waists, or skirts without shorts underneath—all of which can compromise safety. If students are unable or unwilling to participate with the group in dance class, it could be effective to find another way for them to remain engaged, such as observing their fellow students dancing to look for certain aspects of the concepts you are teaching, drawing or writing about what they see, or even directing a group if they are able. I don't recommend using participation in dance class as a reward or nonparticipation from it as a punishment. It should be considered an essential and expected part of their day and not be variable.

In summary, being part of a professional or school community team includes many overlapping considerations—none of which should be ignored. Finding a way to make them all fit together to provide dance education is our goal, and it is a lofty one indeed!

Chapter 4

Your Teaching Space
Creating a safe and effective dance environment

In the world of dance, we don't need a whole lot of "stuff." What we need most to provide high-quality dance instruction is simply this:

SPACE!

In a school setting, the auditorium, multipurpose room, or an empty classroom or bungalow would be suitable. The space must be large enough to allow each dancer to stretch out in all directions and not touch another dancer, a piece of furniture, or a wall. It must be cleared, free of hazards, and the floor must be clean enough for children to sit on. Another consideration is proximity to other classrooms due to the use of music; and also, if there is a classroom below, the sounds of jumping or leaping could be a disturbance.

Note: Something that could occur to a dance teacher, especially one who works in a school setting or other location where their teaching space is used for multiple purposes, is that you are either temporarily or, longer, **displaced**. This is extremely inconvenient, especially if insufficient notice is given. However, rather than canceling your great classes and depriving the students of dance (even temporarily), it helps to have a few tricks up your sleeve that will enable you to teach rich and purposeful lessons in an alternative and perhaps less-than-optimal space. Please refer to **appendix H, "Good Lessons in Limited Space,"** for examples of specific lessons that can work either in a school classroom or in a smaller-than-usual space.

In general, some things that enable groups of students to dance freely in limited space are dividing the group either in half or into smaller groups, where they take turns performing dances that would normally be performed by the entire class. Also, limiting the range of movements used to those that stay in place can enable large groups in small spaces to move more freely. Remember that safety is important, and it is a better idea to alter the structure of your lessons than to have students running into one another or being afraid to extend their limbs.

CREATING A SAFE AND EFFECTIVE PHYSICAL ENVIRONMENT

- **SIZE:** Your students need enough space to move freely without bumping into one another. This will depend on the number of students in a group and how old they are since smaller bodies take up less space. If your teaching space is not large enough, accommodations must be made, such as dividing the class in half or having groups of students practice and perform movements rather than everyone at the same time. Also, having students arrange themselves in lines is the least efficient use of limited space. Either staggering lines or allowing students to find their own "space bubble" gives them an opportunity to develop the skill of spatial awareness!

- **FURNITURE:** You really don't need much. But it helps to have a chair on which to sit between classes, a table for your sound equipment and lesson materials, and shelves, hooks, or another surface on which the students can place their sweaters and other personal belongings. An unobstructed wall, whiteboard, or large easel is needed for displaying visual materials as well.

- **LIGHTING:** Bright is good, and of course, as much natural lighting as possible is the best.

- **VENTILATION and TEMPERATURE CONTROL:** Windows and doors that open to the outside provide fresh air, weather permitting. Also, working heat and air-conditioning with proper filtration are essential. Considering that you will likely be increasing the temperature of the space with many moving bodies, set the thermostats accordingly.

- **HAZARDS:** Any furniture, boxes, or other items in the space should be either removed prior to welcoming in dance students or at least moved well out of the way so as not to be dangerous. Tape can be used to secure any loose wires or broken floor tiles as needed.

- **FLOOR SURFACE:** Whether it be wood, tile, linoleum, or cement, the floor needs to be clean and free of debris or any large cracks, bumps, or holes that could cause someone to trip. Having access to a dust mop, broom, and dustpan is essential.

- **SOUND:** Your sound system must be of high quality and loud enough for everyone to hear. Speakers should be placed above students' heads, if possible, and far enough away to not be too loud in the ears of the students who are closest to them.

The question regarding holding dance classes outside often comes up, possibly because there is no other space available. I believe there is a time when holding a dance class outside is advised, and that is **when you are rehearsing for a performance** that will be held there. Otherwise, outdoor dance classes are ill-advised. Here are several reasons why:

- **Weather:** You have no control over the temperature, wind, or precipitation outside; and extremes in any of those can cause adverse health and safety issues. Also, if you are teaching all day, it is unrealistic to expect you to be outside in the elements for an extended period of time.
- **Distraction:** Keeping children's attention outside where there is so much going on is a challenge, and this can be exhausting for the teacher. Familiar and unfamiliar people going by, traffic, and animals can all prevent your class from staying focused on dance.
- **Sound:** You will be playing music, which would likely be a bit louder than you would need to indoors. So if there are any nearby classrooms or neighbors, they might not appreciate the disturbance. Also, voices need to be projected outside, causing further stress on the dance teacher and possibly requiring the use of a microphone, which may or may not be available.
- **Surface:** The ground outside is not likely to be as smooth and clean as an indoor surface can be, and this can pose increased danger of injury if a student slips and falls.

CREATING A SAFE AND EFFECTIVE EMOTIONAL ENVIRONMENT

Learning environments need to be just as emotionally safe as physically. In any classroom, children need to feel they belong there and that they can express themselves without fear of criticism or humiliation. The arts are unique in that participation requires a certain level of honesty and even vulnerability—and not just in one's words, but in their actions as well. And nothing bares the soul more than movements of the body—it simply cannot lie!

It should be emphasized in dance classes that bodies do not have to look a certain way to be "dancers' bodies" and that participation in any way counts. I have found that singling students out for moving freely and expressively is powerful, especially when it is a child who you may notice to be shy or withdrawn.

Since dance is an expressive art form, encouraging expression in the body is a BIG part of being a dance educator. If a child feels intimidated, they will do what they need to do to protect their own feelings, and that usually means being less expressive. This is the exact opposite of what we want! Helping young people develop into whole beings, which includes their artistic side, requires strengthening their sense of self and boosting confidence in their own abilities and feelings. Exploration of emotions is the only way young people can hope to have control **over** their own feelings rather than being controlled **by** them.

Sadly, children can be cruel and hurtful to one another, which is not entirely their fault. They may not have learned enough empathy to know how their comments and looks can affect their peers. Our job as teachers, no matter what subject, is to help children learn and grow in all areas. So it is important to emphasize that hurtful comments or gestures of any kind are not permitted in your classroom. In the twenty-first century, when people are more and more isolated from one another because of the fear of deadly viruses and further involvement with technology, we need to go above and beyond normal guidance in helping children learn this. This means taking advantage of the teachable moments as they arise and allow the students to right any wrong they may have done that resulted in hurting someone else's feelings. This may take away from your dance teaching time, but it is worth it in the long run. Children need to know how it makes others feel when they do or say hurtful things, and I don't think we should just write them off as them simply being kids and not knowing any better. We must help them realize that they can make a choice to be "peacemakers, not peacebreakers" (thanks to Antonio Aguilar, principal of 186th Street Elementary School in Gardena, California, for this little bit of wisdom).

Chapter 5

Assessment
Measuring progress, learning, and performance quality in dance

What does assessment mean in the arts and, in particular, dance? It may be that we are in the process of inventing it right now! Historically, dance has not been taken seriously enough as a subject in education to warrant a formal assessment process. Subjectivity prevails, and there really is no standard for creativity, right? Maybe. If we look at dance learning more carefully (and creatively), there are several things we can assess to determine whether or not our young dancers have learned, as well as what or how much they've learned.

As Grammy winner Jon Batiste said when accepting his 2022 award for album of the year, "There is no best musician, best artist, best dancer, best actor. The creative arts are subjective, and they reach people at a point in their lives when they need it most." Mr. Batiste's humility is admirable, and it must be considered that he and all other award winners are singled out because of the contribution they have made to their field. Presumably, this is based on some form of measurable data, possibly derived from assessment, objective or subjective opinion, observation, comparison to criteria, and/or the tallying of votes.

This chapter explores three ways to evaluate performance in dance—two of which are about student learning (teachers evaluating students and student self-assessment), with the third being evaluation of the dance teacher. Note: if you are employed by a school district, they will have a teacher evaluation process that will apply to you, which may or may not be meaningful to your job description.

First of all, some clarity is needed regarding the difference between the words **assessment** and **evaluation**. The way I understand the difference is that assessment has to do with the gathering of measurable data regarding the nature, quality, or ability of a subject's performance, while evaluation implies a judgment made about the same. Often, the terms are used interchangeably, and the differences are subtle. However, if you think of it as a four-step process, it makes more sense:

1. Establishment of a goal, rubric, criteria, or standard
2. Observation to accurately determine what the subject is doing
3. Comparison to established goal, rubric, criteria, or standard (assessment)
4. Formation of an opinion or judgment as to how the subject performed (evaluation)

First, regarding the traditional way assessment works, teachers evaluate student progress, learning, and performance.

For upper elementary grades and middle and high school students, written tests are a possibility just to evaluate a student's knowledge and memory of some of the facts, names, history, and other details you have taught them. But that should certainly not be the entirety of your assessment of their dance learning. I believe that the most authentic assessment of a student's learning in dance is what they can demonstrate through movement. This includes their demonstrable attitude, level of participation, and growth over time.

Below and on the following page is a guide intended for teachers who are responsible for grading their students in dance. It can be adapted to fit nearly any dance learning activity, and details can be added that are specific to the performance and the concept the students have been practicing, which will only broaden the range of your evaluation. Dance teachers need to be agile in their assessment criteria, and the topics listed are general enough to apply to both formal and informal performances that your students give. This is also in appendix G, "Handouts."

A Guide to Grading in DANCE

Use the many opportunities you will have to observe and evaluate your dance students, even starting from the first lesson—from the warm-up routine, through movement skill practice, and in informal performances held throughout your class sessions. The following are the most general and universal abilities to look for in dance:

- **Memorized the dance pattern, phrase, or study**
- **Started and stopped on cue and moved with the music**
- **Performed all movements correctly and safely**
- **Was engaged in activity and danced with expression**

It is my opinion that each of these holds equal weight, and their abilities in each category can be evaluated on any numeric scale you choose and then averaged to calculate their grade. Below is an example of a chart you might find useful in keeping track of your students' learning in dance.

Beyond the above four criteria, others that are more specific to each lesson can be simultaneously evaluated. If any of the above is not observed or applicable, other criteria could be used, such as the ability to follow a clear pathway in space, demonstrating the use of correct timing with other dancers, or clearly showing various energy qualities through movements. There is a blank column on the far right of the chart below for this purpose.

STUDENT'S NAME	Memorized the dance	Moved on cue, with music	Movements done correctly	Engaged, showed expression	

If a teacher prefers to evaluate their students' PROGRESS in dance over time, they can use a piece of choreography that they learn at the beginning of the session and practice often enough for them to show improvement. A consistent ritual or warm-up that is performed at every class is a way to make those necessary observations. Observing them at the beginning of the semester, trimester, or quarter and again at the end can give you this data. In addition, video is a powerful tool that allows you to observe multiple students at a time, capturing a moment in time for many, equally.

Besides the type of summative assessment described above, formative assessments (e.g., reflective journal writing, drawing, or documentation of other activities) can provide you with deep insight into your students' understanding of the concepts you are teaching and how you taught them. If your students keep a dance journal, this would serve as a portfolio to their learning and provide you with something to grade if that is part of your job.

Second, students evaluate their own progress, taking ownership of their dance learning.

With practice and a certain level of consistency, students can learn to objectively look at their own work. The key word there being "objectively" so as not to get personally involved so that it becomes emotionally traumatic.

Video can also be used for students to self-assess and can be extremely effective not only in determining progress, but also in branching out into eventually setting personal learning goals. Remember to show a video of a student performance at least twice—first to let them watch whatever their eyes are drawn toward and subsequently to focus on what they need to be assessing. Depending on the students' age, develop a number of points to look for in the video and allow them to give themselves either a thumbs-up or thumbs-down if they demonstrated it or a numeric value to how many times the group demonstrated the concept.

Evaluating the data can then lead to the setting of group goals, such as "more clearly demonstrate low level movements," "enter and exit on cue," or "remain quiet while dancing."

Ideally, a combination of multiple modes of assessment throughout your work with your students would provide the most comprehensive assessment, upon which you could base an evaluation of your students' progress, learning, and performance in dance.

Third, dance teachers can either compare their own competencies to the following checklist or share the seventeen criteria with their supervisor when being observed.

What Effective Dance Teachers Do

	OBJECTIVE	WHAT TO LOOK FOR	HOW TO MEASURE
1	Adapt the environment to ensure the health and safety of all students	Is the environment safe, free of hazards, and appropriate for dance? And does the teacher check on students' condition/well-being?	Observation of environment and teacher behavior
2	Engage students	Calculate the percentage of time students are involved in an activity. Observation of students' affect—do they appear interested in what they are doing?	Calculation and observation of student behavior
3	Include all students	Tally the number of students not participating or minimally participating (categorize).	Tally and observation of student behavior
4	Apply effective teaching strategies	Can students access the curriculum? Do they understand? Is the task developmentally appropriate?	Observation of student behavior and performance
5	Use multiple modalities	Checklist of modalities used: Visual images or objects Auditory explanation (words, music, or sounds) Modeling/demonstration Imagery	Observation of teacher behavior and materials

6	Check for understanding	Does the teacher monitor student work in progress?	Observation of teacher behavior
7	Maintain student involvement	Does the teacher find ways to reengage students who stray off task?	Observation of teacher and student behavior
8	Give useful and meaningful feedback	Is there an individual or group discussion regarding the work? Does the teacher guide but not dominate the conversations?	Observation of teacher behavior
9	Respond to students' needs	Does the teacher prioritize on the spot and respond to the highest need?	Observation of teacher behavior
10	Provide a curriculum that makes sense and is transparent	Do the lessons make connections to prior learning, have clear and immediate goals, include a long-term plan, and build upon each other?	Review of lesson plans (including scope and sequence)
11	Enable students to experience a balance between success and challenge	Does the teacher provide added challenges when an assignment appears too easy and scaffold when too difficult?	Observation of teacher behavior
12	Have a deep knowledge AND understanding of dance	Can the teacher answer students' questions and engage in diverse topics within the realm of dance, making them relevant to students' lives?	Observation of teacher behavior
13	Provide a positive role model	Does the teacher maintain a positive attitude, avoid sarcasm, and dress and behave as she/he expects students to?	Observation of teacher behavior
14	Effectively manage student behavior that interferes with learning	Is there evidence that the teacher is able to extinguish disruptive behavior as it arises? And are there effective routines, clear expectations, and meaningful consequences for student behavior?	Observation of teacher behavior, evidence of routines/known consequences

15	Enable students to engage in exploration of novel movements	Do assignments include an opportunity for students to experience something new?	Observation of student behavior
16	Monitor student progress over time	Does the teacher point out or keep track of what students were able to do at the beginning of the session (or semester) and their progress to their current status?	Observation of teacher behavior, evidence of tracking (notes)
17	Adapt lesson and learning environment when unexpected circumstances arise	How does the teacher handle unexpected situations, ensuring the learning environment and lessons are still rigorous and fit with the overall plan?	Records or lesson plans of alternative lessons given in response to unforeseen changes in the environment or schedule

PART II
Curriculum Overview

A broad and sequential
view of what dance
teachers could teach

Chapter 6

Curriculum Structure
Providing a comprehensive dance learning experience

All accredited schools follow state standards, which have been developed and scrutinized by a committee of experts in each content area and approved by the state Board of Education. The arts are no different, and in California, this process happened and was finalized in 2019.

The way in which the most recent California Arts Standards, in all five art forms, is organized is a direct reproduction of the National Core Arts Standards (NCAS, 2014) (https://www.nationalartsstandards.org/). The advisory committee that approved the California version made some changes to the wording of the individual standards, but the structure and intent of the national standards remain unchanged.

The curriculum structure I have developed and use is similar to the structures of both the California and national standards, but with some changes to the progression of the concepts that make better sense to me than those adopted by the California Department of Education. Let me be clear in that **standards** and **curriculum structure** are two different things; and what I have done for my own clarity and for the purpose of this book is to create a curriculum that is COMPATIBLE with, but not dictated by, the California Arts Standards for Dance (see appendix A, "A Quick Reference Guide to the CAS for Dance").

The biggest structural change I have made is the order of the four *artistic processes*. In both the National and California Arts Standards for Dance, they are in this order:

Creating – Performing – Responding – Connecting

However, for my purpose and functioning as a dance educator, I believe that these four processes make sense but should reflect a logical flow in which children can best experience dance education. What I have done is rearrange (slightly) and refine the naming of the same four artistic processes from the CAS. The shaded box that follows is a brief explanation of why I believe this rearrangement is needed. Following that, in the chart with the shaded headings are lists of what will be explained in more detail in chapters 11–24.

<u>A Logical Progression of a Dance Education Curriculum</u>

When learning dance, the first thing that happens is to simply get in and start moving. Dance students need to see a clear example and TRY IT! With a skilled teacher to guide them, they can explore their body's abilities and experience movement in space, in time, and in relationship to others, as well as with energy and purpose (the elements of dance). I call this part . . .

SKILL BUILDING AND PRACTICE

Once students gain confidence in movement, they can embark on the creative process and begin to develop their own voice, finding inspiration and using various choreographic tools and devices to craft their work. I call this phase . . .

CREATING AND COMPOSING

In the process of becoming a dance artist and becoming part of the dance-making community, they can explore their place in it by making personal and community connections in context to the greater and broader world of dance. I call this part . . .

CONNECTING AND RELATING

With all this experience, the young dancer is in a position to step back and look at what they have done and what others have done and, with an experienced and thoughtful eye, take what they have learned to the next level. I call this part . . .

OBSERVING AND RESPONDING

In both the National and California Arts Standards, there are eleven anchor standards that are consistent between all art forms, which is a beautiful equalizer in my opinion. There are so many more similarities between the arts than there are differences that it makes perfect sense, and this format is based on that truth.

In the curriculum overview on the following pages, I have outlined fourteen categories that could conceivably parallel the eleven anchor standards. However, you will find these to be dramatically different and specific only to dance. The reason I have made these changes to the curriculum structure I use is that in studying the CAS for dance, I find them to be by design broad and somewhat nonspecific. This enables great freedom for educators in developing a teaching curriculum. However, personally, I need an organizational framework that is designed around what I do that will help clarify my intent and weave all the various aspects of my teaching together. The curriculum structure I have developed serves my purpose much better, and it possibly will help other dance educators as well. Please know that it is not meant to replace the standards and only serve as an additional tool through which to use them.

SKILL BUILDING AND PRACTICE – The *elements* of dance and the whole dancer		
<u>BODY</u> *What the dancer uses as an instrument and fine-tuning its capabilities* • warm-up • movement skills • body parts/isolations • shape • yoga • elevation • counterbalance	**<u>SPACE</u>** *Where the dancer creates a visual design* • in-place and traveling • direction • levels • size • pathways • focus	**<u>TIME</u>** *When the dancer starts, changes, or stops movements* • beat • rhythm • tempo • timing • duration • phrasing
<u>ENERGY</u> *How the dancer makes movement happen and gives it meaning* • flow • weight • force • energy qualities • Effort Actions • textures	**<u>RELATIONSHIP</u>** *Who the dancer is and with whom they are dancing* • character • objects • spatial relationships • formations • grouping • musicality	**<u>PURPOSE</u>** *Why the dancer must dance and the dance must exist* • fun • exercise • belonging • celebration • learning • spirituality • practice • history • storytelling • creativity • expression • friendship • culture • tradition • romance • communication

CREATING AND COMPOSING – The *craft* of constructing original work		
INSPIRATION *Generating ideas and transforming them into movement* • visual images • objects • stories • poetry • music or sounds • books about dance • emotions	**CHOREOGRAPIC TOOLS** *Constructing a dance from movements* • improvisation • Principles of Design • design tools	**PERFORMANCE** *Sharing your work with an audience or community* • staging • audience behavior • production elements • performance readiness

CONNECTING AND RELATING – The *context* surrounding creativity		
HISTORICAL AND CULTURAL CONNECTIONS *The role of dance in the human experience* • what dances can reveal • why dances exist • who creates dances • where on earth dances come from • how dances are structured • when dances have been created	**PERSONAL EXPERIENCE** *Expressing students' own lives, identity, and culture* • sharing our ideas and stories • group identity or heritage • current events or issues • our own version of world dances	**INTEGRATION** *Blending dance with other subjects* • science • math • language arts • social studies • visual arts • theatre • music • PE

EXPERIENCING AND RESPONDING – The *impact* of your own and others' work	
PARTICIPATION *Inside perspective* • self-assessment • making adjustments • receiving feedback / defending choices	**OBSERVATION** *Outside perspective* • developing a critical eye • developing and expressing an opinion • offering feedback or suggestions

Chapter 7

Enduring Understandings and Essential Questions
Tools to help identify learning goals and plan instruction

The famous work by Wiggins and McTighe *Understanding by Design* (2005) offers a framework referred to as **backward design** for designing courses and content units. This approach begins by developing student learning goals, then determines acceptable evidence of student learning and, finally, designs instruction intended to achieve the desired goals. Helpful tools to determine these design components are what are commonly known as **enduring understandings**, which are big ideas and specific knowledge students will be expected to acquire at the end of the lesson, AND **essential questions**, which students should be able to answer to determine if they have attained the established goals.

One way of using this framework is by looking at each dance lesson as a microcourse and create your own enduring understandings and essential questions. Once you practice a bit, they are not that difficult to write, and simply because there are some written into the California Arts Standards for Dance doesn't mean those are the only ones you can use. Give yourself permission to write what YOU want your students to understand and answer. They can be as specific or as broad as you want.

The California Arts Standards for Dance include one enduring understanding and one essential question for each of the eleven anchor standards that are broad enough to span all grade levels (see appendix A, "A Quick Reference Guide to the CAS for Dance"). What I offer on the following pages are samples of four enduring understandings and four essential questions specific to each grade level that are aligned with each of the four artistic processes outlined in chapter 6, "Curriculum Structure" (which are slightly different from the CAS). These examples are broad in focus and were simply designed to guide the curriculum in general rather than specific learning goals.

Prekindergarten	
Enduring Understandings:	**Essential Questions:**
• Dances can be memorized and performed again. • What a dancer can see, hear, and touch can give them ideas for movements. • Personal and community experiences can be shared through dance. • Dancers can demonstrate movements that they see others perform.	• *How do dancers stay safe?* • *What comes to mind when we perform different movements?* • *Why do people all over the world dance?* • *When we watched a dance, what did we see?*

Kindergarten	
Enduring Understandings: • Descriptive opposite pairs can guide how movements can be performed. • Dances are made of patterns of movements. • Dances from other places can have meaning to us. • Dancers watch each other and talk about what they see.	**Essential Questions:** • *What are some ways we can change our movements?* • *How does our imagination help us to dance?* • *How do dances express emotions or personal experiences?* • *How do we talk about what we see?*

First Grade	
Enduring Understandings: • Movements can be changed in space, in time, and with energy. • Dance can express ideas and emotions and can tell stories. • We can make connections between other cultures and our own by watching or performing dances. • We learn about dance by dancing and by watching others dance.	**Essential Questions:** • *What must dancers do to move with control and awareness?* • *Why is it important for dancers to try new movements?* • *How do dances from other places compare with dances we know?* • *What can we learn when we watch others perform?*

Second Grade	
Enduring Understandings: • Dancers have an awareness of self and others while moving through space, in time, and with energy. • Dances can be created to express a main idea. • Dances have personal meaning to the people who created them and to the observers. • We can watch for specific things in a performance and share our ideas with others.	**Essential Questions:** • *Why are relationships between dancers important?* • *How do choreographers put movements together?* • *How do dances tell the stories of people and places?* • *What do we look for in a dance to help us understand its meaning?*

Third Grade

Enduring Understandings:	**Essential Questions:**
<ul><li>Choreographers use the elements of space, time, and energy to make changes to their movements.</li><li>We can create our own movements or learn movements that others create.</li><li>Dance is an important way to explore the world and its people.</li><li>There are many similarities and differences between dance styles and genres.</li></ul>	<ul><li>*How can movements be changed to make them more meaningful?*</li><li>*How do choreographers invent new movements?*</li><li>*How do the movements in dances communicate their creators' culture and beliefs?*</li><li>*How are dances or dance genres similar to and different from each other?*</li></ul>

Fourth Grade

Enduring Understandings:	**Essential Questions:**
<ul><li>Dancers develop and use technical skills to utilize the elements of dance.</li><li>Dance movements can be improvised and can be developed, set, and memorized.</li><li>Dances reflect the people who created them and the environments and times in which they are created.</li><li>There are similarities and differences between and within all dance styles and genres.</li></ul>	<ul><li>*How do choreographers manipulate the elements of dance to express their artistic intent?*</li><li>*How are ordinary movements transformed into dance with purpose and meaning?*</li><li>*Where does dance belong in society or culture?*</li><li>*How do movement patterns and other artistic choices create a style or theme?*</li></ul>

Fifth Grade

Enduring Understandings:
- The elements of dance are integrated to create rich and dynamic movements.
- Choreographers make purposeful movement choices to develop and communicate a main idea.
- Dances share important aspects of the environment, history, culture, and beliefs of the people who created them.
- The meaning of a dance can be interpreted by its patterns, characteristics, and relationships.

Essential Questions:
- *How can all the elements of dance be reflected in one movement?*
- *How do choreographers organize ideas to construct dances out of movements?*
- *How does dance contribute to building community and cultural identity?*
- *What makes a dance work artistic and meaningful?*

Sixth Grade

Enduring Understandings:
- Artistic intent of a dance is achieved through use of the elements of dance, dance structures, and context.
- Inspiration for dance can come from connections made between multiple sources.
- Qualities of a dance communicate its cultural, historical, and/or community purpose or meaning.
- Dance reinforces personal views or offers new knowledge and perspectives.

Essential Questions:
- *How can the elements of dance be used to transfer ideas into choreography?*
- *How do dancers and choreographers develop a dance study that supports an artistic intent?*
- *How does dance contribute to society and community?*
- *Why are some movements more or less effective than others in expressing an idea?*

Chapter 8

Class Structure

What a rigorous and effective dance class includes

A well-structured and purposeful class, in any subject, is a cornerstone of pedagogy. How your dance class is structured can determine how much or even whether your students learn. A comprehensive and rich elementary dance class could include a smooth-flowing sequence of the following activities:

- **Introduction** (at rest, five to seven minutes)
- **Warm-up** (moving, five to ten minutes)
- **Presentation of new concept** (at rest, two to five minutes)
- **Exploration and practice** (moving, eight to ten minutes)
- **Composition** (moving, ten to fifteen minutes)
- **Performance** (alternating moving and resting, five to ten minutes)
- **Response** (at rest, two to five minutes)

As you probably noticed, alternating physical exertion and rest is built into this structure, and it is important to find a good balance between the two.

Introduction:
This is a transition for your students into your class. Always give them a warm and welcoming greeting to let them know that they are in a safe space and you are glad they are there in that space with you. If they come in wound up, misbehaving, and being unsafe in your space, it is helpful to ask them to go outside and try entering the space again, pointing out what you expect of them. After all, rehearsal is one of the many gifts of the performing arts, is it not? Get a sense of their mood by observing body language and affect and endeavor to meet them where they are, then gently guide them to where they need to be to learn dance.

Review with them what happened in the previous class if there was one. Or introduce yourself and ask for their prior experience in dance if not. Discuss what they can expect in class that day and what the goals are.

Warm-up:
Helping young students get into a physically and emotionally receptive state can set the stage for them to feel ready to participate in your dance class and do so with confidence. I begin all of my dance classes with what I call the *opening ritual*. The purpose of this is to give the students a bit of space to relax, focus on themselves, and notice how their bodies feel. It is a variation on the eight movement patterns of Anne Green Gilbert's BrainDance (see appendix B) and is done seated. Being a ritual, my hope is that the students will appreciate the moment of consistency and gain some inner peace and clarity by engaging in it.

My warm-ups are choreographed dances that last between about five and nine minutes, depending on the grade level; and besides the physical exercise part, I include skill practice in various components of some of the elements of dance (time, space, and energy). My intent is for them to experience something like a mini dance technique class at the beginning of every lesson. I believe there are more than a few benefits to having a consistent choreographed warm-up. The students will know what to expect. They can feel improvement over time; and after the first three to four times doing it, they can volunteer to lead, enabling the dance teacher to more closely observe the students and make corrections as needed. The downside of doing a choreographed warm-up can be the risk of burnout doing the same dances over and over again. When I experience this, I have found that simply changing the music and re-forming the components of the dance to fit a new and inspiring song can breathe new life into the dance.

And a note on music (sorry for the pun): I encourage dance teachers not to be influenced by requests by their students for music choices. Play what YOU like and expose them to music they may not have heard before. There is so much great music out there in the world. They don't need to hear their favorite songs again and again. Also, their preconceived ideas about a familiar song will likely overshadow what you are trying to do.

After the warm-up is completed, it is a good idea to let your students check in with how their bodies feel. A simple feel of the heartbeat and deep breathing to slow it down are good ways of decompression after physical exertion. If it is your first class meeting or their first time doing the whole warm-up, I recommend taking a few minutes to ask the students (or they can think-pair-share) how their bodies feel. I dedicate the first two classes in any series of classes to teaching and practicing the opening ritual and the warm-up dances. After that, it only takes about the first ten minutes or less of each class. By the end of your classes together, you can ask the students again if they feel any difference in their bodies. The responses might inspire you!

Presentation of new concept: Some dance classes are discrete, and others build upon each other. In either case, presenting the concept you are about to teach them should be fairly brief, but comprehensive enough to give them an understanding of what to expect. You can always say "I will explain more about this later" if you find you are talking too much and the students are getting restless. During this step, the dance teacher may need to demonstrate a concept, and that is usually a good way to transition to the next step where they are up and moving again. Always check for connections to prior knowledge, be transparent about purpose, briefly explain process, and use visual images to help illustrate your intent (see chapter 9, "Using Visuals, Objects, and Props").

Exploration and practice: After your presentation of the new concepts and explanation of the process, then it is their turn to get up and try it out for themselves. During this time, depending on the level of independence and prior experience your students have, you can either dance along with them if they need a model or stand back and observe, providing verbal prompts and checking for understanding. Pointing out students who appear to understand and can demonstrate the concept can serve two purposes: (1) giving those students a big boost of self-esteem and (2) providing the others with a model that is not you. Providing feedback and do-overs is helpful to ensure your students truly understand and are successful at practicing new concepts.

One necessary outcome of this step is to generate material to use in the next step, which is composition of original work. So whether you use the term or not, *improvisation* is what you are doing in this step.

Composition: Now that your students have had an opportunity to practice a skill and have possibly generated some movement material, the dance teacher must guide them toward forming that material into a structured work. Working as a whole group, in small groups, or in pairs and giving clear directions and examples of the end result are ways to achieve success in this phase. Keeping things simple is a good rule of thumb, but if it seems the assignment is too simple, give yourself permission to add complexity to the task. During this step, if the students are ready, they could work independently on a composition project. The dance teacher can then rove around from group to group, providing assistance as needed. Also, when students are in independent work mode, I have found it very effective to provide them with occasional time announcements, letting them know they have five minutes, one minute, or ten seconds to wrap up what they are doing to prepare for a showing.

Performance: Since there usually isn't an audience from outside the class ready and waiting to see a show, students must do that for one another. Dividing the class in half to perform a large group dance or having small groups, pairs, or individuals take turns while the others observe provides a built-in audience. This is also your opportunity to help them learn audience behavior and remind them of the enormous difference between sitting at home watching TV and watching a live performance. You can also provide them prompts of what to look for while watching their classmates perform, thus developing a critical eye while observing dance.

Response: After watching an informal dance performance in class, students might have a lot to say about what they saw, especially if you told them ahead of time what to look for. Asking individual students for their observations is a great way to get a sense of what they are seeing. However, that is the most time-consuming way. Pair-sharing is very effective and gives everyone a chance to express their opinion to someone. Asking for a show of hands is also effective when pointing out what they might have seen. Please refer to chapters 23 and 24 for more details on encouraging meaningful response from students.

Also, in school settings where you know you will be seeing your students again and if you think they will remember and have time, giving homework assignments can be effective in expanding upon your lesson, using a different modality. It also might provide you with needed material for the following lesson. Journal writing is also an excellent way of bringing your students' thoughts back to dance when they are not in class with you.

Here is a simple template that outlines what to include when planning lessons:

Grade or age of students:	**Dance concept(s) / lesson title:**
Standards addressed:	**Student objectives:** *Students will be able to . . .*
Key vocabulary words:	**Materials needed:**

Essential question: *What should the students be able to answer at the end of this lesson?*
Lesson/activity description:*
Follow-up activity / homework:

Chapter 9

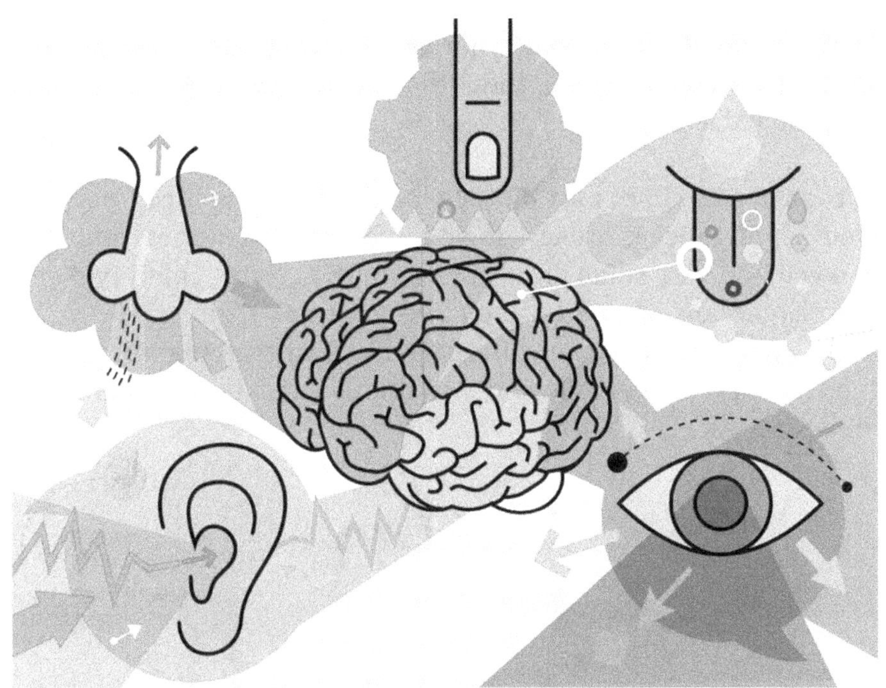

Using Visuals, Objects, and Props
Enhancing multiple sensory and learning modalities

This chapter is FULL of pictures, which makes sense since it is about multisensory learning experiences. It wouldn't do for a chapter about visual and tactile stimuli to have nothing but words! Illustrations make learning so much more comprehensive and can stimulate multiple areas of the brain. I use A LOT of visual illustrations for nearly every concept I teach, and I find that students refer to them often and tend to remember things that have visual representation beyond my verbal explanations. I have also heard many comments of appreciation from classroom teachers, especially special education teachers, about the visuals I use, which is why they are included in this book.

In chapters 11–15 of part III, "Skill Building and Practice," each element of dance is broken down by concept categories; and you will find very small illustrations under each concept heading. I use larger versions of these pictures on small signs that I show when introducing a concept. Here is an example from the element of *time*, followed by a brief explanation of what I might say:

Timing

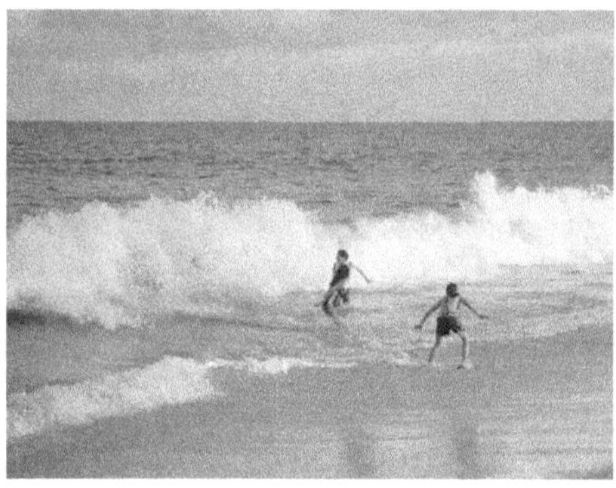

"Dancers need to know how to perform movements at exactly the right time. Just like when you are swimming in the ocean and a wave is coming. To avoid being knocked down by the wave, you need to jump over it at just the right moment. If you jump too soon or too late, the wave will knock you down." Students seem to understand this explanation of what timing means. Of course, many other

examples could illustrate this concept, such as swinging a baseball bat or crossing the street when the light changes. But this was my choice.

By the way, at the risk of stating the obvious, YOU are by far the best visual aid you can share with your students. Demonstration is our most powerful tool and especially the passion with which we use it! Students pick up on that more than what they could from any picture or object, and that is the beautiful spell we have the ability to cast upon them in our teaching.

A note on using video to enhance learning: I admit that this is where I fall utterly short in my personal teaching practice. There are, of course, countless video resources available to educators; and to use them effectively, we must have the time to both research and curate our selections, the technology to store and access them, AND the necessary devices with which to screen them on-site. All of those have been obstacles for me. Making your own videos is valuable, and you can customize them to fit the concepts you are teaching. The only drawback to that is that students will not be seeing authentic dance as part of the greater world of art and culture.

The photos that follow are of many of the visuals I use. With the exception of the fine art examples, all of them are homemade simply by utilizing my computer and printer (with the help of Google images) plus readily available school supplies, such as poster boards, paper cutters, construction paper, glue sticks, and lamination (highly recommended). I have also found it very enjoyable to design and create my own posters, exploring the tip of the iceberg that is graphic design. All of the actual signs, posters, and objects are in color.

To store large posters, I use a portfolio case that measures approximately twenty-six by twenty-one inches, in which larger posters can lie flat and not be damaged. For smaller signs or cards, an accordion-style file folder can be used the same way.

The following visual examples are in alphabetical order and are referenced to the chapter or appendix that further explains their purpose:

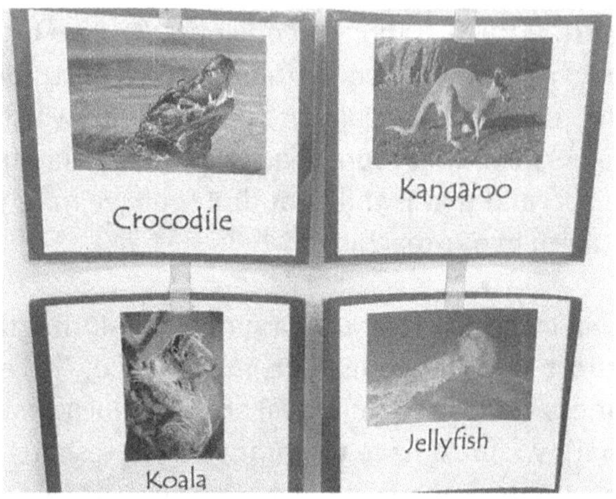

Australian animals. Used with the FORCE MATRIX (see the force matrix poster in this chapter and see chapter 14, "Element of Energy"). Crocodiles BURST, kangaroos REBOUND, koalas PRESS, and jellyfish FLOAT.

Beanbags. These can be used in either of the two dances Obwisana or Sansa Kroma, both from Ghana (see appendix D, "World Dances"). It is much safer to pass these from hand to hand than it is using the traditional rocks. These beanbags are fairly small, about two by two inches.

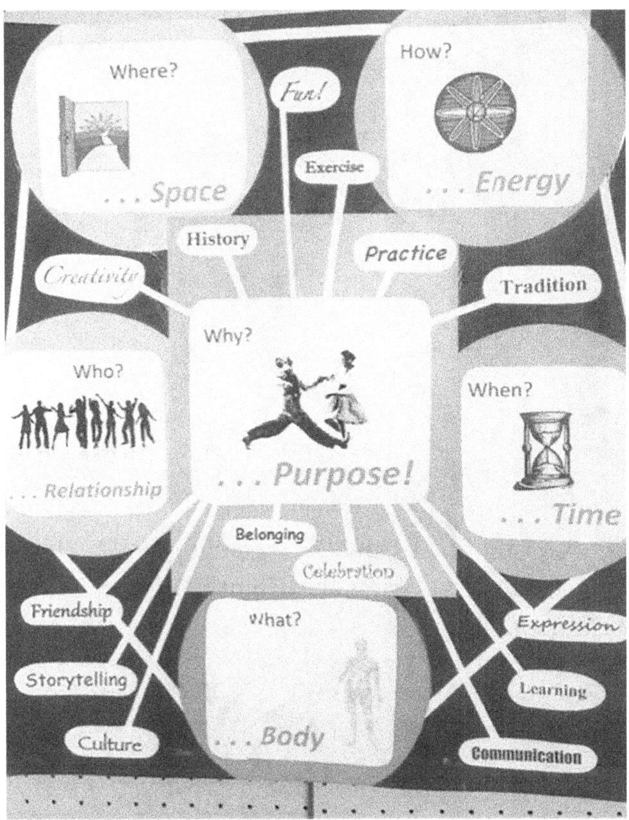

Bubble map poster. This is a general overview of the six elements of dance, all of which are interconnected. Keeping something like this up all the time allows you to refer back to it and even quiz students into which element the concept they are learning about falls. The small white bubbles indicate the many reasons why people dance (see chapter 16, "Element of Purpose").

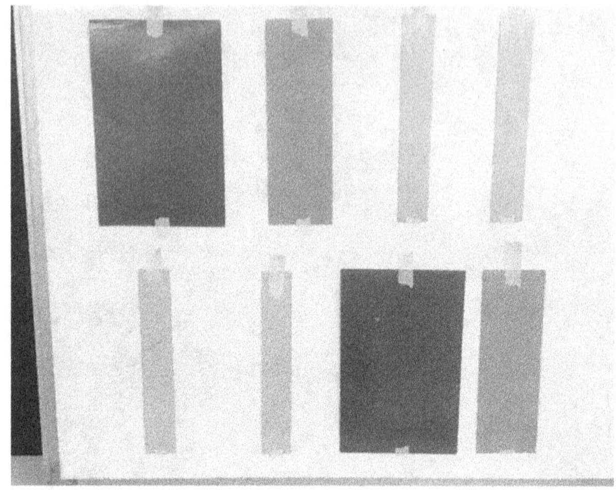

Color cards. Used for DURATION (see chapter 13, "Element of Time"). Black (widest) represents eight beats, brown (midsize) represents four, and orange (narrowest) represents two.

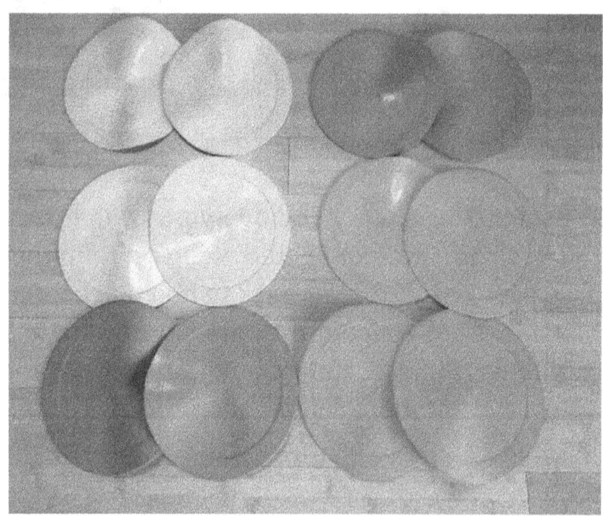

Color spots. Also known as *poly spots.* These are used for marking areas or places on the floor. They are not intended to be handled but rather used as a visual guide when students need one in space. Each pair is a different color.

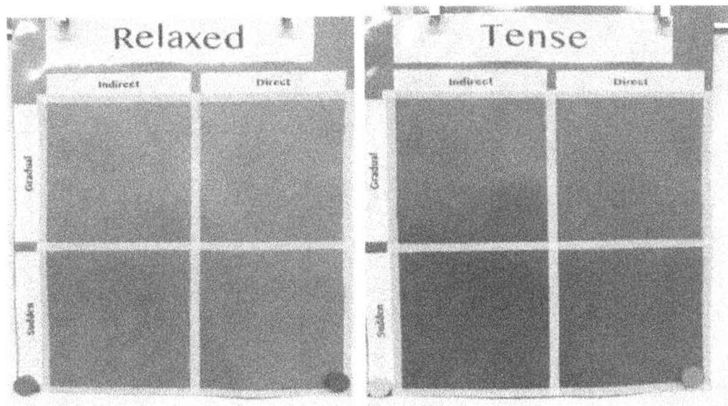

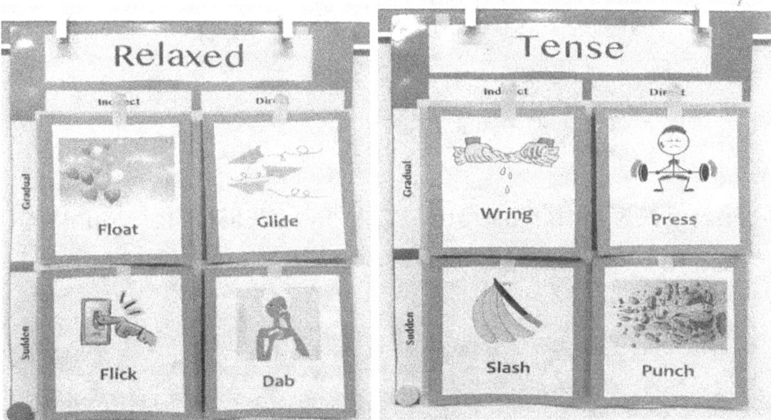

Effort Actions. Two matrix grids used to illustrate Laban's eight Effort Actions, blending relaxed or tense FORCE, direct or indirect FOCUS, and sudden or gradual TIMING (see chapter 14, "Element of Energy," or appendix C, "Element of Energy Deconstruction").

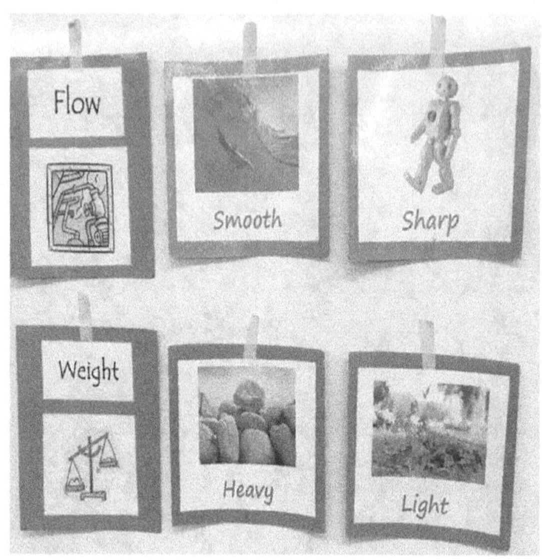

Energy. Used to illustrate FLOW and WEIGHT for younger elementary students (see chapter 14, "Element of Energy").

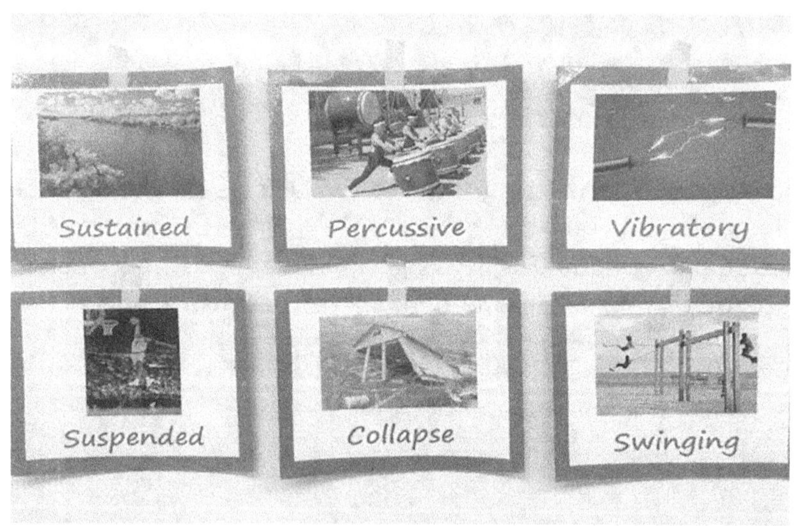

Energy qualities. Used to illustrate the six ENERGY QUALITIES (see chapter 14, "Element of Energy," or appendix C, "Element of Energy Deconstruction").

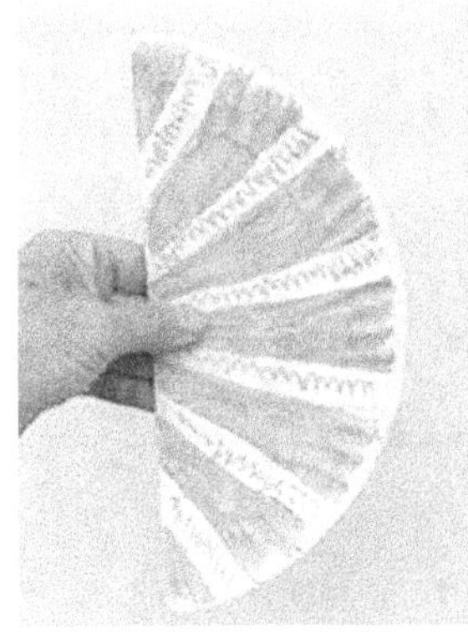

Fans. Made from paper plates and used for the Chinese fan dance connected to FLOW (see chapter 14, "Element of Energy," and appendix D, "World Dances").

Fine art. Diego Rivera's *Flower Festival* (see chapter 17, "Inspiration").

Fine art. Vincent van Gogh's *Starry Night* and Salvador Dalí's *The Persistence of Memory.* Used for ENERGY QUALITIES (see chapter 14, "Element of Energy").

Fine art. Pablo Picasso's *Three Musicians*, segment of Sandro Botticelli's *Birth of Venus*, M. C. Escher's *Relativity*, and Georgia O'Keeffe's *Red Poppy.* These four works of art are used for PATHWAYS (see chapter 12, "Element of Space").

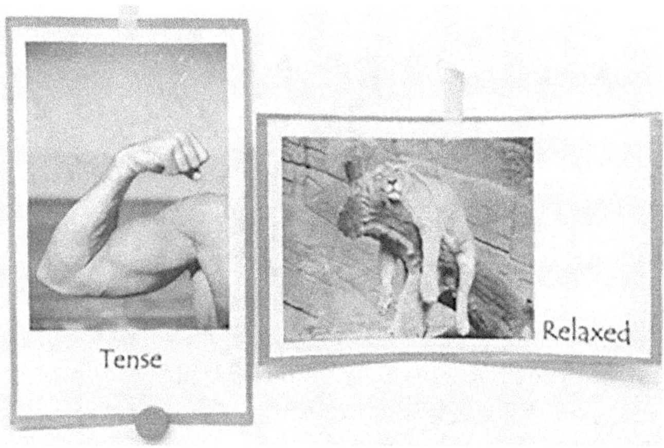

Force. Used to illustrate tense and relaxed FORCE (see chapter 14, "Element of Energy").

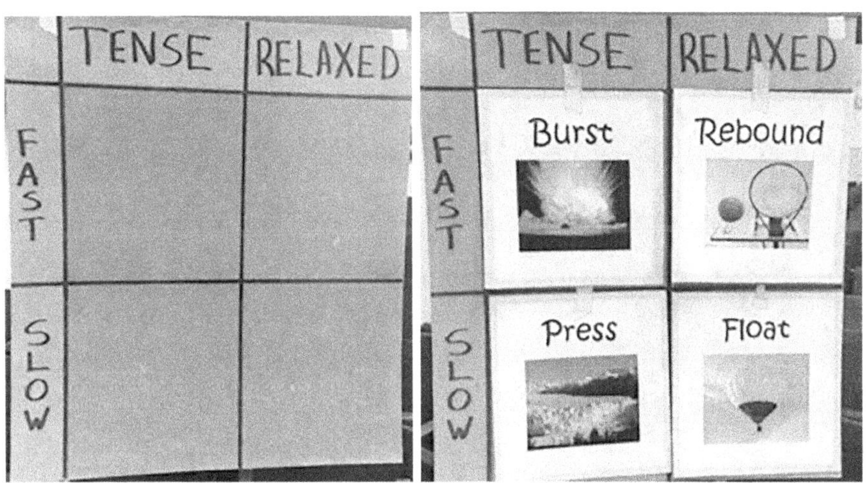

Force matrix. Used to illustrate the blending of tense and relaxed FORCE with fast and slow TEMPO (see chapter 14, "Element of Energy").

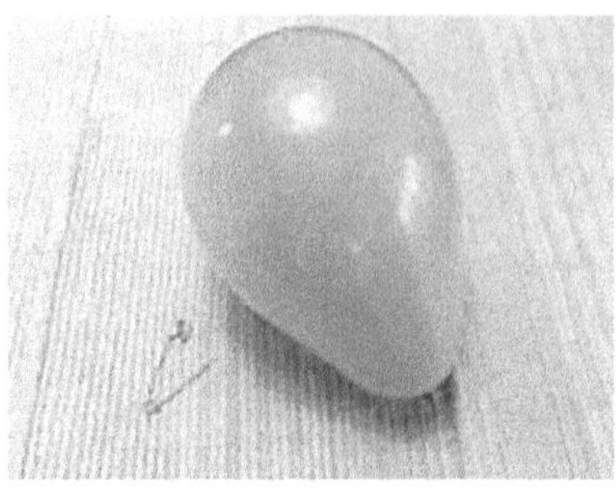

Force matrix demonstration. An inflated balloon demonstrates all four energies on the force matrix above. Tossing the balloon clearly shows *float*. Compressing it from both sides shows *press*. Holding it by the stem and patting it back and forth shows *rebound*. And of course, popping it with a pin shows *burst*, which should be saved for last, for obvious reasons.

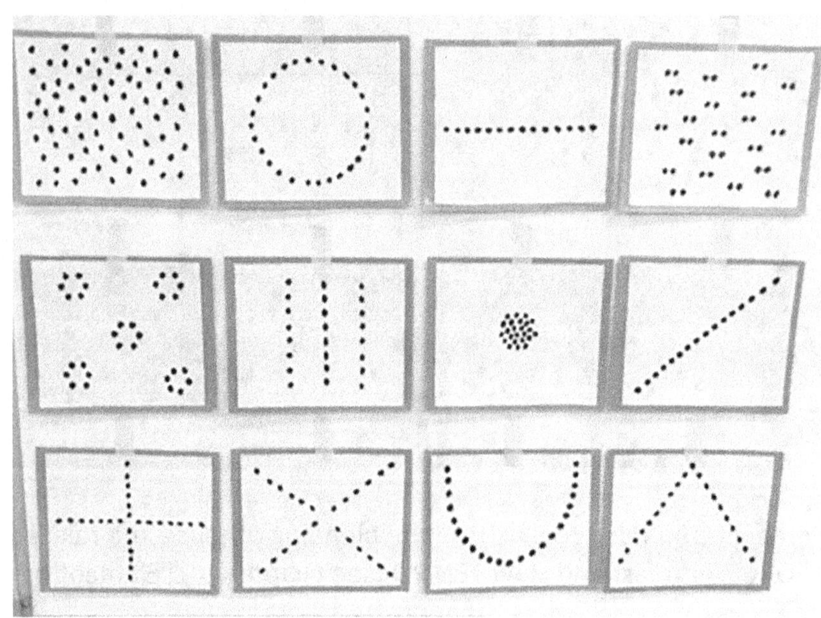

Formations. Used to illustrate multiple bodies in FORMATIONS (see chapter 15, "Element of Relationship").

Geologic events. As an integrated earth science and dance unit, these six natural disasters match well with the six energy qualities (see appendix C, "Element of Energy Deconstruction"). In this photo, the photos are placed over the matching energy quality signs: tsunamis/swinging, earthquakes/vibratory, wildfires/suspended, hurricanes/sustained, lightning strikes/percussive, and landslides/collapse.

In-place and traveling. These objects both move, albeit differently, in space. The thumb puppet stays in place, while the car travels (see chapter 12, "Element of Space").

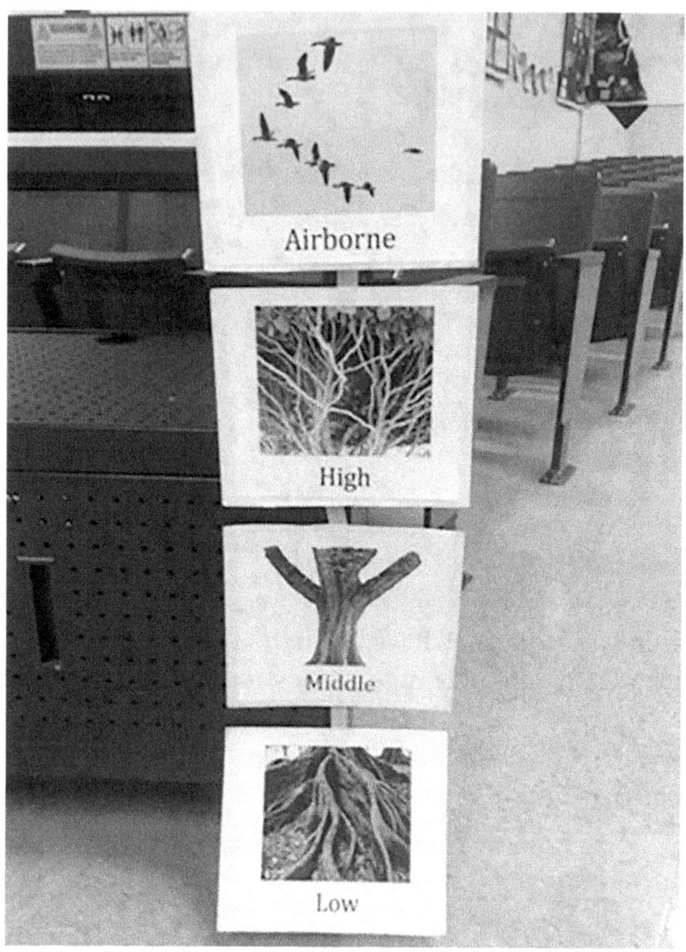

Levels. Used to illustrate four LEVELS in vertical space (see chapter 12, "Element of Space").

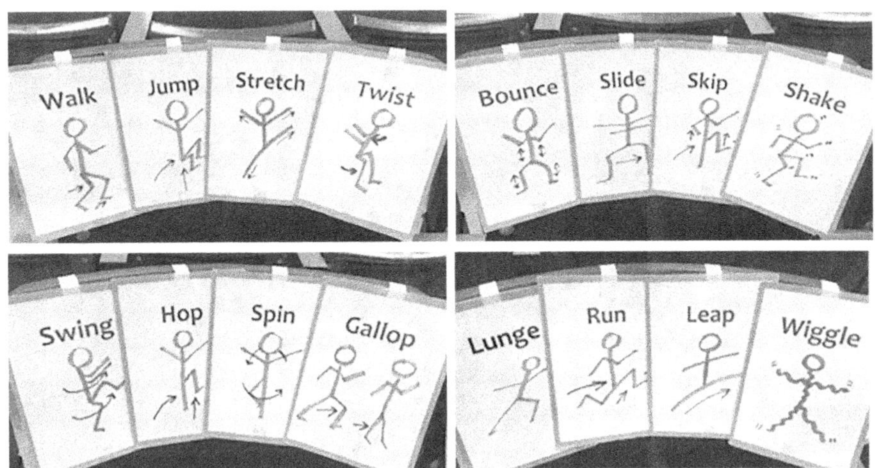

Movements. Used to illustrate eighteen to twenty-two body MOVEMENTS (see chapter 11, "Element of Body"). Missing are roll, waddle, bend, sway, scoot, and crawl. But you get the idea, right?

***Navarasa* moods.** Structure of nine basic emotional states, from India (see the section "Emotions" in chapter 17, "Inspiration," or chapter 22, "Integrating Content Areas," Fifth or Sixth Grade, Theatre).

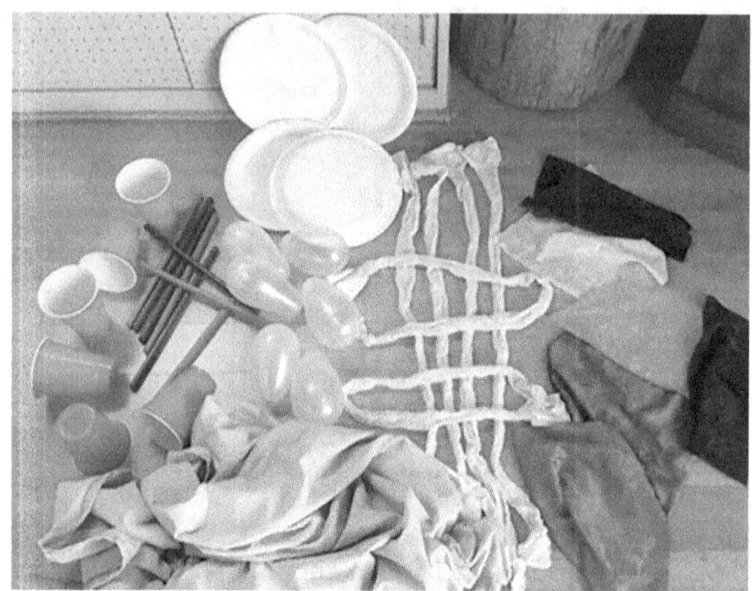

Objects. Pictured here are a variety of objects used to inspire movement (see chapter 17, "Inspiration"). They include plastic Solo cups, paper plates, rhythm sticks, balloons, a bedsheet, nylon stockings, and eight-by-eight-inch scarves. Placing them in sets enough for each child in a small group to have one and in separate areas is advisable. Groups can rotate between them.
Note: it's a good idea to have extra balloons on hand because they tend to pop.

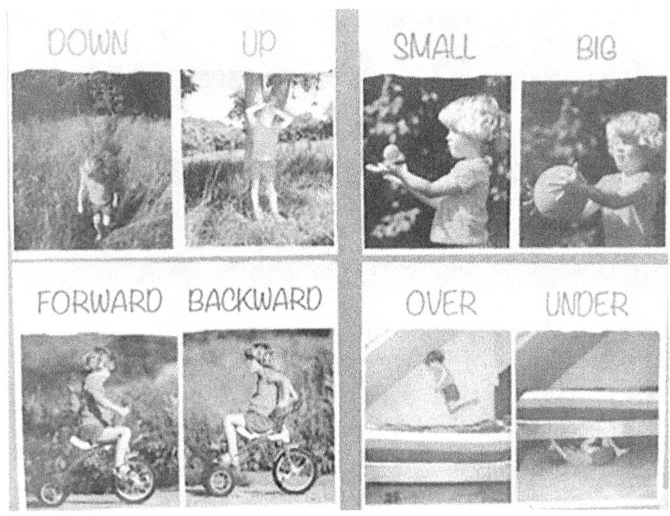

Opposites. Used as an example of OPOSSITE PAIRS in warm-ups (see chapter 11, "Element of Body") or as a structure for composition (see chapter 18, "Choreographic Tools").

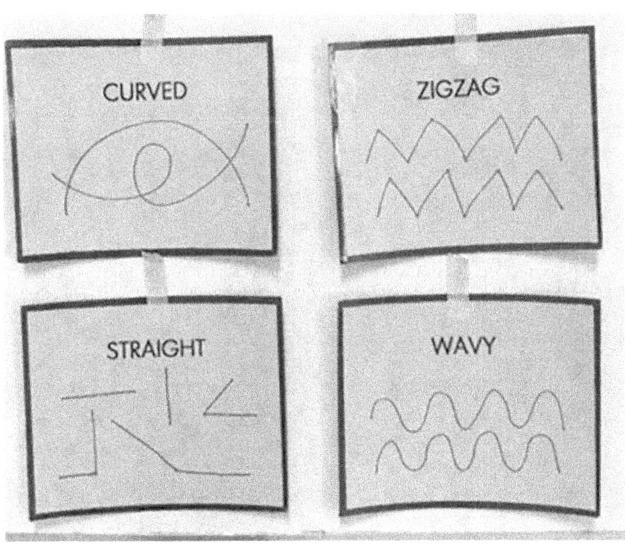

Pathways. Used to illustrate four PATHWAYS (see chapter 12, "Element of Space").

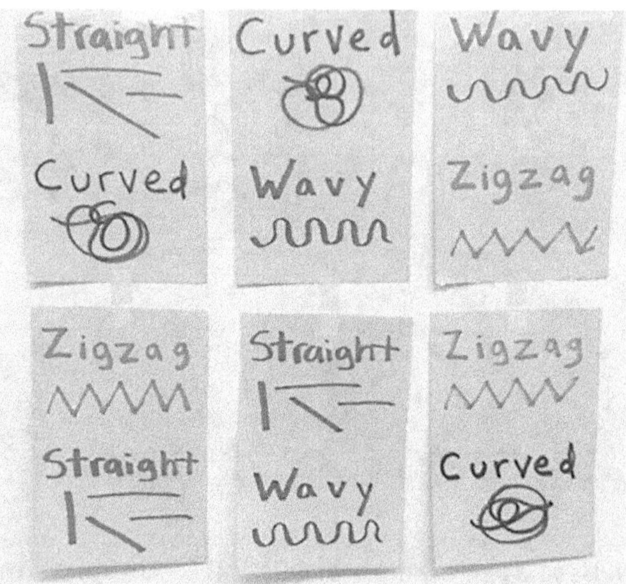

Pathway pairs. Six ways to pair four different PATHWAYS (see chapter 12, "Element of Space"). Each pathway appears three times in the set, and none of the pairs repeat.

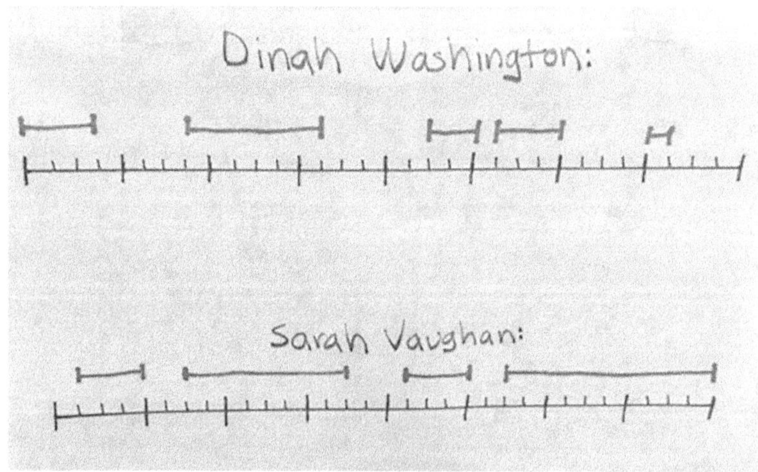

Phrasing. Red lines indicate each singer's use of PHRASING in her version of "All of Me" (see chapter 13, "Element of Time").

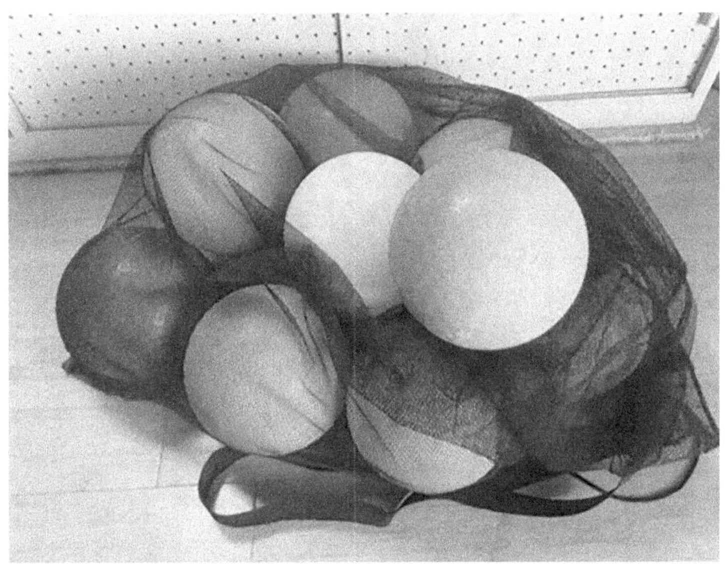

Playground balls. These are fairly small, about eight inches in diameter. They bounce well and are easy to handle. They can be used for rhythmic activities and ball dances (see chapter 22, "Integrating Content Areas," PE).

Rhythm sticks. Used in the Mexican dance Los Machetes (see appendix D, "World Dances") or in many other rhythmic activities.

Ribbon sticks. These are homemade and are very durable. The fabric ribbons are about forty-five inches long and are secured to a small wooden dowel. These can be used as inspiration for movement, drawing pathways in the air, and for Yanko, the Chinese ribbon dance (see appendix D, "World Dances").

Scarves. Many dance teachers use scarves as inspiration for movement. The scarves pictured here are fairly small, about eight by eight inches square. They are made from nonfraying fabric, so there was no need to sew the edges. I also use them for the Qashqai scarf dance (see appendix D, "World Dances").

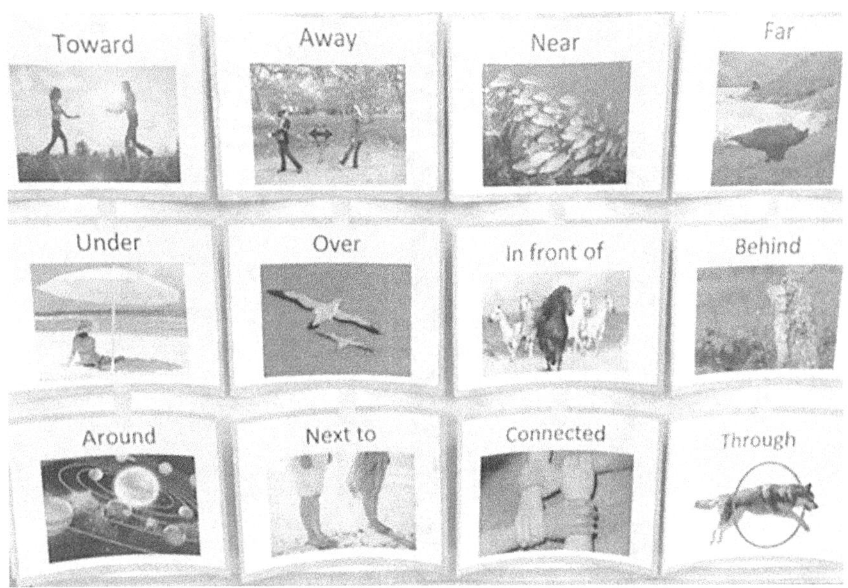

Spatial relationships. Used to illustrate prepositions for RELATIONSHIPS of bodies to one another or to stationary objects (see chapter 15, "Element of Relationship").

Tambourines. Made from paper plates and used in the Italian dance called *Tarantella* (see appendix D, "World Dances").

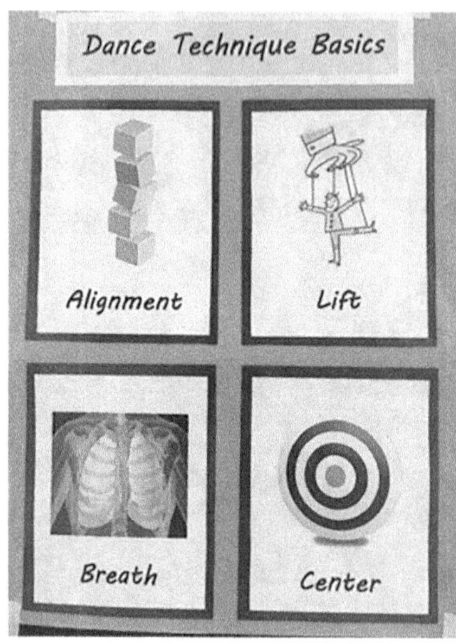

Techniques. Used to illustrate four basic dance TECHNIQUES (see chapter 11, "Element of Body").

Tempo. Used to illustrate three basic TEMPOS (see chapter 13, "Element of Time").

Totem poles. These models of totem poles illustrate the vertical levels of low, middle, and high (see chapter 12, "Element of Space").

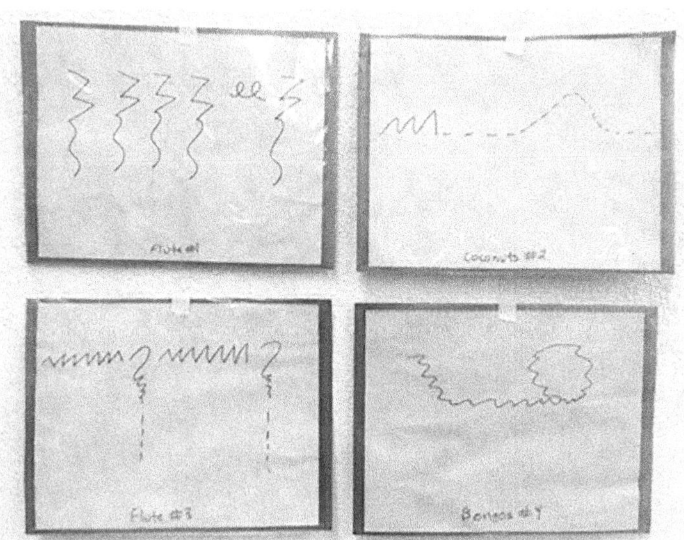

Visualize rhythm. Used to illustrate the four repeating patterns played by various instruments in Carl Orff, *Orff-Schulwerk*, vol. 2, "Rondo" (see chapter 13, "Element of Time").

Chapter 10

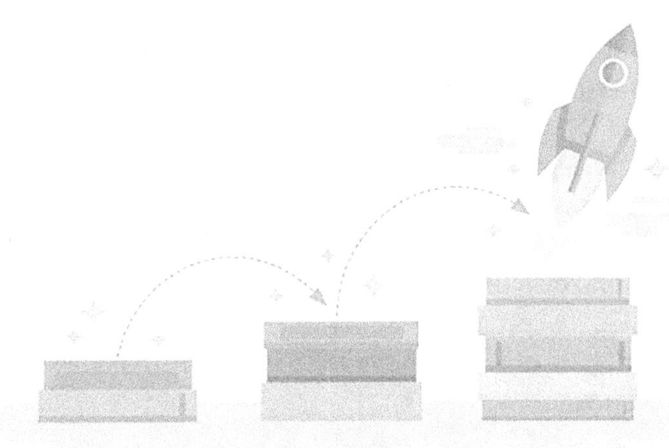

Grade Level Curricula
Suggested lessons and sequences for each elementary grade

So here is where things get specific—actual sequences of lessons that any dance teacher can use. Included in the pages that follow is first a synopsis of how a series of lessons could be sequenced, followed by a sampling of twelve lessons for every elementary grade level that build upon each other and flow from one to the next. In my view, after the first few classes, you can go in a variety of directions, depending on your students' readiness for increased challenges in their dance learning. Of course, if you have more or fewer classes with your students, add or subtract as you please. You will find many more lessons in chapters 11–15, which are organized by the elements of dance and by grade spans rather than by each elementary grade level.

If you teach multiple ages and/or elementary grade levels, you might consider reserving a few lessons that are gems as "exclusive" to a grade. This will avoid redundancy from year to year if you have returning students, and it will also give each grade something special that is just their own (which they will not even realize). This practice has helped me organize around a few successful themes, and when teaching multiple grade levels, anything that can help you keep things organized in your mind is a benefit!

Most dance concepts can span multiple ages and grades, with differences in depth, complexity, or approach. One thing that can be somewhat consistent across age and grade levels is the **progression** from beginning to end of your series of classes. It's all about the journey, right?

Here is a synopsis of what I believe to be a sensible way to BEGIN a series of classes:

- **LESSON 1: Begin with the basics.** Get to know your students' experience and knowledge of dance. Introduce what you will be doing over the weeks ahead. Get them up and moving right away by leading them through your warm-up, which could include patterns of movements that introduce them to new challenges in fitness, body awareness, control, and skill development, also known as **technique** (refer back to chapter 8, "Class Structure," for a description of what I consider to be a good warm-up). Students can feel successful from simply practicing set movements, but with some opportunity for a bit of creative exploration (e.g., when practicing moving one body part at a time, have them freestyle each part, moving it any way they want and discovering what it can do). Early in the sequence of lessons, the dance teacher is doing most of the creative work, but that balance shifts to the students as they gain more experience and confidence in their own exploration. Their creative minds may just be awakening to this new sensation that is *dance*, and they might need a certain level of guidance starting out.
- **LESSON 2: Practice movements and do something with them.** Doing so is still fairly structured and a great opportunity to

observe your students' motor skills and coordination. Practice basic locomotor and nonlocomotor movements, correcting them as needed and clearly defining the vocabulary. Then construct simple patterns, sequences, phrases, or studies that can include opportunities for improvisation, composition, and revision for students with more experience. For some students or some classes, this could be their first attempt at choreography. By giving them choices between a few different movements or giving them the task of putting the movements in order, the process is not so wide open as to confuse them.

- **LESSONS 3–4: Add dance concepts or choreographic tools.** Now that your students have some experience with creating simple choreography, add one thing that will make their work more interesting and give them a new skill to use. From the elements of space, time, and relationship or one of the choreographic tools, which are the easiest to understand, choose **one concept** (e.g., such as level, tempo, formation changes, or stillness) and apply it to a student-constructed dance pattern or phrase. Then basic movements will start to take on a whole new life. The element of *energy* should be included, of course, but is generally more subtle and could be introduced after one or two of the other elements. (Note: the element of *purpose* should be ever present by way of transparency in your expressed learning goals for each lesson.)

The following lesson categories could be arranged in any order that enables students to build on previously learned skills

- **LESSONS 5–11**
  - **Add and blend concepts.** Even very young dance students can layer two concepts together to create and perform dances, and more experienced dance students can layer three or more. (Note: I use the analogy of a sandwich, where every bite includes everything: the bread, the meat, the cheese, the mayo, the lettuce, and the pickle). Every time a new concept is introduced, practice it by itself. Then include

previously learned and practiced concepts along with it.

- ○ **Sources of inspiration.** Really, anything can be something to be danced about. But some of the best resources for ideas for creating original work are stories, poetry, fine art, holidays, objects, emotions, current events, or world dances (see chapter 17, "Inspiration").

- ○ **Integrating with other subjects.** Blending dance with other subjects the students are learning can be a rich and inspiring experience, which deepens students' understanding of multiple subjects at the same time while identifying similarities and overlaps between them (see chapter 22, "Integrating Content Areas," for more lessons that integrate dance with other content areas, including other art forms). I highly recommend collaborating or at least consulting with specialists in other fields or content areas before attempting this. If nondance teachers were to teach a dance lesson, we might be able to provide them with helpful suggestions or guidance, and the same goes in the other direction.

- **FINAL LESSON: Performance.** World dances are excellent finales to a series of dance lessons, but that doesn't mean you have to reserve a world dance until the end; any performance-worthy work can be presented in front of an audience. Since dance IS a performing art that is meant to be shared with others, providing an opportunity to experience that part is important. Plus it gives your young performers a tangible and exciting goal to work toward. Along the way, you can, of course, hold spontaneous performances in your classes simply by dividing the class in half or into groups and having them watch one another. Having an audience in any form is a way to help your students confront nervousness and learn basic performance etiquette, such as staying quiet while others are performing, taking bows, and applauding. Also, by watching one another, they are developing a critical eye and forming opinions about what they observe.

Beginning on the following page, by and for each grade level, you will find a list of twelve lessons. Please note THESE ARE ONLY EXAMPLES, and of course, many other variations and possibilities exist. You will find the same lessons in many of the chapters that follow, so please forgive any redundancy. This collection is an attempt to provide a useful and practical sampling.

In collecting these lessons, I got a sense of what a gallery or museum curator's job is (an art unto itself): picking out examples that best represent the body of work you are attempting to present, setting them up in a way that is accessible to those who want to know, and supporting them with carefully structured background information and details. As a dance teacher, you have great knowledge and expertise that you can use to create your own inspiring dance curriculum. So please use this only as a springboard to the beautiful aerial act that is YOUR instruction!

Prekindergarten

1. **Warm-up/technique.** Include whole-body movements, extensions from the center in different directions, stretches, opposites, and exploration of the four energies of flow and weight.
2. **Movement skill practice / ABAB patterns.** Practice eighteen dance **movements** to any music that has a good beat. No more than nine groups are given two movement cards each, one being movement A and the other being movement B. Practice and perform them as a repeating ABAB pattern.
3. **Element of body / additional movement skill practice.** *Walking, hopping.* Sing and do the three movements in the following song, which is sung to the tune of "Frère Jacques":

"Walking-walking, walking-walking, hop-hop-hop, hop-hop-hop, running-running-running, running-running-running, now we stop!"

Replace *walk*, *hop*, and *run* with three other movements. Then repeat the song several times until all eighteen have been practiced. No music is needed. Students could take turns singing for one another if desired, or five groups could each get three movements and take turns performing for one another, with all groups performing the first version.

4. **Element of body / body parts. *My hands.*** A song sang to the tune of "Twinkle, Twinkle, Little Star" that focuses on one **body part** at a time:

*"Hands upon my HEAD I place, on my SHOULDERS, on my FACE,
on my ELBOWS, on my HIPS, on my STOMACH, on my LIPS.
Then I raise them up so high I think they might touch the sky.
Touch each FOOT and touch each KNEE, clap together 1-2-3.
Wave and wave to all my friends. Hands can rest now, it's the end."*

5. **Choreographic tool / stillness. *Move and stop.*** Play any music and call out a single movement, such as *gallop* or *twist*. Pause the song after about sixteen counts, and students should freeze in place. Divide into groups and take turns to watch one another. Call out new movements for each group or each cycle of groups.

6. **Element of space / levels. *Grow and wilt.*** Practice movements at low and high **levels** as well as changing levels. Play Carl Orff, *Orff-Schulwerk*, vol. 1, "Sieben Vlolkstanze Tanz 2." Starting from a low curled-up position, slowly rise up, as if growing from a seed; and finish at a high level with the body open and stretched up and out to the sun like a flower. Repeat the music and slowly lower back down to the ground like a flower wilting and dying. Divide the class in half. Simultaneously, one group grows, while the other wilts, going in opposite directions, with an adult joining each group.

7. **Element of time / tempo. *Opposites dance.*** Practice moving at slow and fast **tempos**. Use opposite pairs other than fast and slow, such as *down/up*, *small/big*, *forward/backward*, and

over/under as structure. Then divide into as many groups as opposite pairs. Groups take turns moving through their opposite pair, first **slow**, then **fast**. Rotate opposite pairs and repeat. Perform to Angels of Venice, "Dragonfly."

8. **Element of energy/ flow or weight.** Create and perform movements to the following variations on "Eensy Weensy Spider," emphasizing smooth and sharp **flow** or heavy and light **weight** in all movements. Practice seated first, using upper body movements while learning the song. Then repeat standing with whole-body movements, incorporating previously practiced skills, such as changing tempo and levels.

The Tiger (smooth)
The tiger went a-hunting out in the grass so high
Along came a herd of zebras and passed the tiger by
Down went the sun, and the night began to fall
So the tired, hungry tiger ate no dinner at all

The Crab (sharp)
The creepy crusty crab went scooting along the sand
Along came a wave and threw her up on land
Up came the tide and covered up the shore
So the creepy crusty crab went scooting along some more

The Elephant (heavy)
The big, gigantic elephant went walking down the path
Down came the rain, and the elephant took a bath
Out came the sun and dried off all his skin
So the big, gigantic elephant went down the path again

The Eagle (light)
The eagle was a-flying up in the sky so high
Down in the water a fish was swimming by
Down flew the bird as fast as she could go
But the fish swam to the bottom and said, "You are too slow!"

9. **Inspiration / nursery rhymes.** Read one or both of the following examples and have students echo them back, emphasizing the rhythm pattern in each line. Then line by line, create rhythmic and repetitive movements for each.

Hey, diddle, diddle, the cat and the fiddle, the cow jumped over the moon.
The little dog laughed to see such a sport, and the dish ran away with the spoon.
Los Pollitos dicen, "pio, pio, pio," cuando tienen hambre, y cuando tienen frio.
La gallina busca, el maiz y el trigo, les da la comida, y les presta abrigo.

10. **Integrated lesson/ music. *Merry-go-round.*** In a circle (holding hands is optional), learn the following song/dance while singing the words. Then perform to music with singing, then again to music without singing, transforming the movements with words into movements with music without words. The tune is to "The Wheels on the Bus." Use Carl Orff, *Orff-Schulwerk*, vol. 2, "Comodo." Song lyrics / movements are as follows:

We're on a merry-go-round and round,
round and round, round and round
We're on a merry-go-round and round,
round and round we go (skip or gallop in a circle)
We're on a merry-go-up and down . . .
(Lift hands up and bend down)
We're on a merry-go-in and out . . .
(Whole group moves into the center of circle and out)
We're on a merry-go-side to side . . .
(Swing or slide sideways, alternating sides)
We're on a merry-go-around ourselves . . .
(Spin around self)
We're on a merry-go-slow and fast . . .
(Walk slowly in a circle, then run)

11. **Inspiration / story dance.** *The Farmyard Cat.* Read the story and list events that happen in the story in single words ending in *-ing*. Create movements for each word. Play "Sneaky Snake" from the *Rhythmically Moving* music series, vol. 4 (see appendix F, "Stories").

12. **World dance.** See appendix D, "World Dances." Here are a variety of dances from around the world, some of which involve simple formations or the use of handheld objects that can be adapted and are well suited to teach prekindergarteners: **Arirang** (Korea), **Caimarusa** (Colombia), **Here Comes Sally** (American South), **Hokey Pokey** (England), **Yanko ribbon dance** (China).

Kindergarten

1. **Warm-up/technique.** Include whole-body movements, extensions from the center in different directions, body parts, stretches, opposites, levels, and exploration of the four energies of flow and weight.

2. **Movement skill practice / ABC patterns.** Practice eighteen dance **movements** to any music that has a good beat and with a rest after every three movements. Divide into six groups, and each group is given a set of three movements, and they decide the order of the movements representing an ABC pattern. Each group performs their pattern for the other two groups and repeats all three of their movements to create a repeating ABC pattern.

3. **Choreographic tool / echoing.** *Echo dance.* For in-place movements only. Form a circle and place all of the IN-PLACE movement cards around the inside of the circle (*stretch, bend, swing, spin, twist, bounce, shake, wiggle* and *walk, hop, jump, and run,* which can be done in place). Divide the group into pairs or trios, each behind a movement card. Each gets a turn performing their movement by themselves for four beats. Then the rest of the group imitates them by echoing. Play Eric Chappelle, *Music for Creative Dance: Contrast and Continuum,*

vol. 4, "Back at Ya." After the song is over, rotate the movement cards and repeat the whole dance.

4. **Element of space / in-place and traveling.** *Enter and exit.* Play Schubert, *Moment Musical* and form nine groups (to fit music). Each group gets one traveling and one in-place movement, and all begin on one side of space. Place a marker or spot in the center of the space. One group at a time enters with their traveling movement to the spot, does their in-place movement at the spot, then exits with the same traveling movement to the other side of the space.

5. **Element of body / shape.** *ABC patterns*. In four groups, each chooses two movements (A and B), practices them, and adds a still shape (C) at the end. Play Carl Orff, *Orff-Schulwerk*, vol. 1, "Gassenhauer," and each group gets two turns to perform their pattern.

6. **Element of space / directions.** *ABAB pattern.* Put all movements together in pairs. Movement **A** will be done forward and backward, and movement **B** will be done right and left. Play Bob Marley & the Wailers, "Three Little Birds." Divide and take turns performing to avoid fatigue.

7. **Element of time / timing.** *Partners.* Arrange the class into pairs and decide which is dancer 1 and which is dancer 2. Place an object like a cone or a chair in the center of the space, and pairs form a large circle around it. Give each pair two movements, one that travels and one that stays in place. **Taking turns**, person 1 travels to the center, then person 2. Then they do the in-place movement at the **same time**. Then they repeat both movements with the same two kinds of timing, returning to their place in the circle. Play Eric Chappelle, *Music for Creative Dance: Contrast and Continuum*, vol. 2, "Caribbean Leaps."

8. **Element of relationship / spatial relationships.** *"I See You."* Exploring **in front, behind, through**, and **around**. Dancers are grouped in two pairs facing each other from a distance. Play Marian Rose, "I See You." With the lyrics, each pair stands facing the other with one person who is the "tree" holding still, with the arms extended like branches **in front**. Their partner, who is the "squirrel,"

is peeking **through** the "branches" from **behind** at the squirrel on the opposite side. Then both squirrels come out and take both hands and gallop **around** each other until the music changes. They then return to their partners and move **in front** of them, becoming the tree. Then the person who was the tree before is now behind and becomes the squirrel. The song cycles through seven times.

9. **Element of energy / flow and weight.** *Mirror dance.* In partners, students face each other and choose who is the leader first. With movements that stay in place, mirror with **smooth** and **sharp flow**, following cues in the music to Eric Chappelle, *Music for Creative Dance: Contrast and Continuum*, vol. 1, "Western East." *Shadow dance.* In partners, with one behind the other, the dancer in front is the leader and does traveling movements with **light** and **heavy weight**, following cues in the music to Eric Chappelle, *Music for Creative Dance: Contrast and Continuum*, vol. 1, "A Tale of Two Villages."

10. **Inspiration / fine art.** *Flower Festival* by Diego Rivera. After studying the picture and discussing who the artist is and the general feeling of the picture, ask the students to tell you what they see and list what they say, up to seven or eight observations. Create movements that express each of the items listed. Play Dan Schwartz, "Latino America" as background.

11. **Integrated lesson / language arts.** *Alphabet dance.* See appendix G, "Handouts," for both English and Spanish versions. Practice movements described by the word or phrase beginning with each letter. For the English alphabet, play Carl Orff, *Orff-Schulwerk*, vol. 2, "Tranquillo"; and for the Spanish alphabet, play *Flamenco Guitar*, "Canción de la Luna."

12. **World dance.** See appendix D, "World Dances." Here are a variety of dances from around the world, some of which emphasize body parts, echoing, or the use of handheld objects, which can be adapted and are well suited to teach kindergarteners: **Che Che Kule** (Ghana), **El Juego Chirimbolo** (Ecuador), **La Mariposa** (Bolívia), **Peopleton stick dance** (England/Wales), **Shoemaker's dance** (Denmark).

First Grade

---

1. **Warm-up/technique.** Include whole-body movements, extensions from the center in different directions, body parts, stretches, tempo, force, levels, and exploration of the four energies of flow and weight.

2. **Movement skill practice / ABCD patterns.** Practice eighteen dance **movements** to any music that has a good beat. Divide into six groups and give each group three movements. Group members choose an order, and the ABC represents the three movements, and D represents melting to the floor. Play Creeper Lagoon, "Under the Tracks."

3. **Element of space / in-place and traveling.** *Meet and greet and part.* With partners across the floor, one pair at a time dances. Call out one traveling movement to have students travel toward each other to "meet." Call out an in-place movement to do together to "greet" each other, and repeat the traveling movement to "part," going away from each other back to their same sides. Play the Blues Project, "Flute Thing."

4. **Element of time / tempo.** *Things that move.* Play three classical music selections. Then practice moving to each at moderate first, then fast and slow **tempos**. List eight things each that move at slow, moderate, and fast tempos. Make four groups. Give each group two items from each tempo, and they create one movement to express each item (total of six movements per group). Perform one group at a time to the same three classical selections.

5. **Element of space / size.** *Shrinking space.* Place four chairs in the four corners of the space and tell students to visualize imaginary lines that connect them around the outside of the space. Play Eric Chappelle, *Music for Creative Dance: Contrast and Continuum*, vol. 4, "Islands." Students dance any movement they like without going outside the "space" and without

touching anybody else. When the music pauses, selected students move the chairs closer to the center, causing the space to shrink. When the music resumes, the same rules apply, forcing movements to get smaller. Repeat this process two more times with pauses in the music. On the last pause, move the chairs back out to their original places, and movements can become large again.

6. **Element of energy / force. *Yes/no dance.*** In partners, one is the "dancer," and the other is the "master." The master places their hands on the dancer and makes them dance by moving their body parts as they wish. The dancer responds as if saying "yes" with relaxed force, going along with what the master is making them do. Then when the music changes, the dancer tenses their muscles and resists the master's guidance as if saying "no." Play Eric Chappelle, *Music for Creative Dance: Contrast and Continuum*, vol. 3, "I Say, You Say" and switch parts halfway through.

7. **Elements of time and energy / force matrix.** Show a four-squared grid with the words **tense** and **relaxed** across the top and **fast** and **slow** down the left side (see chapter 9, "Using Visuals, Objects, and Props"). Fill in four squares with four energies as follows:

BURST – tense/fast
REBOUND – relaxed/fast
PRESS – tense/slow
FLOAT – relaxed/slow

Diamond dance. Tape pictures of the four energies above to four different walls. Then groups of four form a diamond shape with one person toward each wall. Play Carl Orff, *Orff-Schulwerk*, vol. 1, tracks 12–15. With each musical selection, the front person in the diamond shape is the leader, and all others in the group follow that person's movements with their matrix energy. When the songs end, the whole group turns to face the next wall, and a new leader is in the front.

8. **Inspiration / story dance. *My Mama Had a Dancing Heart.*** See appendix F, "Stories." After reading the story to the students, match the four force matrix energies with the four seasons depicted in the book: *rebound*/spring, *burst*/summer, *float*/autumn, and *press*/winter. Following the descriptions of the three things present in each season, students create movements expressing those things plus a movement to express "celebrating," which can be both at the beginning and at the end of the dance.

9. **Element of relationship / spatial relationships and world dance. *Chinese friendship dance.*** See appendix D, "World Dances." Partners practice the spatial relationships *toward*, *around*, *next to*, *away*, *over*, and *under* with each other. Then they apply those relationships to the structure of the dance.

10. **Element of space / pathways. *Going hiking.*** Share a story of a trip hiking in the woods, where we leave our homes and walk down streets along **straight** pathways to get to the trail, then along a **wavy** pathway winding through the forest. On our way up, we have to leap across a stream from rock to rock along a **zigzag** pathway. Upon reaching the top of the mountain, we see an eagle soaring along a **curved** pathway. Suddenly, a bear comes out of the bushes, and we move slowly backward along a **straight** pathway, then turn and retrace all steps until we are home. Students create movements expressing each part and perform to Eric Chappelle, *Music for Creative Dance: Contrast and Continuum*, vol. 2, "Circular Journey."

11. **Inspiration/objects. *As and with the object.*** Use five objects: small scarves, balloons, rhythm sticks, plastic cups, and a large bedsheet. Discuss two ways to use objects in making dances: (1) **Imitate AS** the object. Move like it and make a still shape that looks like the object. (2) **Partner WITH** the object by dancing with it or making a still shape with it. Show each object and have students imitate movements the teacher makes it do. To practice dancing WITH the objects, place them in different areas or "centers" around the room. Then groups of students rotate

around to each set of objects. Play any music as background. Stop the music to cue students to stop, put down the object, and rotate to the next object/area. After all groups have explored all objects, remain at the final object. Then groups create movements **as** and **with** their object and perform to Carl Orff, *Orff-Schulwerk*, vol. 1, "Tanz 3" in a sequence as follows:

- Start far away from the objects and travel toward them **as** they would move.
- Dance **with** the object as a partner. Set two to three different movements that all do together.
- Make a group shape **with** the objects and dancers together.
- Place the object down and travel away again **as** the object, the same as the entrance.

12. **World dance.** See appendix D, "World Dances." Here are a variety of dances from around the world, some of which emphasize pathways, emotions, objects, small or large movements, which can be adapted and are well suited to teach first graders. **Itik-Itik** (Philippines), **Lott Ist Todt** (Germany), **Qashqai scarf dance** (Iran), **Tokyo Dontaku** (Japan), **Virginia Reel** (colonial USA).

Second Grade

---

1. **Warm-up/technique.** Include whole-body movements, extensions from the center in different directions, body parts, two-part patterns, stretches, tempo, force, and exploration of the energies of flow and weight.
2. **Movement skill practice / sequences.** *Build a sequence.* Practice twenty dance **movements** to any music that has a good beat. Use their understanding of a four-part **sequence** (*first, next, then, and finally*). Divide into five groups, and each group selects four movements from the twenty practiced to create a dance sequence. Perform taking turns to Bobby McFerrin, "Circlesong Six."

3. **Element of body / body parts.** *AABA pattern.* In four groups,
    each chooses two body parts (A and B) and follows this pattern:
    A – from lying down, rise, being lifted up by the first body part;
    A – travel, being pulled by the first body part; B – travel, being
    pulled by the second body part; A – connect with others in the
    group by the first body part. (Note: to avoid having children's
    heads touching one another, use only the head as body part
    B). Play Eric Chappelle, *Music for Creative Dance: Contrast and
    Continuum*, vol. 2, "Weavers" and perform one group at a time.

4. **Element of time / rhythm.** *Patterns with partners.* While
    seated, practice clapping various rhythm patterns and have
    students follow, as in a call-response. Then add whole-body
    movements. After the above practice, students work with a
    partner to create a pattern of at least two different movements
    that they can repeat four times. Accompany on drum, matching
    the rhythm pattern their movements created as each pair
    performs.

5. **Element of space / pathways.** *Pathway pairs.* There are six
    possible ways to pair four things. So divide into six groups
    and give each group a pair of pathways (see chapter 9, "Using
    Visuals, Objects, and Props"). Each group creates a phrase of
    three movements and performs all of them along their first
    pathway and then repeats them along their second pathway.
    Perform to Prem Joshua, "Deccan Queen."

6. **Inspiration / fine art.** See chapter 9, "Using Visuals, Objects,
    and Props." Use *Three Musicians* by Picasso, *Relativity* by M. C.
    Escher, *Birth of Venus* by Botticelli, and *Red Poppy* by Georgia
    O'Keeffe. Students trace the pathways they see in each picture
    in the air (Picasso/straight, Escher/zigzag, Botticelli/curved,
    O'Keeffe/wavy) first with their fingers or other body parts, then
    with whole-body movements through space. In four groups
    by artwork, create a sequence of three movements showing
    the pathways seen in their artwork. Select music that fits each
    piece, such as baroque for Botticelli and Native American music
    for O'Keeffe.

7. **Integrated lesson / math.** *Addition dance.* Randomly select three movements and make a three-part sequence. Practice the sequence counting eight beats for each movement. Play Carl Orff, *Orff-Schulwerk*, vol. 1, "Gassenhauer." List several ways to add up three numbers to equal twenty-four. Choose one of the examples and practice the same sequence, counting each movement by a number other than eight. Create as many groups as there are addition examples remaining and give each group three movements to create their own sequences. Each group performs to the same music, and there should be no more than eight groups.

8. **Elements of body and relationship / shape and spatial relationships.** *Circle shapes.* Begin in a circle with one person in the middle making a shape. The next person in the circle dances **toward** the center person, then **around** them, and then stops and makes a shape in one of the following five called-out relationships: **next to**, **behind**, **in front of**, **over**, or **under**. Then the person who was there before dances **away** and goes back to the circle. Play any music with a long steady beat as background and continue around the circle until all have had a turn.

9. **Inspiration, element of space, and integrated lesson / story dance, size, and theatre (upstaging).** *Officer Buckle and Gloria.* See appendix F, "Stories." List main events that happen in the story with single words ending in *-ing*. Create movements expressing each event in the story, and when creating movements for "upstaging," dancers are in pairs in front of and behind each other. The person in front does small-size movements, and the person behind does large-size movements, attracting the attention of the viewers (upstaging). Perform to Eric Chappelle, *Music for Creative Dance: Contrast and Continuum*, vol. 1, "Jammin' on the Porch."

10. **Element of energy / flow.** *Trios.* Practice three kinds of flow—*vibratory*, *sharp*, and *smooth*—to the first three clips of Eric Chappelle, *Music for Creative Dance: Contrast and Continuum*, vol. 4, "Potpourri." Divide into groups of three, and members

decide who will dance which type of flow. Play Eric Chappelle, *Music for Creative Dance: Contrast and Continuum*, vol. 3, "Dakota Dawn." Following the musical cues, drum for *sharp*, flute for *smooth*, and shaker for *vibratory*. First improvise, then set movements. Perform two to three trios at a time.

11. **World dance / objects. *Fan dance.*** See appendix D, "World Dances." Use paper plates cut in half, and each dancer gets two "fans." Practice and perform movements of the dance using vibratory and smooth flowing movements for the civilian type of fan dance and sharp flowing movements for the military style. Play David Byrne, main title theme from *The Last Emperor*.

12. **Inspiration / poetic forms. *Cinquain.*** Read examples of a few poems and diagram their structure. The five lines are composed of the following: The first line is a single noun, which is the topic of the poem. The second is two adjectives describing it. The third line is three verbs. The fourth is a four- to five-word quote that expresses an emotion the noun might say. The fifth line is a different and related single noun. Students either vote to choose their favorite example or decide on a topic and write an original poem. Explore and set movements that express each word or phrase of the poem. Then perform to music that fits the topic.

Third Grade

1. **Warm-up/technique.** Include whole-body movements, extensions from the center in different directions, body parts, two- to three-part combinations, stretches, yoga, energy qualities.

2. **Movement skill practice / phrases. *ABCA thematic phrases*.** Practice twenty dance **movements** to any music that has a good beat. Divide into no more than six groups, and each group is given three movements. They decide their favorite of the three

movements, and that is movement A. Their second choice is B, and their third choice is C. Movement A, being the favorite, is repeated at the end, creating an emphasis or theme for their phrase that follows an ABCA pattern. Perform to any music with a 4/4 time signature.

3. **Elements of space and body / levels and shapes. *Add-on shapes.*** In groups of four, each gets a level: *low, middle, high,* or *airborne.* One person at a time, starting with *low,* enters from the side and makes a still shape at their level in the center of the space. Each person in their group enters at their respective levels and connects to the person already there, creating a group shape. Note, the *airborne* person moves at that level but makes a shape at any of the other levels. All exit after their multilevel shape is completed. Play Eric Chappelle, *Music for Creative Dance: Contrast and Continuum*, vol. 2, "Pizz.Ah!" and follow the musical phrases.

4. **Integrated lesson / science. *Trees.*** The whole group brainstorms different species of trees and lists them as well as the different ways in which a tree can die (fire, cut down, lightning, drought, insects, old age). Select three to four tree species and divide into as many groups. Each group does research as to their tree's size, shape, where it grows, etc. and finds pictures. Combine with levels and create movements for a dance phrase in five parts: *roots*/low, *trunk*/middle, *branches and leaves*/high, *things coming into or out of the tree from the air*/airborne, *death of the tree.* Play Michael Manring, "Life in the Trees."

5. **Element of time / duration. *Color cards.*** Use a set of four cards of varying widths—one representing eight beats, another representing four beats, and two representing two beats each—in different colors for the numbers of beats (see chapter 9, "Using Visuals, Objects, and Props"). Groups create four-movement phrases and first practice each movement for four beats each. Then match a color card to each movement, creating a duration sequence. Groups perform their phrases

following that pattern. Rearrange color cards and repeat with a new duration sequence. Discuss which is preferable and why. Play any 4/4 music with a slow beat.

6. **Element of time and personal experience / duration.** *Everyday life.* List things the students do in their everyday lives that take a long duration of time, a medium duration, and a short duration. Choose one item from each list and put them in a logical chronological order representing one "day." Students create movements that express each idea in their day—the long movement taking eight beats, the medium taking four, and the short taking two. Perform to Eric Chappelle, *Music for Creative Dance: Contrast and Continuum*, vol. 4, "Oslo Walk."

7. **Element of space / pathways.** *Pathway maps.* Draw examples of three different overlapping pathways, from point A to point B. Then orient them to fit the space you are working in. Practice those with different movements. Groups of three students draw their own maps the same way, each contributing a pathway. Each person creates a movement that follows their pathway, from A to B in eight beats. Dancers take turns traveling their pathway. Then all three return from point B to point A at the same time, also in eight beats. Perform to Muse, "Supermassive Black Hole."

8. **Element of relationship / spatial relationships. "*Walking in Beauty*" (*excerpts from the poem about the Navajo changing ceremony*).** See chapter 15, "Element of Relationship." In Navajo culture, this ceremony is performed when a child is changing into an adult. Practice doing movements with partners in the following spatial relationships: *in front of, behind, next to, over, under,* and *around.* Form groups of five to seven, and one person is the designated "changeling" who travels in a diagonal direction from upstage to downstage, surrounded on all sides by the other four or more dancers. The changeling creates their own special walk, and as the lines of the poem are read, the dancers surrounding him/her perform six different "beauty" movements when cued. All finish in a final shape at the end of

the journey. Play Mary Youngblood, "Walk with Me." The poem reads as follows:

IN BEAUTY I WALK
WITH BEAUTY BEFORE ME
I WALK WITH BEAUTY BEHIND ME
I WALK WITH BEAUTY BESIDE ME
I WALK WITH BEAUTY ABOVE ME
I WALK WITH BEAUTY BELOW ME
WITH BEAUTY ALL AROUND ME, I WALK
IT IS FINISHED IN BEAUTY

9. **Element of energy / energy qualities. *Echo dance.*** The whole group is in a circle or in two circles if the group is large. Play Eric Chappelle, *Music for Creative Dance: Contrast and Continuum*, vol. 4, "Back at Ya" and go around the circle. Each person gets a turn to create a movement with one of the energies as called out by teacher in a repeating order, and all in the circle echo that movement. Repeat the song as many times as needed to allow all to have multiple turns leading.

10. **Inspiration / poetic forms. *Haiku.*** This is a Japanese form of poetry with a line structure as follows:

First line: five syllables
Second line: seven syllables
Third line: five syllables

Choose any topic and write a haiku. Then explore movements that express images in the poem. Emphasize the dance elements they have learned and use them to create expressive movement phrases inspired by each line of the poem. Perform to music that fits the feeling of the poem.

11. **World dance and element of relationship / character and objects. *Danza de los Viejitos.*** See appendix D, "World Dances." Perform the dance in character as an elderly person and using an object in the form of a walking stick.

12. **Inspiration / story dance.** *The Legend of the Bluebonnet.* See appendix F, "Stories." List the main events that occur in the story, and dancers create movements that express the feeling behind each event. Perform to Michel Cusson, "The Wolf and the Bear."

Fourth Grade

1. **Warm-Up/technique.** Include whole-body movements, extensions from the center in different directions, body parts, two- to three-part combinations, stretches, yoga, energy qualities.
2. **Movement skill practice / phrases with improvisation.** *16-8-8-16-16.* Practice twenty-two dance **movements** to any music that has a good beat. Divide into five groups, and each is given four movements that they put into a sequence as follows: enter from the side for sixteen beats, next movement for eight beats, next movement for eight beats, any movement/improvisation for sixteen beats, final movement exit for sixteen beats. Perform one group at a time to Dan Savell, "Driving a Jet."
3. **Element of body / shape.** *Muscle memory.* In groups of three to five, each group creates one shape that all members do exactly the same way. They also choose three different movements, and groups dance their first movement for twelve beats, followed by their shape and hold it for four. Then the second and third movements each, followed by the same shape. The challenge is to form the same shape after doing different movements, requiring the muscles to remember. Perform to Prem Joshua, "Deccan Queen."
4. **Element of time and energy / timing and energy qualities.** *Transitions.* Groups create three different whole-body shapes and practice making transitions between them. Practice making those transitions first with gradual timing (sustained energy) and then again with sudden timing (percussive energy). Perform

to Eric Chappelle, *Music for Creative Dance: Contrast and Continuum*, vol. 1, "Western East" and cycle through shapes continuously with gradual timing until the music changes. Then do the same with sudden timing.

5. **Integrated lesson / language arts. *Graham quote.*** Use the following quote by Martha Graham: *"Dance is the hidden language of the soul."* Identify the main-idea words (*dance, hidden, language,* and *soul*) and the transition words (*is, the, of,* and *the*). Discuss how all are essential to make a complete sentence. The whole group improvises to create a movement or a short phrase that expresses each of the main-idea words. Then create movements that express the transition words, and since they repeat, the movements repeat as well. Put all movements/phrases together and perform with groups taking turns to watch each other. Play Mickey Hart, "Amazon Nguni."

6. **Element of energy / energy qualities. *Chance dance.*** Match six energies to the numbers of dots on a die. On a separate list, match six selected movements. In four groups, pass out one die, scratch paper, and a pencil to each group. They roll six times to create an energy list, then six more times to determine the movements matched to the energies on their list. If energy/movement pairings repeat, groups will need to figure out a way to make them different, such as changing level, tempo, or direction. Play Prem Joshua, "Deccan Queen."

7. **Integrated lesson / science. *Geologic events.*** After discussing the difference between weather and geologic events, list the following, matching them with the six energy qualities: *landslide*/collapse, *hurricane*/sustained, *lightning strike*/percussive, *earthquake*/vibratory, *tsunami*/swinging, and *wildfire*/suspended. Improvise various movements for each event listed. Play Michel Cusson, "Ly-O-Lay Ale Loya" as background. Divide into three or six groups and create short studies to express their event. Studies must include three different movements: one that travels, one that stays in place, and one that makes a formation. Movements can be in any order.

8. **Element of space and world dance / directions.** *Four-sided dances.* Practice and perform several dances that change direction with each repeating cycle of movements. Some examples are Macarena, Pata Pata, Texas line dances, and Payaso del Rodeo. See appendix D, "World Dances," Four-Sided Dances. Practice and perform selections from this group of dances. Then groups can create their own version of a repeating pattern dance that changes directions and perform them to the same music.

9. **Inspiration / music or sounds.** *Call and response.* Play one of the following musical selections or any other that has a simple and repeatable echoing melodic phrase: Eric Chappelle, *Music for Creative Dance: Contrast and Continuum*, vol. 4, "Back at Ya" or Christine Stevens, "Call and Response" (middle section). Dancers stop and listen as the phrase plays for the first time, then create a movement expressing that phrase with their bodies as the phrase repeats. Movements can be set and practiced, and groups or individuals can take turns performing.

10. **Element of relationship and inspiration / formations and books about dance.** *EARTHDANCE.* Use the book by Joanne Ryder as a guide and practice the following formations: **cluster**, **circle**, **small circles scattered**, **parallel lines front to back**, **pairs**, and **single line across**. Create movements as described in the book while moving through the formations. Play Mass Ensemble, "Wind in the Earth Harp."

11. **Inspiration/emotions.** *Seven emotions, back-to-back.* Improvise movements expressing the seven basic emotions of *anger*, *fear*, *happiness*, *disgust*, *interest*, *sadness*, and *surprise* in this order to Eric Chappelle, *Music for Creative Dance: Contrast and Continuum*, vol. 3, "Potpourri." In partners, begin standing back-to-back with each other with no emotion; and as soon as each clip begins, they turn and make eye contact, imagining their partner as the reason they are feeling the emotion. They dance an improvised duet together, and when the music pauses, quickly go back-to-back again and go back to no emotion.

12. **World dance / emotions / formations / directions.** *Bele Kawe.* See appendix D, "World Dances." This Afro-Caribbean dance includes the three emotions of *interested*, *surprised*, and *angry*, along with concentric circle formations and forward, backward, and sideways directions.

Fifth Grade

---

1. **Warm-up/technique.** Include extremes of the four basic dance techniques of *alignment*, *lift*, *breath*, and moving from the *center*, as well as whole-body movements, rhythmic patterns in five directions from the center, exercises strengthening the core, body part isolations, two- to three-part combinations, stretches, yoga, prep/jumps, and Effort Actions.

2. **Movement skill practice / rondo structure.** *All-moves rondo.* Practice twenty-two dance **movements** to any music that has a good beat. Choose four movements and create a phrase that enters and exits (traveling at the beginning and end), which will be part A. Divide into six groups and give each group three movements with which to create a phrase, noting they will have to repeat the first movement at the end to finish the musical phrase in the song. Play Sean Paul, "Gimme the Light" and label groups B–G, and groups practice and perform their phrases, beginning and ending with part A.

3. **Element of space / levels, focus, and directions.** Divide into four groups. After exploration of the three concepts within the element of space, change *levels* from low to airborne or from airborne to low, change *focus* from near to far, and changing *directions* while moving. Play John Mayall & the Bluesbreakers, "Hideaway."

4. **Element of space / focus.** *Focus palindrome.* Practice eye exercises. Practice whole-body movements with the focus changing as follows: on *hand*, on *foot*, on *ceiling*, on *floor*, on *shoulder*, on *knee*, on *window*, on *door*, on *another*, on *multiple*

points, constantly changing. Play Eric Chappelle, *Music for Creative Dance: Contrast and Continuum*, vol. 4, "Focus" for this practice. Divide the group in half and assign partners from the other group. Play Eric Chappelle, *Music for Creative Dance: Contrast and Continuum*, vol. 3, "Fairytale" and point out that the song follows a palindrome sequence, ABCDCBA. The first group enters on section A with multiple focus, then change to near focus on own body for section B, and then focus on three far points in the room for section C. Then the other group enters, and partners focus on each other for section D. The first group exits, and the next group follows the same pattern, but in retrograde.

5. **Element of time / timing. *Mirror, echo, conversation.*** As a whole group, practice any simple movement, such as standing and squatting, in *unison*, *random*, and *canon* **timing**. Discuss how *unison* timing is doing the same movement at the same time (*mirror*), how *canon* timing is doing the same movement at a different time (*echo*), and how *random* timing is doing either the same movement or a different movement at a different time (*conversation*). In pairs, improvise movements all three ways. Play Eric Chappelle, *Music for Creative Dance: Contrast and Continuum*, vol. 2, "Celtic Suite" and follow the changes in the musical sections to change types of timing.

6. **Element of energy / force. *Controlling the group.*** In groups of four, one person at a time is the "mover," and the rest of the group members are "the moved." Play Eric Chappelle, *Music for Creative Dance: Contrast and Continuum*, vol. 1, "Lucky Stiff" and follow the four cycles of changes in the music to rotate leaders. Each mover faces their group of the moved and creates movements as if casting a spell on them using relaxed and tense force, following the changes in the music. Group members respond to the movements with the same level of force.

7. **Elements of space, time, and energy/Effort Actions. *Layered choreography.*** Create thirty-two beats of simple choreography to any music, and students learn and memorize it. Divide into groups and with all using the same choreography, students first

decide to add either tense ore relaxed force to each set of eight beats (e.g., first eight/relaxed, second eight/relaxed, third eight/tense, and fourth eight/relaxed). Repeat this process with the same movements two more times, adding either direct or indirect focus to each eight, then adding either sudden or gradual timing as the final layer. Groups determine which four Effort Actions they constructed with their choices for each set of eight beats.

8. **World dance / Orixás.** See appendix D, "World Dances." Match eight orixás with the eight Effort Actions as follows: Oxum/*float*, Iansan or Oya/*punch*, Oxumare/*flick*, Omolu/*wring*, Iemanja/*glide*, Ogum/*slash*, Oxossi/*dab*, and Oxala/*press*. Four or eight groups are given either two or one of the orixás, and they create a brief study of three to four movements expressing their orixá and demonstrating the matching Effort Action.

9. **Element of energy and inspiration / objects. *Texture.*** Have stations set up with a variety of objects of different textures available to touch, as well as chart paper and markers near each object. Some examples of objects include a bristle brush, cotton balls, sand, marbles, a feather, playdough, leaves, and hair gel. Groups of students rotate around to each object, and after feeling them, they write words that describe how they feel to the touch. Ask them not to duplicate words that are already written. In as many groups as there are objects, each uses the list that all groups generated and compose a dance study including movements for each word listed. Play Mickey Hart, "Kaluli Groove."

10. **Inspiration / story dance. *The Spider Weaver.*** See appendix F, "Stories." Divide in half, and groups can create alternating movements or phrases that express the important events in the story. Perform to Bobby McFerrin, "Circlesong Seven."

11. **World dance / rondo form. *Highlife.*** See appendix D, "World Dances." Teach and practice five different movements of the Highlife, alternating with the A movement to form a rondo pattern. Play Christy Lane, "Rhythms of the Highlife."

12. **Personal experience / our own world dance. *Highlife.*** After learning and practicing the traditional version of the

> Highlife, list other things that students enjoy every day that go uncelebrated. Choose four topics and divide into four groups. Each group creates five original movements that are rhythmic and repeatable and that express different aspects of their topic. Perform each to the same music.

Sixth Grade

1. **Warm-up/technique.** Include extremes of the four basic dance techniques of *alignment*, *lift*, *breath*, and moving from the *center*, as well as whole-body movements, rhythm patterns in five directions from the center, exercises strengthening the core, body part isolations, two- to three-part combinations, stretches, yoga, prep/jumps, and Effort Actions.

2. **Movement skill practice / dance studies. *Choice studies.*** Practice twenty-two dance **movements** to any music that has a good beat. Divide into five groups, and each group chooses four movements to create a movement sequence. For each of the movements, the group makes a **choice** to apply one of the following concepts: *body part* movement, a *traveling* movement, an *in-place* movement done in a *formation*, and a movement that is replaced by a still *shape* (which could be the group's least favorite movement). These can be done in any order and to any music.

3. **Element of space / levels, size, direction, focus, pathways. *Five concepts in space.*** Play Carl Orff, *Orff-Schulwerk*, vol. 2, "Allegro Moderato." Divide into five groups, and each gets sixteen slow beats (after a four-beat intro). The groups are **LEVELS** (airborne, high, middle, low), **SIZE** (small, grow, big, shrink), **DIRECTIONS** (forward, backward, diagonal, sideways), **FOCUS** (self, another person, far, everywhere), and **PATHWAYS** (straight, curved, zigzag, wavy). Groups create a movement for each of the four aspects of their concept of space, and each movement gets four beats in the music.

4. **Element of time / phrasing.** *Directions dance.* Teach the following pattern: Reach diagonally back, arc over to the opposite front, then diagonally back to the other side to the opposite front. Step forward, step backward, reach side to side, reach up and down. First perform each pair of directions for eight beats each. Then groups change the counts of three of the four sets of eight beats, and the whole phrase must still add up to thirty-two, resulting in changes in the phrasing of the whole pattern (e.g., both *diagonals* eight beats, *forward/backward* four beats, *sides* sixteen beats, and *up/down* four beats). Perform to Shaggy, "Keepin' It Real."

5. **Element of body / balance.** *Balance/off-balance.* Choose seven pairs of movements. Then perform them in an AABB pattern, performing each movement off-balance first, then on balance. Create a whole-group dance where everyone performs all of the movement pairs or divide into groups by pair. Either divide and perform for each other, or groups within the dance take turns. Play Gemini (Sandor and Laszlo Slomovits), "Tipsy."

6. ***Moving formations.*** As a whole group, practice the following formations moving in space but maintaining the formation: **circle** (side to side), **straight line** (rotating), **cluster** (all around the space), **semicircle** (inverted), **small circles** (rotate), **cross/X** (rotate), and **V** (inverted). Create a whole-group dance by choosing seven traveling movements (one for each formation) and a transition motif. Play Mass Ensemble, "Chaos Nebula."

7. **World dance, element of relationship, and objects / formations and one maraca.** *Los Concheros.* See appendix D, "World Dances." This dance includes the use of one handheld maraca and being in and out of multiple formations. In one section, it also practices counterbalancing with partners.

8. **Element of relationship / spatial relationships.** *Chair dances.* This dance is done only where there are twelve stable chairs available. Practice all relationships, starting with all dancers on one side of room and two chairs in the center with some space between them. Play Gorillaz, "Tomorrow Comes Today." Two at a time dance **toward** the chairs and position themselves in one of

the other relationships as called out to the chair, make a frozen shape, then dance **away** to the other side as the next two enter with the next relationship. Dancers divide into eleven groups, and each gets a chair (the one between gets two) and a relationship. They create a phrase of at least three movements demonstrating their relationship to their chair and end in a shape that also clearly shows that relationship. Perform to the same music.

9.   **Element of time / rhythm.** *External/internal.* Play music that has a strong and predictable rhythm. Students can choose from four to five selected movements and move to the beat, which is an **external** rhythm. Then ask them to dance the same movements to music without any beat, requiring them to make their own decisions when to change to the next movement, which is following an **internal** rhythm.

10. **Inspiration / integrated lesson / poetic forms.** *Five senses poem.* See chapter 17, "Inspiration." This form of poetry makes connections to science and language arts by using sensory perception and metaphor to translate images generated by the words into movement. Read examples. Then either separate groups to create movements expressing each line of a selected poem, or groups each get (or write) their own poem. Have the "looks like" line be a frozen shape. Play any music that fits the poem.

11. **Personal experience / current events or issues.** *Events or issues.* Either ask students to bring in headlines from news articles of interest to them or have a discussion around the most important issues they are facing in their lives at school. If using a headline, no alterations need to be made. But if using an issue of personal interest, create a short sentence that could be a news headline in five to eight carefully selected words. Divide into groups by word in the headline, and each creates a movement phrase expressing their word. All groups teach their phrase to all other groups to create a group dance of the whole sentence. Divide and perform and play any music that fits the topic.

12. **World dance / Oxendans.** See appendix D, "World Dances." This dance combines partner balance and counterbalance, theatrical stage fighting, and the humorous expression of emotions.

PART III
Skill Building and Practice

The elements of dance
and the whole dancer

Chapter 11

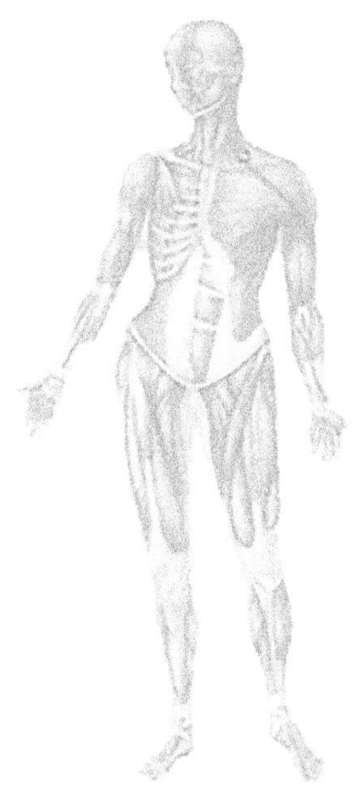

Element of BODY
What the dancer uses as an instrument and developing its capabilities

The dancer is fortunate indeed, for he has for his instrument the most eloquent and miraculous of all instruments, the human body.
—José Limón

Thank you, Mr. Limón, for that affirmation of the exceptionality of dancers! And he is right—it doesn't get any better than our own bodies. Unlike other art forms (with the exception of theatre and vocal music) where the artist can put the instrument or medium away when done using it, we and our bodies are inseparable. Caring for and developing our instrument as you would any instrument of great value involves learning specific methods of fine-tuning and safe use. Hence, an entire element of our art form is devoted to it.

The term with which dancers are most familiar when referring to skills training is *technique*. Some may think that this is a thing reserved for more advanced dancers in either age or ability; however, I believe that good technique should be included in dance education at ALL AGES. It isn't just first position, folks!

The four most basic dance techniques are correct **alignment** of the body, a sense of **lift**, using **breath** with movements, and moving from one's **center**, which is the dancer's source of power and control. Even the youngest and most inexperienced dance students can learn and practice these, oftentimes without even knowing it.

A note on posture in children: I have observed in the past several years an increase in bad posture in children, especially in middle to upper elementary grades. It is most noticeable when they are seated on the floor, either in a crisscrossed position or in various seated stretching positions. Their backs appear slack of tone, and it is difficult for them to sit straight for more than a few seconds. I suspect it is because they spend a great deal of time in front of screens, in chairs, or reclining on the couch playing video games. Of course, we have no control over any of that, and it is no fault of theirs. But I feel it is imperative that we as dance educators instill in our students an understanding of the importance of back and core strength to avoid future back pain and other postural challenges they are likely to face when they get older. We owe it to them! My former husband was a tall man and indulged in rather bad posture at times, which I often brought to his attention (might be part of the reason he is my former husband). He jokingly referred to me as the "posture police" for the constant reminders of his apparent giving in to gravity. Reminding children of the force of gravity, which will NEVER stop affecting them, and how their bodies must be strong enough to live in harmony with it, I believe, is an essential part of our job and a gift we can give them for their lives.

Here are concepts around which I have developed lessons that can help ANY body become a dancing body:

- **Warm-up,** preparing and fine-tuning the dancer's instrument*
- **Movement skills,** for correct execution and creative exploration
- **Body parts/isolations,** moving one part at a time while keeping the rest of the body still
- **Shape,** design of the body's form in stillness
- **Yoga,** for relaxation, strength, flexibility, and clearing the mind
- **Elevation,** five ways of leaving the ground (for upper elementary grades)
- **Counterbalance,** opposing weight, balance, and gravity (for upper elementary grades)

*<u>Why a warm-up is essential</u>

- **Increasing body temperature (slightly)** improves nerve transmission and muscle metabolism, allowing muscles to perform more efficiently.
- **Building strength** enables dancers to control movements, increases stability, increases muscle capacity (especially important when they are still growing), increases bone strength, and decreases the risk of injury.
- **Increasing flexibility** improves mobility, range of motion, posture, and muscle coordination and reduces the risk of injury and muscle soreness.
- **Building endurance** enables dancers to exert physical energy at a high level for a longer period of time without tiring out while using less energy. It also improves the overall health of the heart and lungs.

WARM-UP

Preparing and fine-tuning the dancer's instrument

Some form of a warm-up should begin every dance class. This could be guiding your students through just the right amount of movement—balancing aerobic exercise, strengthening, stretching, and rhythmic precision. The length of the warm-up is important too because you don't want your young dancers to be too tired to do anything else afterward, and yet you do want to give them enough of a workout to feel a difference in their bodies.

Here is what I include in my warm-ups, which increase in complexity with each grade. In all of my warm-up dances, I start off with large uncomplicated movements to engage the large muscle groups. Then I get into more specific and complex patterns to build a variety of skills as the dance progresses.

For younger elementary students, four to six minutes in length:
- **Awakening,** either small to big or low to high
- **Whole-body** movements with deep breathing
- **Directions,** reaching forward, backward, and both sides with the whole body
- **Center** of body strengthening
- **Body parts,** isolating head, shoulders, elbows, hands, stomach, hips, knees, and feet
- **Patterns** of two movements repeating
- **Stretches,** three positions sitting down
- **Opposites** in movements (down/up, small/big, forward/ backward, over/under)
- **Force,** moving in place tense and relaxed
- **Tempo,** running in place slow and fast
- **Energy,** exploring *smooth, sharp, heavy,* and *light*

For middle to upper elementary students, six to nine minutes in length:

- **Techniques,** incorrect and correct *alignment*, *lift*, and *breath* and pulling in to and stretching out from the *center*
- **Whole-body** movements with deep breathing
- **Directions/rhythm,** reaching and stepping *up*, *side*, *down*, *back*, and *front* in a repeating rhythmic pattern
- **Core/center** of body strengthening
- **Isolations** of head, shoulders, elbows, hands, rib cage, hips, knees, and feet
- **Multiple combinations** of two to four movements that repeat
- **Stretches,** three positions sitting down
- **Yoga,** three to six poses
- **Prep/jumps,** beginning with knee bends into jumps, slow and quick
- **Energy qualities,** any movement with *sustained*, *vibratory*, *suspended*, *percussive*, *swinging*, and *collapse* energy (see appendix C, "Element of Energy Deconstruction") OR
- **Effort Actions,** any movement with *float*, *punch*, *flick*, *wring*, *glide*, *slash*, *dab*, and *press* (see appendix C, "Element of Energy Deconstruction")

MOVEMENT SKILLS

For correct execution and creative exploration

Dancers spend a lot of time throughout their careers practicing movements and movement combinations. Dancers practice movements to first learn how to do them and then get better at doing them, also to explore doing them in new ways, to learn the vocabulary, and to move with music.

Some movements are difficult to define; here are some clarifications that might help:

Stretch extends out from the center, while **Bend** pulls in.

Jump leaves the ground, while **Bounce** maintains contact.

Hop is **Jump**, but on one foot.

Shake is tense, while **Wiggle** is relaxed.

Gallop leaves the ground, while **Slide** maintains contact.

Sway stays in place, while **Waddle** travels.

Leap is a larger, more stretched-out version of **Run**.

Run leaves the ground, while **Walk** never loses contact.

Lunge interrupts momentum to shift weight off and then back on center, while **Slide** continues on a trajectory.

For younger elementary students:

Use eighteen movement cards (see chapter 9, "Using Visuals, Objects, and Props") to explore and practice various ways of doing each movement safely and correctly. Practice in sets of three, followed by rest or divided by whether they stay *in place* (nonlocomotor) or *travel* (locomotor). Use the following movements: **walk, jump, stretch, twist, bounce, slide, skip, shake, swing, hop, spin, gallop, crawl, run, leap, wiggle, waddle**, and **bend**. Play any music that has a long steady beat.

- *Walking, Hopping.* Sing and do the three movements in the following song, which is sung to the tune of "Frère Jacques":

"Walking, walking, walking, walking, hop-hop-hop, hop-hop-hop, running-running-running, running-running-running, now we stop!"

    Replace *walk*, *hop*, and *run* with three other movements. Then repeat the song several times until all eighteen have been practiced. No music is needed. Students could take turns singing for one another if desired, or five groups could each get three movements and take turns performing for one another, all groups performing the first version.

- ***ABAB Patterns.*** No more than nine groups are given two movement cards each, one being movement A and the other being movement B. Practice and perform them as a repeating ABAB pattern. Play any music with a long steady beat.
- ***ABC Patterns.*** Practice eighteen dance **movements** to any music that has a good beat and with a rest after every three movements. Divide into six groups, and each group is given a set of three movements, and they decide the order of the movements representing an ABC pattern. Each group performs their pattern for the other two groups and repeats all three of their movements to create an ABCABC pattern.
- ***Across the Floor.*** For locomotor movements only. Place movement cards along the sides of the space and divide the class into pairs or trios between all the movements, and they begin along the side. When the music plays, one pair at a time performs their movement across the floor to the other side and stop. Then the pair on that side performs their movement to the opposite side. All pairs get a turn and end up with a new movement. Repeat starting from the other side. Play any version of the song "Alley Cat" or any upbeat music.
- ***ABCD.*** Divide into six groups and give each group three movements. Group members choose an order, and the ABC represents the three movements, and D represents holding still. Play Creeper Lagoon, "Under the Tracks."
- ***Half-and-Half.*** Divide the group in half, and all remain standing to take turns performing two movements as called out. The group that is not dancing must remain standing still. Play Pat Metheny, "To the End of the World."

For middle elementary students:
Use twenty movement cards (see chapter 9, "Using Visuals, Objects, and Props") to explore and practice various ways of doing each movement safely and correctly. To the above eighteen movements

for younger elementary students, add **lunge** and **sway**. Practice in sets of four, followed by a rest or freestyle moment. Play any music that has a steady beat.

- ***Build a Sequence.*** Use their understanding of a four-part sequence: *first*, *next*, *then*, and *finally*. Then have up to five groups select four movements from the twenty practiced to create a dance sequence. Perform to Bobby McFerrin, "Circlesong Six."
- ***Repeat After Me.*** Make five groups. Give each four movement cards (at least one traveling) and designate a leader for each movement given. Play Eric Chappelle, *Music for Creative Dance: Contrast and Continuum*, vol. 4, "Back at Ya." The first leader enters with a traveling movement, which the rest of the group repeats. Continue with the second movement, third movement, and fourth movement, then the first movement again to exit.
- ***ABCA Thematic Phrases.*** Divide into no more than six groups, and each group is given three movements. They decide their favorite of the three movements, and that is movement A. Their second choice is B, and their third choice is C. Movement A, being the favorite, is repeated at the end, creating an emphasis or theme for their phrase. Perform to any music with a 4/4 time signature.
- ***Three Ways.*** After group exploration of different ways to do each movement (e.g., with a body part, backward or sideways, changing level, or connected to another person), divide into pairs and assign each pair one movement. They create a dance phrase showing their movement done three different ways. Play Carl Orff, *Orff-Schulwerk*, vol. 1, "Gassenhauer."

For upper elementary students:
Use twenty-two movement cards (see chapter 9, "Using Visuals, Objects, and Props") to explore and practice various ways of doing each movement safely and correctly. To the above twenty

movements for middle elementary students, add **roll** and **scoot**. Play any music that has a steady beat.

- ***Chance Dance.*** Choose and list six different movements, matching them to the dots on a die. Groups each roll their own die four times and make note of the order of movements the die has chosen for them. Groups perform their phrases one at a time to the Pharaohs, "Freedom Road." If time allows, repeat the process and create new phrases.
- ***Rondo.*** Play Sean Paul, "Gimme the Light." Choose four cards to make a phrase that enters and exits, which will be part A and will be repeated between the verses by both entering and exiting groups. Make four groups, and each gets four cards to create their own phrases, and they call themselves groups B–E. Each group will do part A twice, before and after their phrase. The rondo pattern is as follows: A – B – A – C – A – D – A – E – A.
- ***Circle Dances.*** After practicing all movements, make three or four small circles. Play "Bobby McFerrin, Circlesong Six." The teacher calls out a traveling movement that all circles perform around their individual circles for four slow beats, then an in-place movement for four slow beats. Then repeat both movements, traveling in the opposite direction. Call out two new movements and repeat, continuing until all movements have been practiced. Emphasis is on changing direction and stopping traveling momentum quickly.
- ***Exploring Space.*** Play Carl Orff, *Orff-Schulwerk*, vol. 2, "Funf Stucke-Allegro Moderato." Divide into five groups, each getting sixteen slow beats of music after a four-beat intro. The groups are each assigned a concept with four components from the element of SPACE: **levels** (airborne, high, middle, and low), **size** (small, grow, large, and shrink), **directions** (forward, backward, diagonal, and sideways), **focus** (self, another person, far, single, and multiple), and **pathways** (straight, curved, zigzag, and wavy). Each group chooses a movement for each of the four components of their category of *space* and performs them for four slow beats each.

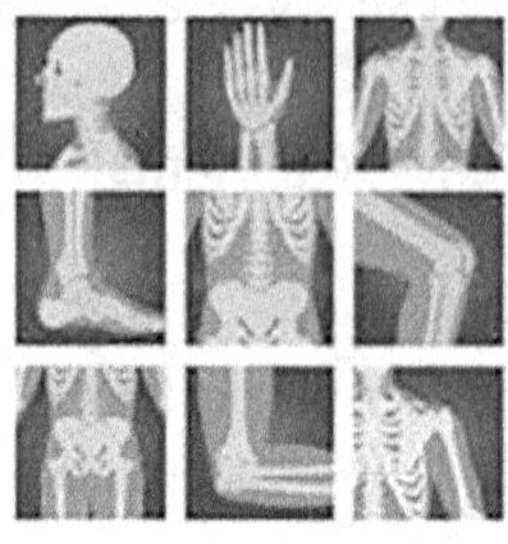

BODY PARTS/ISOLATIONS

Moving one part at a time while keeping the rest of the body still

Isolating certain parts of the body requires certain skills and concentration, especially while concentrating at the same time on NOT moving the rest of the body.

For younger elementary students:
Practice moving the following eight body parts both in-place and traveling as if the body part is being pulled by a string: **head, shoulders, elbows, hands, stomach, hips, knees,** and **feet**.

- *"My Hands" Song.* Learn and practice the following to the tune of "Twinkle, Twinkle, Little Star." Do this first seated, just touching each part as it is sung, then standing, adding your choice of rhythmic body movements:

  "Hands upon my HEAD I place, on my SHOULDERS, on my FACE.
  On my ELBOWS, on my HIPS, on my STOMACH, on my LIPS.
  Then I raise them up so high I think they might touch the sky.
  Touch each FOOT and touch each KNEE, clap together 1-2-3.
  Wave and wave to all my friends. Hands can rest now, it's the end."

- *Touch of Life.* In partners, one is the "dancer," and the other is the "life giver." The life giver touches their dancer on a selected body part, and when touched, only that part moves any way the dancer likes. Play Eric Chappelle, *Music for Creative Dance: Contrast and Continuum*, vol. 3, "I Say, You Say." Partners change roles with changes in the music.

- ***Che Che Kule.*** See appendix D, "World Dances," for details on this dance from Ghana. It includes movements of the head, shoulders, hips, knees, and feet.
- ***El Juego Chirimbolo.*** See appendix D, "World Dances," for details on this dance from Ecuador. It is a partner dance that includes touching each other's feet, hands, and elbows.
- ***Pulled by a String.*** Divide into four groups, and each is assigned two of the eight body parts. All groups begin from the side of the space. Begin being pulled into the space by an invisible string tied to a called-out body part for eight beats. Stop near the center of the space and move the same part in place for eight beats. Then exit to the opposite side, being pulled by same body part. All groups repeat, going back to the original side with their other body part. Play Quincy Jones, "Comin' Home Baby."
- ***Seven Jumps.*** See appendix D, "World Dances," for details on this circle dance from Denmark that has dancers lift or touch the floor with various body parts.
- ***AABA.*** In four groups, each chooses two body parts (A and B) and follows this pattern: A – from lying down, rise, being lifted up by the first body part; A – travel, being pulled by the first body part; B – travel, being pulled by the second body part; A – connect with others in the group by the first body part. (Note: to avoid having children's heads touching one another, it is not advisable to use the head as body part A). Play Eric Chappelle, *Music for Creative Dance: Contrast and Continuum*, vol. 2, "Weavers" and perform one group at a time.

For middle elementary students:
- ***"I'm a Dancer Now."*** Teach and practice the following song to the tune of "Ten Little Indians": *I circle my head and spin around, I circle my head and spin around, I circle my head and spin around, 'cause I'm a dancer now.* Do the movements as described. Then for the last phrase, do

any whole-body movement ending in two claps. The four following verses go like this: *I bend my elbows and skip backward. I shake my shoulders and take a walk. I bounce my hips and gallop like a horse.* Small groups can create their own versions of the song by choosing a body part and a movement that it does and a whole-body movement. Perform without background music.

- **Pull In / Pull Out.** In four groups, assign two of the eight body parts. Each group chooses two movements, one that travels and one that stays in place. All begin off to the side of the space in different areas. Each group dances their traveling movement as if being pulled by their first body part. Next, do their in-place movement with the same body part, then change to the next body part with the same in-place movement. Then exit, being pulled by the second body part with the same movement as with the entrance. Play any music with a steady beat that can be counted in four sets of eight.

For upper elementary students:
Replace the stomach with a rib cage isolation in practice.

- **Body Pinball.** In groups of four to five, each chooses four of the eight body parts and draws a map plotting the course of where a movement will travel between the body parts. For example: *shoulder* to *knee* to *hips* to *head* and back to *shoulder*. Choose a different movement for each body part and practice them separately. Then link them together with a movement as a pinball bounces around its table from point to point. Play soundtrack to *The Final Option*.
- **Partners Connect.** If safe, practice doing various in-place and traveling movements with different body parts connected to a partner (do not include the head and maybe not the rib cage). Partners begin from opposite sides of the space and enter toward each other for twelve beats, being pulled by a chosen body part and with a chosen traveling movement.

When they reach each other, partners connect those body parts to create a connected still shape and hold for four beats. While maintaining contact with their partner, transition to connecting with a different body part, creating a different still shape. Finally, exit together connected by the second body part. Play any music.

- ***Different Parts Connect.*** In partners, follow the same sequence as "Partners Connect" above. But rather than connecting by the same body part, each dancer chooses a different body part and connects to each other with those.

SHAPE

Design of the body's form in stillness

Describe how a dancer's space is like an artist's canvas and how the lines we make with our bodies are the same as those drawn by artists—only ours can move as well as hold still. Practice transitioning into still body shapes from movements or from other shapes. Emphasize the importance of using the whole body in their shapes and of holding still in the shape. Challenge them to create and hold balancing shapes without hopping or touching to keep from falling. Give them an opportunity to watch each other while practicing.

For younger elementary students:

- ***Movements and Shapes.*** Divide the group in half. One half observes while the other dances, then switch. Play any upbeat music, and students dance any movement while the music is playing. Then the teacher stops the music, and all freeze in any shape. Hold silence long enough to make very brief comments on the shapes observed. Allow each group four to five turns, then switch.

- ***ABC Patterns***. In four groups, each chooses two movements (A and B). Practice them and add a still shape (C) at the end. Play Carl Orff, *Orff-Schulwerk*, vol. 1, "Gassenhauer," and each group gets two turns to perform their pattern.
- ***ABCD Pattern.*** Divide into groups of three to four, giving each group two movements, which are parts A and B. Each group designs and practices a shape that they all do for part C, and all melt to the floor for part D. Play Eric Chappelle, *Music for Creative Dance: Contrast and Continuum*, vol. 2, "Weavers," and groups take turns and exit the space after melting.

For middle elementary students:
- ***Travel-Curved-Straight-Travel.*** Focus specifically on *curved* and *straight*-lined shapes. Small groups each enter from the side with a traveling movement of their choice, stop at the center of the space and first form a curved shape, followed by a straight-lined shape. Then they exit with the same traveling movement. Play Quincy Jones, "Comin' Home Baby."
- ***Adjective Movements and Shapes.*** Practice making shapes based on the following adjectives: *big, small, straight, curved, twisty, pointy,* and *scary*. Brainstorm a list of more adjectives that could be used to describe both movements and shapes. Groups of three to four choose two adjectives and create a movement ending in a shape for each (e.g., bumpy slide / bumpy shape, sparkly spin / sparkly shape). Play Kraked Unit, "Douala Paris." Then practice counting music as patterns of twelve for the movements plus four for the still shapes.
- ***Sculptures.*** In partners, one is the clay, and the other is the sculptor. The sculptor changes the shape of their clay by

manipulating its parts. When finished, they imitate the shape they created on the other person and become the clay. The other person steps away and becomes the sculptor. Repeat the process until the selected music ends. Play classical music, such as Vivaldi, "Finale-Allegro Molto."

- **In-Place and Traveling.** Alternate individual shapes following in-place movements with connected group shapes following traveling movements. In groups of three to four people, do improvised movements and shapes. Then take turns to watch one another. Play any music with a 4/4 time signature and count twelve beats for each movement and hold the shape for four.

- **Add-On Shapes.** Start from a single line at the side of the space. Then one person at a time enters with any movement of their choice and forms a shape in the center. After four people connect, all exit, and the next in line starts a new shape. Play Eric Chappelle, *Music for Creative Dance: Contrast and Continuum*, vol. 2, "Pizz.Ah!" and follow cues in the music. Other concepts can be added to this dance, such as levels, energy qualities, or pathways.

For upper elementary students:
- **Muscle Memory.** In groups of three to five, each creates one shape that they all do exactly the same way. They also choose three different movements. Groups dance their first movement for twelve beats, followed by their shape and hold it for four. Then they dance the second and third movements, each followed by the same shape. The challenge is to form the same shape after doing different movements, requiring the muscles to remember. Perform to Prem Joshua, "Deccan Queen."

- **Positive and Negative Space.** Read and show Bill T. Jones's book *Dance*, pointing out the white shapes in the pictures as being the *negative* space and the black and brown shapes as the *positive* space. Practice making shapes, paying particular attention to the negative space created by each shape, both alone and in pairs or trios making connected shapes. Groups create a dance phrase that includes two movements and two shapes (one shape with dancers alone and one connected to each other), with multiple areas of *negative* space in each shape. Play any music with a steady beat that is long enough for each group to perform their movements and shapes four times slowly and hold the shape for at least eight beats.

- **Symmetry/Asymmetry.** Symmetry of the body comes when opposite sides of the body's midline are in a mirror image likeness. Practice making three symmetrical shapes and one asymmetrical shape, quickly changing with three to four slow beats between shapes. Repeat this several times for practice. Groups of three to four all begin in a neutral standing position. With strong beats in the music, one group at a time assumes a symmetrical shape, followed by an asymmetrical shape at the same time. Play Eric Chappelle, *Music for Creative Dance: Contrast and Continuum*, vol. 4, "Totem Pole."

- **Sculpture Gallery.** Half of the group spreads out, and each person forms a shape of their choice. When the music starts, the other half enters as the sculptors, and each chooses one of the shapes onstage and changes the shape by gently moving its body parts. Then the sculptor assumes the shape they just created, and the previously frozen person then dances away to another shape. Play Vivaldi, "I. Allegro." The dance ends with the music, and all who are not shapes exit. The lesson could be extended to include *levels* in space or *symmetry/asymmetry*, and "sculptors" must change the level and/or the symmetry of the shapes they create.

- **Circle-Connect.** Form one large circle, and one person is in the center, forming a still shape. One dancer from the perimeter dances for twelve beats and connects to the person in the center. Together, they hold a connected shape for four beats. Then the person who was there first dances back to the perimeter in eight beats, leaving the other person there holding their shape, which is now not connected to anyone. Repeat as many times as is needed so that everyone in the circle gets a turn.

- **Same and Different.** Make five groups and give each four movement cards. Groups practice each movement and create a shape that follows each movement, performing them in twelve plus four beats. The first shape is **the same** (all dancers imitate the same shape, not connected), the second shape is **different** (all individual, not connected), the third is **imitated-connected** (all the same shape, connected), and the fourth is **different-connected** (all different, connected). Play Gorillaz, "Re-Hash."

YOGA

For relaxation, strength, flexibility, and clearing the mind

Discuss how yoga is an ancient practice originally from India and how the word *yoga* means "joining" of the body, mind, and spirit. Refer to the various positions as *asanas* and discuss how that word means "seat," or a settling into a position. Emphasize the importance of breathing with each asana and use inhaling and exhaling as a structure for moving through the various poses. Play any relaxing and continuous music in the background, such as William Presland, "Morning Star."

For younger elementary students:
Practice a selection of any of the following twelve asanas using the *Yoga Pretzels* cards (Tara Guber and Leah Kalish, 2005): ELEPHANT/breath, TREE/balance, GIRAFFE/forward bend, COBRA/back bend, DRAGON/stretch, BUNNY/breath, PLANK/balance, RIVER/forward bend, DOLPHIN/backward bend, PRETZEL/twist and stretch, OPEN HEART/partner, CHILD'S POSE/relax.

- ***Four-Part Pattern.*** Divide into four groups by four selected asanas, and all groups begin from side of space. Enter with a traveling movement of their choice, then perform their asana. Do the *child's pose*, then exit with the same traveling movement. Play any New Age or relaxing music.
- ***Three Groups, Two Asanas.*** Divide into three groups. Each chooses their own traveling movement. Assign each group two of the asanas, except *child's pose*. All begin from the side. Then one group at a time enters the space with their traveling movements, perform their first and second asanas, and melt into *child's pose*. When all are in *child's pose*, all rise and exit back to where they started at the same time.

For middle elementary students:
Practice a selection of any of the following twelve asanas: LION/breath, STORK/balance, FISH/back bend, CAT-COW/stretch, BACK-TO-BACK CHAIR/partner, ARROW/balance, EAGLE/twist, CAMEL/back bend, WARRIOR/stretch, OPEN HEART/partner, SLEEPING SNAKE/group, and CHILD'S POSE/relax.

- ***Five-Part Pattern.*** In three groups, each gets two asanas, except *sleeping snake* and *child's pose*. Part 1: first asana, part 2: traveling movement to another location, part 3: second asana, part 4: *sleeping snake*, part 5: finish in *child's pose*. Play any relaxing or New Age music as background.
- ***Three Groups–ABCA.*** Divide into three groups and assign each group three of the previously practiced asanas. Each

group creates a phrase that includes their asanas in any order that they choose, with their favorite being first and repeating it at the end to create an ABCA pattern. Play any relaxing or New Age music as background.

For upper elementary students:
Practice a selection of any of the following fourteen asanas: FROG/breath, STORK/balance, TURTLE/forward bend, TWISTING DRAGON/twist and stretch, CAMEL/back bend, COBRA/back bend, SHARK/back strength. Also practice the following seven partner poses: SEESAW, OPEN HEART, BACK-TO-BACK CHAIR, LIZARD ON A ROCK, DOUBLE BOAT, ELEVATOR, and DOUBLE DOG.

- ***Seven-Part Pattern.*** Divide into six groups by six elected asanas, and all groups will do the last three (*seesaw*, *sleeping snake*, and *child's pose*). Each group creates a phrase that includes their asana plus the three that all do and create three original movements as transitions between them.
- ***Linking the Groups.*** Divide into five groups, and each gets two asanas, except *sleeping snake*. The first group performs their two asanas with a set transition between them and ends in *sleeping snake*. The next group enters and joins them in the *sleeping snake*, then performs their two asanas and also end in *sleeping snake*. Each group, in turn, links with the previous group in the *sleeping snake* and then ends with it for the next group to join them. Play any long relaxing or New Age music as background.
- ***Together and Apart.*** Create a whole-group dance that begins in partners and alternates individual asanas with partner poses. Choose an order of all asanas practiced, and partners can either return to the same person or change partners. Divide the class in half to perform for one another. Play any long relaxing or New Age music as background.

ELEVATION

Five ways of leaving the ground

Break down and practice safe and correct execution of the following elevated movements, using ballet terminology. Break down and practice all five ways of leaving the ground:

SAUTÉ/jump (two feet to two feet)

SAUTÉ ARABESQUE/hop (one foot to one foot)

JETÉ/leap (one foot to the other foot)

SISSONNE (two feet to one foot)

ASSEMBLÉ (one foot to two feet)

For upper elementary students:

- ***Enter and Exit.*** Divide into five groups by elevation type, and each group creates an entrance movement that does not leave the ground. Perform their elevation type in two different ways at the center and then exit with their nonelevating movement again. Play Franz Schubert, "Moment Musicale."

- ***Retrograde Elevations.*** Practice and set an original way of performing each elevation type, creating a whole-group dance. Also, create smooth nonelevating transitions between each elevating movement. Perform the sequence forward and backward, working out how it can be done. The pattern goes as follows: A-B-C-D-EE-D-C-B-A (dashes representing the transitions), demonstrating a sequence in retrograde. Play Edvard Grieg, "Peer Gynt."

COUNTERBALANCE
Opposing weight, balance, and gravity

Here are some definitions: **Balanced** is a state of *equilibrium* (forces of gravity and weight are distributed equally). **Off-balance** is a state of *disequilibrium* (forces of gravity and weight are not distributed equally). **Dynamic** balance is moving, and **static** balance is holding still.

For upper elementary students:
Individual practice: Hold a position with five points touching the floor, then four, three, two, and one. Then add movements ending in a balance. For example: *wiggle* – five points, *twist* – four points, *sway* – three points, *leap* – two points, and *swing* – one point. The challenge is to interrupt the natural flow (or momentum) of the movement to find a balance point on various numbers of points.

Practice with a partner: For this, it helps to have partners be of somewhat equal size. **(1)** Face each other holding both hands, with the elbows bent and toes touching. Lean back and straighten the arms. Then bend the knees, as if both are sitting in a chair. Then pull back up to a standing position. **(2)** From sitting down back-to-back, stand up together. **(3)** From front to back, perform the trust fall, taking turns falling and catching. **(4)** With the ankles or lower legs linked, lean away. **(5)** Arrange themselves back-to-back, with one person curved forward as the other lies back on their back and switch. **(6)** Experiment with their own ways to share weight.

- *Balance/Off-Balance.* Choose seven pairs of movements. Then perform them in an AABB pattern, performing each movement off-balance first, then on balance. Create a whole-group dance, where everyone performs all of the movement in pairs or divide into groups by pair. Either divide and perform for one another or groups within the dance take turns. Play Gemini (Sandor and Laszlo Slomovits), "Tipsy."

- **Three Counterbalanced Shapes.** Divide into groups of three to four, and each creates three different connected shapes. Then experiment with transitioning between them **without letting go**. Emphasize that it will likely require changing which body parts are connected and that the shapes must be very different. Play Jenny Allinder, "Star of the County Down." The whole study could go as follows: One dancer at a time enters and forms a still shape, each connecting to the others as they enter. All transition to the second shape, then transition to the third shape. Then one by one, all exit, leaving the final shape.

- **Five, Four, Three, Two, One, Five Points.** In groups of four to five dancers, each group chooses five movements, each done with a different number of points on the body touching the floor. Play Prem Joshua, "Deccan Queen." Then groups begin with a five-point movement to a four-point movement to a three-point movement to a two-point movement to a one-point balancing movement, then finally back to the original five-point movement, eight beats each.

- **Helping Shapes.** In trios, each dancer creates an off-balance shape that needs help from their partners to hold. Play Quincy Jones, "Comin' Home Baby." Then each person dances into and holds their shape, with help, in eight beats.

- **Six Actions.** Use the following sequence *six actions* as a framework: PASS, REACH, TURN, FALL, RISE, SEPARATE. Partners or trios create a movement for each part of this pattern that alternates between being balanced and off-balance. Perform to any upbeat music with a long steady beat. I like Latin music for this one.

Chapter 12

Element of SPACE
Where the dancer creates a visual design

Dance is a visual art! It is a picture that moves before your eyes. And exactly like all other visual arts, dancers create something for the observer's eyes to see in the three-dimensional **space** that our bodies occupy. A dancer's awareness of space and their ability to use it effectively is an essential component of dance as an art form.

There are many aspects of the element of space that dancers, whether intended or not, are using at all times. One aspect that is not included in this chapter, but rather in chapter 15, "Element of Relationship," is what is called *spatial relationships*. These are various ways of placing dancers in juxtaposition with one another in space. That concept could just as easily have fit in this chapter since it truly is a blend of both, but I had to make a choice.

Another concept that is often identified with the element of space is *shape*. However, I believe it is a better fit in the element of *body* (see chapter 11, "Element of Body"). Yes, when we are forming shapes, we are doing so in space as always while dancing, and we are manipulating the lines our various body parts create, thereby designing space. But in my view, the main emphasis in the concept of shape is on the creation and control of lines created by the *body* that happens to occupy space.

Here are six concepts that are part of the element of *space*:
- **In-place and Traveling,** moving in self-space and the general space shared by all
- **Direction,** from a dancer's center or their orientation to the surrounding horizontal space
- **Levels,** occupying various gradations of vertical space
- **Size,** the amount of space or volume used in movements or shapes
- **Pathways,** lines traced in the air around the body or on the floor moving through space
- **Focus,** using the dancer's gaze to draw attention

In-Place and Traveling

Moving in self-space and the general space shared by all

For young dancers, spatial awareness is a developmental milestone. Understanding and navigating where they are in any space mean the difference between successfully performing movements in groups and risking injury to themselves or others. Students need to learn how to leave and return to a space and to remain there when needed.

Dance movements can be categorized as either **traveling** (or locomotor) or **in-place** (or nonlocomotor). And there are several movements that can be done both ways, such as *walk*, *run*, *jump*, *hop*, and *lunge*. No matter what movement a dancer is performing, they need to know whether they are traveling through space with it or staying in place.

For younger to middle elementary students:
Color spots are helpful to designate places in the room, and matching color spots can indicate destinations. Movement cards can be used to select movements that travel or stay in place.

- **Coming Home.** Use pairs of colored poly spots placed across the floor from one another to designate each group's "home" and their "destination." Divide into groups by color, and one group at a time performs. Play any upbeat music, and each group first performs a called-out movement that stays in place (such as *wiggle*), then a called-out traveling movement (such as *gallop*) to the matching spot. Repeat both movements, returning home to the original spot. If students can do this easily, remove the spots after all have had a turn and repeat. Another option would be to have one student on each spot, with all performing the same movements. Switch places with the dancer on their matching color spot. This can be a bit chaotic, but if there is enough space, more students can dance at the same time.
- **Meet and Greet and Part.** With partners lined up across the floor from each other, one pair at a time dances a called-out traveling movement toward each other to "meet." Then they dance a called-out in-place movement to "greet" each other. And finally, repeat the traveling movement back to the same side to "part" from each other. Play any music as background.
- **Enter and Exit.** Play Franz Schubert, *Moment Musicale*, and divide into nine groups or pairs to fit the music. Each group is assigned one traveling and one in-place

movement. Place a color spot in the center of the floor, and all groups start from one side, entering and traveling to the spot. Then they do their in-place movement near the spot, then exit with the same traveling movement to the opposite side. Each group gets sixteen quick beats in the music, so the next group enters as the previous group is exiting.

- ***Duck, Duck, Goose.*** Replacing an in-place movement for the word "duck" and a traveling movement for the word "goose" and doing the movements as called out can transform this traditional game into a very fun dance. Dancers form one large circle or two smaller circles if there is enough space, with all dancers standing. One person is chosen from each circle to be "it." That person walks around the outside of the circle, touching the head of each person they pass and repeating the name of the in-place movement. When touched, the dancer does the movement and continues to do the movement until "it" says the word of the traveling movement. Whoever is chosen begins to chase "it" doing that movement until they reach the empty space in the circle from where the chosen person left. Then that person becomes "it." Play any classical music as background. I like Vivaldi.
- ***Mirror and Shadow.*** With a partner, begin facing each other, with a designated leader *mirroring* two different in-place movements. Then the leader turns around and does two different traveling movements with the other person following, or *shadowing*. Repeat both parts with the other person as the leader. Play George Benson, "Breezin'."

Direction

From a dancer's center or their orientation to the surrounding horizontal space

There are two kinds of directions a dancer needs to know about:
(1) one which is internal and does not relate to the general space
and (2) one which is completely related to the surrounding space.
Both are concerned with *horizontal* space. Often, young dancers,
when asked to move backward, will do a 180-degree turn and move
forward! Of course, they are correct in a way but are missing out on
a chance to experience backward motion.

For younger elementary students:
For practice of internal body directions, ask students to touch their
stomach and imagine there is a light shining from it. That light always
needs to be pointing toward a designated point in the front of the room.
Practice *bend*, *stretch*, and *swing* forward, backward, and to both sides
without changing where their light is pointing. Next, slide each foot out
and back in to all directions. Finally, step out and back in to all directions.

- **ABAB Pattern.** Put all movements together in pairs.
  Movement **A** will be done forward and backward, and
  movement **B** will be done right and left. Play Bob Marley
  & the Wailers, "Three Little Birds." Divide and take turns
  performing to avoid fatigue.

For middle elementary students:
When practicing orientation in the space, it can help to draw a
picture of the space showing where the audience is as well as where

the back and right and left sides are. Practice changing orientation by facing **front** to **side** to **back** to other **side** and return to front. Practice selected movements facing all four orientations.

- ***Points in Space.*** Designate four places anywhere in the room and choose four movements that travel to each of them. Then match a different internal body direction to each of the movements.

For upper elementary students:
Adding diagonals can confuse younger students but can open up a whole new way of using angles in space to older dancers. Have students imagine being inside a large square, with the front, sides, and back being the flat sides and the corners being the diagonals. In this case, there are eight directions to choose from.

- ***Directions Dance.*** This simple structure can be used to explore many other concepts, such as focus, tempo, duration, and force. Facing front, reach toward the back right diagonal, over the top, and cross over to the forward left diagonal with the same arm. Repeat with the other arm on the other two diagonals. Take four steps forward and four steps backward. Lunge right twice, then lunge left twice.
- ***Internal and External Orientation.*** In small groups, they create a four-part dance sequence. Each part matches an internal body direction with an orientation in space, using all four of each. For example: **slide** right facing left, **jump** backward facing forward, **crawl** forward facing right, and **stretch** left facing backward. Groups might need paper and pencils to write down their choices.
- ***Four-Sided Dances.*** Practice and perform several dances that change direction with each repeating cycle of movements. Some examples are Macarena, Pata Pata, Texas line dances, and Payaso del Rodeo. See appendix D, "World Dances."
- ***Element of Space.*** This includes **directions**, **levels**, and **focus**. Divide into four groups, and each group selects three movements to create a phrase. Practice the phrase for

memory. Then add changing *levels* (high to low or low to high) to the first movement, changing *focus* (from their own hand to far or multiple focus) to the second, and changing *directions* (turning right, left, moving sideways, or backward) to the third. Perform to John Mayall & the Bluesbreakers, "Hideaway."

Levels

Occupying various gradations of vertical space

Some movements are defined by their level in vertical space, such as *roll*, *crawl*, *walk*, and *leap*. By changing the level of some movements, you change what the movement is. For example, *run* and *jump* are airborne versions of *walk* and *bounce*. It is really fun to try movements at levels other than what is expected, and pointing out to students how the definition can change will help them better understand the importance of levels in the correct execution of movements. To illustrate levels, I use the image of a tree (see chapter 9, "Using Visuals, Objects, and Props"): the roots being the lowest, the trunk being middle, the branches and leaves being high, and things that fly in and out of the trees (such as birds) being airborne.

For younger elementary students:
High and *low* are opposites, and for students who understand that concept, just the two levels can be enough. Adding a middle level challenges their physical strength in maintaining a squatting position.

- ***"Eensy Weensy Spider."*** Go through the motions of the song with just hands first, seated. Then add the rest of the body, moving from low to high slowly, then quickly from high to low as the spider, then again as the sun drying up the rain, then one more time as the spider climbing up. Sing the song or use any recorded version.

- **Grow and Wilt.** Practice movements at low and high levels as well as changing levels. Play Carl Orff, *Orff-Schulwerk*, vol. 1, "Sieben Vlolkstanze Tanz 2." Starting from a low curled-up position, slowly rise up, as if growing from a seed; and finish at a high level with the body open and stretched up and out to the sun like a flower. Repeat the music and slowly lower back down to the ground like a flower wilting and dying. Divide the class in half. Simultaneously, one group grows, while the other wilts, going in opposite directions, with an adult joining each group.

- **Grow and Melt.** Play Carl Orff, *Orff-Schulwerk*, vol. 1, *Funf Kleine Kanons*. In three or six groups, practice moving from a low to a high level (growing) in eight beats. Hold a still shape for four beats, then move from high back down to low (melting) in eight beats. Each group can select movements for their growing and melting parts.

- **Levelance.** Play Eric Chappelle, *Music for Creative Dance: Contrast and Continuum*, vol. 1, "Levelance." Following the pitch and timbre of the three different sections, the whole group can dance any movement at the level the music tells them. Then divide in half, one half getting a high level and the other getting a low level. Both dance during the middle. The group not dancing must hold still wherever they are, and groups can mix together throughout the space.

- **Water, Land, and Air.** List things that move in these three levels on earth (water being low level, land being middle level, and air being high level). Improvise all items listed one level at a time. Then choose the best four at a low level and the best three at both the middle and high levels. Play Eric Chappelle, *Music for Creative Dance: Contrast and Continuum*, vol. 4, "Amphibious." Follow the changes in the music, beginning with the first item/movement in the water, then to land and to air. The music cycles through twice more, then finishes with the water tune. The whole group can create and practice the dance, then divide and perform it for one another.

- **Objects and Levels.** See chapter 15, "Element of Relationship," in the subcategory of "Objects."
- **Movement Mix-Up.** In groups, each chooses four movements and arranges them in order of preference, performing the first at low, the second at middle, the third at high, and the fourth as a melting movement descending back to low. Each group performs their chosen pattern to Mary Youngblood, "And We Shall Dance." Then groups rearrange the order of their movements, practice, and perform again.
- **Square in the Air.** Divide into six groups and give each two movements, one in place and one traveling. Do the in-place movement first, starting low and ending high. Then do the traveling movement at a high level across the floor for a short distance. Repeat the in-place movement, going from high to low this time. Then turn around and repeat the traveling movement back to the original place, but at a low level. Play David Benoit, "Safari."
- **Palindrome.** Divide into three groups. Each group creates a phrase of four selected movements and labels them A, B, C, and D. Movement A is done at *low* level, B at *middle* level, C at *high* level, and D changes level from *high* to *low*. Repeat D from *low* to *high*. Repeat C at *high*, B at *middle*, and A at *low*. Perform to Mary Youngblood, "And We Shall Dance."

For middle and upper elementary students:
- **Tempo and Levels.** See chapter 13, "Element of Time," in the subcategory of "Tempo." Add *airborne* level and practice selected movements at all four levels.
- **Trees.** See chapter 22, "Integrating Content Areas," Third Grade, Science.

- ***Add-On Shapes.*** In groups of four, each gets a level: *low, middle, high,* and *airborne.* One person at a time, starting with *low,* enters from the side and makes a still shape at their level in the center of the space. Each person in their group enters at their respective levels and connects to the person already there, creating a group shape. Note that the *airborne* person moves at that level but makes a shape at any of the other three. All exit after their multilevel shape is completed. Play Eric Chappelle, *Music for Creative Dance: Contrast and Continuum,* vol. 2, "Pizz.Ah!" and follow the musical phrases.
- ***Echo Dance.*** In groups of five, each is assigned to one of the four levels, *low* to *airborne* plus descending. Each person creates a movement they perform at their level. Play Eric Chappelle, *Music for Creative Dance: Contrast and Continuum,* vol. 4, "Back at Ya." One group at a time performs in a call-response form, with each group member leading and the rest of the group imitating their movement.

 **Size**

The amount of space or volume used in movements or shapes

Another word that can be used to describe the size of movements or shapes in space is **volume**, a term used in math to describe the measurable dimensions of objects or spaces. Practice with several selected movements, starting out **small** with body parts close to center. Then expand outward, doing the movement as **big** as possible. Then shrink back to small, still doing the same movement.

For younger and middle elementary students:
- ***Changing Size.*** Play Carl Orff, *Orff-Schulwerk,* vol. 1, "Funf Kleine Kanons." Then divide the class into three large groups.

Each group chooses a single movement and performs it very small. Pause with change in the music and expand. Then perform the same movement very big. Each group performs their movement. Then give each a new movement and perform again. Do this as many times as there are movements.

- ***abc-Grow-ABC-Shrink.*** Use sets of three movements and divide into as many groups as there are sets of movements. Perform each set small for four beats each. Then grow for four beats. Repeat the same three movements big and shrink for four beats. Groups take turns performing and can rotate sets of movements and perform again. Play Mary Youngblood, "Beneath the Raven Moon."

- ***Shrinking Space.*** Place four chairs in the four corners of the space and tell students to visualize imaginary lines that connect them around the outside of the space. Play Eric Chappelle, *Music for Creative Dance: Contrast and Continuum*, vol. 4, "Islands." Students dance any movement they like without going outside the "space" and without touching anybody else. When the music pauses, selected students move the chairs closer to the center, causing the space to shrink. When the music resumes, the same rules apply, forcing movements to get smaller. Repeat this process two more times with pauses in the music. On the last pause, move the chairs back out to original places, and movements can be large again.

- ***All Things Big and Small.*** By student suggestion, list six to seven things that are small (such as ant, grain of sand, worm) and six to seven things that are big (such as mountain, building, whale). After making lists, the teacher selects the first item on each list and creates a movement expressing each for the whole group to practice. Then divide into as many groups as there are pairs of items. Assign each group one small thing and one big thing, and they create movements expressing their items. Each group performs their pair of items twice. Then all perform the whole-group movements together. Play any music that is long enough for all to perform as background.

- ***Tokyo Dontaku.*** See appendix D, "World Dances." Practice and perform the dance, noting that all movements are very small in size.

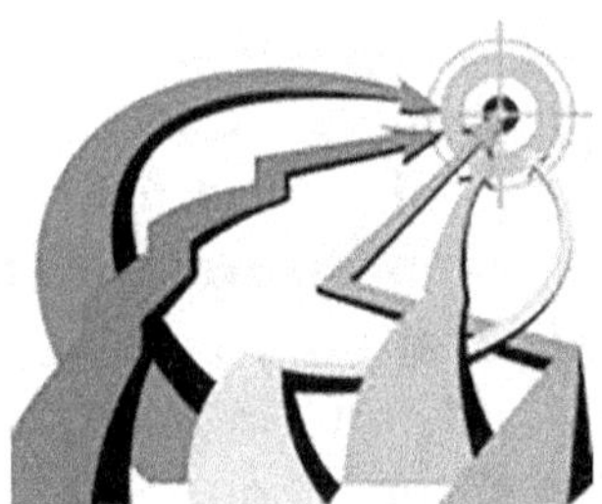 **Pathways**

Lines traced in the air around the body or on the floor moving through space

Wherever the whole body or the body parts are going, they are following a pathway. In-place movements and various body parts follow **air** pathways, and the whole body moving through space follows **floor** pathways. The four pathways include **straight**, **curved**, **zigzag**, and **wavy**. Take one pathway at a time and first "draw" them in the air the with various body parts, such as hands, head, elbows, and feet. Then practice with whole-body traveling movements all around the floor.

For younger elementary students:
- ***The Snake and Her Friends.*** Tell the following story: *There once was a snake who was very friendly, but all the other animals were afraid of her because they knew she could be very dangerous with her poisonous bite or her crushing coils. She always traveled along a* wavy *path. First, she met a horse, who was traveling along a* straight *path; and she showed him she was not dangerous by dancing for him. Next, she met a bird, who was flying in a* curved *path, watching her from above; and she showed her she was not dangerous too. Finally, she met a rabbit, who was jumping in a* zigzag*

path to try and avoid her; and she showed him she was not dangerous also. Play Eric Chappelle, *Music for Creative Dance: Contrast and Continuum*, vol. 2, "Pathway Puzzle." Divide the group in half. Each half performs to one full cycle of the music to watch each other, and then both groups perform together at the shortened cycle at the end.

- **Color Spots.** Place two spots apart from each other, forming a **straight** path between them. Place three spots in a triangle formation and demonstrate movements following **curved** pathways around and circling between them. Place four spots in offset lines and demonstrate movements following a **zigzag** pathway toward each spot. And place four spots in a line with space between and demonstrate movements weaving through them in a **wavy** pathway. Play any long music, and one student at a time can travel along each pathway.

- **Melting Pathways.** Play Eric Chappelle, *Music for Creative Dance: Contrast and Continuum*, vol. 2, "Pathway Puzzle." Three groups cycle through all pathways (will need to start the music over after six sections). When it is not their turn, dancers sit on the floor without moving, and dancers who are moving must navigate around and between them while staying on their pathway. With melting sound in the music, the group that is dancing follows their pathway, lowering themselves to the floor until their next turn. At the end of the music, all groups dance together, following *straight*, *curved*, and *zigzag* pathways together, then slowly melting along a *wavy* pathway with the last long melting sound.

- **Pathways and Body Parts.** Divide into four groups, and each is assigned a pathway and two body parts. The sequence goes as follows: The first body part is in place along the pathway. Then travel being pulled by that body part along the same pathway. Repeat with the second body part. Play any version of "Alley Cat."

- **Itik-Itik.** Apply the four pathways to the four different movements of this dance. See appendix D, "World Dances."

For middle elementary students:

- ***Pathway Pairs.*** There are six possible ways to pair four things. So divide into six groups and give each group a pair of pathways (see chapter 9, "Using Visuals, Objects, and Props"). Each group creates a phrase of three movements and performs all of them along their first pathway and then repeats them along their second pathway. Perform to Prem Joshua, "Deccan Queen."

- ***Fine Art.*** Using four examples of fine art described below (see chapter 9, "Using Visuals, Objects, and Props"), point out the predominant lines present in each and discuss how they can be expressed as pathways in space through movement. For *straight* – *Three Musicians* by Pablo Picasso, for *curved* – the upper part of *Birth of Venus* by Botticelli, for *zigzag* – *Relativity* by M. C. Escher, and for *wavy* – *Red Poppy* by Georgia O'Keeffe. Divide into four groups, and each is given one of the examples of fine art. Each group creates a three-movement phrase that expresses the various pathways seen in the picture. Play any music that fits the feeling of each picture.

- ***Pathway Maps.*** Draw examples of three different overlapping pathways, from point A to point B. Then orient them to fit the space you are working in. Practice those with different movements. Groups of three students draw their own maps the same way, each contributing a pathway. Each person creates a movement that follows their pathway, from A to B in eight beats. Dancers take turns traveling their pathway. Then all three return from point B to point A at the same time, also in eight beats. Perform to Muse, "Supermassive Black Hole."

- ***Parallel/Not Parallel.*** See chapter 22, "Integrating Content Areas," Third Grade, Math.

- ***Pathways and Stage Areas.*** In groups of three, they choose four of the six areas of the stage (downstage right, left, and center and upstage right, left, and center). Each dancer begins in one of them, the fourth area being the destination for all, traveling along a different pathway. Then all exit the space along the fourth. Be sure they all do different movements as well. Play the Lively Ones, "Surf Rider."

For upper elementary students:
- ***Pick Up and Drop Off.*** Play the Pharaohs, "Freedom Road." Count slow eights. Make five groups, and each gets eight sets of eight (the music starts to fade after last eight of the last group). Groups draw a map with four points labeled A–D and connect all the points with four pathways. For the first eight, all enter from offstage and go to their designated points. Person A travels to B, AB travel to C, ABC travel to D, ABCD travel to A, BCD travel to B, CD travel to C, D travels to D. Then all exit overlapping with entrance of next group.
- ***The Journey.*** See chapter 22, "Integrating Content Areas," Fifth Grade, Language Arts.

Focus

Using the dancer's gaze to draw attention

Where a dancer chooses to look can be a powerful way of drawing the attention of the audience. Changing the dancer's focus can give an entirely different meaning to any movement and can establish a connection between dancers.

Begin this lesson by doing some simple eye exercises, such as looking up, down, to both sides, and in circles without moving the head. Also, hold the hand in front of the face at a short distance. Practice focusing on it and then on the wall or another object in the distance beyond it. Demonstrate a simple movement, such as opening the arms and legs into second position, repeating it several times and focusing on something different each time. Have students identify what you are focusing on.

For younger to middle elementary students:
Practice focusing directly on one thing NEAR and another thing FAR for ten seconds each without moving. Repeat with several different focal points. Choose four focal points in the room, starting very near, gradually getting farther away. Then practice any in-place movement, then any traveling movement, maintaining focus on each object. Remind students that they don't need to travel toward the object on which they are focusing.

- ***Near and Far Objects.*** In four groups, each decides on one **far** object and one **near** object (which is one of their own body parts). They are given one traveling movement and one in-place movement (which should not be *spin*). They create an ABBA pattern as follows: (1) Travel from the side to the center of the space, focusing on the *far* object for eight beats. (2) Do in-place movement, focusing on the same *far* object for eight beats. (3) Change focus to the *near* object or body part and do the same in-place movement for eight beats. (4) Exit with the same traveling movement, focusing on the same *near* object. Play Eric Chappelle, *Music for Creative Dance: Contrast and Continuum*, vol. 2, "Skippy Ska" or Cusco, "Dance of the Sun Priest."

For upper elementary students:
Practice to Eric Chappelle, *Music for Creative Dance: Contrast and Continuum*, vol. 4, "Focus," focusing on the following ten focal points (do any movement for eight beats each): *hand, foot, clock, door, shoulder, knee, ceiling, floor, another person, everywhere* (multiple foci).

- ***Single, Single, Multiple.*** Play John Mayall & the Bluesbreakers, "Hideaway." In pairs, create a phrase of three movements, eight beats each, where the first is focusing on

a single object in the room, the second is multiple focus, and
the third is on each other.

- **Focus Palindrome.** Play Eric Chappelle, *Music for Creative
  Dance: Contrast and Continuum*, vol. 3, "Fairytale." Follow
  cues in the music to change parts. The sequence of musical
  motifs is a palindrome: ABCDCBA. Divide the group in half
  and assign partners in opposite groups. For part A, each
  group does any movement, where they maintain **multiple**
  focus. For part B, each group chooses one part of their own
  body and does any movement with **near** focus. For part C,
  select three **far** focal points inside or outside the room and
  dance any movement, focusing on each thing for ten slow
  beats each. For part D, the second group enters. They make
  eye contact with their partner from the first group, doing
  any movement while maintaining eye contact. Then the first
  group exits; and the second group repeats parts C, B, and A
  and exit at end of music.

- **Spidey Suite.** Play Danny Elfman, "Spidey Suite" or any other
  dramatic soundtrack music. In pairs, enter and exit in a loop
  from and to the same side. Enter with focus on a **single far**
  point in the room. Change movement and focus to an in-
  place movement, focusing on a **single near** object. Change
  movement and make **eye contact** with each other, then exit
  with **multiple** focus.

Element of TIME

When the dancer starts, changes, or stops movement

Dance is immediate! A fleeting second goes by, and a movement is performed, and the dancer is already onto the next and the next and the next movement in a dance at exactly the right moment. *When* a dancer does a movement can determine the effect and meaning of a dance, generate interest, and create a compelling visual effect. Time is the element dance most closely shares with music, our most common partner.

Many people say they "can't dance" because they don't think they have a sense of rhythm, and that is quite possibly a self-fulfilling prophecy.

Rhythmic and musical abilities are, to some extent, built into our DNA, but not completely. They can be taught, practiced, and mastered; and that, my friends, is a big part of our job with children. We can never allow them to think they can't do something, or it will likely come true!

The way I see this element broken down is into six concepts, one of which also falls into the element of *relationship*—that one being *timing*. It is a perfect blend of the elements of time and relationship because it is all about WHEN a dancer dances in relation to either another dancer or a group or in relation to the music (for more about a dancer's relationship with music, refer to chapter 15, "Element of Relationship"). Timing is a component of *energy* as well in how gradual timing can result in smooth-flowing or sustained movement and how sudden timing can result in sharp or percussive. For this chapter, the following six concepts are outlined:

- **Beat,** a predictable pulse that can be measured
- **Rhythm,** a repeating pattern of different movements
- **Tempo,** the speed or velocity at which a dancer moves
- **Timing,** dancers' relationships to each other and to music
- **Duration,** the length of time spent on and between movements
- **Phrasing,** a more complex and subtle form of using duration as an artistic choice

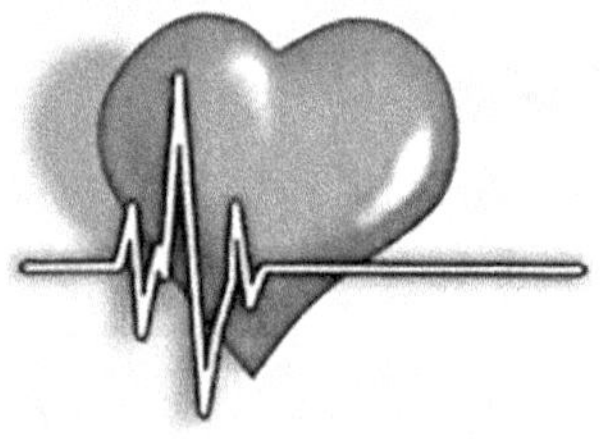

BEAT

A predictable pulse that can be measured

Clapping, marching, tapping, bending the knees, and many other movements can be used to help students learn to hear, feel, and move with a beat.

For younger students:

Practice the following twelve movements with music with a clear and steady beat in the background: *walk, jump, twist, bounce, slide, skip, swing, hop, gallop, run, waddle,* and *bend*. Also practice clapping and counting to eight.

- **Clap and Move.** Divide into groups of three to four, and each group gets one movement at a time. Clap eight times with the music and then do their movement on the beat eight times and repeat both. Each group gets a turn. Then they all get new movements and repeat. Play Eric Chappelle, *Music for Creative Dance: Contrast and Continuum*, vol. 2, "Caribbean Leaps."

- **Clap, Stomp, Move.** Divide into four groups and give each two movements. Play Cusco, "Tula." On the beat, clap the hands three times quickly in two slow beats. Then stomp the feet the same way. Then do the first movement for four slow beats. Then do the same clapping and stomping with the second movement and repeat both. Groups take turns and then could get new movements and do it again.

- **La Mariposa.** See appendix D, "World Dances." Play Colibrí, "La Mariposa." Create two movements that a butterfly might do and perform them for sixteen beats each with vocals. Follow the words of the song and clap and stomp three times each. Then slowly spin with the arms stretched out like wings. Dancers can then take hands with others in pairs or small groups and gallop around in circles for thirty-two quick beats. Then repeat the clapping and stomping section and finish by repeating the first two butterfly movements until the music fades.

- **No Beat / Beat.** Use and practice the following five movements that naturally have a steady beat: *walk, leap, twist, skip,* and *swing*. Then do the same with these five that don't: *bend, stretch, spin, wiggle,* and *shake*. As a whole group, create two three-movement patterns, one of which does not naturally have a steady beat and one that does. Divide into three groups and perform for one another to Eric Chappelle, *Music for Creative Dance: Contrast and Continuum*, vol. 4, "Bottle Rocket," following cues in the music. Perform again but switch the movement patterns to perform the no-beat movements to the music that has a steady beat and vice versa.

For middle elementary students:
Counting beats comes into play with these students. Seated, start with practice patting knees and doing various movements, such as pushing alternating hands forward, tapping the floor with the fingers, and flapping the elbows—each in **eight counts**, then **four counts**, then **two counts**, then **one count** each. Notice how the movements aren't done faster, but the dancer has to think faster to change the movements at the right time.

- *Four-Count Dance.* In groups of four to five, each person creates a movement in four counts and teaches it to the others. All dancers perform all movements together, and if someone chooses a traveling movement, all dancers should travel in the same direction. Play Eric Chappelle, *Music for Creative Dance: Contrast and Continuum*, vol. 2, "Caribbean Leaps."
- *Obwisana.* See appendix D, "World Dances." In circles of five to six students, begin with one beanbag and practice passing it around the circle on a steady beat, singing the song from the music (see appendix D, "World Dances"). Next, add enough beanbags for all to have one and pass simultaneously, keeping the beat. Then create variations on passing the beanbag, still staying on the beat. Finally, perform one group at a time to Music Together: Family Favorites, "Obwisana."
- *Echo Lady Who.* Divide in half and give each group four movements, and they will take turns performing all four movements. Play Eric Chappelle, *Music for Creative Dance: Contrast and Continuum*, vol. 1, "Echo Lady Who." Follow the

counts with the repetitions of movements: 8s – 6s – 4s – 2s – 1s – 1s.

- **Addition Dance.** List as many three-number combinations as the students can think of that add up to twenty-four. Choose four that are very different from one another and divide into as many groups. Groups choose three movements and practice and perform each movement for the number of counts in their addition example. Play Carl Orff, *Orff-Schulwerk*, vol. 1, "Gassenhauer." Each group performs twice.
- **Adapting Movements.** Divide into four groups, and each chooses three movements to make a short phrase. Play Eric Chappelle, *Music for Creative Dance: Contrast and Continuum*, vol. 3, "Tambourine." Each group performs their three movements quickly to the section with no beat, then the same three movements for sixteen beats each to the section of the music that has a steady beat. Notice the adaptations that needed to be made for certain movements to fit both types of music.

For upper elementary students:
Practice various movements that keep a steady beat, such as stomping, clapping, or tapping different body parts.

- **Body Percussion.** Use three kinds of sound-making movements: *clap*, *tap*, and *stomp*. Encourage creativity in what body parts are used to produce sounds that keep a steady beat, and groups of three to four create a phrase of four parts that includes at least one of each of the three types of percussion. Groups perform one at a time without background music but create the music themselves.
- **Across the Floor.** Play two selections of music, one that has an obvious and steady beat and one that does not. Practice two to three selected movements to both and discuss how the movements need to change to fit each song. For example, Michel Cusson's "Koani" and "Musk Ox." Create groups of three to five dancers, and each creates a short

phrase of three movements that travels across the floor. Each group performs their phrase, taking turns to the song with the steady beat first, then returns back to the other side to the song without the beat. Remind students that they will need to find their own time to move while dancing to the song without a beat.

- **Beat Circle.** Form either one large circle or several small circles. With no music, one person starts a beat, such as clap-double clap; and once it goes around the circle, it changes. Start simple, with movements in **two beats**, and then introduce more complex movements each time around. The goal is for each person to do the movement without missing a beat. Examples are single or double claps, grab knee, punches, walk in place down-up-up, cross spin. No music is needed, but something with a steady beat in the background could be used.

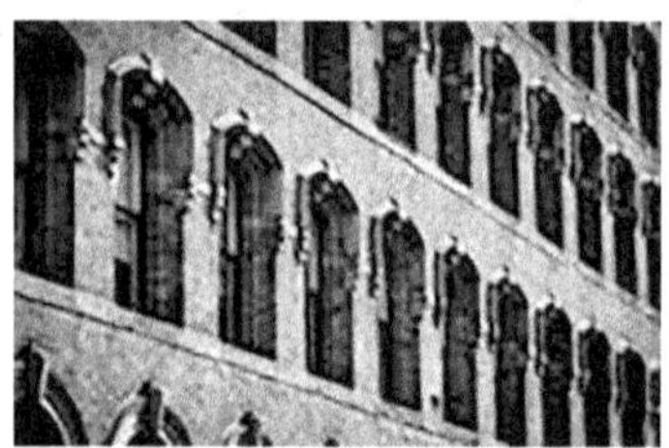 # RHYTHM

A repeating pattern of different movements

Children respond very well to predictable patterns, with movements, chants, and songs. They are able to memorize and perform complex sequences once they understand how it works.

For younger elementary students:
- **Dance My Name.** Say each child's first and last name out loud and repeat it to feel the rhythm it creates. After the teacher models with their name, the whole group creates a movement that expresses the rhythm of each child's name. Play a piece of music with a steady beat as background and perform each child's name with the movements.

- **Rhythmic Phrases.** Repeat the following phrases: "lion, elephant, hippopotamus," "Mom, Dad, me, and my family," and "pepperoni pizza, yum, yum." Repeat each one several times, creating rhythmic chants. Using these phrases or making up new ones, divide into groups by phrase and create movements that match the rhythm of the words when chanted. No music is needed, but something with a steady beat in the background could be used.
- **Breathing.** Seated, practice various rhythms of the BREATH, including *snore*, *hiss*, *pant*, *sneeze*, *sigh*, and *yawn*. Then stand and experiment with various whole-body movements following the rhythm of each type of breathing. Divide into three groups, and each group gets one type of breathing and creates a rhythmic pattern matching it that can be repeated, such as *snore-snore-snore-pant* four times quick. Then groups create whole-body movements expressing their pattern. Play Eric Chappelle, *Music for Creative Dance: Contrast and Continuum*, vol. 4, "Breath Meditation" as background for the performance. Repeat the process with the remaining three breath types.

For middle elementary students:
- **Patterns with Partners.** Seated, practice clapping various rhythm patterns and have students follow, as in a call-response. Then add whole-body movements. After above the practice, students work with a partner to create a pattern of at least three different movements that they can repeat four times. Accompany on drum, matching the rhythm pattern their movements create as each pair performs.
- **Gumboot Dance.** See appendix D, "World Dances." Share the history of this style of dance, and after practicing some basic steps, create patterns that could express certain phrases. Perform several as a whole group. Then smaller groups create their own rhythmic patterns and describe what they are "saying" with the rhythm. Play Ladysmith Black

Mambazo, "Diamonds on the Soles of Her Shoes" and begin after the steady beat starts.

- **_BINGO Waltz._** Teach this dance as described in "Waltz" in appendix D, "World Dances." Play Marian Rose, "Red Rose Waltz."

For upper elementary students:

Seated, practice with the teacher leading various rhythm patterns with upper body movements, followed by standing and doing whole-body patterns the same way. Students can also volunteer to lead.

- **_Visualize the Rhythm._** Use four picture representations (see chapter 9, "Using Visuals, Objects, and Props") of the four parts of Carl Orff, _Orff-Schulwerk_, vol. 2, "Rondo." Then listen for the patterns that repeat in the piece. In four groups, each group creates its own repeating movement pattern to follow their part of the song, using the visual representation as a guide. Each group performs to their part of the song, then rotates visual designs and repeats the process three more times so all the groups will have a chance to create movements to all four parts of the song.
- **_The Add-On Machine._** Form eight groups, one for each sound pattern played in the music. Play Eric Chappelle, _Music for Creative Dance: Contrast and Continuum_, vol. 1, "The Add-On Machine," listening for each rhythm. Groups create and set repeating movement patterns expressing their rhythm and perform with the song.
- **_Call-Response._** Play Christine Stevens, "Call and Response." In the call-response section in the middle of the song, there are twenty-four sets of short rhythms played and repeated. Dancers should hold a still shape on the "call" and interpret music with movement in the "response." Divide into four groups and take turns interpreting the calls. Groups could either set movements and all do the same or continue to improvise.
- **_Ball Dance._** If enough playground balls are available for each student to have one, create a dance that follows a 6/8 time signature to Eric Chappelle, _Music for Creative Dance:_

Contrast and Continuum, vol. 2, "Pharaoh's Waltz" or any other song in 6/8 that is not too fast. First, practice bouncing or tossing the ball on the one beat. Then create and add other movements, such as bouncing it under one leg, tracing an arc over their heads while traveling, spinning, and passing to a partner—all of which should be done with rhythmic accuracy. Perform as a whole group or divide and watch one another.

- *External/Internal.* Play music that has a strong and predictable rhythm, and students can choose from four to five selected movement, and move to the beat, which is an **external** rhythm. Then ask them to dance the same movements to music without any beat, requiring them to make their own decisions when to change to the next movement, which is following an **internal** rhythm.
- *Pass the Drum.* Divide the group in half, and one half forms a large circle while the other half dances inside. Use a drum that students can easily hold and play by hand, and those forming the outer circle pass the drum and, in turn, play a short rhythmic phrase coming from their own **internal rhythm**. Then the dancers imitate it with movement as an **external rhythm**. Encourage the dancers to do movements rather than clapping or stomping to express the rhythm they hear. After everyone on the outside has had a turn, switch and repeat.
- *Resultant Rhythm.* For practice, divide the group in half, and each half forms a circle. One group claps three, the other half claps four, both tapping the knees on count 1. Then with the same rhythm, each group creates a whole-body movement in their count. To illustrate, draw a resultant rhythm chart of twelve dashes on a board with different colored checks or *X*s on the dashes that represent the 1s. Divide halves into halves again and put a group of threes with a group of fours to perform together. Each of these groups could create their own new movements if desired or simply perform the movements already created to show the observers how the two rhythms go together. Play Dan Savell, "Drunkard Fisherman."

 **TEMPO**

The speed or velocity at which a dancer moves

A music teacher would no doubt scold me for doing this—and rightly so, but I normally focus on only three tempos: SLOW, MODERATE, and FAST. Of course, there are several more words that describe subtle differences in tempo; but for our purposes in elementary dance, helping kids learn to control their bodies in these three ways is an important learning goal.

For younger elementary students:
Practice sitting down with clapping, tapping the knees, and other arm or upper body movements—first very *slow*, then *moderate*, then *fast*. Then standing, practice four to six whole-body movements the same way.

- ***Opposites Dance.*** Practice moving at both slow and fast **tempos**. Use opposite pairs other than fast and slow, such as *down/up*, *small/big*, *forward/backward*, and *over/under* as structure. Then divide into as many groups as opposite pairs. Groups take turns moving through their opposite pair, first **slow**, then **fast.** Rotate opposite pairs and repeat. Perform to Angels of Venice, "Dragonfly."
- ***Tortoise, Human, Hare.*** Place objects, tape, or spots on the floor, forming a large circle, creating a trail around which to travel. Divide into three groups by character (*tortoise, human*, and *hare*), and groups create a traveling movement appropriate to their character. Play Eric Chappelle, *Music for Creative Dance: Contrast and Continuum*, vol. 1, "The Road to Neah Bay." Follow cues in the music to travel around the

circle at their respective tempos. When multiple themes play, multiple groups dance.

For middle elementary students:

Play any three pieces of music, each of which exemplifies one of the three tempos. First, listen and find the beat. Then pretend to conduct the orchestra. Then "free dance" any movement to each selection, with the teacher providing verbal cues to encourage varied movements.

- ***Things That Move.*** After the above practice, list five to seven things each that move at slow, moderate, and fast tempos. Then create movements that express each item listed to the same musical selections used in the above practice. The teacher observes and chooses the clearest and most expressive movements at each tempo. Take turns and watch one another perform selected items, going from slow to moderate to fast across the list. For the performance, play any music that has a steady beat and can be moved with to both double time for fast and half time for slow. I use Christine Stevens, "4/4 Groove" or Shaggy, "Keepin' It Real."

- ***Three-Tempo Songs.*** Divide into three groups, and each creates a sequence of four movements and practices. Assign a tempo to each group, and they perform their sequence to the corresponding musical selection practiced above. Rotate tempo assignments and repeat to all three songs. Rotate tempos and repeat one more time so each group has a chance to perform their sequence to all three tempos.

- ***Tempo and Levels.*** This combines the elements of *time* and *space*. Use *Rhythmically Moving*, vol. 5, "The Entertainer" as the structure for this dance. Divide the class into three groups by level: *low*, *middle*, and *high*. Each group chooses three movements they will perform at their level. With the music, the *low* group dances their first movement at *slow* tempo, then *fast*. The *middle*-level group does the same, as does the *high* group. Then all simultaneously repeat the same movement. Repeat this pattern with each group's second movement, following changes in the music. During the next section of the music, the whole group chooses four movements that they all dance at their respective levels for eight beats each, then repeats them. Finally, each group performs their third movement in the pattern of the first two. Repeat the whole dance, with groups keeping the same movements but changing levels.

 **TIMING**

Dancers' relationships to each other and to music

Knowing **when** to dance with others is an important skill that dancers need. This concept overlaps with the element of *relationship*, and many other artists and skilled professionals—such as musicians, actors, singers, all athletes, chefs, and martial artists— need the same skill.

For younger elementary students:
Practice simple movements in a circle so everyone can see everyone else, both at the **same time**. **Take turns**, either divided in half (boys/ girls) or one person at a time around the circle.

- *Partners.* Arrange the class into pairs and decide which is dancer 1 and which is dancer 2. Place an object, such as a cone or a chair, in the center of the space. Then pairs form a large circle around it. Give each pair two movements, one that travels and one that stays in place. **Taking turns,** person 1 travels to the center, then 2. Then they do the in-place movement at the **same time**. Then they repeat both movements with the same two kinds of timing, returning to their place in the circle. Play Eric Chappelle, *Music for Creative Dance: Contrast and Continuum*, vol. 2, "Caribbean Leaps."

- **Trios.** Each group of three is given or chooses two movements. They decide who is dancer 1, 2, and 3. On their first movement, each takes a turn dancing it for four beats. Then all dance the same movement at the same time for four more beats. Repeat the pattern with the second movement. Play any music that has a 4/4 time signature.

For middle elementary students:
Assign partners and practice several in-place movements, such as *twist*, *jump*, *spin*, *wiggle*, and *spin*—first **taking turns**, then in **unison** with their partner. With the same partners, travel across the floor the same way with different movements, such as *run*, *gallop*, *slide*, *leap*, and *waddle*.

- **Movements and Shapes.** Pairs choose two movements, each followed by a still shape that both will hold. Play Eric Chappelle, *Music for Creative Dance: Contrast and Continuum*, vol. 4, "Oslo Walk." The first person in the pair dances the first movement ending in the shape in four beats. Then the second repeats the same movement and shape, taking turns. Then they dance the second movement and same shape in unison.
- **Two-Movement Combinations.** As practiced above, pairs choose their own two movements, and the first person dances the first movement for four beats. The second does same movement for four beats, then repeats the pattern with the second movement. Then in unison, both dance the first movement for four beats and the second for four beats. Play John Mayall & the Bluesbreakers, "Hideaway."

For upper elementary students:
Practice three kinds of timing—*unison*, *canon*, and *random*—as a whole group (divided in half for canon), with five to six selected movements, such as *swing*, *slide*, *run*, *spin*, *bend*, and *leap*.

- ***Five-Movement Dance.*** Divide into groups of four to six students, and each is given or chooses five different movements. They choose an order and then practice and perform the first two movements in *random* timing, the third and fourth in *unison*, and the fifth in *canon*, one person at a time. Play Carl Orff, *Orff-Schulwerk*, vol. 1, "Melodie." Follow cues in the music to change timing and movements. Each group performs to the whole song.

- ***Three Kinds of Timing.*** Discuss and practice how moving with a partner face-to-face in *unison* is a *mirror* dance, how *canon* timing in the same relationship is an *echo* dance, and how *random* timing with a partner is a movement *conversation*. Partners face each other and first improvise and then set movements—first *mirroring* each other, then in *canon* with each other, and finally in a movement *conversation*. Play Eric Chappelle, *Music for Creative Dance: Contrast and Continuum*, vol. 3, "Celtic Suite," changing timing with changes in the music. For the first two segments, partners switch who is the leader.

- ***Four Types of Timing.*** Organize the four types of timing in the following matrix grid:

	SAME MOVEMENT	DIFFERENT MOVEMENT
SAME TIME	**Unison** (Mirror)	**Contrast** (Freestyle)
DIFFERENT TIME	**Canon** (Echo)	**Random** (Conversation)

  With partners facing each other, practice and perform a partner dance following the structures listed above in this order: Unison/Mirror, Random/Conversation, Canon/Echo, and Contrast/Freestyle. Play the first four clips of Eric Chappelle, *Music for Creative Dance: Contrast and Continuum*, vol. 2, "Potpourri" and change the types of timing with the changes in the music.

DURATION

The length of time spent on and between movements

Dancers and choreographers can make choices about how **long** or how **short** a time to spend doing certain movements before changing to another one. These choices can be made by personal preference, artistic inspiration, or simply following a musical cue.

For middle elementary students:
Select three movements and practice the sequence counting 4-4-8 beats per movement, then again counting 4-8-4, and then again counting 8-4-4. Discuss how the phrase changed and which they liked the most. Discuss how duration can be used to make dance sequences or phrases more enjoyable by extending the time doing a favorite movement. Play a drum or any music with a slow and steady beat in a 4/4 time signature as background.

- *Five Movements.* Students choose five cards, place them in a sequence, and put their favorite movement in the middle. The counting goes 4-4-8-4-4. Perform to John Mayall & the Bluesbreakers, "Hideaway."
- *Color Cards.* Use a set of four cards of varying widths—one representing eight beats, another representing four beats, and two that are the same representing two beats each, in different colors for the numbers of beats (see chapter 9, "Using Visuals, Objects, and Props"). Groups create four-movement phrases and first practice each movement for four beats each. Then arrange the color cards to create a duration sequence, and groups perform their phrases following that pattern. Rearrange color cards and repeat with a new

duration sequence. Discuss which is preferable and why. Play any 4/4 music with a slow beat.

- ***Color Cards, Individual to Group.*** Divide into groups of four and give each group one set of color cards (see chapter 9, "Using Visuals, Objects, and Props"). First, three members of the group each creates a movement for their number of beats, and one person creates a still shape. Perform one person in the group at a time to Angels of Venice, "Dragonfly." Second, group members teach one another their movements, and the whole group performs all parts of the dance together to the same music. Make changes to the order of the movements as desired and perform again.

PHRASING

A more complex and subtle form of using duration as an artistic choice

Phrasing and duration are more or less the same thing, the difference being the level of pure expression used in lingering on a movement, quickly moving on to the next, or even pausing for dramatic effect. Jazz music is a perfect example of how a singer or musician can use phrasing to define their interpretation of a song. The same is true with dancers.

For upper elementary students:
Choose a three-movement combination in sixteen beats (such as spin-stretch-walk) and practice it three times using different phrasing (extend the first movement to eight beats, then extend the

second, and then the third). Discuss how changing the phrasing of the movements changes the feeling of the phrase.

- **Directions Dance.** Teach the following pattern: Reach diagonally back, arc over to the opposite front, then diagonally back to the other side to the opposite front. Step forward, step backward, reach side to side, reach up and down. First perform each pair of directions for eight beats each. Then groups change the counts of three of the four sets of eight beats, and the whole phrase must still add up to thirty-two, resulting in changes in the phrasing of the whole pattern (e.g., both *diagonals* eight beats, *forward/backward* four beats, *sides* sixteen beats, and *up/down* four beats). Perform to Shaggy, "Keepin' It Real."
- **Change Phrasing in Eight Beats.** In smaller groups, they choose their own three movement combinations and perform them three times to show different phrasing variations, emphasizing a longer duration on the first, second, and then third movements. Play Gorillaz, "Double Bass." Afterward, discuss which version was the best and why.
- **Levels and Phrasing.** Groups of three to five start with a thirty-two-beat phrase of four movements (eight beats each). Then change the phrasing of all movements to counts other than eight. Add four levels, starting with *low* and progressing to *airborne*, and decide which movement can change level the quickest (fewer beats in phrasing variation). Perform to Jimmy Cliff, "Sitting in Limbo."
- **Sarah and Dinah.** Play two versions of "All of Me," one by Dinah Washington and the other by Sarah Vaughan. As the songs are playing, illustrate by drawing lines to indicate the lyrical phrasing of the first eight measures (see chapter 9, "Using Visuals, Objects, and Props"). Divide into four groups, two for each version of the song. Using the illustration of phrasing use by both singers, each group creates a movement phrase or study that follows their respective singer's lyrical phrasing. Groups each perform to their song. Then those dancing to the same song could come together to create movement phrases to more of their song.

Chapter 14

Element of ENERGY
How the dancer makes movement happen and gives it meaning

Energy is the life force within us that allows us to move! It is created by light, heat, and motion, as well as the reverse—energy must be generated to create light, heat, and motion.

You know very well that many factors contribute to the energy we use as humans. Eating healthy foods, drinking enough water, getting enough rest, personal interactions, and the influence of outside stress are the most significant. However, dancers have greater control over their energy than the average person. They are able to intentionally increase or decrease energy levels, steer the course of how it flows through the body, alter its quality and texture, and utilize gravity and weight. All of these abilities come with exploration and practice. I find that there is a very clear parallel between a dancer's use of energy and a painter's use of color. Energy gives depth and meaning to movements just as colors give meaning to lines and shapes on a canvas. A dancer can determine the meaning of a dance with the energy choices they make because it is energy that makes the emotion or intent on the inside visible to those watching from the outside.

The California Arts Standards for Dance (see appendix A, "A Quick Reference Guide to the CAS for Dance") sometimes use the word *dynamics* in reference to energy. However, I feel this is not completely accurate. *Dynamic* means "changing" and is the opposite of *stasis*, which means "unchanging." Obviously, other aspects of dance besides energy can change or remain the same, depending on the choices made by the dance artist. For these reasons, I have made the choice not to use the word *dynamics* to describe energy.

Here are concepts within the element of *energy* that dancers can learn to control and use to accomplish their artistic goals:
- **Flow,** how energy travels through the body
- **Weight,** either defying or giving in to gravity
- **Force,** the amount of energy used in the muscles
- **Energy qualities,** expanded and more specific versions of *flow* and *weight* (see appendix C, "Element of Energy Deconstruction")
- **Effort Actions,** combining opposite aspects of *force*, *timing*, and *focus* (see appendix C, "Element of Energy Deconstruction")
- **Textures,** expanded vocabulary describing subtleties related to the sense of touch

 **FLOW**

How energy travels through the body

Imagine a source of light coming from just under your skin; and as you watch it, it begins to travel all around your body, changing size and shape as various parts move. This movement of energy inside the body is called *flow*. It can be illustrated by the image of water flowing through pipes: a wide-open flow with no obstructions is **smooth**; a bend in the pipes requires the movement of the water to be interrupted and change direction, becoming **sharp**; and a pinched or overloaded pipe could cause the pipe to shake and rattle, resulting in **vibratory** flow.

For younger elementary students:
Practice *smooth* and *sharp* with a teacher-led mirroring dance of both energies to Eric Chappelle, *Music for Creative Dance: Contrast and Continuum*, vol. 1, "Western East," following cues in the music. Create and perform movements to the following variations on "Eensy Weensy Spider," emphasizing smooth and sharp flow in all movements. Practice seated first, using upper body movements while learning the song. Then repeat with whole-body movements:

- ***The Tiger (smooth).*** *The tiger went a-hunting out in the grass so high*
  Along came a herd of zebras and passed the tiger by
  Down went the sun, and the night began to fall
  So the tired, hungry tiger ate no dinner at all

- ***The Crab (sharp).*** *The creepy crusty crab went scooting along the sand*
  Along came a wave and threw her up on land
  Up came the tide and covered up the shore
  So the creepy crusty crab went scooting along some more
- ***Mirror Dance.*** In partners, students face each other and choose who is the leader first. With movements that stay in place, mirror with **smooth** and **sharp flow**, following cues in the music to Eric Chappelle, *Music for Creative Dance: Contrast and Continuum*, vol. 1, "Western East."

If putting **smooth** and **sharp** flow together with **heavy** and **light** weight, practice to Eric Chappelle, *Music for Creative Dance: Contrast and Continuum*, vol. 4, "Energy."

- ***Weather Dance (with Weight).*** Explore movements that express four different types of weather: *windy*-smooth, *rainy*-sharp, *snowy*-heavy, and *cloudy*-light. Also explore a movement and a still shape that express *sunny* weather. Choose two movements for each weather type. Then either as a whole group or divided into four groups by *smooth*, *sharp*, *heavy*, and *light*, perform the whole dance to Michel Cusson, "Sawtooth Mountain," finishing halfway through the song.
- ***Wildlife (with Weight).*** Use the following four animal examples: penguin/*smooth*, squirrel/*sharp*, elephant/*heavy*, and spider/*light*. Create three movements for each animal plus a sleeping position. Perform each to a different song by Michael Manring: penguin/"Blue Orleans," squirrel/"Magnets," elephant/"Renegade Intellectuals," and spider/"Far." Divide and perform for one another.
- ***My Mama Had a Dancing Heart (with Weight).*** See chapter 17, "Inspiration." Read the book and match flow and weight energies to the seasons as follows: *spring*/sharp, *summer*/smooth, *autumn*/light, and *winter*/heavy.
- ***Pairs of Colors (with Weight).*** In six groups, each gets a unique pair of two energies on cards with matching colored

background. The pairs are *sharp/light*, *sharp/smooth*, *sharp/heavy*, *light/smooth*, *light/heavy*, and *smooth/heavy*. Groups create a pattern of two to three movements and repeat the same pattern twice, with each of their energies. Play Eric Chappelle, *Music for Creative Dance: Contrast and Continuum*, vol. 4, "Oslo Walk."

- ***Diamond Dance (with Weight).*** Tape four energy pictures (see chapter 9, "Using Visuals, Objects, and Props") to the four walls, and groups of four form a diamond shape with one person toward each wall. Play Eric Chappelle, *Music for Creative Dance: Contrast and Continuum*, vol. 4, "Energy." As a group faces each of the walls, the front person is the leader of their group, and all others follow that person's in-place movements.

For middle elementary students:
Add *vibratory* to *smooth* and *sharp*. For whole-body practice, play the first three clips of Eric Chappelle, *Music for Creative Dance: Contrast and Continuum*, vol. 4, "Potpourri" in this order: *vibratory*, *sharp*, *smooth*. To add *weight*, play the same music and practice to the first five clips.

- ***Trios.*** Play Eric Chappelle, *Music for Creative Dance: Contrast and Continuum*, vol. 3, "Dakota Dawn." Groups of three decide who will dance which of the three types of *flow*, following the music for cues: drum for *sharp*, flute for *smooth*, and shaker for *vibratory*. First improvise, then set movements. Perform two to three trios at a time.
- ***Four Groups (with Weight).*** Play Carl Orff, *Orff-Schulwerk*, vol. 1, "Sielbuch fur Xylophon." Divide into four groups by *smooth*, *sharp*, *heavy*, and *light*. Each group is assigned one of the five energies, reserving *vibratory* for the whole group. Each group decides on two movements that demonstrate their energy. One group at a time performs their first movement. At a pause in the music, all do a vibratory movement and hold a still shape. Then each group performs their second movement, moving out of the shape.

WEIGHT

Either defying or giving in to gravity

Stepping on the bathroom scale generates a number that can't be disputed. However, dancers can alter their weight regardless of what the scale reads simply by using gravity to give the illusion of heaviness or lightness in their movements.

For younger elementary students:
Practice with a teacher-led mirroring dance of both energies to Eric Chappelle, *Music for Creative Dance: Contrast and Continuum*, vol. 1, "A Tale of Two Villages," following cues in the music. Create and perform movements to the following variations on "Eensy Weensy Spider."

- ***The Elephant (heavy).** The big, gigantic elephant went walking down the path*
  Down came the rain, and the elephant took a bath
  Out came the sun and dried off all his skin
  So the big, gigantic elephant went down the path again
- ***The Eagle (light).** The eagle was a-flying up in the sky so high*
  Down in the water a fish was swimming by
  Down flew the bird as fast as she could go
  But the fish swam to the bottom and said, "You are too slow!"
- ***Shadow Dance.** In partners, with one behind the other, the dancer in front is the leader and does traveling movements with **light** and **heavy weight**, following cues in the music to Eric Chappelle, *Music for Creative Dance: Contrast and Continuum*, vol. 1, "A Tale of Two Villages."

See **flow** on the previous page for several more dances that can be done putting *flow* and *weight* together.

FORCE

The amount of energy used in the muscles

For younger to middle elementary students:
Seated, practice tensing and relaxing body parts (face, neck/shoulders, hands, arms, stomach, legs, feet, and whole body). Free dance to Eric Chappelle, *Music for Creative Dance: Contrast and Continuum*, vol. 3, "The Bayou Both-Step," following changes in the music for relaxed or tense movements.

- ***Blue and Red.*** List things the students know of that are blue (such as the ocean, the sky, blueberries, recycling bins, and first-place ribbons) or red (such as stop signs, apples, heat, fire alarms, peppers, and traffic lights). Choose three from each list and create movements where the blue items are performed with *relaxed* force and where the red things are performed with *tense* force. Perform to the same music as above.

- ***Yes/No Dance.*** In partners, one is the "dancer," and the other is the "master." The master places their hands on the dancer and makes them dance by moving their body parts as they wish. The dancer responds as if saying "yes" with relaxed force, going along with what the master is making them do. Then when the music changes, the dancer tenses their muscles and resists the master's guidance as if saying "no." Play Eric Chappelle, *Music for Creative Dance: Contrast and Continuum*, vol. 3, "I Say, You Say" and switch parts halfway through.

- ***Three-Movement Pattern.*** In four groups, each chooses a three-movement pattern. Play Eric Chappelle, *Music for Creative Dance: Contrast and Continuum*, vol. 3, "I Say, You Say." Each group performs their pattern first with relaxed force, then with tense force.
- ***Feel the Force.*** Choose six movements and practice each with *relaxed* and *tense* force in the whole body. Perform to Bobby McFerrin, "Circlesong Two," following the three strong beats in the music. Then change the force on the fourth. Perform each movement relaxed, tense, relaxed, tense. Divide and watch one another perform, switching groups halfway through the song.
- ***Melt and Grow.*** Groups create a sequence of movements in six parts: (1) *relaxed* at high level and melt, (2) *relaxed* at middle level and melt, (3) *relaxed* at low level and form a still shape, (4) *tense* grow to middle, (5) *tense* grow to high, (6) *tense* and shape. Play any music with a long steady beat.

Show and fill in **MATRIX** poster, blending extremes in *force* and *tempo* (see chapter 9, "Using Visuals, Objects, and Props") as follows:

BURST – Tense and Fast
REBOUND – Relaxed and Fast
PRESS – Tense and Slow
FLOAT – Relaxed and Slow

Practice each energy seated with upper body movements and with the whole body to four consecutive tracks from Carl Orff, *Orff-Schulwerk*, vol. 1, starting with "Vier Tanzstucke," then "Lieder Und Spielstucke." Do so in this order: *burst, rebound, press,* and *float*.

- ***Australian Animals.*** Practice choreography from below, emphasizing the energy from the matrix chart as listed. Place pictures of animals (see chapter 9, "Using Visuals, Objects, and Props") on the floor and spread them out. Divide the group between pictures. Play Eric Chappelle, *Music for Creative Dance: Contrast and Continuum*, vol. 3,

"Dancing Digits," and each group dances simultaneously the movements for their animal. The teacher cues students when to rotate to the next animal. The music cycles five times, so the group will likely end up where they started, so that is their assigned animal for the performance.

Koala/press. Walk on all fours. Climb and pull leaves at the center. Scratch/shoo flies away. Then walk on all fours again. Sleep with the hands crossed on the shoulders, with the chin tucked into the arms, squatting.

Kangaroo/rebound. Jump with the hands crossed and the legs wide. Then touch the floor with the hands, and the feet jump to move slower. Sleep on the side with the arms and legs stretched out.

Jellyfish/float. Expand as if filling with water, then pushing out, moving backward. Spin down to the floor and back up. Sleep standing up, on tiptoes, with the arms out to sides, as if floating on the surface of water.

Crocodile/burst. Do a fast and furious crawl. Stop, pounce, roll, and wrestle on the floor. Sleep flat on the belly with the arms and legs bent at sides and the chin resting on the floor.

Play Eric Chappelle, *Music for Creative Dance: Contrast and Continuum*, vol. 2, "Circular Journey," and groups perform as follows: All dance during first section. *Koalas* dance only during next, then *kangaroos* only, then *jellyfish* only, and then *crocodiles* only. On fanfare section, each animal group enters and makes a still shape in the same order as above. For the last section, all animals return to their beginning areas and go to sleep as the music fades.

- ***Earth Elements.*** Match four energies with four earth elements as follows: *float*/air, *rebound*/water, *press*/earth, and *burst*/fire. List some images associated with each earth element. Here are some examples: **fire** (sparks, embers, flames, lava, stove, bonfire), **water** (rain, river, ocean, waves, mist, shower), **earth** (dirt, rocks, mountain, trees, sand, plants), and **air** (wind, tornado, bubbles, breeze, breath, steam). Call out listed words to cue free dance. Play Mickey Hart, "Island Groove." Either divide the class in half, and each gets two elements (water/air and fire/earth). OR divide into four groups by element and put movements that express the chosen images together in a sequence for each element.

For upper elementary students:
- ***12-16-12-16-12.*** Play Carl Orff, *Orff-Schulwerk*, vol. 2, "Grazioso." These numbers represent the number of beats in each section of the music. Divide into three to four groups, and each creates two movements emphasizing tense and two movements emphasizing relaxed force. Perform the first tense movement for twelve beats, the two relaxed movements for eight beats each, and the second tense movement for twelve beats. Repeat the two relaxed movements. Finally, repeat the first tense movement for twelve beats.
- ***Stick and Milk.*** Play any fairly quick hip-hop beat as background. Then count four beats holding or "sticking" a still shape with tense force and four beats moving or "milking" out of the shape with relaxed force. Repeat multiple times. Then change to two beats each. Groups can set shapes and perform one group at a time to the same music.
- ***Controlling the Group.*** In groups of four, one person at a time is the "mover," and the rest of the group members are "the moved." Play Eric Chappelle, *Music for Creative Dance: Contrast and Continuum*, vol. 1, "Lucky Stiff." Follow the four cycles of changes in the music to rotate leaders. Each *mover* faces their group of the *moved* and creates movements as if casting a spell on them using relaxed and tense force,

following the changes in the music. Group members respond to the movements with the same level of force.

- **Friend or Foe.** In partners, practice tense and relaxed force by improvising either "fighting" with tense force or in "friendship" with relaxed force. There is no touching on *fighting*, but touching is allowed on *friendly* movements. Play Eric Chappelle, *Music for Creative Dance: Contrast and Continuum*, vol. 1, "Lucky Stiff" and follow cues in the music, alternating between relaxed and tense force. Pairs can set movements and perform to the same music, entering and exiting rather than performing for the whole song.

ENERGY QUALITIES

Expanded and more specific versions of *flow* and *weight*

The following six words describe a broad range of energies that can be applied to any movement. They are **sustained**, **percussive**, **swinging**, **suspended**, **collapse**, and **vibratory** (see appendix C, "Element of Energy Deconstruction"). Practice whole-body movement to the first six clips of Eric Chappelle, *Music for Creative Dance: Contrast and Continuum*, vol. 4, "Potpourri" in the same order as above.

For middle to upper elementary students:
- **Chance Dance.** Match six energies to the numbers of dots on die. On a separate list, match six selected movements. In four groups, pass out one die, scratch paper, and a pencil to each group. They roll six times to create an energy list, then six more times to determine the movements matched to the

energies on their list. If energy/movement pairings repeat, groups will need to figure out a way to make them look different, such as changing level, tempo, or direction. Play Prem Joshua, "Deccan Queen."

- ***Wildlife.*** Match animals with energy qualities as follows: snake or penguin/*sustained*, chicken or squirrel/*percussive*, hummingbird or butterfly/*vibratory*, monkey or elephant/*swinging*, opossum or bear/*collapse*, and deer or eagle/*suspended*. Six groups are assigned one of the six wildlife choices. Each creates a dance with at least three parts, including a traveling movement, an in-place movement, and a still shape—all of which demonstrates the matched energy quality. Perform to Michael Manring selections as follows: **sustained**/"Blue Orleans," **percussive**/"Magnets," **vibratory**/"Geometry," **swinging**/"Renegade Intellectuals," **collapse**/"The Precise Moment of Dusk," and **suspended**/"A Brief History of the Wind."

- ***Echo Dance.*** The whole group is in a circle or in two circles. Play Eric Chappelle, *Music for Creative Dance: Contrast and Continuum*, vol. 4, "Back at Ya." Go around the circle, and each person gets a turn to create a movement with one of the energies (in order), and all in the circle echo that movement.

- ***Three and Three.*** For the qualities *sustained*, *percussive*, and *vibratory*, play Eric Chappelle, *Music for Creative Dance: Contrast and Continuum*, vol. 3, "Dakota Dawn." Groups divide by the three qualities. Set phrases of four movements and perform, following the cues in the music. Keep repeating phrases and use only the first thirty-two very slow beats in the music. For the qualities *suspended*, *swinging*, and *collapse*, play Eric Chappelle, *Music for Creative Dance: Contrast and Continuum*, vol. 4, "Pathways." Individually practice. Groups perform set movements showing the same energies, following the cues in the music in that order.

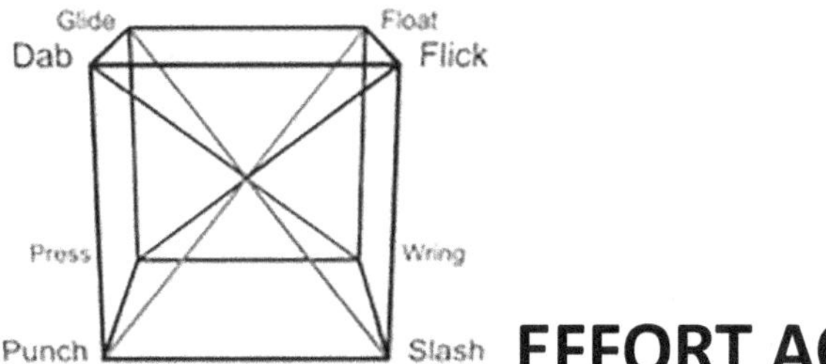

EFFORT ACTIONS

Combining opposite aspects of *force*, *timing*, and *focus*

Rudolf Laban's eight Effort Actions need to be thought about in three dimensions, like a cube—one side being about *force*, the adjacent side representing *timing*, and a third nonparallel side representing *focus*. On each corner of the cube, one of the Actions resides, demonstrating a unique combination of one extreme or the other of force, timing, and focus. See appendix C, "Element of Energy Deconstruction," for more details. The eight Effort Actions are **float**, **punch**, **flick**, **wring**, **glide**, **slash**, **dab**, and **press**. It helps to show two matrix posters (see chapter 9, "Using Visuals, Objects, and Props"). Then fill in each square of both grids.

For upper elementary students:
Practice each *action* seated first, with upper body movements. Then for whole body-practice, put them together in pairs (float/punch, flick/wring, glide/slash, and dab/press), counting three slow beats for the first *action*, then one for the second, and repeat. Practice all four pairs that way. Then reverse the order of each pair and practice them again that way. Play Gorillaz, "Dare."

- ***Layered Choreography.*** Create thirty-two beats of simple choreography to any music, and students learn and memorize it. Divide into groups and with all using the same choreography, students first decide to add either tense or relaxed force to each set of eight beats (e.g., first eight/relaxed, second eight/relaxed, third eight/tense, and fourth eight/relaxed). Repeat this process with the same movements two more times, adding either direct or indirect focus to each eight, then adding either sudden or gradual timing as the final layer. Groups determine which four Effort Actions they constructed with their choices for each set of eight beats.

- *Four Songs.* Use any four selected songs and give each of four groups one of the songs and two Effort Actions. The four songs that I find work well are as follows: the Clash, "Listen" for **float and punch**; Michel Cusson, "Sawtooth Mountain" for **flick and wring**; the Blues Project, "Flute Thing" for **glide and slash**; and Michael Manring, "Life in the Trees" for **dab and press**. Each group creates a dance study that must include both of the Effort Actions (emphasizing the contrast between them) and at least one movement where all dancers are in unison.

- *Echo Dance.* In one large circle or two to three small circles, each person, in turn, gets an action. They demonstrate, and all others in the circle echo. Play Eric Chappelle, *Music for Creative Dance: Contrast and Continuum*, vol. 4, "Back at Ya," and go through all actions three times.

- *Paintbrushes.* In pairs, with one paintbrush between them, first take turns brushing the floor with imaginary paint as the Effort Actions describe. Play classical music, such as Bach's *Christmas Oratorio*, as background. Then stand up. One person acts as the "artist" and strokes the other person, who acts as the "paint," encouraging it to move around the space, or "canvas," as the teacher calls out each of the Effort Actions. In same pairs, choose 3 Actions and use paintbrushes to practice and set movements that both will perform. Perform without paintbrushes to the same music.

- *Effort Actions and Phrasing.* For the seated practice of just the counting first, use *stretch* for the first number and freeze in a selected *shape* for the second number: 1/7, 2/6, 3/5, 4/4, 5/3, 6/2, and 7/1. Divide into four groups. Then give each a pair of Effort Actions and sets movements to go with their two Effort Actions. Play *Rhythmically Moving*, "Sunflower Slow Drag," and everyone does all seven combinations, four at a time (1/7, 2/6, 3/5, 4/4). Then all groups perform again with the rest (4/4, 5/3, 6/2, 7/1).

- ***Orpheus and Euridice.*** Read the mythical story of Orpheus and Eurydice and list the main events, matching them with the eight Effort Actions as follows:
- Happy, love, musical, beautiful, **FLOAT**
- Bite of the snake and death, **SLASH**
- Courage or quest, **PUNCH**
- Frightening journey through the Furies, **FLICK**
- Success, don't look back, **GLIDE**
- Looking back, **DAB**
- The Furies take her back, **PRESS**
- Pursued by the Furies, punished, tormented, **WRING**
  Divide into four groups (each group responsible for two of the eight events in the story), and groups compose short dance phrases that express their part of the story through the Effort Actions. Play Christoph Willibald Gluck, *Orpheus and Eurydice Opera*, "Melody for Violin and Piano."

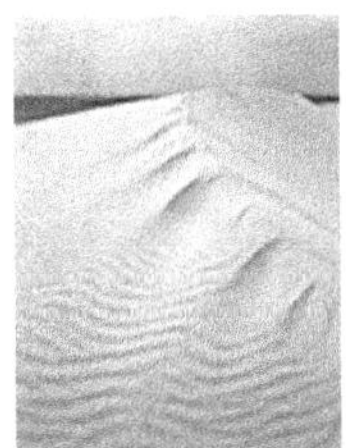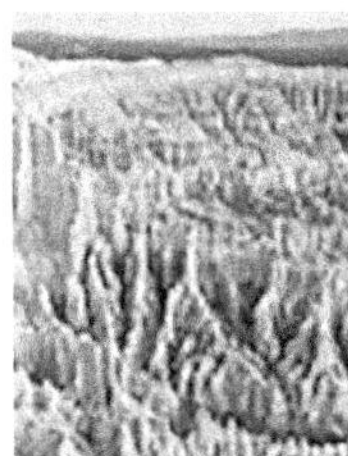 **TEXTURES**

Expanded vocabulary describing subtleties related to the sense of touch

Both music and visual arts use the word ***texture*** to describe certain characteristics of their art form. In all cases, artists transfer sensations perceived through their tactile sense to some type of response, which is kinesthetic for dance. A wide range of descriptive words are associated with texture, such as *bumpy, rough, soft, jiggly,* or *sticky.* Try to envision a movement that could be described by any of those words.

For upper elementary students:
Discuss the meaning of the word **texture**: "the feel, appearance, or consistency of a surface or substance." List students' ideas of items that they know have a distinct texture and have them imagine touching each object with their hands. Then have them imagine they are touching it with different body parts and then have the movement grow into the whole body.

- ***Imaginary Objects.*** Groups choose two imaginary objects and set movements as if touching the object with their hands, first seated, then rise to standing. Then transfer the movement to a different body part with an in-place movement, then into a traveling movement with their whole body. Return to the place they started with the body part, then lower back down to seated with the hands. Play Santana, "Singing Winds, Crying Beasts" as background for the performance.

Have stations set up with a variety of actual items of different textures available to touch, as well as chart paper and markers near each item for students to write words that describe how they feel. Some examples include a bristle brush, cotton balls, sand, marbles, a feather, playdough, leaves, and hair gel.

- ***Objects.*** Groups of students rotate around to each object, and after feeling them, they write words that describe how they feel to the touch. Ask them not to duplicate words that are already written. In as many groups as there are objects, each uses the list that all groups created and composes a dance study that includes movements for each word listed. Play Mickey Hart, "Kaluli Groove."

Chapter 15

Element of RELATIONSHIP
Who the dancer is and with whom they are dancing

Our sense of self defines and gives purpose to our lives and is constantly evolving along the way. We make choices, live with the consequences, and hopefully learn from them, thus creating and defining our character. It takes a lifetime to finish this dance, and many partners and groups will join and leave. Hopefully, at some point, we will be comfortable with who we are and feel brave enough to redefine and reinvent that person all along the way.

In dance, we can have many different relationships; and since it is a performing art, our relationship with the audience or community is ever present. While performing in dances, we often take on different personae, much the same as what actors do, and move through countless ideations of spatial and timing interactions with fellow dancers, thus creating relationships.

Many of the concepts in this element of dance cross over into other elements, but I guess that is just the nature of relationships. Here are the six aspects of this element that I think can be clearly articulated and taught:

- **Character,** the dancer's embodiment of another being, living or nonliving
- **Objects,** items used as enhancements to movement or as partners
- **Spatial relationships,** the use of prepositions to define relationships in space
- **Formations,** creating designs with multiple bodies
- **Grouping,** who dances together, in large or small groups or alone
- **Musicality,** a dancer's relationship to their accompaniment

CHARACTER

The dancer's embodiment of another being, living or nonliving

The overlap between the dance element of *relationship*, which is self-identity, and *theatre arts* is obvious. Acting and character dancing are almost exactly the same. The main differences are the use of voice and the presence or lack of music.

For younger elementary students:
With young children, pretending is your ticket to their imaginations. Taking on the movements, body shapes, habits, and awareness of the habitat of a multitude of animals or other living or nonliving beings provides an opportunity to practice transcendence out of our human form, into that of someone or something else. There are also many connections to other elements of dance that can be made through embodying other personae.

- *Wildlife Flow and Weight.* Linking with the element of *energy*, matching the **flow** qualities of *smooth* and *sharp*, and **weight** opposites *heavy* or *light* to animals open the door to many movement possibilities. **Smooth** works well with penguins, dolphins, and snakes. **Sharp** flow is demonstrated by squirrels, cats, and chickens. **Heavy** weight is seen in elephants, gorillas, and whales. **Light** weight shows in the forms of spiders, frogs, and birds. Some music that works well with these four energy/animal matches are selections by Michael Manring: *smooth*/"Blue Orleans," *sharp*/"Magnets," *heavy*/"Renegade Intellectuals," and *light*/"Far."

- *Australian Animals.* Combining *fast* and *slow* **tempo** (element of *time*) with *tense* and *relaxed* **force** (element of *energy*) on a matrix grid (see chapter 9, "Using Visuals, Objects, and Props," and appendix C, "Element of Energy Deconstruction") creates four new energies: **burst, rebound, press,** and **float.** The following four animals that famously live on and around the continent of Australia match well with these four energies: *burst*/crocodile, *rebound*/kangaroo, *Press*/koala, and *float*/jellyfish. Play Eric Chappelle, *Music for Creative Dance: Contrast and Continuum*, vol. 2, "Circular Journey." Then explore movements, shapes, and sleeping positions of each of these animals and perform them one at a time in groups.

- *Weight and Halloween Characters.* These six spooky characters that are common to most Halloween celebrations can be divided by **weight** (element of *energy*): for **heavy,** *pumpkin, mummy,* and *monster*; and for **light**, *bat, skeleton,* and *ghost.* Explore movements, and students can set patterns in groups by character. Play Angelo Badalamenti, "Audrey's Dance."

- ***Water, Land, and Air.*** This explores high, middle, and low **levels** (element of *space*): water, being the lowest level on the surface of the earth; land, being in the middle; and air, being high above the others. Students can list things that move in the water, on land, and in the air. They can explore movements that express the items listed. Not all things have to be animals or even living. For example, seaweed lives in the water, cars drive on land, and clouds float by in the air. Play Eric Chappelle, *Music for Creative Dance: Contrast and Continuum,* vol. 4, "Amphibious." Follow changes in the music to change to the next thing that moves on the next level.

- ***Animals along Pathways:*** Exploring the four basic **pathways** (element of *space*), match the traveling movements of various animals as follows: **straight**/horse, wolf; **curved**/eagle, butterfly; **zigzag**/rabbit, frog; and **wavy**/fish, snake. Play Eric Chappelle, *Music for Creative Dance: Contrast and Continuum,* vol. 2, "Potpourri" (first four clips: wavy, straight, zigzag, curved).

- ***Itik-Itik.*** See appendix D, "World Dances," for this Philippine dance that explores the movements of ducks.

For middle to upper elementary students:

- ***Earth Elements.*** Following the same matrix grid as described above in the Australian animals dance, blend together slow and fast tempos with tense and relaxed force to create **burst**, **rebound**, **press**, and **float**. The four elements of the earth match these four energies well: *burst*/fire, *rebound*/water, *press*/earth, and *float*/air. Explore movements that reflect various forms of each element: flames, volcanic eruptions, and lightning for fire; river, rain, and waterfall for water;

trees, mountains, and sand for earth; and wind, bubbles, and steam for air. Play Mickey Hart, "Island Groove" or any other earthy music.

- **Energy Qualities Wildlife.** Match the six energy qualities with the following six animals: **sustained**/penguin or snake, **percussive**/squirrel or chicken, **vibratory**/hummingbird or butterfly, **suspended**/deer or eagle, **collapse**/opossum or bear, and **swinging**/monkey or elephant. Explore and create movement phrases and shapes. Use Michael Manring music selections as follows: sustained/"Blue Orleans," percussive/"Magnets," vibratory/"Geometry," swinging/"Renegade Intellectuals," collapse/"The Precise Moment of Dusk," and suspended/"A Brief History of the Wind."

- **Orix**ás. Match the eight Effort Actions with the following eight spirit characters from the Brazilian religious practice candomblé: **oxum**/*float*, **iansan (oya)**/*punch*, **oxumare**/*flick*, **omolu**/*wring*, **iemanja**/*glide*, **ogum**/*slash*, **oxossi**/*dab*, and **oxala**/*press*. See appendix D, "World Dances," for more explanation on this dance tradition.

- **Los Viejitos.** See the "Objects" section below. This dance from Mexico honors the elderly and uses walking sticks and optional masks as well as the body postures and movements of old people. See appendix D, "World Dances," for more details.

- **Totem Pole.** This dance incorporates the dance concepts of *shape, levels, spatial relationships, timing,* and *weight,* as well as integrating social studies in exploring the Native American tradition of totem poles as well as wildlife and their habitat. In groups of three, with all facing the same direction, begin in a relationship where the person **in front** is at a **low** level, the person **behind** is at a **high** level, and the person **between** is at a **middle** level. When viewed from the front, this configuration makes the dancers appear to be vertically stacked. Each dancer begins in a frozen **shape** at their level, and when drums begin in the music, they all quickly change shapes eight times with **sudden** timing. Then dancers change positions in eight beats with **gradual** timing. Repeat two more times. Then dancers leave their totem formation and move all around the space, taking on the characters of the following animals with matched **weight**: bear/**heavy**, eagle/**light**, whale/**heavy**, frog/**light**, beaver/**heavy**, nonflying raven/**light**, salmon/**heavy**, and butterfly/**light**. Follow cues in the music and pause after every two animal characters. Return to totem positions after butterfly and repeat *shapes* and changing positions until the music ends. Play Eric Chappelle, *Music for Creative Dance: Contrast and Continuum*, vol. 4, "Totem Pole."

OBJECTS

Items used as enhancements to movement or as partners

Manipulating objects or props with purpose can add a dramatic effect to dances and enhance the visual beauty of the movements. Examples include fans, ribbons on handheld sticks, scarves, and, of course, the skirts worn in folklórico from Mexico and Latin America.

This section emphasizes using objects as a type of partner, without which the dance would have little meaning.

For younger elementary students:
- *Me and My Partner.* See "Spatial Relationships" below. This dance is equally about the dancer's relationship with an object in space and to it as a partner.

- **Object Centers.** See chapter 9, "Using Visuals, Objects, and Props." Provide a small supply of about ten of each of the following objects: balloons, plastic cups, scarves, small playground balls, paper plates, stretchy stockings or elastic bands, lengths of rope, rhythm sticks, and, for group exploration, either a large bedsheet or parachute. Place sets of objects around the space like "centers" and divide into groups by how many objects there are. Groups explore movements dancing with their objects, with prompts from the teacher to encourage creativity as needed. Play Eric Chappelle, *Music for Creative Dance: Contrast and Continuum*, vol. 1, "Oasis." Stop the music to cue students to form a still shape with their object. Then replace it where it was and rotate as a group to the next center. Repeat this until all groups have experienced all objects.
- **Objects and Levels.** Explore movements with each object at three levels: *low*, *middle*, and *high*. Divide into as many groups as you have object sets. Each group creates a dance with four movements: (1) Choose a movement to dance with the object at a *high* level. (2) Choose a different movement to dance with it at a *low* level. (3) Choose a different movement to dance with it at a *middle* level. (4) Finish in a group shape with the objects at multiple levels. Play Eric Chappelle, *Music for Creative Dance: Contrast and Continuum*, vol. 2, "Circular Journey." Follow the cues in the music for groups to perform after all have entered the space at the same time at the beginning. Finish with all exiting together with the same music at the end.
- **Fan Dances.** Arirang (Korea) and civilian and military styles (China). For this and the following, see appendix D, "World Dances."
- **Ribbon Dance.** Yanko (China)
- **Scarf Dance.** Qashqai scarf dance (Iran)
- **Stick Dances.** Los Machetes (Mexico) and Peopleton stick dance (England/Wales)

For middle and upper elementary students:

- ***Worship the Object.*** Select a few single objects of the students' choosing, such as a soccer ball, a backpack, a trash bin, or a chair. Then in groups by object, list adjectives that describe their object in ways that place great value on them, such as *beautiful, long, sacred, soft, magical,* etc. Groups improvise to create movements inspired by their listed words and develop the movements they like most into a dance that honors the object. Play Beethoven, Symphony no. 6, *Pastorale.*

- ***Los Viejitos.*** See the "Character" section earlier in this chapter and appendix D, "World Dances." The walking sticks used in this dance are essential to the movements and enhance the dancer's ability to portray their elderly character.

- ***Maypole Dances.*** A Maypole is more of a set piece than an object, and the dances are designed around its physical structure. I have never attempted a Maypole dance at a school simply because of the necessity for elaborate construction.

- ***Tinikling.*** This dance from the Philippines requires two long bamboo sticks that are held on each end and tapped on wooden blocks together to create a rhythm and a tricky obstacle for dancers stepping between them.

- ***Limbo.*** This dance from Trinidad requires one long bamboo pole that must be held horizontally by two people as others line up and dance **under** (*spatial relationship*) it as it progressively gets lower and lower. Play any version of "Limbo Rock" you like.

SPATIAL RELATIONSHIPS

The use of prepositions to define relationships in space

There are fourteen prepositional words that students need to know so they can place themselves in a dance in a meaningful way with others or objects. They are the following: **toward**, **near**, **around**, **face-to-face**, **in front of**, **behind**, **next to**, **through**, **between**, **over**, **under**, **connected**, **away**, and **far**.

Here's a little bit more information about what these words mean: *toward*, *around*, *through*, and *away* are traveling relationships, while *near*, *between*, and *far* stay in place. *Over* and *under* can't be separated, nor can *in front of* and *behind*. *Connected* means touching. *In front of*, *behind*, and *next to* assume there is a "front" in the space and all dancers and stationary objects are facing it. *Face-to-face* can only be between dancers and not objects.

For younger elementary students:
- *Runway.* Partners start FAR apart on opposite sides of the room, travel **toward** each other, travel forward **next to** each other, "pose" in a shape at the front, then travel **away** to opposite sides. Play any music that has a strong and fast beat, such as EDM.
- *Opposites with Partners.* Use two opposite pairs of spatial relationships: **in front of/behind** and **over/under**. In pairs, they create a pattern that includes two different movements representing each of their two opposite relationships, switching positions. Play David Benoit, "Safari."
- *"I See You."* Exploring **in front**, **behind**, **through**, and **around**. Dancers are grouped in two pairs facing each other from a distance. Play Marian Rose, "I See You." With the lyrics,

each pair stands facing the other with one person who is the "tree" holding still, with the arms extended like branches **in front**. Their partner, who is the "squirrel," is peeking **through** the "branches" from **behind** at the squirrel on the opposite side. Then both squirrels come out and take both hands and gallop **around** each other until the music changes. They then return to their partners and move **in front** of them, becoming the tree. Then the person who was the tree before is now behind and becomes the squirrel. The song cycles through seven times.

- *Me and My Partner.* See the "Objects" section earlier in this chapter. Each dancer needs an object that holds its shape and one they can easily pick up and move with. Articles of clothing aren't good choices because they don't hold their shape. Hats, backpacks, water bottles, or stuffed toys are good choices. Place the object on the floor and practice the following movements in the spatial relationships: *slide* **in front of** it, *swing* **behind** it, *twist* **next to** it, *leap* **over** it, pick it up and *spin* **under** it, put it back down and *skip* **around** it. Then pick up the object. While the dancer stays in place, make the object do the same movements in the same spatial relationships to them, as if bringing a puppet to life. Play David Benoit, "Wild Kids." Go through both parts (dancer dances and object dances) twice. Then hold the object and dance with it any way they want until the end of the song.
- *Chinese Friendship Dance.* See appendix D, "World Dances," and use **far**, **near**, **around**, **next to**, **away**, and **over/under**.

For middle to upper elementary students:
- *Chairs.* Provide one chair for each student, and they are spread around with as much space between them as possible. Dancers start offstage and enter traveling **toward** their chair, then dance **around** it, **in front of** it, **behind** it, **next to** it, **over** it, **connected** to it, and finally exit **away** from

it. The whole group creates a different movement for each spatial relationship. Practice, divide in half, and perform to Mickey Hart, "Island Groove."

- **_Troika._** See appendix D, "World Dances" (**next to, over/under, around, in front of/behind**).
- **_Los Machetes._** See appendix D, "World Dances" (**next to, around, over/under, in front of/behind**).
- **_Circle Shapes._** Begin in a circle, with one person in the middle making a shape. Next, the person in the circle dances **toward** the center person, **around** them, then stops and makes a shape in one of the following five called-out relationships: **next to, behind, in front of, over,** or **under.** Then the person who was there before dances **away** and back to the circle. Play any music with a long steady beat as background. Continue around the circle until all have had a turn.
- **_Gustav's Skoal._** See appendix D, "World Dances." Relationships include **next to, toward, away, connected, under/over, through,** and **around.**
- **_Stationary Object._** Use something in the room that does not move, such as a piano or a piece of furniture. Then groups (by two relationships, not matching pairs) create a study where they enter and assume one relationship with the object and a shape, then transition to a second relationship and shape. Play any music as background.
- **_Walking in Beauty (excerpts from the poem about the Navajo changing ceremony)._** In Navajo culture, this ceremony is performed when a child is changing into an adult. Form groups of five or divide in half. One person is the designated "changeling" who travels in a diagonal direction from upstage to downstage, surrounded on all sides by the other four or more dancers. The changeling creates their own special walk, and as the lines of the poem are read, the dancers surrounding him/her perform six different "beauty" movements when cued. All finish in a final shape

at the end of the journey. Play Mary Youngblood, "Walk with Me." For the text of the poem, see chapter 10, "Grade Level Curricula," Third Grade.

- **Three Groups.** Divide into three groups (A, B, and C), and each gets three relationships (except *toward* and *away*, which all will use). Relationships can be grouped as follows: (A) *in front of, behind, through*; (B) *around, over, under*; (C) *next to, between, connected*. Each group creates movements for *toward* and *away*. Beginning from the sides of the space, enter (*toward*) and create movements for each of their relationships and then a final movement to exit (*away*). Perform one group at a time to any music. For *through* and *between*, they will need to create a space with their bodies to enable the others in the group to assume the relationship.

- **Chair Dances.** This dance is done only where there are twelve stable chairs available. Practice all relationships, starting with all dancers on one side of the room and two chairs in the center with some space between them. Play Gorillaz, "Tomorrow Comes Today." Two at a time dance **toward** the chairs and position themselves in one of the other relationships as called out to the chair, make a frozen shape, then dance **away** to the other side as the next two enter with the next relationship. Dancers divide into eleven groups, and each gets a chair (*between* gets two) and a relationship. They create a phrase of at least three movements demonstrating their relationship to their chair and end in a shape that also clearly shows that relationship. Perform to the same music.

- **Effort Actions.** Use eight Effort Actions as verbs and randomly match them with relationships (e.g., *float around* or *punch through*). Divide into four groups, and each group gets two *Effort Actions/relationship* pairs. They create a movement phrase to express each with an entrance and exit. Play Mickey Hart, "Temple Caves."

FORMATIONS
Creating designs with multiple bodies

Creating a visual design and a structure in which to dance is making use of FORMATIONS. Dancers need to see the picture, visualize their place as part of it in relation to the group, and create and maintain it in performance.

Using graphic displays of dots, which represent the dancers, in various formations can be very helpful. See chapter 9, "Using Visuals, Objects, and Props," for examples of cards that can be made illustrating the following twelve formations: **scattered**, **circle**, **single line across**, **parallel lines deep**, **diagonal line**, **pairs**, **cluster**, **semicircle**, **five small circles**, **cross**, **X**, and **V**. Also, a whiteboard can be used to draw original formations.

For younger elementary students, use *scattered, circle, pairs, single line across, parallel lines deep,* **and** *cluster*:
- *Four Formations / Eight Movements.* Use **scattered**, **circle**, **pairs**, and **single line across**. Divide the group in half and give each half two of the formations. Then each group chooses two movements that travel and two that stay in place. Play Eric Chappelle, *Music for Creative Dance: Contrast and Continuum*, vol. 1, "All in One," and one group at a time performs. Both groups begin in the first formation, sharing the space. During the space music, they perform their in-place movement, then travel to the second formation during

the rhythmic music, do the second in-place movement, then travel back to the first formation.

- ***Formations and Changing Levels.*** Play Carl Orff, *Orff-Schulwerk*, vol. 1, "Erster Kanon." Then divide the class into three groups (by three selected formations). Each group gets two movements (one traveling and one in-place). Enter with their traveling movement into their formation. Change levels with their in-place movement, staying in the formation. Then exit with same traveling movement, but at the opposite level. Follow the music for changes. Groups can keep the same movements but change formations and repeat.

For middle to upper elementary students, add *diagonal, semicircle, five small circles, cross, V,* and *X*: Practice walking through formations, challenging the students to get into the next formation in as few counts as possible. Play a drum to keep the count.

- ***Choose Four.*** The class votes on their four favorites out of all the formations practiced, and all begin with the first choice. Choose four traveling movements and display them between the two formations, with one at the end to travel back to the first formation. Play Carl Orff, *Orff-Schulwerk*, vol. 2, "Rondo." Then choose three in-place movements to do in the formations on changes in the music.
- ***EARTHDANCE.*** Use the book by Joanne Ryder as a guide and practice the following formations: **cluster, circle, small circles scattered, parallel lines front to back, Pairs,** and **single line across.** Create movements as described in the book while moving through the formations. Play Mass Ensemble, "Wind in the Earth Harp."
- ***Draw Your Own.*** Students can draw their own "digital pictures" and transform them into formations. Groups could be smaller, four to five people. They can focus on the transitions between the formations, which must be part of the dance. The dance must contain three different formations. Perform to David Benoit, "Sailing through the City."

- **_Perimeter and Area._** See chapter 22, "Integrating Content Areas," Fifth Grade, Math. Divide in half, and each group practices the following five geometric shape formations: _circle_, _square_, _triangle_, _rectangle_, and _oval_. For the performance, half the group makes the first formation and sets an in-place movement. Meanwhile, the other half dances inside it (perimeter and area) with a set movement for that formation. Groups take turns forming the perimeters and areas. Play Carl Orff, _Orff-Schulwerk_, vol. 1, "Ekstatischer" as background.

- **_Moving Formations._** As a whole group, practice the following formations moving in space but maintaining the formation: **circle** (around circumference); **straight line**, **cross**, and **X** (rotating); **cluster** (all around space); and **semicircle** and **V** (inverting). Create a whole-group dance by choosing seven traveling movements (one for each formation) and a transition motif. Play Mass Ensemble, "Chaos Nebula."

GROUPING

Who dances together, in large or small groups or alone

Being a part of a group is something that comes very naturally to children and is usually a situation in which they can find structure and comfort. In dance, we can move as a whole group (or **ENSEMBLE**), divide into two large groups (or **HALVES**), or smaller groups still (such as **QUARTETS**, **TRIOS**, or **DUOS**). Also, dancers can dance alone as a **SOLO** performer.

For younger elementary students:

- ***Changing Groups.*** Practice getting into different groupings, from *solo* to *duo*, to *solo* again, to *trio*, then to *solo* again. Set three movements, one traveling (which all will use transitioning between groupings) and two different movements to be done with partners in *duos* and *trios*. Play Eric Chappelle, *Music for Creative Dance: Contrast and Continuum*, vol. 2, "Skippy Ska." The dance begins with all dancers doing their own movements as soloists, then travel to their partners and do a set movement as *duos*, separate and do any movement solo again, then travel into *trios* and do a set movement together. Separate again and finish doing any movement as a soloist.

- ***Partners within Groups.*** Divide the whole group into three groups and each of those groups into *duos*. Play Carl Orff, *Orff-Schulwerk*, vol. 1, "Erster Kanon." Pairs from the first larger group enter, sliding together and holding both hands. They change partners on a four-beat break, then slide off to the opposite side with their new partner. The next group repeats, and the final group also repeats. Repeat the whole dance with new partners, crossing back to the other side.

- ***Groups and Spatial Relationships.*** See "Spatial Relationships" above. The whole group does *around* and *connected* by taking hands and dancing around in one large circle in a set movement pattern, such as *gallop, jump, gallop, jump*. Divide into *quartets*. All get *next to* each other and do another pattern, such as *twist, spin, twist, spin*. Then divide into *duos* and set movements for *over/under* at the same time and *in front of/behind* also at the same time. Then all separate and do all different movements with no relationship to each other. Finally, all return to the whole group circle and finish repeating the *around* and *connected* pattern. Play Mickey Hart, "Elephant Walk."

For middle to upper elementary students:

- ***Category Circle.*** Form one large circle and play any long piece of music with a steady beat as background. The teacher calls out various categories, such as "went to a party last weekend," "has two sisters," "has a dog," "loves school," "is wearing red," "loves broccoli," etc. Students who fit into the category called out go to the center and dance any movement they like until the next category is called out. Select groups that have a varied number of dancers and list them. One group at a time improvises and sets a movement or phrase. Since many people will likely be in multiple groups, keep the phrases very simple. This is also a great way for students to find out what they have in common with one another.

- ***Waves of Tory.*** See appendix D, "World Dances." This dance from Ireland involves both grouping and formations. **Halves** of the group form lines across from each other, then **quartets** in circles, then **duos** traveling forward and backward.
- ***Regrouping.*** Begin by choosing four movements to create a phrase for the whole group to dance (ENSEMBLE) and perform. Then regroup and repeat the phrase into groups of four (QUARTETS) and perform. Then regroup into partners (DUOS) and perform. Then divide by girls/boys or some other way (HALVES) and perform. Finish by returning to the whole group and repeat the same four movements. Play any music as background.

MUSICALITY

A dancer's relationship to their accompaniment

Discuss how dancers can work together in groups, but another member of their group is always the music, and their collective relationship to the common sound allows a dance to take shape.

This is a somewhat abstract concept, and I reserve its exploration for upper elementary grade students. Their ability to transform the sounds, patterns, energy, and feelings heard in the music into movement is what sets skilled dancers apart as artists. It is the dancer's ability to "see" music.

For both of the lesson examples below, first play the selected music and allow the students to close their eyes and imagine that the music is "pouring" into their bodies. Play the selections again and allow the students to improvise movements that they feel interpret the music they hear. Then ask the students to improvise without the music, but from the memory of what they heard. Note: This activity takes a lot of concentration, and some groups are not well suited for it. I find it best to have all students dance at the same time. That way, it is harder for them to watch one another and be tempted to criticize.

- *"Potpourri."* Use the first four or five clips of any of Eric Chappelle's "Potpourri" selections. After improvising, play them a third time, pausing between clips to allow the students to improvise in silence, interpreting the song clip they just heard. Divide into as many groups as the clips of music played, and each group is responsible for creating a dance phrase that can be repeated to fill the counts of the entire clip of music. The dance must have a clear beginning and end with the music. Play the clips multiple times so groups can count the beats and memorize how their music feels. Perform to the same musical selections, allowing groups to make revisions, and perform again.
- *"Sonidos de Los Angeles."* Play Juan David Gonzalez Ariza's "Sonidos de Los Angeles" (because of its rich texture and varying sounds that will evoke images when played). Allow the students to improvise with and without the music and ask them to remember one movement they created that expresses something they heard in the song. In groups of three to four students, have them show and teach one

another the movement they created while improvising. Together, they create a dance phrase that includes all of their movements. Practice and perform to the same music (obviously), and while the song is playing, groups perform their movements when they fit the various parts of the song. So groups could be starting and stopping and restarting.

Chapter 16

Element of PURPOSE
Why the dancer must dance and the dance must exist

Dance has existed among human beings since long before recorded history. It is deep in our DNA and is essential for our survival. All people all over the world throughout history have danced, and the moment in which we live right now is no different. We couldn't NOT dance if we tried. We must do it! And the dances we create now will become part of the history of the future. The point is, there are many reasons why *dance arts* exist. It's kind of exciting to be part of that, isn't it?

This chapter is different from the previous five in this section regarding the elements of dance in that there are no specific lessons that teach WHY we dance, and honestly, I don't see how that could be done. The reason why is ever present, surrounding what we do just by the mere fact that we are doing it. Purpose is deeply embedded in each lesson we teach, and as educators, we have the exciting job of exposing pertinent and specific learning goals and articulating them for our students within the context of a rich and enjoyable firsthand dance experience. I could refer you back to chapter 7, "Enduring Understandings and Essential Questions," for some thought-provoking ideas; and there are several questions there that begin with the word *why*. However, if you are looking for answers or deep and profound wisdom related to the meaning of life through dance in this chapter, sorry to disappoint—but no one can claim to know why another dancer dances or why another artist creates. Each of us is seeking our own answer, which may be a lifelong journey of the most beautiful kind!

Your students will eventually begin to develop their own inner narrative regarding this biggest-of-all questions, and they will also try out different ways of articulating their creative purpose. I believe that modeling transparency in why we do what we do is important, and if we are clear and able to express our purpose to our students, they will have a much better chance of understanding and demonstrating the point of each lesson and of feeling comfortable with asking and answering the question of *why* in other situations.

Why do you think the two people in the illustration on the previous page are dancing? Using a picture like this can inspire a fascinating discussion, lead to many insights, and get your students thinking about purpose in a very direct way. I can think of several possible reasons why the dancers in the picture are dancing, and likewise, any dance you share with a class or have them create can serve multiple purposes. On the following pages is a chart of sixteen squares, each containing a single word as a reason why people dance, plus a brief list of the kinds of dances and dance experiences that historically serve that purpose. As dance educators, we have the great privilege of providing our students with many opportunities to experience dance—and for many reasons.

Fun!	Exercise
• Spontaneous outburst • Hearing a good song • Imitation of a favorite artist • Stress release • Dance games	• Aerobic dance • Zumba • Yoga • Fitness
Belonging	Celebration
• Group dances • Partnering • Part of a community • Dance teams	• Winning or scoring • Wedding • Quinceañera • Bar/Bat Mitzvah • Presidential inauguration • Harvest
Learning	SPIRITUALITY
• Total Physical Response (TPR) • Social studies • Language concepts • Math concepts • Physiology	• Liturgical dances • Religious practice • Communion with higher power • Transcendence • Yoga
Practice	History
• Becoming a better dancer • Perfecting technique • Rhythmic accuracy • Precision • Rehearsal • Mastery of skills	• Record events • Deepen understanding of the past

## Storytelling - Classical ballets - Folklore - Fables - Expression without words	## Creativity - Artistic process - Craftsmanship - Final product - Originality
## Expression - Share feelings - Share ideas - Define personal identity - Outlet for burning issues	## Friendship - Make new friends - Reconnect with old friends - Partnerships - Peaceful and positive interaction
## Culture - Illustrating where people come from - Costumes - Music - Civilization - Customs - Way of life	## Tradition - Annual festival - Holiday performance - Prom
## Romance - Ballroom dance - Couples' dances - Pas de deux	## Communication - One-to-one between dancers - Share with an audience - Alternative to written or oral language

PART IV
Creating and Composing

The craft of
constructing
original work

Chapter 17

Inspiration
Generating ideas and transforming them into movement

From where do dancers and choreographers find inspiration for their work? It is unpredictable. Dance artists can get ideas for movement from virtually anywhere: nature, music, other dancers, pictures, objects, sensations, fine art, poetry, stories, personal experiences, current events . . . just to name a very few.

In this chapter, rather than elaborate on specific lessons, I am providing various categories of inspirational stimuli and connections that can be made with the elements of dance. There are also references to the appendices at the end of this book for further details and examples that I have found to work well as inspiration for student work.

First, a definition: **INSPIRATION** *(noun), the process of being mentally stimulated to do or feel something, especially to do something creative.* Brilliant! Just what we need.

The following are seven categories of inspirational stimuli:
- **Visual images**
- **Objects**
- **Stories (examples in appendix F, "Stories")**
- **Poetic forms**
- **Music or sounds**
- **Books about dance**
- **Emotions**

VISUAL IMAGES

Stimuli through the sense of sight

As students look at pictures, a dance educator can guide their observations toward skills and content they have already learned and to what you want them to learn. One strategy is to simply ask students what they see in the picture, write down their responses in single words, and improvise to create movements that express what is listed. Finding just the right background music can really help set the mood and increase students' willingness to explore movements.

Also, it is helpful to have visual image examples that are large enough for students to view from a short distance. If you have easy access to a projector, that would allow everyone to see the same large image at the same time. If not, large prints can be used and in fact might also be helpful if dividing into groups by picture, where each group can look closely at their own.

Fine art examples (see chapter 9, "Using Visuals, Objects, and Props"):

- *Flower Festival* by Diego Rivera (for younger students, pre-K to first grade, simply have them tell you what they see in the picture)
- *Starry Night* by Vincent van Gogh (connected to the six energy qualities, look for *swinging*, *suspended*, and *percussive*, for third to fourth grade)
- *The Persistence of Memory* by Salvador Dalí (connected to six energy qualities, look for *collapse*, *sustained*, and *vibratory*, for third to fourth grade)
- *Birth of Venus* by Botticelli (head only since the rest of her is naked) (connected to curved pathways, for first to third grade)
- *Three Musicians* by Pablo Picasso (connected to straight pathways, for first to third grade)
- *Relativity* by M. C. Escher (connected to zigzag pathways, for first to third grade, and a chance dance lesson for fourth to fifth grade with selected movements and directions)
- *Red Poppy* by Georgia O'Keeffe (connected to wavy pathways, for first to third grade)

Photography:

Any photograph of something that is of interest to you or your students can serve as an inspirational springboard. Wildlife, nature, people in various settings, and abstract images are all great choices. Be sure to have a clear vision of what skills or concepts you want your students to work on, inspired by the picture. Of course, lines/pathways, shapes, colors, depth, rhythm, and textures can all be observed and translated into movement.

Visualization:

Guiding your students through using their imagination to "see" things you wish them to see that connect with the skills and concepts you are teaching them can be a very easy and powerful tool. First of all, you don't need any images to show them—just your suggestions. I have used an imaginary journey to various places, such as to the mountains, outer space, or under the ocean. Also, I have used music clips, such as Eric Chappelle's "Potpourri" selections. By playing them and asking the students to simply listen with eyes closed and then share what they imagined when the music was playing, many workable ideas can be generated. (Note: Be sure to tell them ahead of time not to envision the instruments they hear. That would be a good music lesson, but we are hoping for inspiration for movement that goes a bit further).

OBJECTS

Physical items that can be manipulated to explore movement

Enhancing movement:
Many dances and dance styles rely upon certain objects or props to define their meaning and reveal their identity to an audience. For example, many East and Southeast Asian countries (Korea, China, Japan, Vietnam, and the Philippines) use fans, large and small, to characterize the movements of a multitude of different dances. The walking sticks used in Los Viejitos from Mexico, the handheld sticks for Los Machetes (also Mexico), the Peopleton stick dance (England-Wales border region), and, of course, the tambourines used in *tarantella* (Italy) are some of the more famous examples of objects being used to enhance or define a dance. Other examples include the several dances that use scarves or handkerchiefs, such as the Qashqai scarf dance (Iran), El Vals de los Paños (northern Mexico),

Boboobo (Ghana/Togo), and in the Hora (Israel) as an alternative to holding hands. See appendix D, "World Dances," and chapter 9, "Using Visuals, Objects, and Props."

Then there is footwear! One of the most important factors in dance, an entire book could be devoted to the history, diversity, and function of all the various kinds of shoes, slippers, and boots (or the lack thereof) worn by dancers around the world. Just to name a few examples, *tap*, *ballet*, *gumboot*, and *clogging* all rely on footwear to define themselves.

Movement born out of observation or manipulation:
Any object can serve as a vehicle to creating movement, and I believe there are two ways a dancer can use an object as that basis: exploring movement **as the object** (such as imitating the movements it can make when you move it) or dancing **with the object** (as a sort of partner or as a costume piece or prop). One of the most beautiful examples of a costume as an essential part of a dance is in the folklórico tradition of Mexico and, of course, Alvin Ailey's *Cry*. But I digress.

Using even ordinary objects can be a springboard for beautiful and imaginative dances. Some objects I have used include paper plates, nylon stockings (not pantyhose), plastic cups, bedsheets, balloons, rhythm sticks, and small playground balls. Chairs can also be used to create interesting dances, but I prefer to use them to explore spatial relationships rather than encouraging children to lift and move them around in a group setting.

AS the object: Students observe and imitate movements the teacher is making the selected objects do, such as rolling a cup on its side, shaking a sheet and letting it drop, and batting a balloon up and watching it float. This requires that the students embody what they see the object doing, imagine being made of its material, and take on its shape and weight. For older students, exploring **TEXTURES** (see chapter 14, "Element of Energy") through their tactile sense can inspire beautiful and rich movement development. Some objects that are good for this are as follows: sandpaper, cotton balls, dried leaves, cooked spaghetti, a stiff-bristle brush, and marbles. For this, students take turns touching the object and either write down words that describe how it feels or begin exploring movements that do the same. Phrases and studies can be developed out of this exploration.

WITH the object: All children need to touch, play, and explore the possibilities of what various objects can do and what can be done with them. Especially for younger children, providing them a bit of time to simply play with and touch the objects you provide will satisfy their need to do so; and afterward, they will likely be more open to following suggestions and manipulating the objects in ways that are more conducive to creating a dance. Offering movement suggestions to students who don't seem to know where to begin can be helpful, such as spinning, leaping, throwing and catching, sliding, and connecting to other dancers.

One way to structure this kind of activity is by creating "centers" in your space. You can do this by placing several of the same objects in a designated area and divide the students into as many groups. Play any music. Then direct the students to dance with their designated objects while the music is playing and freeze in a still shape with it when the music stops, then replace the object and move as a group to the next area or the center to explore the next set of objects. Do this as many times as it takes for all groups to explore all objects. Note: Using a bedsheet is a bit different because the students must work together rather than each having their own object. Dances can be created in groups by object, following this simple sequence: First, they enter the space dancing **AS** the object. Next, they pick the object up and dance **WITH** it. Then they create and hold a still shape. Finally, they replace the object and exit **AS** it once again.

Another fun and creative way to use objects is in a simple *"pass the object"* circle dance. Simply form circles of about five to six dancers and give each group one of each object. First, they practice and create the most interesting way that they can of passing each object around the circle from one person to the next (behind the back, under the leg, with a jump, etc.) and remember it. Play any music, and groups start with one object and pass it the same way until the music stops (controlled by the teacher). When the teacher pauses the music, whoever is holding the object exchanges it for another and begins again with a new object and a new way of passing.

STORIES

Using literature as a basis for movement

For this section, please refer to **appendix F, "Stories,"** for a few examples of great literature that can be brought to life through dance. And to be clear, it goes both ways—dances can be created to tell stories, and stories that explain dances can be written. Here are simple steps for doing both.

CREATING A DANCE FROM A STORY

Dance can enhance comprehension of written material for both performer and observer and encourage a deeper exploration of concepts. And for English-language learners, dance can make unfamiliar words or ideas comprehensible. The following four steps describe the process of translating written material into movement:

1. **Present LITERATURE**
2. **Identify ACTION WORDS**
3. **Explore MOVEMENTS**
4. **Compose CHOREOGRAPHY**

<u>STEP 1: Present LITERATURE</u>

Choose from picture books, chapter books, articles, nonfiction, or even your students' own writing. **Always know your written material before sharing it with students.** No special introduction is necessary other than informing the students of the intent, which is to create a dance based on the writing. Simply read your selection aloud to the group, emphasizing the important points along the way and making connections to students' prior knowledge.

<u>STEP 2: Identify ACTION WORDS</u>

In a teacher-led group discussion, quickly review your selection and create a list of five to ten key words that describe the important events in your story. The goal is to boil down your selection to just a handful of points or events. That way, only what is most relevant will be revealed. Make a list of the events in the same order as presented in the writing. List them as words that end in -*ing*, indicating an action, which can easily translate to movement. If your students are struggling to come up with ideas, it is sometimes helpful to ask the following: "What is happening in this part of the story?" "What is this character doing?" or "What do you imagine when you hear those words?"

<u>STEP 3: Explore MOVEMENTS</u>

Following your list of words ending in -*ing*, guide your students through movement exploration, encouraging them to use their **whole body**. A drumbeat or background music can help get them going. Observe as they are moving. Then make suggestions as needed to use or vary the movement concepts they already know, such as high or low levels, traveling or in-place movements, fast or slow tempo, or energy qualities. Try to discourage them from making literal interpretations of the words, such as gestures or pantomime, which might not go as deep into the meaning of the story as you wish them to go. As your students are improvising, watch for the most interesting, original, or expressive movements you see your students creating. Then pause to ask those students to show the group what they are doing. Your experienced eye can detect the movements that best express the concept. After a movement is created, have the whole group either practice and learn it or put more than one movement together to create a movement combination or phrase. Repeat this process for each action word.

STEP 4: Compose CHOREOGRAPHY

When your students have created movements or phrases that express the images or events from the writing, it is time to put them together in a structure that will make sense to both the dancers and the audience. Obviously, the dance should go in the same order as the writing; and if events in the story repeat, the movements should as well. The dance can be performed as the work of the whole group, as smaller groups focusing on individual sections, or as a combination of both. If possible, it is beneficial to divide the group in half and take turns performing the dance for one another so they have an opportunity to see it from the audience's perspective. Note: It is a good idea to have musical accompaniment chosen before the final performance, and using the same music as background in the previous movement exploration step can simplify the whole process.

CREATING A STORY FROM A DANCE

Dance can provide a vibrant and dynamic source of inspiration to writers and storytellers. Moving one's body and observing others move can engage kinesthetic brain functions that open up creative pathways in a way that only a firsthand physical experience can. The following four steps describe the process of using dance as inspiration for storytelling:

1. **Create CHOREOGRAPHY**
2. **Use IMAGINATION**
3. **Get FEEDBACK**
4. **Story WRITING**

<u>Step 1: Create CHOREOGRAPHY</u>

Introduce this activity as a brainstorming step rather than a dance-making project, with the ultimate goal being to create a sequence of movements that can later be interpreted to tell a story. Divide your students into groups, with the intention that each group will generate their own story. Then each group chooses three actions from the following:

RISE, BEND, TURN, REACH, SEPARATE, BALANCE, PASS, FREEZE, FALL

Put the selected actions in any order, knowing that they represent the beginning, middle, and end of a future story. Choose an adverb to describe each action, such as *rise joyfully*, *turn sharply*, or *pass slowly*. Explore movements and set a sequence of either single movements or single phrases. Remind the students of the movement concepts they know as they are creating their dance, encouraging them to use different levels in space, different energy qualities, traveling movements, or changes in tempo. This will encourage them to deepen the level of movement expression beyond simple gestures or pantomime and perhaps lead to generating more detailed images in their minds.

<u>Step 2: Use IMAGINATION</u>

After your students have created and set their choreography, have them practice it two to three times, directing them to use their imaginations while performing each movement. Between each practice, allow them time to discuss what they envisioned among themselves. The following prompts may help: "What happened at the beginning?" "What did you imagine while you were dancing?" or "What happened to cause the next movement?" Group members (or the teacher) should take notes of their discussion and begin to develop a story line that connects the movement events. Note: Do not encourage your students to write a final draft of their story at this point. Getting outside observations can spark many new creative ideas.

Step 3: Get FEEDBACK

Each individual group performs their dance, taking time after each performance for discussion and comments from the audience. Before the performance, the audience should be prepared by knowing that their job is to use their imagination as they watch the dance and afterward make comments on what they saw. Notes of the audience's observations should be taken for each group. Also, both general and specific observations are valuable.

Step 4: Story WRITING

The final task is to write a story based on the dance they created. Using their own ideas and those of their audience, each group attempts to formulate a cohesive story that includes a beginning, middle, and end, as well as characters and a setting. Also, they should illustrate their story—but not by drawing dancers and rather by drawing images they saw, felt, or heard from themselves, each other, and the audience. Note: To avoid confusion, your students' stories should probably not be about dancers or dancing. The dance is used as a springboard for inspiration at a different level, not as the basis of the story.

POETIC FORMS

Structures and imagery derived from the art of words

Just as dance is the art of movement, poetry is the art of words. Similarly, both art forms have certain structures that guide artists toward giving their work form. Using prewritten poems as inspiration for dances is a great place to start, and from there, having students try their hand at writing their own poems from which to create their own dances is a double dose of creativity across disciplines! Below are some basic structures and examples used in poetry that can be understood and used by students of each grade level as listed. See appendix G, "Handouts," for further description and examples of the following poetic forms.

Pre-K to Kindergarten – NURSERY RHYMES

Children at this age (or adults for that matter) might not be able to write their own nursery rhyme. But there are many to choose from, and here are just a few. First, practice singing each nursery rhyme. Then create movements that express each line (matching the lines with each of the four energies if desired).

Los Pollitos:

Los pollitos dicen, pio pio pio - Light
Cuando tienen hambre, cuando tienen frio - Heavy
La gallina busca el maiz y el trigo - Sharp
Les da la comida y les presta abrigo - Smooth

Hey, Diddle, Diddle:

Hey diddle, diddle, the cat and the fiddle - Smooth
The cow jumped over the moon - Heavy
The little dog laughed to see such sport - Light
And the dish ran away with the spoon - Sharp (taking turns)

Other nursery rhymes include "Little Miss Muffet," "Hickory Dickory Dock," "Jack and Jill," and "Humpty Dumpty."

First Grade – ACCENTS AND SYLLABLES

Choose a concept or idea. Then choose five words with varying numbers of **syllables** and arrange them with the single syllable word last. The following is based on "community helpers," written by a first-grade class:

CONSTRUCTION WORKERS   **FIREFIGHTERS**
NURSES   **BUS DRIVERS**
COPS

This is based on "school," written by a first-grade class:

TEACHERS   **LESSON**
ATTENDANCE   **AUDITORIUM**
LEARN

Explore and set movements that represent each of the words, emphasizing the **accent** of the word by increasing the amount of force used in the appropriate part of the movement.

Second Grade – CINQUAIN

A descriptive poem in five lines, using mostly single words. Choose a topic and write a poem structured as follows:

NOUN
ADJECTIVE   **ADJECTIVE**
VERB   **VERB**   **VERB**
Four- to five-word sentence quoting the subject and expressing an emotion
Different and related NOUN

Here is an example of a cinquain written by a second-grade class on the topic of Santa Claus:

SANTA
JOLLY   **UNUSUAL**
JUMPS   **LAUGHS**   **FLIES**
"I CAUGHT YOU BEING GOOD"
CHRISTMAS

Explore and set movements that represent each of the words. Remind students to use their **whole bodies** to create movements rather than just facial expressions or everyday gestures.

Third and Fourth Grades – HAIKU

A Japanese form of poetry with a line structure as follows:

First line: five syllables
Second line: seven syllables
Third line: five syllables

Choose any topic and write a haiku. Then explore movements that express images in the poem. The following haikus were written by fourth-grade students:

The pounding rain comes
Drip, drop, drip, it is raining
The lake is shiny

Apples are yummy
They grow on trees and smell good
Apples are the best

Fifth and Sixth Grades – FIVE SENSES POEM

This form makes connections to science and language arts by using sensory perception and metaphor to translate images generated by the words into movement.

Choose any topic, and in seven lines, describe your topic as follows:
1. *Color . . .* describe the color(s) of your topic
2. *It Feels like . . .* (tactile sense)
3. *It Sounds like . . .* (auditory sense)
4. *It Tastes like . . .* (gustatory sense)
5. *It Smells like . . .* (olfactory sense)
6. *It Looks like . . .* (visual sense)
7. *It Makes me feel like . . .* (emotional response)

Dancers can create either a combination of movements, a phrase, or a still shape for each line of their poem. Encourage your students to use **whole-body movements** rather than just facial expressions or everyday gestures since this is what sets dance apart from pantomime. Use any music that fits the topic and feeling of the poem. The following examples were written by fifth-grade students:

War is brown
It feels wet and cold
It sounds like thunder
It tastes like bitter grapes
It smells like yesterday's garbage
It looks like ancient ruins
It makes me feel like crying

Lemons are bright yellow
They feel cool and bumpy
They sound like a thud when they hit the ground
They taste sour
They smell fresh and clean
They look like little yellow footballs
They make me feel refreshed

MUSIC OR SOUNDS

Stimuli through the auditory sense

Music and dance go together like peanut butter and jelly—once put together, it is difficult to take them apart. Of course, many dances are inspired by music. In fact, spontaneous dancing in any setting is often inspired by a great song that is overheard (haven't we all done that?). Rather than outline how to count music and make up steps for choreography, in this section, I will simply outline three different ways to use auditory stimuli as inspiration for dance-making through the use of **imagery**, **breathing**, and **call and response**.

Imagery. Play any selected piece of music, and as the students are listening, tell them to let their imagination go and visualize any images the music shows them in their mind. Immediately after they listen, write down in simple terms the **imagery** their minds produced. You may need to repeat this two to three times for each musical selection. I have found that the first time trying this, students will usually describe the instruments they hear playing. Encourage them to go beyond these literal images and see what else the music shows them. Once you have generated a list of words or terms, improvise to create movements that express each. Play the original musical selection and perform the dance they created.

Breathing. Depending on the age or grade level of the students, practice three to eight different ways of letting air pass in and out of the body: **snoring**, **hissing**, **panting**, **snorting**, **sighing**, **gasping**,

sneezing, and **yawning**. Explore and set movements to each selected breath type in a way that can be repeated, as in how breathing actually happens. Construct movement patterns in a way that is appropriate for the grade level, such as dividing into groups by breath type, adding on and repeating breath movement patterns, or choosing three or more to make longer patterns. Use Eric Chappelle, *Music for Creative Dance: Contrast and Continuum*, vol. 4, "Breath Meditation" as background.

Call and Response. Play one of the following musical selections: Eric Chappelle, *Music for Creative Dance: Contrast and Continuum*, vol. 4, "Back at Ya" or Christine Stevens, "Call and Response" (middle section). You may also play any other that has a simple and repeatable echoing melodic phrase pattern. Dancers stop and listen as the phrase plays for the first time. Then they create a movement expressing that phrase with their bodies as the phrase repeats. Movements can be set and practiced, and groups or individuals can take turns to perform.

BOOKS ABOUT DANCE

Fiction, nonfiction, and reference books

Here are some examples of excellent books on the subject of dance from which inspiration for dance can be derived, as well as some suggestions on how to use them and with which grade levels.

Eyewitness: Dance by Michael Tambini, **pre-K to kindergarten.** Photographic illustrations of a wide variety of aspects of the art of dance. Students can look at the pictures and imitate the shapes and potential movements they see. Play classical music, such as selections from Beethoven's Symphony no. 6 in F Major.

The Human Alphabet by Pilobolus, with photographs by John Kane, **pre-K to first grade.** Dramatic illustrations of bodies creating letter shapes with connections to words. Students can look at the pictures and work with others to imitate the shapes they see. Play Mass Ensemble, "Hawk's Gaze."

Jiggle Wiggle Prance by Sally Noll, **pre-K to first grade.** Includes expanded movement vocabulary. Students can learn new movement words and practice new movements. Identify the rhyming words, and groups can perform movements in groups by page spread. Play Jenny Allinder, "Rose of My Heart."

Color Dance by Ann Jonas, **kindergarten to first grade.** Connection to the concept of the color wheel. Using colored scarves, if available, groups by color can create movements and join other groups as colors blend. Play Mickey Hart, "The Hunt."

Dance by Bill T. Jones and Susan Kuklin, **first to second grade**. Illustrations are great examples of shapes, positive/negative space, and levels. Divide in half or into groups and create movements or movement patterns, with a shape expressing each page spread. Play Aisha Duo, "Despertar."

Shoes Off, Mommy? by Alison Rose, **first to second grade.** Connects the four seasons, dance genres, movements, and feelings. Experiment dancing with and without shoes. Play David Benoit, "As If I Could Reach Rainbows."

My Mama Had a Dancing Heart by Libba Moore Gray, with illustrations by Raúl Colón, **first to second grade.** Uses images of the four seasons and can connect to multiple dance concepts, such as force, pathways, flow, and weight. Match seasons with these concepts and create movements for the whole group that express each season. Divide and perform for one another. Play Carl Orff, *Orff-Schulwerk*, vol. 1, "Lieder Und Spielstucke-Rondo."

Sometimes I Dance Mountains by Byrd Baylor, **second to third grade**. Explores multiple ways of moving in connection with the natural world. Explore movements of images presented in the book. Choose six to eight favorite images and divide into as many groups. Each group creates a dance sequence or phrase expressing their image and perform taking turns. Play David Lanz and Paul Speer, "Eagle's Path."

Water Dance or ***Cloud Dance***, both by Thomas Locker, **third to fourth grade.** Uses imagery to connect to science. Use page spreads and divide into groups to create dance phrases following action words in text and images from illustrations. Play Eric Chappelle, *Music for Creative Dance: Contrast and Continuum*, vol. 3, "Breathe" for either book.

Sherman Dances by Douglas Goble, **third to fifth grade.** Explores many varied dance styles and genres. Students choose three to six dance styles from those featured in the book and create an original dance phrase based on what they know about that style. They could do research if possible. Play a steady beat on a drum that can change with the exploration of each dance style.

EARTHDANCE by Joanne Ryder, with illustrations by Norman Gorbaty, **third to fifth grade.** Works with various formations. Choose a formation for each page and create movements that move in and out of them. Divide and perform as a semilarge group. Play Mass Ensemble, "Wind in the Earth Harp."

Art Moves by Cynthia Miltenberger, **fourth to fifth grade.** Explores the common elements between dance and visual arts. Point out the elements common to both art forms and divide into as many groups. Each group creates a dance phrase that emphasizes their element of dance and then creates a visual picture of their phrase that emphasizes the same element of visual arts. Perform to any classical music.

The First Music by Dylan Pritchett, with illustrations by Erin Bennett Banks, **fourth to sixth grade.** Various rhythmic patterns. Identify the eleven animal characters in the book, and groups create repeating movement phrases that fit the written rhythm pattern for each animal. Play Michael Wall, "Barre - Warm Up" as a subtle background with a steady beat.

I See the Rhythm by Toyomi Igus and Michele Wood, **fifth to sixth grade.** Explores African American dance and musical genres. List genres and words describing what students know about each. Choose six to eight genres, and groups create movement studies expressing what they know about them. They could do some research and finish studies performing them to the appropriate music for each genre.

Drumbeat in Our Feet by Patricia Keeler and Júlio Leitão, **fifth to sixth grade.** Explores African culture, history, and visual arts. Divide into five to seven groups, and each selects one of the traditions discussed. Each group creates and sets a dance study expressing their tradition. Put the studies together to create one longer dance work. Create illustrations of the costumes (or make masks) of each selected tradition. Play African Drums Traditional, "Were – Were" as background for whole dance.

Rotten Richie and the Ultimate Dare by Patricia Polacco, **fifth to sixth grade.** Sibling dynamics and how a brother and sister resolve a conflict by stepping out of their respective comfort zones into that of the other, one of which being *ballet*. Play Beethoven, *Symphony no. 8 in F, Opus 93*.

EMOTIONS

Our feelings and moods

I would argue that our human ability to read, understand, and express emotions is the most significant thing that sets us apart from other living things. The complexity and depth of our ability to perceive, process, and express our deepest feelings is truly extraordinary on this earth. *Feelings, moods,* and *emotions* are all words that describe the responses of our brains to situations and stimuli—all of which are perfect fodder for artists. In dance, we express our feelings not only in our faces but also with our entire bodies, and skilled dancers can evoke a multitude of emotions in their audience.

I know I said at the beginning of this chapter that there would not be specific lessons. However, *emotions* seem to defy categorization within other elements and are important enough to warrant discrete and in-depth study. So here are some specific lessons developed around various structures of categorizing human emotions, beginning with younger and progressing to upper elementary students:

Four Emotions. For youngers students, the emotions most easily understood are **anger**, **fear**, **happiness**, and **sadness**. Use any structure or pattern such as four opposite pairs of spatial concepts to which each of the emotions can be applied. For example, the opposite pairs of *up/down, small/big, forward/backward,* and *over/under* can each be performed with one of the four emotions listed above. Groups can create simple dance patterns that demonstrate the spatial concepts first, then apply the emotions to them.

Happy Ending. Create a movement for each of the four emotions based on free-dance practice, and in three groups, each has an emotion that is not *happy*. Groups perform their movement plus the happy movement to give their dance a happy ending. Play Eric Chappelle, *Music for Creative Dance: Contrast and Continuum*, vol. 3, "Morning Fours."

Six Emotions: **ANGRY, FEARFUL, HAPPY, DISGUSTED, INTERESTED, SAD.** Students practice making facial expressions of each emotion as presented. Then they do a simple arm gesture, such as circling the arms parallel to the floor and pushing forward from the center. Add each emotion to the movement and discuss how the body changes in the force or energy it uses and in the posture, such as leaning forward for *interested* and keeping the hands close to the body for *fearful*. Next, do free dance of each emotion in the above order to the first six clips of Eric Chappelle, *Music for Creative Dance: Contrast and Continuum*, vol. 3, "Potpourri," finishing each section with a shape that also expresses the emotion.

Lott Ist Todt. See appendix D, "World Dances." Traditional version includes *sad*, *fearful*, and *happy*. Additional versions can include *angry*, *disgusted*, and *interested*.

Emotions Tell the Story. For middle elementary students. Brainstorm and list two to three scenarios that make the students feel each emotion. Divide into six groups by emotion, and they choose one scenario from the list and create a movement expressing it. Next, assign a second emotion for each group (see chart on the following page as an example) and repeat the process of the first emotion. Each group then discusses scenarios that might cause them to change from the first emotion to the second and then creates a movement that expresses that, to be performed between the other two movements. Each group performs their three-part dance, then tells the story to the audience and performs it again. Play Kraked Unit, "Douala Paris" or any music that sets a melancholy mood.

Angry	Fearful	Happy	Disgusted	Interested	Sad
Sad	Interested	Disgusted	Happy	Fearful	Angry

Back-to-Back. For middle to upper elementary students. To the above six emotions, add a seventh, *surprised*. Free dance to the first seven clips of Eric Chappelle, *Music for Creative Dance: Contrast and Continuum*, vol. 3, "Potpourri." In partners, begin standing back-to-back with each other with no emotion; and as soon as each clip begins, they turn and make eye contact, imagining their partner as the reason they are feeling the emotion. They dance an improvised duet together, and when the music pauses, quickly go back-to-back again and go back to no emotion.

Navarasa Moods. For upper elementary students. Practice the *nine moods* of the *Navarasa* from India to the first nine clips of Eric Chappelle, *Music for Creative Dance: Contrast and Continuum*, vol. 1, "Potpourri" in the following order: *pride, tranquility, sorrow, disgust, love, surprise, anger, joy,* and *fear*. Divide into three groups, and each group is randomly given three moods. They choose the order of their three moods and create a dance phrase consisting of six movements (two for each mood) that are expressive and representative of each. Play Prem Joshua, "Deccan Queen."

Chapter 18

Choreographic Tools
Constructing a dance from movements

In this chapter, you will find descriptions of several basic guides called *choreographic tools* or *devices* to which dancers can avail themselves when attempting to create a dance. The creative process is similar among art forms, and the diagram below outlines what I find to be a useful flow of the steps in the **choreographic process** for dance.

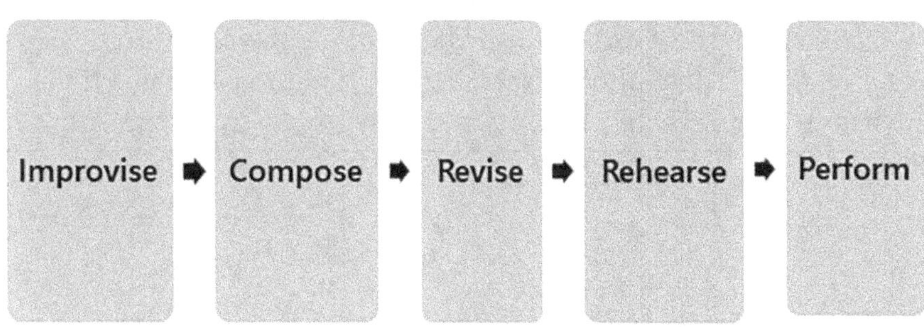

There is also a parallel process for **writing** with some different words but basically the same steps:

Brainstorm – Rough Draft – Revise – Edit – Publish

The first step for a dancer (sorry about the pun) is to generate ideas, and many sources can be utilized to do that, as described in the previous chapter (chapter 17, "Inspiration"). The most overarching process in all art forms is, of course, **IMPROVISATION**. This is when you have an idea or an inspiration in your mind, and as a dancer, you put it into your body. I have found young children to be quite capable improvisers when given the opportunity and a little guidance. However, when students get a little older, say fifth to sixth grade, they tend to restrict their movements and make excuses for themselves for fear of embarrassment. Encouragement goes a long way, so keep your eyes open for the student who you can tell is shy but has something to say. Watch for something they do well and let them know. Also, if you set up situations where students are all moving at the same time, they might be less intimidated than if they are in groups with their peers looking on. At some point, in all dance arts education, improvisation MUST be part of the process.

IMPROVISATION
Taking the first step in the creative process, generating movement ideas

Improvisation is a tool all artists use to generate material with which to form their work of art, whether it be dance, music, poetry, filmmaking, photography, cuisine, or visual arts. It is the first step in the creative process and teaches you to look to and

---

> trust in yourself. Here are some basic *dos and don'ts* for dance improvisation:
>
> **DO:**
> - TRUST in yourself and in one another.
> - TRY new movements.
> - RESPOND to *your understanding* of the instructions.
> - ALLOW yourself to be controlled by the movements you are doing.
> - MULTI-TASK by moving while listening for directions and/or thinking about new ways of moving.
> - STOP when your movement has come to its conclusion, not just when everybody else stops.
>
> **DON'T:**
> - INTERFERE with others.
> - JUDGE anybody else.
> - BOTHER thinking about life problems while you are dancing.
> - COMPARE yourself with anybody else.
> - WORRY about being wrong.
> - STOP dancing when new directions are being given—keep moving.

After improvising, dancers have generated a collection of movements that can be considered raw materials, which need to then be molded and shaped into some kind of form. This step requires skilled craftsmanship (or *craftswomanship*, just saying) and a knowledge of various guiding principles and tools. There are ten things called **Principles of Design**, specifically for dance, as described by Elizabeth Hayes (1993) in *Dance Composition & Production*. They are as follows:

VARIETY	**CONTRAST**	**UNITY**	**BALANCE**	**SEQUENCE**
HARMONY	**REPETITION**	**CLIMAX**	**TRANSITION**	**PROPORTION**

Ideally, a masterfully crafted work of dance art by a professional choreographer will include many of these principles. In elementary-level dance education, however, we have the realistic expectation that young students might learn better focusing on one big idea at a time while creating original choreographic works.

In addition to the Principles of Design, which guide dance composition, there are tools and devices choreographers can use to fashion their work into a finished product. I simply call these **design tools**, and I have found several to be effective in helping kids create dance studies. As with the Principles of Design, these tools can, of course, be adapted to be used with nearly any age. In an effort to streamline curriculum and enable students to learn new things each year, focusing on one per year makes sense to me. With this in mind, I have sought to find a good match between the different ages and grade levels and a single Principle of Design (PoD) and *design tool*. Here is what makes sense to me:

GRADE	PRINCIPLE of DESIGN	DESIGN TOOL
Pre-K	*Variety* - they can identify things that are different	**Stillness:** moving/not moving
Kindergarten	*Variety* - They can identify things that are different.	**Echoing:** imitate and repeat
First	*Unity* - They can do things with others and find commonality.	**Amplification:** enlargement in space, time, and energy
Second	*Sequence* - They can see a logical order.	**Accumulation:** add on in succession and remember
Third	*Repetition* - They can make choices to create emphasis.	**Embellishment:** add detail
Fourth	*Transition* - They can look between the main points to the details.	**Chance Dance:** make choices by random selection

Fifth	**Contrast** - They can keep things interesting by envisioning extreme differences.	**Abstraction:** depart from representational qualities
Sixth	**Balance** - They can look at their work broadly and emphasize purposefully.	**Theme and Variation:** altering a dance phrase with purpose

You may notice that three PoDs (*harmony*, *climax*, and *proportion*) didn't make the elementary school cut. That certainly doesn't mean that younger children can't or shouldn't learn them. I simply feel that they are the most complex of the ten, and older students would likely have more success practicing and learning them.

On the following pages are outlined several lesson ideas that I have found effective in using the Principles of Design and *design tools* matched to each grade level. Keep in mind that these matchings are only my own opinion, based on what I have found to work for children at various ages and stages of development. It is certainly true that any of the design principles and choreographic tools can be adapted to be appropriate for any age or grade level.

Prekindergarten

PRINCIPLE of DESIGN – VARIETY
Look around the space and point out things they can see that are **different** from one another and other things that are the **same**.
- *Same and Different.* Divide into four groups and give each group two different movements. They perform them by doing the first movement for sixteen beats (two sets of eight are the same movement) and the second movement for an additional eight beats to give the pattern **variety**. All groups repeat to complete the song. Play Carl Orff, *Orff-Schulwerk*, vol. 1, "Gassenhauer."

<u>DESIGN TOOL</u> – STILLNESS. Alternate moving and stopping to draw attention when desired.
Practice free dance with any music, and students need to stop and hold completely **still** when the music stops. Repeat several times.

- *Walking, Hopping.* See "Movement Skills" lesson in chapter 11, "Element of Body."
- *Move and Stop.* Play any music and call out a single movement, such as *gallop* or *twist*. Pause the song after about sixteen counts, and students should freeze in place. Divide into groups and take turns to watch one another. Call out new movements for each group or each cycle of groups.
- *AB Pattern.* A is any selected movement, and B is holding still. Play the Wipeouts, "Walk Don't Run." Half of the group or three or four groups take turns performing. Repeat the music if needed. You could place three or four color spots on the floor to indicate groups.

Kindergarten

<u>PRINCIPLE of DESIGN</u> – VARIETY
Talk about things that are **different** from one another (opposite pairs) and about things that are the same (the weather for several days in a row, going to school every day, etc.). Then point out how doing the same thing every day can get boring and cause you to lose interest. The same is true in dance because if the dancers do the same movement over and over, it's not as interesting as when they change the movements.

- *Change It Up.* Divide into four groups, and each group chooses one movement. They perform their movement for sixteen beats. Next, each group chooses a second movement that is extremely different from the first to add **variety** and performs it after the first for eight beats each. And finally, each group chooses a third movement and adds it on to their pattern and performs the first two movements for four beats each and the third for eight beats. Play Bobby McFerrin, "Circlesong Six."

<u>DESIGN TOOL</u> – ECHOING. Use imitation skills and taking turns.
Practice **echoing** first with vocalizing some short sentences, then with seated movements. The teacher is the leader.

- *Echo Dance.* For in-place movements only. Form a circle and place movement cards around the inside of the circle, dividing the group into pairs or trios, each behind a movement card. Each gets a turn performing their movement by themselves for four beats. Then the rest of the group imitates them by echoing. Play Eric Chappelle, *Music for Creative Dance: Contrast and Continuum*, vol. 4, "Back at Ya." After the song is over, rotate the movement cards and repeat the whole dance.
- *Che Che Kule.* See appendix D, "World Dances."

First Grade

<u>PRINCIPLE of DESIGN</u> – UNITY
Discuss what it means to be united with others—being together for the same purpose. In the element of time, dancers can do the same movements at the same time, and that is one form of unity. Another way is on a personal level, and that is finding out what you have in common with others and dancing together to celebrate that.

- *Different-Same.* In groups of four to five, they choose two movements they like and put them in a pattern that goes ABAC—with A being any spontaneous movement and B and C being the set movements they chose, bringing them together in **unity**.

- ***Circle Dance.*** The whole group forms a circle, and when called upon, selected students dance in the middle with a selected called-out movement in **unity**. The teacher calls out attributes such as "wearing red," "likes ice cream," "has a dog," "likes to play basketball," or "likes to dance." When the students who fit each category enter the circle, they can do any movement at first. Then the teacher calls out a movement, and they all do it in **unity**. Play any music that is long enough for several rounds as background.

DESIGN TOOL – AMPLIFICATION. Use extremes of space, energy, and time to emphasize movements.
Seated, practice how to *amplify* a movement by increasing its SIZE/volume, its FORCE/intensity, and its TEMPO/speed.

- ***Amplify One Movement.*** Divide into three groups, and each creates a three-movement pattern and practices it. Focus on the third movement; and each group *amplifies* their third movement in a different way by increasing the size, force, and tempo. Perform to any music that has a long steady beat. After all have had a turn, pause and rotate the amplification modes between the groups and repeat. Then repeat a third time so all groups have a chance to perform all three amplifiers.

Second Grade

PRINCIPLE of DESIGN – SEQUENCE
Diagram the four-part story sequence that they might know: FIRST, NEXT, THEN, and FINALLY.

- ***Build a Sequence.*** Groups choose four movements with **enter** *first*, **exit** *finally*, and at least one in-place movement in the middle for either *next* or *then*. Play Gorillaz, "Tomorrow Comes Today."

- ***Story Sequence.*** Create an example of how a story can be generated from a sequence by randomly selecting four movements. All practice the sequence and then think-pair-share what the story was that the movements could have told. Share out quickly. Then put pairs together to form four larger groups and give each group four different movements for them to create their own **sequence**. Each group performs, discusses, and generates the story, then tells it to the audience and then performs the story sequence again. Play Kraked Unit, "I Love Bidoche!"

<u>DESIGN TOOL</u> – ACCUMULATION. Purposefully build a dance sequence by adding movements one at a time.
- ***Four-Beat Dance.*** In groups of four to six, each person contributes one movement, and all learn and perform the sequence one movement at a time until all have contributed and have learned all movements in the sequence. Play Eric Chappelle, *Music for Creative Dance: Contrast and Continuum*, vol. 2, "Caribbean Leaps."
- ***Accumulate Movements.*** The whole group decides on a single traveling movement that all will use as the beginning of multiple accumulated sequences. Divide into small groups. They must add three more movements to complete a four-part sequence that they can (1) do without stopping, including (2) one movement that stays in place and (3) one that exits at the end with a different traveling movement as the entrance. To facilitate the process, play background music for one minute to allow the groups to experiment with various movements that will follow the initial movement. At the end on one minute, stop the music. Then groups must make a choice and practice their two movements. Repeat this process two more times to finish the sequence, and each group performs to the same music.

Third Grade

<u>PRINCIPLE of DESIGN</u> – REPETITION
Discuss how repetition is common in all art forms and point out visual examples in the room.

- ***Thematic Phrases.*** In no more than six groups, each decides on their favorite movement, which is movement A. Then they choose two more as movements B and C. Perform their phrase, **repeating** movement A at the end, creating an **ABCA** pattern. The theme of the phrase is the movement that is repeated for emphasis. Play any music that has a long steady beat, and groups take turns performing.

<u>DESIGN TOOL</u> – EMBELLISHMENT. Give greater meaning to movements by adding detail.

- ***Add Detail.*** Detail can be added to a movement to give it more depth and meaning, such as a head turn, a change of focus, an energy quality, or a hand movement. Brainstorm and list the results you might wish to achieve in **embellishing** a movement, such as "make it more exciting," "show an emotion," "make it different from another movement," or "do something unexpected." From this list, explore how each result might be accomplished using the different elements of dance. Create a dance phrase of three movements that all will use. Practice it as is and then divide into groups by results listed. Each group chooses which movement from the phrase they wish to embellish and alter the way that movement is done to achieve their selected result. Perform to any music.

Fourth Grade

PRINCIPLE of DESIGN – TRANSITION

Discuss how there is a transition between any two things, and in dance, the transitions are of equal importance as the movements. Consider other examples of transitions, such as doorways, waking up, going to school, or finding your seat.

- ***Shapes in Transition.*** Transitions between movements can be either GRADUAL (momentum continues) or SUDDEN (momentum is interrupted). Divide into four groups, and each creates three still shapes that they all do exactly the same. Practice transitioning from one to the next, to the next, and back to the first, creating a continuous cycle. Play Eric Chappelle, *Music for Creative Dance: Contrast and Continuum*, vol. 1, "Western East." During the sustained section, make **transitions** between shapes **gradually**; and when the music changes to the percussive section, make transitions **suddenly**.

DESIGN TOOL – CHANCE DANCE. Construct a dance through random selection.

Discuss how Merce Cunningham used this device as a tool for much of his choreography.

- ***Chance Dance.*** Choose and list six different movements, matching them to the dots on the die. Groups each roll their own die and list the order of the movements the die has chosen for them. Practice and perform to Michael Manring, "Funk and Disorderly." Use this tool to explore levels, the six energy qualities, or grouping.

Fifth Grade

PRINCIPLE of DESIGN – CONTRAST
Discuss how one of the ways choreographers can make dances interesting is by showing CONTRAST in their movement choices. Consider other examples of contrast and how others use it to increase interest and draw attention to their work, such as the color scheme of black and white, bright lights at night, and extremes in volume or intensity in music.

- ***Different and Same.*** In up to six small groups, give each three movement cards, and they put them in an order that they like. To show **contrast** between **chaotic and synchronized** movements, first all do a different movement from their phrase. Then all do the first movement, then all different again. Then all do the second movement, then all different again. Then all do the third movement. Play Prem Joshua, "Deccan Queen," eight beats for each movement.

DESIGN TOOL – ABSTRACTION. Intentionally depart from representational qualities.
Show examples of abstract versus realistic art, such as Miro's *The Singing Fish* and Rembrandt's *The Return of the Prodigal Son.* Discuss definitions of *movement, gesture,* and *art*:

Movement: *The act of changing place or moving in any way; any change of position*

Gesture: *The use of motions of the limbs or body as means of expression to enhance or illustrate communication*

Art: *The conscious use of skill and creative imagination; the skillful, systematic arrangement and adaptation of means for the attainment of some end*

Demonstrate movement example of **BREATHING**. Show how the abdomen expands and contracts in a repeating rhythm with each breath. Then try it with other body parts, making the hands, arms, legs, or neck "breathe" as well. Explain how artists use creative choices to change the way the observer sees things. Some artists create abstraction by enlarging, simplifying, reshaping, or inverting objects or images or by using shapes and lines that may resemble certain familiar images but leave the observer wondering. Others simply start with an abstract image and build on the theme it creates. *Modern dance* may be considered abstraction as opposed to *ballet*, which is more realistic in its recounting of stories through dance.

- *Everyday Things.* Explain how making a dance about an everyday object is instantly placing it into the realm of the abstract. List realistic things you would like to make a dance about, such as *water, toothpaste, forest, bicycles, video games*. Choose three to five of the most diverse items listed and assign them to as many groups. Create a phrase with a minimum of three movements and one frozen shape that represents their subject ABSTRACTLY. Play David Benoit, "Safari" or David Lanz and Paul Speer, "Rain Forest."

- *Movement + Gesture.* Explore gestures such as a **high five, waving goodbye, nodding in agreement, shrugging the shoulders,** or **raising your hand**. Discuss what each one is intended to communicate. Then alter them by adding a movement to instantly transform the gesture into DANCE, such as blow a kiss/*spin*, cross arms/*jump*, shake a finger/ *sway*, pray/*slide*. Small groups, such as trios, start with a familiar gesture, then choose a movement card and put the two together. Form a circle, and each performs their variation. Choose another gesture and repeat the process. Play Mickey Hart, "Elephant Walk."

Sixth Grade

PRINCIPLE of DESIGN – BALANCE

Discuss how choreographers use balance when creating dances and dance studies. **Progressive balance** (from start to finish), **visual balance** (in space onstage), and, of course, **physical balance** (in control of movements and still shapes) are all important skills to master.

- *Balancing Diagonals.* Play any lively upbeat music, and partners start from opposite corners upstage and choose one traveling movement and one in-place movement. Start traveling from one corner, meet in the middle (**spatial balance**), and do an in-place movement together. Then stop and freeze, holding a balance (**physical balance**, helping each other or not). Then pass each other and continue along their original diagonal (**progressive balance**) path with the same traveling movement to opposite corners.

DESIGN TOOL – THEME AND VARIATION. Make changes to a recurring phrase or motif.

Discuss what a theme in dance is: a movement subject or motif that recurs becomes a theme. It can be developed with variations to make a composition, as in music. Explore ways of varying single movements by changing some aspect of each of the elements of dance (relationship, space, time, energy, and body parts).

- *Four Groups / Four Variations.* Play David Byrne, "Five Golden Sections." The whole group creates a phrase that takes eight sets of eight quick beats. Then perform it in four groups taking turns. Groups then make choices on how to vary the phrase by changing the components of each of the five elements.

- ***Theme and Variation.*** Play Bobby McFerrin, "Circlesong Six." In small groups (no more than nine groups), each chooses a movement for A and a different movement for B. Explore **variations** on how to do both movements, such as a different level, tempo, direction, relationship to another, or energy. Repeat both A and B with a variation so they become A.1-B.1, then again to create A.2-B.2.

Chapter 19

Performance
Sharing your work with an audience or community

Being a performing art, dance is meant to be presented, right? Certainly, and that can take many forms. The inspirational quote "Dance like no one is watching" takes us to a place of freedom of expression without the consequence of being seen in a state of complete abandon, exposing our deepest selves. It is definitely a thing I encourage everyone to do, and admittedly, dancing when there is actually no one watching is one of the most liberating and inspiring things I allow myself to do. In fact, as a choreographer, letting myself go to that place of total freedom is an essential part of the creative process; and I'm sure I'm not alone in that practice. It is also completely harmless to others, which makes my heart feel better about indulging in that way.

There are also many situations where dancing is much less goal oriented and where a certain level of freedom of movement and expression can be achieved without risking embarrassment (such as at a nightclub, a party, a religious gathering, or out in the streets or other public space)—usually because you are in the company of others doing the same thing! These experiences are equally uplifting to the spirit but serve more of a communal and celebratory purpose than that of creating choreography intended to be performed formally on a stage.

Anyway, dancing like there IS someone watching is what we are ultimately meant to do as dance artists, wherever we are. Here are some ways to do it in a classroom, school, or community setting:

- **In classes**, informal performances can occur at any time. If you have a group, you can divide it into smaller groups that serve as audiences for one another, which gives everyone practice on how to both observe and be observed by others. These performances can occur at the end of any and every class and simply be the culmination of a short composition project. Designating separate performance/audience spaces within the dance classroom is helpful, and if you want the students to look at the dance from an outside perspective, it is necessary. Honestly, though, sometimes I have simply asked certain students to just stop and hold still when it is the other group's turn while remaining where they are and observing the dance from the inside. Of course, it depends on what you want your students to observe and/or experience.
- **School assemblies or recitals** are more formal than in-class performances because they include an audience

from outside the class setting. Usually, there is a purpose for a performance of this nature, such as a holiday show, a seasonal festival, or an end-of-the-year concert. The audience can consist of the greater student body, parents and families, and even invited guests from the community. Performances like these are usually held in a large space, such as the school auditorium or yard. There will be a designated space for the performers that is separate from the audience and usually some sort of program, either announced or written, telling the audience what they will be seeing. Costumes, props, and set pieces can be utilized if needed; and special sound and lighting equipment might need to be set up ahead of time. Student dancers will need to rehearse several times in the space prior to the performance, and very little time should go by between the final rehearsal and the performance in front of an audience.

- **In the community**, social gatherings of many types can become venues for dance, both planned and spontaneous. We dance teachers might not have a direct presence in settings such as these, but our role is one of background support, helping our students gain experience and confidence in dancing in a group and enabling them to fully engage and participate in community events outside our classroom. If you are teaching in a studio setting, you might not have access to a performance space, so a nearby venue will need to be identified and scheduled for your purpose. This could require weeks or even months of extra planning, depending on the extent of your production, and will likely be an event your students will look forward to all year. In this scenario, the dance teacher may have to take on the role of producer, coordinating multiple aspects of a production—on top of working directly with the students as teacher, support system, therapist, and artistic director. I encourage anyone in this position to seek help from parent volunteers or colleagues. Most of all, trust in yourself and keep a positive and encouraging attitude for your students. It can be stressful, but remember, it WILL be over at some point and become a memory that both you and your students will cherish.

How do you know when your students' work is ready to be performed? As an experienced dancer/performer, you likely have a sense of what criteria should be met before a dance is ready. To help students evaluate performance readiness, below is a very short checklist they can fill out as a group when it gets close to performance time. There are two inseparable components to every dance: the **dance** itself and the **dancer**—neither of which can exist without the other. When your students can check off all of them, they and their dance are ready to perform!

	DANCE	**DANCER**
Pre-K to first grade	_______ Finished _______ Sound, costumes, props	_______ Memorized the dance _______ Highest level of skill
Second to third grade	_______ Finished _______ Sound, costumes, props _______ Well crafted	_______ Memorized the dance _______ Highest level of skill _______ Maintain concentration
Fourth to sixth grade	_______ Finished _______ Sound, costumes, props _______ Well crafted _______ Properly staged	_______ Memorized the dance _______ Highest level of skill _______ Maintain concentration _______ Expression

Some composition skills the **dance** should demonstrate through its performance are:
- Pre-K to first grade: A complete work with no missing parts where the auditory and visual components fit together.
- Second to third grade: In addition to the above, use of stage depth for choreographic purposes, understanding of the structure of the **dance** including a beginning, middle, and end, and understanding the meaning of the work.
- Fourth to sixth grade: In addition to the above, visual and sequential composition, purposeful use of staging, use of the choreographic and rehearsal processes to refine and define their work.

Some performance skills the **dancer** can learn and demonstrate are:
- Pre-K to first grade: Awareness of designated spaces for performers and audience, facing the audience, enter and exit the performance space, respond to cues, and take bows.
- Second to third grade: In addition to the above, understanding and using stage directions, dancing all the way off stage, and not being distracted or distracting others while performing.
- Fourth to sixth grade: In addition to the above, putting forth effort to use the whole body and face as an instrument of expression of the intent of the **dance**, and bringing together all the elements of dance with clarity and purpose.

PART V
Connecting and Relating

The context surrounding creativity

Chapter 20

Historical and Cultural Connections
The role of dance in the human experience

This chapter focuses on the incredibly vast universe that is historical and cultural dance! Of course, many volumes of many books could be and have been written about this subject. So please forgive me for not even scratching the surface here. The ideas in this chapter are what make sense to me to share with young dance students to help them get a more comprehensive understanding of *dance arts* in general and their importance to us as humans. A rich dance education should include the connections to the past and to other people with whom we share our world. Yes, students want to learn the latest moves they see in the media, and they should. But an understanding of the bigger, broader world of dance will help them better appreciate what they see and eventually create.

There is considerable overlap between history and culture, and in fact, they coexist in harmony with each other. Very simply put:

Historical refers to time lines, and **cultural** refers to geography, community, or shared experiences.

Obviously, both of these happen at the same time. Every culture throughout human history up to the present day have danced, which is one of the universal bonds all humans share. Dance can express our feelings and our ideas, tell stories, document our history, and reveal trends in popular culture. It is one of the most valuable and illustrative art forms known to humankind.

Certain terms can use some clarification regarding historical and cultural dance, and here are some that I have found to be helpful:
- **Folk dances** are created and performed by ordinary people and/or the community and are not intended to be performed onstage.
- **Folkloric dances** are traditional folk dances that have been adapted to be performed onstage, usually by highly trained dancers.
- **Cultural dances** reflect specific aspects of a particular cultural group.
- **Multicultural dances** are a set of various dances that come from around the world, encompassing many cultural groups.

The term I most prefer is **world dance**, which, to me, is the most inclusive of labels, encompassing all of the above. It assumes a globally equal perspective and does not delineate based on time period or point of view. For the examples of those *world dances* with which I have had the most success, here is a big huge reference to **appendix D, "World Dances."** There, you will find sixty-seven dances listed in alphabetical order, with a brief explanation of the meaning or purpose of the dance (i.e., its historical relevance), the region or country of the world from which it originates, the basic choreography, the music that I have used, the skills needed to perform it, and, in some cases, the variations on how the dance can be creatively adapted to explore various concepts within the elements of dance. Then refer to **appendix E, "World Dances by Grade Level,"** for lists of several dances for each elementary grade that have proven successful. Of course, the suggestions in appendix E are simply that . . . suggestions. I believe that nearly any world dance can be adapted to meet the ability and maturity level of students of any age.

Also, here is a reference to **chapter 21, "Personal Experience,"** where there are descriptions of how various traditional dances can be reimagined to create **our own world dance**, which is a version of a traditional dance made to be meaningful to a group that is not necessarily of the dance's origin. I have found this practice to be extremely powerful in getting to the essence and meaning of a traditional dance, and it appears to be easily relatable from a young person's perspective. Of course, as dance educators and ambassadors of dance from around the globe, we must always be quite clear that because we are creating a different version of a dance originated by other people from other times and places, we are doing nothing but **honoring** its creators and its original form. We are most certainly not appropriating the history and culture of any other people and never taking credit for the creations of anyone else.

The term *historical*, of course, refers to a given span of time included in our known recording of human history. In fact, dance goes so far back that it even predates cave painting! That is how ancient and fundamental dance is to the human experience. Dances reflect trends in the political, social, and economic states of the people who created them and therefore provide an invaluable look back in time.

A REALLY Brief History of American Dance

Prior to European colonization of this continent, Native tribal dances illustrated the lives of the people by expressing what was important to them, such as changes in the natural world and their place in it, and interactions between peoples, such as defending their land or relocating (e.g., the Hopi snake dance, the Tsimshian trail chant, and the Apache sunrise dance).

Following the many millennia of tribal life, European colonists brought with them the dances they knew from their countries of origin. They were then adapted to fit their lives in their new environment, which was more of an agrarian and religion-based existence than what they left behind (e.g., the Appalachian big circle dance).

Then with the development of civilization dominated by European Americans, which attempted to extinguish Native presence, and the introduction of captured African slaves, a world of racial tension, oppression, and division developed, which was reflected in the dances over the many decades leading up to the Civil War and beyond (e.g., for white Americans, there were ballroom-style dances, which followed strict etiquette; and for black Americans converted by force to the religious practices of white Americans, various dances emerged that included body percussion and stepping since drums were not allowed).

Then the Industrial Revolution occurred, and dance styles seemed to remain separated by race to some extent but gradually began

---

to merge (e.g., black-influenced dances, such as the cakewalk, Charleston, Lindy Hop, and the jitterbug; musical theatre traditions, which arose out of black minstrel shows; performance/theatrical-style dances, including ballet; and the emergence of *modern* dance, which were both predominantly white).

During the second half of the twentieth century, dance styles came and went rapidly, as did trends in American life. With the '60s came individualism and breaking away from traditional male/female roles, as did the dances of the time. During the '70s, people seemed to miss the structure of the dance hall/nightclub setting, and a resurgence in "disco" dance with partners became popular. In the '80s, technology was booming, and many of the dances seemed to reflect nonliving images, such as the moonwalk and the robot. From the '90s through present day, the media has taken over as the main platform for dance and its connection to popular music, resulting in the invention of music videos; and of course, the emergence of hip-hop dance and music has catapulted black Americans into prominence worldwide.

By definition, *cultural* dance refers to certain dances that are shared by a community and are unique to certain people and their traditions, which encompass a multitude of genres, regions, eras, and purposes. A dance of a particular cultural group can be seen as a form of communication, and when observed by those outside the cultural group, it can reveal great truths about those who created it.

What dances can reveal. Information and insight regarding many aspects of a given cultural group appear in their dances and in ways no other evidence of its existence can. For example, how a dance is structured can indicate the structure of the community, such as forming opposing lines of men and women, dancing in circles where all can see one another, utilizing leaders and followers, practicing call and response, or grouping dancers by age or status. Good examples of how dances reflect the culture of the people who created them are the dances of the northwest coast Native peoples of Alaska, British Columbia, and Washington State. Many dances reflect various animals, which also reflects the social structure of extended families forming clans that are represented by their animal totem.

Why dances exist. As humans, we have a deep need to express ourselves, socialize, and, of course, move! Put those things together with our highly developed ability to organize by creating rhythmic and spatial patterns, and a dance is inevitable. All arts fulfill these basic needs. By using specialized tools and skills, they give us the ability to develop and evolve as humans, and that is why they all exist. Some dances **tell stories**, such as the classical ballets of the nineteenth and twentieth centuries, many of which are based on fairy tales or much simpler stories, such as one of jealousy (Bele Kawe), mourning a lost loved one (Lott Ist Todt), or the search for a new home (Hoe Ana). Not to mention the role of musical theatre in America and abroad, where dances are essential in the plot line of the overall story (Bollywood). Many dances are a **celebration**, such as for a good harvest (Alunelul, Bahay Kubo), freedom or independence (Boboobo), honoring the elderly or other important people (Los Viejitos, Gustav's Skoal), and just **being together** (Appalachian big circle dance). Some dances express our appreciation for the beauty and importance of **nature** (Waves of Tory, Itik-Itik), and other dances simply help us acknowledge and cope with our daily **work activities** (Bhangra, Sugarcane Harvest). A dance can also be a physical manifestation of music (swing, jazz, waltz, hip-hop, merengue), in which case it is difficult to know which came first.

Who creates dances. Everyone creates a dance the moment they move their body compelled by some inspirational idea or feeling. When an idea or feeling is strong enough and many people share the experience, the creative process infused with our human intellect and drive kicks into gear, and dances are born. Observing and, better yet, learning a dance from a cultural group or historical time other than our own allow us to understand both the differences and similarities between us. Knowing that people who are different from us can have the same thoughts and feelings we have can only deepen understanding and empathy and ultimately bring us together. How is that not good?

Where on earth dances come from. Actually, everywhere! Every place on earth where people live or have lived is the origin of some form of dance. And many dances are even about the environment or region of the world from which they originate. Weather, climate, terrain, seasons, and wildlife are evident in so many dances since we all know how important all of those things are to human life. The Israeli dance Mayim is all about the importance of water in a dry region of the world, the Qashqai scarf dance illustrates the seminomadic lifestyle of a group of people from Iran, and Tokyo Dontaku explores urban life in the biggest city in the world.

How dances are structured. There are a few categories into which most dances fit, and they are based on various rhythmic or spatial patterns. For example, there are line dances, circle dances, partner dances, ensemble dances, figure dances, dances with props or objects, repetitive dances, call-and-response dances, dances with leaders and followers, and dances that follow the structure of music.

When dances have been created. Dances come to be when there is a compelling reason to make one, and throughout human history, there have been countless times when that has been the case. This leads back to the historical aspect of dance. As dance educators, we are creating future history in our students every time we give them the opportunity to make a work of dance art. They are being woven into the fabric of this most basic of human practices; and their stories, ideas, feelings, and observations will help shape the existence of humans on our planet.

It is helpful to have a few guiding principles when discussing and sharing world dances with students. Below are a few basic points on which various grade ranges can focus. Please see chapter 7, "Enduring Understandings and Essential Questions," for additional examples by grade level.

- **Younger elementary students:** Discuss the dance's location of origin, costumes, story, and purpose. Then compare those aspects to our own. Ask why the dance is important to the people who created it and what we can learn about them.
- **Middle elementary students:** Discuss how the movements of a dance communicate various aspects of the lives of the people/culture who created it. Then compare and contrast multiple dances to one another. Ask what is the same and what is different between us and the people who created the dance.
- **Upper elementary students:** Discuss how details and movement qualities reveal the time, place, and people who created it and the significance of the dance to its creators and to us. Ask how dances can help us better understand other people in the world and why that is important.

Chapter 21

Personal Experience
Dancing students' own lives, identity, and culture

Other than those of us who have chosen *dance arts* as our life's work (or life's joy or both), most people probably don't feel like they have a personal relationship with them. And that is absolutely OK. Whether everyone knows it or not, dance in some way is part of our lives—in our history as human beings, as part of the traditions of whatever cultural group with which we identify, and in all of the media we consume every day. We dance at parties celebrating all sorts of occasions, we see tons of dance in movies and on TV, and there are several extremely popular video games designed around dance as well. Also, dance is the main focus in halftime shows at sporting events, some reality TV competition shows, musical theatre, concerts, music videos, and even in advertising. (Note: Why do you think dance is used so much in commercials? Because it captures the viewer's attention like nothing else does!) Also, there is the very natural tendency that most people have, which is unconsciously beginning to move when hearing a good song—is that not dance?

On my first dance class session with a group of students, I try to get an idea of where they are at regarding how dance is part of their lives. I ask them some simple questions, like have they ever seen a dance performance or been in one or have they danced at a party or while playing a video game. Most children I have worked with have some level of firsthand experience with dance. Then opening up a discussion about whether or not dance is even an art and whether or not it is a sport (it can be both, by the way) can be extremely revealing as to the students' depth of understanding.

In this chapter, my hope is to share some ideas that dance educators can use to help their students relate dance to their lives in a meaningful way and give them an opportunity to express themselves through this most visceral of art forms. Here are several *essential questions* that can guide our thinking around our own personal experience with dance and those of our students:
- How does dance deepen our understanding of ourselves and of others?
- How does dancing make me feel?
- How do dance relationships compare with personal relationships?
- How can we tell a story by dancing?
- What needs to happen for me to be able to call myself a dancer?
- What role does dance play in my life? In my community? In my culture?

- Why is dance important?
- What is my own personal dance style, and how can I develop it?

In the following lesson examples, there are descriptions of ways to help students accomplish many goals using dance. First of all, **sharing our ideas and stories** is one of the most important functions of *dance arts* and, in fact, all arts! The same can be said about exploring our own **group identity or heritage**, taking a close look at **current events or issues**, and ways to create **our own versions of world dances** using dance traditions from other cultures or historical periods.

SHARING OUR IDEAS AND STORIES

See the section called "Stories" and the subsection called "Creating a Story from a Dance" in chapter 17, "Inspiration," for a breakdown of the process of generating material for an original story from movement choices. This process can be adapted for various grade or age levels.

For younger to middle elementary students:
Students practice four or six emotions with facial expressions and simple movements.

- ***Emotions Tell the Story.*** See the section "Emotions" in chapter 17, "Inspiration." This lesson creates a dance that tells a story with a beginning, middle, and end, based on situations or scenarios outlined by the students' own experience. Brainstorm and list two to three situations or scenarios that make the students feel each of the emotions practiced. Divide into as many groups as emotions and assign each group one of the emotions. They choose the situation for their emotion and create a movement that expresses it. Next, they are given a randomly selected second emotion. Then they choose a situation and create a movement that expresses that emotion. The final step is for each group to discuss the first situation, the second situation, and then what needs to happen in between. They then create a movement that expresses that situation and put all three movements together to form a three-part sequence. Perform to Kraked Unit, "Douala Paris."

For middle to upper elementary students:
Discuss the five main events in a person's life from the **PAST:** being a baby, younger siblings being born, traveling, holidays, and starting school. Then discuss the five main things that interest them from their life in the **PRESENT:** favorite subject in school, favorite thing to do with family, favorite food, favorite sport, thing they are good at, and current pets. And finally, discuss the five main things to look forward to in their **FUTURE:** going to college, working, having a family, staying healthy, and enjoying life.

- *My Life Time Line.* The whole group creates movements for all of the items in the PAST. Then they divide into five groups based on their choice of the five topics from the PRESENT, and each creates a phrase that represents their topic. And finally, the whole group creates movements for the first four topics in the FUTURE; and each group creates their own movement or phrase for the final topic, which is *enjoying life*. Put all parts together and perform to David Benoit, "Looking Back."

GROUP IDENTITY OR HERITAGE

For younger elementary students:
List the following categories and write a maximum of three ideas in each:
Favorite foods
Favorite places to go
Favorite things to do alone
Favorite things to do with others
Favorite part of the school day

- ***All about Us.*** Improvise movements expressing all things listed, and either the teacher or the group chooses their single favorite in each category. Set the selected movements to create a dance. Also, you could add *girls/boys*, and each group gets together and creates a movement that expresses them. Perform to a song of the group's choice by offering two to three choices, and they select their favorite.

For middle to upper elementary students:
- ***Who's in the Circle Dance.*** For the teacher's reference, list some categories that describe the students in the class, such as pets, foods they love, movies they have seen, sports they play, games they like, favorite color, what they are wearing, etc. Form one large circle and call out items on the list. Then dancers to whom the item pertains enter the middle of the circle and dance any movement they like. Play any music that is long and has a lively beat.

- ***Sherman Dances***. See the section called "Books about Dance" in chapter 17, "Inspiration." After reading the book and listing the various dance styles and concepts they recognize, students choose which style they would like to create an original piece of choreography representing it. Remind them that they are using their own prior knowledge of the style and should pick a style they already know something about. Play music appropriate to the style for each group performance.

For upper elementary students:
- ***Personal Heritage.*** This is a research project that could take several class sessions. Begin by modeling what the students will do by teaching them a dance from your own personal heritage (which may require a bit of research on your part). Discuss various ethnic and/or cultural groups that are represented in the class and list them. Decide on three to four that are the most heavily represented. Then divide the class into as many groups. If there are students who choose not to delve into their own heritage or if they are the only one in the class, they could join another group, do the project on their own, or the class could add a separate group that is interested in researching a group or culture that is not their own. Each group then searches for a dance that was created by their cultural group, researches its origin and meaning, and learns a few movements or steps from the dance. At a subsequent class session, groups perform the dance and then teach the steps to the whole class. They could show videos they found and play the music that would traditionally accompany the dance.

CURRENT EVENTS OR ISSUES

For younger elementary students:
- ***Holidays.*** This can be done when approaching any important holiday or reason for celebration. Show illustrations of iconic symbols or characters that pertain to the holiday of choice. Discuss why and how we celebrate the holiday and list key words that represent student's suggestions. The whole group creates movements expressing each of the key words listed to create a dance honoring the chosen holiday. Perform any music that is appropriate to the holiday.

For middle elementary students:
- ***One Important Thing.*** Discuss important things going on in school, community, or city. List them and choose one for all to make a dance about. Then list answers to four questions (*why*, *what*, *how*, and *who*): (1) why it is important, (2) what happened, (3) how we know about it or observe it, and (4) who is affected. Divide into four groups by question and answer, and each group creates a sequence or phrase expressing their question and answer. Perform to any music appropriate to the important thing.

For upper elementary students:
- ***Events or Issues.*** Either ask students to bring in headlines from news articles of interest to them or have a discussion around the most important issues they are facing in their

lives at school. If using a headline, no alterations need to be made. But if using an issue of personal interest, create a short sentence that could be a news headline in five to eight carefully selected words. (Note: headlines are useful because they encapsulate the point of the article in just a few words.) Divide into groups by word in the headline, and each creates a movement phrase expressing their word. All groups teach their phrase to all other groups to create a group dance of the whole headline. Divide and perform. Play any music that fits the topic.

OUR OWN VERSIONS OF WORLD DANCES

See appendix D, "World Dances," for descriptions of the traditional versions of these dances.

For younger elementary students:
- *Caimarusa.* Discuss and list places the students would like to travel. Use their ideas, and pairs create a movement that they will perform coming down the aisle. The rest of the dance remains the same.
- *Che Che Kule.* Brainstorm other topics besides body parts, such as foods, pets, or sports. Choose one and list five things that are meaningful to the students about the selected topic. Create movements expressing each of those things, and five leaders at a time take turns leading the dance.
- *Itik-Itik.* Discuss other animals besides ducks. Choose one

and create four different movements that represent how that animal moves.

- **Shoemaker's Dance.** Think of other things we can make with our hands and create three movements, done facing a partner in place. Then create one more movement that travels to show off the finished product.
- **Tokyo Dontaku.** Create a Dontaku dance about the city or town where you live. This is done by first creating a movement that represents opening the door and going outside your house, then four more movements expressing things you like to do outside.
- **Virginia Reel.** Create a "California Reel" (or any other state), following the same structure as the traditional dance. Then replace the movements with others that represent what they like to do when they see friends who live far away.

For middle elementary students:
- **Adze-ee.** Think of other conversations you might have with your parents or teachers and create movements that express what is said back and forth. Keep the same game format.
- **Bele Kawe.** Focusing on the three emotions of *interested*, *surprised*, and *angry*, list several scenarios that make the students feel each of those emotions. Choose one for each emotion. Then create movements that move forward for *interested*, backward for *surprised*, and sideways for *angry*.
- **Gumboot Dance.** Groups of dancers write a few simple phrases of words that communicate something they need to say to one another. Then they create rhythm patterns using body percussion as in *gumboot* dance, expressing the word phrases.
- **Hoe Ana.** Discuss and list several places the students would like to live and how they would get there. Create two movements for each destination, one that expresses the pace and the other showing the mode of travel to get there.
- **Mayim.** Discuss things that are scarce and important to

us, such as water in the dry country of Israel. Create four movements that express various aspects of that thing.
- *Tarantella*. Think of something besides a spider that you are afraid of and make a dance that represents getting rid of it and protecting yourself from it.

For upper elementary students:
- *Alunelul.* Think of what we harvest in our community. Then create movements that represent that and follow the structure of five, three, one. Or simply replace movements in the traditional version with two different movements.
- *Bhangra.* Choose other work activities you or your family members do. Then create movements that express them. Use formations that represent the activities as well.
- *Boboobo.* List accomplishments the students are proud of. Then create movements that can be done with small scarves or handkerchiefs in hands that celebrate various aspects of each accomplishment listed.
- *Highlife.* After learning and practicing the traditional version of the Highlife, list other things that students enjoy every day that go uncelebrated. Choose four topics and divide into four groups. Each group creates five original movements that are rhythmic and repeatable and express different aspects of their topic.
- *Irish Battle Reel.* Discuss reasons why students get into fights with one another. Then groups create three movements for each situation—first advancing forward face-to-face with an opponent; moving right and left, staring them down; and then moving backward in retreat.
- *Sugarcane Harvest Dance.* List a type of outdoor work that is done in our lives. Then break the job down into three parts: the initial part of the job, the secondary part, and the final part. Create a phrase for each part, including different levels, pathways, and tempos.

Chapter 22

Integrating Content Areas
Blending dance with other subjects

Integrating content areas can be an enormously powerful teaching method. It explores two (or more) subjects in depth at the same time and opens up possibilities for multiple learning modalities. Both subjects take on new life and provide an opportunity for educators to creatively collaborate in planning instruction.

In addition, let me be abundantly clear: **dance and all of the *arts* are NOT tools to be used by other content areas to make them more fun.** The *arts* ARE content areas and must be considered equal in importance to all others! I firmly believe in integrating content areas, but there is a right way and a wrong way of doing it. For example, simply forming letter shapes with one's body does not constitute an integrated dance and language arts lesson for kindergarten. However, there is value to doing that; and scaffolding such a lesson by practicing moving into and out of still body shapes and involving the elements of time and space, along with focusing the language arts learning goals around a final outcome, could make it one.

As dance specialists, we are experts in our subject; and in order to honorably integrate subjects with one another, it is best to have specialists in each field participate in collaboration. At an elementary school setting, a collegial specialist would be either the general education teacher or another arts or PE educator. At a minimum, dance specialists can be self-collaborators if we are willing to put ourselves in the shoes of another specialist and study up on the grade level standards for the content area with which we intend to integrate. That is what I have done for many of the integrated lessons I have taught, which are outlined on the following pages.

To get started planning an integrated lesson, it can be helpful to use a Venn diagram to map out how your two subjects differ and where they are similar and can overlap. It is a remarkably easy and revealing tool to use, and I have always been surprised by the multiple ways in which dance and other subjects are similar. The following diagram is an illustration of a Venn diagram that can be used to map out how dance and science can integrate. Below the diagram are some examples of very general truths about both subjects. To create an honestly integrated lesson, generate your own truths about your two subjects, place them where they belong on the diagram, and then focus on the ideas in the center section, where both subjects overlap. From there, specific lesson content can be created. Of course, if you are doing this, you probably have a specific topic and grade level in mind. So use facts about those things, not necessarily the examples below.

DANCE   SCIENCE

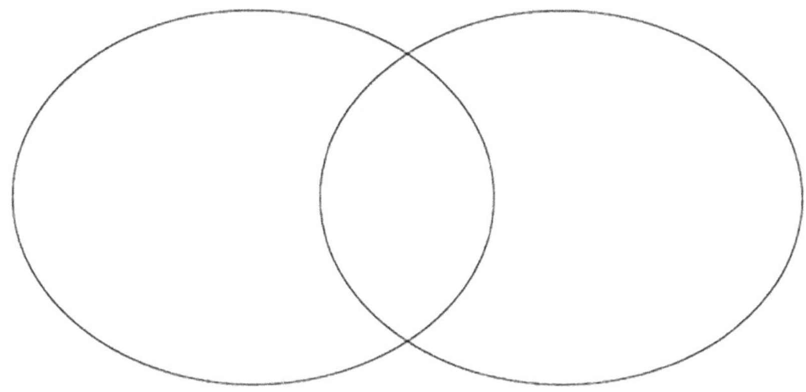

Where would the following topics be placed in this diagram?

Involves movement   Is microscopic   Is constantly changing   Grows

Is alive   Has an environment   Involves patterns   Involves energy

Uses music   Flows in a cyclical way   Lives underground   Breathes air

Is a solid   Is a form of exercise   Involves chemicals   Involves sound

Involves space   Is electrically charged

Beginning on the following page are outlines of integrated lessons I have created for each grade. Dance is integrated with science, math, language arts, social studies, visual arts, theatre, music, and PE. Besides general education content areas, it is especially rich and vibrant to integrate the *arts* with one another. In some cases, it is almost impossible to find things that are different between art forms; but integrating them only deepens the understanding of both simply because as educators, we must go deeper to find the differences. (Disclaimer: As using technology is not one of my personal strengths as a dance educator, you will not find integrated dance and *media arts* lessons in this book. I simply don't have enough experience exploring *media arts* to include them. However, I encourage you to do so!)

Prekindergarten

SCIENCE

Discuss how plants stay in place and how animals travel. Then list a variety of both plants (such as grass, seaweed, bushes, vines, and trees) and animals (such as insects, fish, birds, mammals, and reptiles).

- ***Plants and Animals.*** Using the lists above or generating your own with student suggestions, create pairs of one plant and one animal. Divide into groups by pairs of plants/animals, and each group creates a movement expressing their plant (which stays in place) and their animal (which travels). Everyone in each group performs both parts. Play Camille Saint-Saëns, *The Carnival of the Animals no. 1*, "Introduction and Royal March of the Lion."

MATH

Exploring the concepts of one and two / solo and duo.

- ***Solos and Duos.*** Begin in a circle, and one student dances into the center SOLO. Then another person joins them, and they dance together, holding hands or elbows as a DUO. Then the first person leaves, and the remaining person is now the SOLOist. The next person in the circle joins. Repeat until all have had a turn. Play any music with a steady beat that is long enough for each person to have a turn.

LANGUAGE ARTS

Learn and practice a traditional song—emphasizing the words that rhyme, adding new verses, and expressing them in detail through movement.

- ***Ring around the Rosie.*** No music, only singing. Perform the traditional circle dance, holding hands and skipping in a circle with the song. Then "fall down" at the end, letting go of hands. All do the original song as a whole group, then could break up into four smaller groups to show the remaining additional verses with **rhyming words**:

*Cows are in the meadow, eating **buttercups**, ashes, ashes, we all **stand up*** (from crawling on hands and knees)

*Clouds are in the sky, and rain is **falling down**, ashes, ashes, we all **spin around*** (arms stretched out and looking up to the sky)

*Bunny rabbits hopping, dive into a **hole**, ashes, ashes, we all do a **roll*** (rabbit jumps on hands and feet, then tucks and rolls)

*Nighttime is falling, babies in their **beds**, ashes, ashes, we all nod our **heads*** (tiptoe around, then stop and place hands together as a pillow is next to the head as if falling asleep) Repeat original song as a whole group again at the end.

SOCIAL STUDIES

Explore common activities in everyday life in two different environments and express them through movement.

- ***Home and School.*** Make lists of things they do at home and the things they do at school. Explore movements for all and narrow it down to four in each category. Play Eric Chappelle, *Music for Creative Dance: Contrast and Continuum*, vol. 1, "All in One," with the space music representing home and the rhythmic music representing school. The music cycles through four times. You could break them into four groups or do the dance as a whole group.

VISUAL ARTS

Practice drawing circles of various sizes and straight lines in different directions. With bodies in space, follow curved and straight pathways with both in-place and traveling movements and still shapes.

- ***Circles and Straight Lines.*** Observe straight lines and circles in the room. Then the whole group creates and follows a repeating pattern of circles and straight lines and then creates movements that express it. Then draw another pattern example and create another pattern of movements. Play any music with a steady beat and change with musical phrases every four or eight beats.

THEATRE

Use nonrepresentational objects to create a character in a situation. Use sets of multiple scarves, cups, plates, and rhythm sticks.

- ***Rotation.*** Groups are divided between the objects. The teacher guides them through experiences of the following actions: where they "wear" the object, "fight" with the object, or "make friends" with the object. Play Eric Chappelle, *Music for Creative Dance: Contrast and Continuum*, vol. 1, "Oasis" and stop the music to cue the rotation of groups to the next object. Repeat until all have practiced with all objects. The teacher chooses the best match of action and object, and groups perform with the object they started with.

MUSIC

Move to the directions of a song while singing it, then without singing it.

- ***Merry-Go-Round.*** In a circle, holding hands, learn the following song/dance while singing the words. Then perform to music with singing, then again to music without words, transforming the movements with words to movements with music. The tune is similar to "The Wheels on the

Bus." Without singing, play Carl Orff, *Orff-Schulwerk*, vol. 2, "Comodo." Song lyrics/movements are as follows:

*We're on a merry-go-**round and round**, round and round, round and round*
We're on a merry-go-round and round, round and round we go . . . (Skip or gallop around in a circle. Holding hands is optional.)

*We're on a merry-go-**up and down** . . .* (Lift hands up and bend down.)

*We're on a merry-go-**in and out** . . .* (The whole group moves into the center of the circle and out.)

*We're on a merry-go-**side to side** . . .* (Swing or slide sideways, alternating sides.)

*We're on a merry-go-**around ourselves** . . .* (Spin around self.)

*We're on a merry-go-**slow and fast** . . .* (Walk slowly in a circle not holding hands, then run.)

PE

Build skills in a variety of locomotor movements and combine them, following straight or curved pathways.

- ***Locomotor Movements.*** Place four to five colored spots on the floor in a straight line and five to six colored spots in a circle in a different space nearby. Divide the group in half, and each half goes to either the circle or the line. Play any music and pause to provide a cue for the groups to switch locations. Both groups do the same movements, just along different pathways. The teacher calls out movements, starting with **walk-jump**, and dancers should take small steps between spots and jump OVER each spot. Change locations and repeat the same combination. Then change to **slide-hop**, then to **run-leap**, and finally to **roll-crawl**.

Kindergarten

SCIENCE

Discuss the *water cycle* and its components and how they match with the four energies of *flow* and *weight*: EVAPORATION/*light* weight, CONDENSATION/*heavy* weight, PRECIPITATION/*sharp* flow, and ASSIMILATION/*smooth* flow. Note that the cycle never stops moving, so you can begin at any point.

- ***Water Cycle.*** Explore and create one to two movements for each part of the cycle using the following images or forms of each component:

Evaporation – steam, mist, vapor
Condensation – raindrops, hailstones, falling
Precipitation – landing on water/splashing, pavement/bouncing, ground/soaking in
Assimilation – lake, ocean, river, snowdrift

All learn and practice the whole sequence. In three groups, each performs the dance one at a time. Play Mary Youngblood, "Beneath the Raven Moon."

MATH

From a seated position, the teacher calls out the names of one student at a time, and all count together as the student called upon stands. All remain standing until all have been called and it is known how many there are. Depending on the total number, divide the class either in half, thirds, or fourths. Keep the numbers fairly large and determine the "magic number," which is the number of students in each group, which should be the same for all groups. Dance concepts explored are timing, grouping, and traveling movements.

- ***Counting On.*** Each group chooses a traveling movement and begins with one person doing the movement in a small circle around the space. Count as each member of the group joins, continuing until all are dancing. Then count again, and one by one, they drop off and return and sit down in their original space. Play David Benoit, "Sailing through the City" as background.

LANGUAGE ARTS

Sing traditional version of the alphabet song or the Spanish alphabet as students know them. See appendix G, "Handouts," for my versions of the English and Spanish alphabets.

- ***Alphabet Dance.*** Practice movements described by the word or phrase beginning with each letter. For the English alphabet, play Carl Orff, *Orff-Schulwerk*, vol. 2, "Tranquillo"; and for the Spanish alphabet, play *Flamenco Guitar*, "Canción de la Luna."

SOCIAL STUDIES

Choose a holiday from the following: Halloween, Día de los Muertos, Thanksgiving, Fourth of July, MLK Day, Cesar Chavez Day, Valentine's Day, Christmas, or Kwanzaa. Discuss the importance of the holiday and what we do to celebrate it, expressing cultural significance through movements.

- ***Celebration.*** List aspects of the chosen holiday. Create movements that express each item on the list, being careful not to make it simply a pantomime. Then set a class dance to honor the spirit of the holiday. Divide and watch one another perform. Select music that is appropriate.

VISUAL ARTS

Show an example of a color wheel with the six primary and secondary colors and discuss how the primary colors blend together to make the secondary colors. Share the book *Color Dance* by Ann Jonas (see the section "Books about Dance" in chapter 17, "Inspiration"). Scarves and images inspire movements, and groupings determine how colors blend.

- ***Color Dance.*** Use large sheer scarves, if available, in primary colors. Then group by color: yellow, blue, and red/pink. List one thing that each of the three primary colors is, and as many groups create and perform movements for the item that is their color, using the scarves as additional inspiration. Then groups join to create movements for the secondary colors. Yellow and red join for orange, yellow and blue for green, and red and blue for purple. Perform to Angels of Venice, "Dragonfly," following the sequence in the book.

THEATRE

Explore and set movements representing the following four animals: *penguin*, *squirrel*, *elephant*, and *spider*. Match them to the *flow* and *weight* energies of *smooth*, *sharp*, *heavy*, and *light*. Discuss the habitat in which each animal lives as well as its size and what it eats, which are all aspects of a character an actor might portray.

- ***Move Like the Animals.*** Divide into four groups by animal, and each group creates two to three movements expressing their animal, including facial expressions and sounds. Perform to Mickey Hart, "Elephant Walk." Each group performs their animal movements.

MUSIC

Repeat the following two phrases: "lion, elephant, hippopotamus" and "pepperoni pizza, yum, yum." Then repeat each one several times to get the feeling of the rhythm—listening for, feeling, and moving to different rhythms.

- ***Rhythmic Phrases.*** Divide into two groups by word phrase, and each group creates two different whole-body movements that express it. Dancers not performing say the word phases as a whisper as accompaniment. No music is necessary because it might interfere. If inspired, create new phrases that have different rhythmic patterns.

<u>**PE**</u>

Work on throwing and catching skills and explore traveling and in-place movements while doing so.

- ***Small Scarves.*** Provide enough small scarves for each student to have one. Explore and set two different ways to throw and catch the scarf to themselves, one in place and one while traveling. Select and set movements. Then perform to Mary Youngblood, "Laugh with Me." Then put students together in pairs and have one be the thrower and the other the catcher. Then switch parts after both scarves have been thrown and caught. Perform the same movements adapted to do with another person.

First Grade

<u>**SCIENCE**</u>

Discuss the life cycle of plants—how they begin from seeds and with soil, water, and light grow and develop into plants, which produce seeds. Incorporate three *levels* (low, middle, and high), plus changing *levels* going up and going down.

- ***Seeds to Plants.*** In four groups, assign roles of *seeds/plants, soil, rain,* and *sunlight.* The **seeds** group begins onstage curled up at a *low* level on or near the floor. Play Carl Orff, *Orff-Schulwerk,* vol. 1, "Tanz 3." As the music starts, the **soil** group enters and dances over the *seeds* at a *middle* level and stays. In the next section of the music, the **rain** group dances around and between *seeds* and *soil* at a *high* level, quickly changing to *low,* and exits. In the third section of the music, the **sunlight** group dances across the floor continuously at a *high* level and exits. For the final section of the music, **seeds** slowly grow into **plants,** changing level from *low* to *high,* and exit. Meanwhile, *soil* changes level from *middle* to *low* and becomes the *seeds* for the next rotation of roles. Repeat with the new *seeds* group onstage. Then the other groups rotate parts: *rain* into *soil*, *sunlight* to *rain*, and *seeds/plants* to *sunlight*. Repeat the music for each rotation of roles four times.

MATH

Place two color spots on opposite sides of the space. Have a student demonstrate and count how many walking steps it takes to get from one to the other and write it down. Try other locomotor movements, such as gallop, run, waddle, etc. Then write down all the numbers. Use locomotor movements as standards of measurement.

- ***Measure the Distance.*** Set up five more pairs of color spots across the floor from one another, not directly across one another so paths will cross. Divide into groups by spot colors. Each group creates a dance with two different movements, traveling from one spot to the corresponding spot and back, using the numbers as a guide. Play Mickey Hart, "Elephant Walk."

LANGUAGE ARTS

Discuss how words are like body parts and how sentences are like the whole body.

- ***Words/Sentences.*** Begin by writing a sentence of four to five words. Select the same number of body parts and match them to the words. Create separate movements done with just the body part for each word. Then create a movement pattern done with the whole body that expresses the whole sentence. Perform the parts and finish with the whole. Play John Hanks, "Rhumba Gumbo."

SOCIAL STUDIES

Show a world map. Point out all seven continents by name and list the following two animals that live on each: **North America** – bear, eagle; **South America** – monkey, tree frog; **Africa** – camel, lion; **Asia** – cobra, panda; **Australia** – koala, kangaroo; **Antarctica** – whale, penguin; and **Europe** – hare, swan. The first animal listed moves with tense force and the second with relaxed. Learn geography and exploring force in movements.

- ***Seven Continents Wildlife.*** Divide into seven groups by continent, and each creates a pattern of two movement expressing each of their two animals, four movements total emphasizing the difference between tense and relaxed force. Perform each to Eric Chappelle, *Music for Creative Dance: Contrast and Continuum*, vol. 2, "Travel Notes" selections as follows: North America – *American*, South America – *Andean*, Africa – *Sahara*, Asia – *Indian*, Australia – *Balinese*, Antarctica – *Koto*, Europe – *Celtic*. Repeat the patterns enough times to finish the song.

VISUAL ARTS

Using crayons, practice drawing **value** scales, from **dark** to **light** to dark again, across a page. Then do the opposite drawing, from light to dark to light again, across the page. Point out that **force** is similar to value in its changing intensity and its usefulness as a way to draw attention or give meaning to pictures in art and movements or shapes in dance. Notice what the body and arm and hand must do to draw light versus dark value. Free dance to Eric Chappelle, *Music for Creative Dance: Contrast and Continuum*, vol. 1, "Lucky Stiff" to feel the changes in force following the cues in the music. Divide the group in half; and as one half dances, the other half draws any design to the music, changing value from light to dark with changes in the music.

- ***Value and Force.*** Play Bobby McFerrin, "Circlesong Five." In groups of three to four, one group at a time travels all around the space with selected (or called out) traveling movements, changing the *force* from relaxed to tense to relaxed to tense, changing every twelve beats in the song.

THEATRE

Practice six emotions through facial expressions and whole-body movements: *angry, fearful, happy, disgusted, interested,* and *sad.* List ideas of situations that make them feel each emotion.

- **Happy Endings.** Divide into five groups and give each an emotion other than *happy.* Each group uses the scenarios listed and creates a movement that expresses one of them for their emotion. Then they create a movement that expresses *happy* and put it together with their other emotion to tell a story that has a happy ending. Play Mickey Hart, "Amazon Nguni."

MUSIC

Sing the first few lines of three very common songs: "Rudolph the Red-Nosed Reindeer," "Twinkle, Twinkle, Little Star," and "Happy Birthday to You." Explore rhythm in sounds and movements.

- **Singers and Dancers.** Sing them all again doing arm movements, as if conducting an orchestra. Sing them a third time and repeat the lines as needed to create a beginning movement. Divide into three groups by song, and each finishes the dance the whole group started for their song. Other groups sing while each group performs.

PE

Work on eye-hand coordination and hitting slow-moving objects and exploring various body parts.

- **Balloons.** Have enough inflated balloons for everyone to have one, with some extra in case any should pop. Practice hitting balloons with hands in the air without letting them touch the floor—first with one hand, then with the other hand, then alternating hands, then with the elbows, knees, and feet. Also, practice hitting one back and forth with a partner. Partners create a three-part pattern with three body parts, one of which goes back and forth. Play Kraked Unit, "Douala Paris."

Second Grade

SCIENCE

Discuss how the weather changes all the time and how important it is to our lives. We must decide what to wear based on the weather and sometimes even what we do. Discuss what the weather is like right now and what we do to be ready for it. Discuss various kinds of clothing or accessories we need for different forms of weather. Also discuss what causes different types of weather, such as temperature, pressure, and season.

- ***Weather Dance.*** List five major types of weather: *windy, rainy, snowy, cloudy,* and *sunny.* Match the five energies that are *flow* and *weight* as follows: *windy*/smooth, *rainy*/sharp, *sunny*/vibratory, *snowy*/heavy, and *cloudy*/light. Divide into four groups by weather type (except *sunny*), and each group creates two different movements that express their weather type, showing the energy that goes with it. The whole group creates two movements plus a still shape that expresses *sunny* weather, which all will do together. Perform one weather type at a time to Michel Cusson, "Sawtooth Mountain."

MATH

Discuss how there are many ways for different combinations of three numbers to add up to the same number. The concept in dance is counting beats, memorizing sequences, and making choices of movements that are performed longer than others.

- ***Addition Dance.*** Randomly select three movements and make a three-part sequence and practice the sequence counting eight beats for each movement. Play Carl Orff, *Orff-Schulwerk*, vol. 1, "Gassenhauer." List several ways to add up three numbers to equal twenty-four Choose one of the examples and practice the same sequence, counting each movement by a number other than eight. Create as many groups as there are addition examples remaining and give each group three movements to create their own sequences. Each group performs to the same music, and there should be no more than eight groups.

LANGUAGE ARTS

Discuss the purpose of punctuation in language arts, which is to direct the reader and give meaning and emphasis to words. Dance concepts explored include shape, tempo, force, and formations.

- ***Punctuation Dance.*** Discuss the purpose of punctuation, which is to enhance the meaning of written language using symbols other than letters. Show symbols for the following eleven punctuation marks and practice the movements described:

  . *Period,* stop, freeze, shape, stillness

  , *Comma,* pause, slow down, floating, moment of light weight

  ; *Semicolon,* change idea in the middle, traveling across the floor, change direction

  - *Hyphen,* ideas or words put together, bodies connected in movements and shapes

  ( ) *Parentheses,* isolated idea, contained, pressing, groups surrounding

  ' *Apostrophe,* skip, hiccup, trip, fragments, rebounding, briefly touch and let go

  : *Colon,* separate parts from the whole, body parts / whole-body movements

  " " *Quotation marks,* literal translation, text, quotes, realistically interpreted movements, gestures

  ´ *Accent,* emphasis, strongest part of a movement, bursting, sharp

  ? *Question mark,* curiosity, uncertainty, quick rise up to a higher level

  ! *Exclamation point,* excitement, intensity, big finish to a movement, finality

Divide into five groups. Each is assigned two punctuation symbols, except *exclamation point*, which all will do together. Groups create original movements to express their two symbols. Perform to either Bobby McFerrin, "Circlesong Two" or Eric Chappelle, *Music for Creative Dance: Contrast and Continuum*, vol. 4, "Quarks."

SOCIAL STUDIES

This project will likely take two lessons. It explores major events in one's lifetime and ways to express them through movement.

- ***My Life Time Line.*** Discuss and list four to five main events in a person's life from the **PAST: being a baby**, **younger siblings being born**, **traveling**, **holidays**, and **starting school**. All select and set three to four movements that express past events. For the **PRESENT**, get into a circle and call out some of the following immediate events or attributes; and if it applies, that person dances in the middle of the circle.
- Wearing red (or any other color)
- Have a pet
- Visited family last weekend
- Used hair gel this morning
- Finished homework
- Did something fun today
- Ate a healthy snack
- Slept well

For the **FUTURE**, discuss and list the four to five main goals that people have, such as **going to college**, **working**, **having a family**, **traveling**, **staying healthy**, and **enjoying life**. As with the *past* section, select and set three to four movements that all will perform together. Play David Benoit, "Looking Back."

VISUAL ARTS

Discuss the similarity between **dotted lines** that can be drawn and **formations** that can be created with multiple bodies in space (see the section "Formations" in chapter 15, "Element of Relationship).

(Note: many thanks to the brilliant LAUSD Elementary visual arts teacher, Brittany Maddocks, for this collaboration.) Use straight lines, circles, pairs, and semicircle formations.

- **Dotted Lines/Formations.** For the visual arts project, groups of three to four students share a fairly large paper and take turns using Q-tip swabs and four colors of paint (a different color for each formation) to create a design of different colored dotted-line formations that overlap one another. For the dance, the whole group practices making the same formations with their bodies in space. Choose two movements for each formation, one to travel into it and the other to do in place while maintaining the formation. You could divide the group in half and have them perform for each other if there are enough students to effectively make all of the formations. Practice the sequence entering from offstage one dancer at a time, traveling to the first formation. Then all do the in-place movement. Repeat to the second formation, the third, and the fourth, then exit. Perform to Mary Youngblood, "Laugh with Me."

THEATRE

This connects to the concept of *size*, which is part of the element of *space*. Discuss what the theatre concept of *upstaging* is. Practice in partners, one behind the other and both doing the same movement—with the back person exaggerating and doing the movement with large size drawing attention and the front person doing the same movement with very small size using little space. Divide and watch one another to see the impact.

- **Officer Buckle and Gloria.** See appendix F, "Stories." Read the story and list the events that happen in chronological order. Create movements for each event that occurs, which all students perform individually. But when it gets to the "upstaging" sections, dancers work in partners, one behind the other doing movements at different sizes. Play Eric Chappelle, *Music for Creative Dance: Contrast and Continuum*, vol. 1, "Jammin' on the Porch."

MUSIC

Explore various ways of using rhythm sticks by tapping them together, tapping the floor, and tapping each other's sticks. Use rhythm patterns with sounds and movements, emphasizing timing with a partner.

- ***Partners with Rhythm Sticks.*** In pairs, each person having two rhythm sticks, create a pattern that includes all three ways of using the sticks practiced. Perform one pair at a time, and they must repeat their pattern four times. No music because the sticks create the rhythm.

PE

After assessing the outdoor playground equipment, sort the equipment pieces out by area and function, such as hanging, climbing, balancing, swinging, etc. Then map out a path between them. Discuss the equipment in class and list movements that are normally done on them. Replace the movements on the list with various movements the students know and take the corresponding movement cards outside to try them out.

- ***Playground Fitness Dance.*** Divide into groups by equipment/ area. Then groups explore and practice on the equipment in unusual ways, such as backward, sideways, or upside down. Groups create and set a phrase of three different movements on their piece of equipment. Play any upbeat and playful music.

Third Grade

SCIENCE

Discuss and research various species of trees, their habitats, shapes, and various ways of dying. Students practice movements and shapes at four levels: *low*, *middle*, *high*, and *airborne*.

- ***Trees.*** The whole group brainstorms different species of trees and lists them and the different ways in which a tree can die (fire, cut down, lightning, drought, insects, old age).

Select three to four tree species and divide into as many groups. Each group does research as to their tree's size, shape, where it grows, etc. and find pictures. Combine with levels and create movements for a dance phrase in five parts: *roots*/low, *trunk*/middle, *branches and leaves*/high, *things coming into or out of the tree from the air*/airborne, *death of the tree*. Play Michael Manring, "Life in the Trees."

MATH

Understand parallel and nonparallel lines and explore various pathways in space.

- ***Parallel/Not Parallel.*** After drawing parallel and nonparallel lines as examples, dancers pair up or in trios and practice walking parallel to each other along all four pathways: *straight*, *curved*, *zigzag*, and *wavy*. Then the same groups practice traveling around the space in nonparallel pathways. Set a different movement for each pathway and perform them first parallel, then not parallel. Play Eric Chappelle, *Music for Creative Dance: Contrast and Continuum*, vol. 4, "Oslo Walk" as background.

LANGUAGE ARTS

Write the personal letter example below and point out the seven main parts: **salutation, subject, examples, clarification/definition, in addition, citation**, and **sign-off**. Explore movements that express both punctuation and parts of a personal letter.

- ***A Letter about Dance Class.*** Students improvise to create movements that express each of the parts of the letter, with as many "examples" and "in additions" as desired.
  1. **Dear *blank*** (salutation)
  2. **Have you ever taken a dance class?** (subject)
  3. **In my dance class, I am learning these things** (examples): *blank, blank,* **and** *blank.*
  4. **I have learned how to** *blank,* **which means** *blank* (clarification/definition),

5. **and I can also** (in addition) **change the** *blank* **of my movements. I can even** *blank* **and** *blank* **too!**
6. **My teacher said, "You are really good at** *blank*."** (citation, repeat something from above)
7. **Wish you were here!** (sign-off). **Love,** *blank*

Divide the letter into parts/sentences, and as many groups create movements that express their part. Put the whole thing together to perform. Play Jenny Allinder, "Three-Wheel Hannah."

SOCIAL STUDIES

Show models or pictures of totem poles and discuss their history and purpose in northwest coast Native culture. Include levels, shapes, energy qualities, and pathways. The first section of the dance quickly changes shapes with three dancers at three levels in a line, front to back, so all can be seen from the front, resembling a totem pole.

- **Totem Pole.** Groups of three dancers create a three-level shape in a line, front to back, so all can be seen from the front, resembling a totem pole. Each dancer forms a different shape at their level. Play Eric Chappelle, *Music for Creative Dance: Contrast and Continuum*, vol. 4, "Totem Pole." During the first section of the music, dancers quickly change shapes using *percussive* energy eight times, then change positions in the totem pole with *sustained* energy for eight slow beats. Repeat these steps three times, and all dancers should end up where they started. Practice and create four pairs of animal movements with energy qualities and pathways for eight slow beats each, followed by a brief pause after each pair as follows:

Bear: Collapse, Straight / **Eagle:** Suspended, Curved
Whale: Collapse, Wavy / **Frog:** Suspended, Zigzag
Beaver: Swinging, Straight / **Raven:** Percussive, Zigzag
Salmon: Sustained, Wavy / **Butterfly:** Vibratory, Curved

At a pause in the music following the last animal, quickly return to original three-person totem pole shapes in four beats. Then repeat the shapes and changing levels section twice, and finish in a frozen shape as the music ends. Divide and watch one another perform dance.

VISUAL ARTS

Using the dance concept of *levels* (*low, middle, high*, and *airborne*) together with the four *earth elements* (*water, earth, fire*, and *air*), discuss how various places/elements on earth occupy different vertical levels: *water* is at the lowest level, *land/earth* is in the middle, *fire* is high, and *air* is, of course, airborne.

- *Landscapes.* Discuss and list two forms that each earth element can take such as the following: *water* – ocean, river; *earth* – rocks, plants; *fire* – flames, lightning; and *air* – wind, clouds. Dancers, in groups by each level/earth element, create a movement at their level that expresses each of the forms their element can take. Perform to Michael Manring, "Life in the Trees." For the art project, individual students each create their own landscape picture—choosing to illustrate one form of each level/earth element, paying attention to the composition, and transposing the levels onto the paper. Use paint, collage, or pastels. (Note: thanks to the brilliant LAUSD Elementary visual arts teacher, Brittany Maddocks, for this collaboration.)

THEATRE

- *In Character.* Discuss what students know about elderly people in their families and list their observations. Use this information and practice various movements and body posture embodying the characteristics listed. Practice and perform **Los Viejitos** (see appendix D, "World Dances"), emphasizing the importance of staying *in character,* with the body posture and energy of a very old person throughout the dance. Divide and watch one another to see how many stayed in character for the whole performance.

MUSIC

Use several different percussion instruments, including, but not limited to, the following: **tambourine, grate, rain stick, sleigh bells, triangle, hand cymbals**, and **clave**. Play Eric Chappelle, *Music for Creative Dance: Contrast and Continuum*, vol. 1, "The Add-On Machine" as an example of various rhythms that can be played.

- ***Percussion Instruments.*** Demonstrate the sound each instrument makes and demonstrate a different repeating rhythm with each one. Have student volunteers play the rhythm, and the teacher shows how someone might dance to it. Group by instrument, and each member of the group gets a turn being the "player." Each group decides on a rhythm they create and a movement pattern to express it. Perform one at a time to their own instruments.

PE

Using playground balls, with one ball per student, practice bouncing, tossing, and rolling the balls with precision—to themselves, then with partners, putting one ball aside. Practice ball-handling skills, triplet rhythm, and movements with objects.

- ***Ball Dance.*** Create a dance pattern that includes all three ball skills (bouncing, tossing, and rolling) that follows a 3/4 or 6/8 time signature, with the bounce or toss being precisely on the one count. Play Camille Saint-Saëns, *The Carnival of the Animals*, "L'Elephant" or any other music with the same time signature.

Fourth Grade

SCIENCE

After discussing the difference between weather and geologic events, list the following, matching them with the six energy qualities: *landslide*/collapse, *hurricane*/sustained, *lightning strike*/

percussive, *earthquake*/vibratory, *tsunami*/swinging, and *wildfire*/suspended.

- **Geologic Events.** Improvise various movements for each event listed. Play Michel Cusson, "Ly-O-Lay Ale Loya" as background. Divide into three or six groups and create short studies to express their event. Studies must include three different movements: one that travels, one that stays in place, and one that makes a formation, in any order.

MATH

Discuss the difference between two-dimensional and three-dimensional perspectives. Show a picture of an object and the real object. Divide in half. Practice making still shapes up against a blank wall to create two-dimensional shapes while the other half observes and then switch. Then form a circle, and half of the group in the center forms shapes as those in the circle walk around to observe them from all sides and then switch.

- **2-D and 3-D.** All dancers begin off to the sides of the space, leaving the blank wall open, and take turns entering and forming a **2-D** shape against the wall. After all have had a turn, create a simple and repeatable traveling movement pattern that all begin doing to form a moving circle. Again, taking turns, dancers move into the center and form a **3-D** shape as the rest of the group is traveling around them. Play any music.

LANGUAGE ARTS

Define what a quote is and the rules surrounding how it should be both researched and cited. Students can do research to find an inspiring quote about a topic of their choice, making sure they correctly copy it and cite its author. Explore and express main movements and transitions between them and the parallel in words.

- **Graham Quote.** Use the following quote by Martha Graham: *"Dance is the hidden language of the soul."* Identify the main-idea words (*dance*, *hidden*, *language*, and *soul*) and the transition words (*is*, *the*, *of*, and *the*). Then discuss how all are essential to make a complete sentence. The whole group improvises to create a movement or a short phrase that expresses each of the main-idea words. Then create movements that express the transition words, and if they repeat, the movements can repeat as well. Put all movements/phrases together and perform with groups taking turns to watch one another. Play Mickey Hart, "Amazon Nguni."

SOCIAL STUDIES

Refer to a map of California or students' knowledge of the geography and various ecosystems in our state. Then discuss what each looks like, what lives there, and what the people from those areas do. Practice and connect four pathways in space with in-place and traveling movements: *straight*, *curved*, *zigzag*, and *wavy*.

- ***California Ecosystems.*** Discuss various California ecosystems, including *ocean* (wavy), *mountains* (zigzag), *desert* (straight), and *valleys* (curved). Four groups are each assigned one of the ecosystems. They create dances about their part, including three different movements, each of which should clearly demonstrate their pathway and various aspects of their ecosystem. Play *Rhythmically Moving*, "California Strut."

VISUAL ARTS

Use the six *energy qualities* (see appendix C, "Element of Energy Deconstruction") and match the following (or other) animals to them: *sustained*/snake, *percussive*/chicken, *swinging*/monkey, *suspended*/deer, *collapse*/bear, and *vibratory*/butterfly.

- ***Energy/Animal Masks.*** Premake enough masks out of fabric or heavy paper for every student to have one. Make sure they can wear it without it falling off while dancing. Use glue sticks and a wide variety of items to design and decorate the blank masks, such as feathers, pieces of felt, aluminum foil, pipe cleaners, as well as several colors of paint and brushes. Divide the students into groups by energy/animal. Using photographs of the animals, students construct a mask for themselves that represents their animal. For the dance, each group creates and sets movements their animal might do, emphasizing the energy quality matched with it. Follow a simple pattern, such as **rise** from the floor, **travel** around the space, **circle** around another in their group, and **exit**. Play Mickey Hart, "Elephant Walk." (Note: many thanks to the brilliant LAUSD Elementary visual arts teacher, Brittany Maddocks, for this collaboration.)

THEATRE

In both theatre and dance, performers need to be able to improvise and quickly change from one idea or movement to another to maintain a flow or rhythm as a member of a group. In a circle, do the theatre game, where each person says a number, taking turns counting to three. One number at a time, replace with a movement.

- *Counting Game.* After practicing the above, groups of four to five set movements and perform to Dan Savell, "March through Canyons." Then allow four quick beats per movement. Dancers should have a different movement each time it is their turn.

MUSIC

Play any example of a piece of music that has an underlying beat with a repeating rhythm layered on top, such as the Mermen, "Unto the Resplendent."

- *Beat and Rhythm.* In pairs, each person has a pair of rhythm sticks. One taps a steady beat as the other creates a repeatable rhythm pattern to play over the steady beat. Switch and practice again. Then put the sticks aside and create and perform two movements, doing the same thing.

Perform the dance with or without background music. Then repeat the pattern at least four times.

PE

This is similar to the second-grade PE activity, but with added complexity. After assessing the outdoor playground equipment at the school, sort the equipment pieces out by area and function, such as hanging, climbing, balancing, swinging, etc. Then draw a map of the equipment. Discuss the equipment in class and list movements that are normally done on them.

- ***Playground Fitness Dance.*** Groups of four to five are assigned two pieces of playground equipment that are near each other. Then they create a dance, including one movement not normally done on that equipment and a still shape on each piece, plus a transition movement that gets them from one to the other. Equipment pieces can be given to more than one group to see how different their movements turn out. Play any upbeat music that is long enough for each group to get a turn.

Fifth Grade

SCIENCE

Law of physics: "A body in motion will remain in motion, and a body at rest will remain at rest" (unless either the motion or the rest is interrupted). When a movement leads you into another movement through space, you are using momentum, like going down a slide or jumping off a swing. Explore by doing a twist into a spin, swing into a slide into a hop, and go and stop to experience interrupted momentum.

- ***Momentum.*** Randomly choose two movement cards and try to find the right momentum to initiate the second from the first (emphasize technique and physical balance). Groups start with one card, then add a second and figure out how to direct the momentum to move from one to the next, then add a third and do the same. Play the Blues Project, "Flute Thing."

MATH

Explore geometric concepts of shapes that are defined by their perimeter and contain their area. Dance connections include creating formations with multiple bodies and inhabiting the area created by each form.

- ***Perimeter and Area.*** Divide in half, and each group practices making the formation of the following five geometric shapes: *circle, square, triangle, rectangle,* and *oval.* For the performance, half the group makes the first formation (perimeter) and sets an in-place movement while the other half dances inside it (area) with a set movement phrase. Groups take turns forming the perimeters and the areas: For example, group A forms the circle, and group B dances inside. Then group B forms the *square,* and group A dances inside, and so on. Play any music that is long enough as background.

LANGUAGE ARTS

Explore narrative story writing following the structure of a journey, including descriptive language, landmarks, and events along the way. Use four pathways (*straight, curved, zigzag,* and *wavy*), traveling movements, and still shapes. Translate a drawing into movements into a story.

- ***The Journey.*** Divide into three large groups. On large paper, each draws their own map that represents a journey from one place to another in one continuous line, including all four pathways (*straight, curved, zigzag,* and *wavy*), with three landmarks between each pathway. Set movements following the pathways and still shapes indicating the landmarks on their map. Write and illustrate the story of the "journey." The map should have clear beginning and end places, which are not the same place. Play Michael Wall, "6 125."

SOCIAL STUDIES

On a map of the world, look at North and South America and point out the different areas where Europeans colonized themselves. Discuss the diaspora of western African culture on the Americas as well. Draw a parallel between Brazil and the United States in how there were three predominant cultures in the early years of both currently recognized nations: Native, European, and African. Practice in-place and traveling movements emphasizing the eight Effort Actions.

- *Orixás.* See appendix D, "World Dances." Divide into four groups, and each learns and performs two of these eight brief Brazilian dance variations, each emphasizing one of the eight Effort Actions. Remember the parallel between the three Brazilian cultures featured and the three American cultures that exist here. Also, emphasize how the purpose of the various dances is to honor the spirits that live within all things around us (polytheism). Groups can then brainstorm things in their everyday life that might embody a spirit and create movements expressing them. Play Grupo Batuque, "Candomble."

VISUAL ARTS

Use Laban's eight Effort Actions (see appendix C, "Element of Energy Deconstruction") as a guide for both movement and painting.

- *Effort Actions Mural.* After gaining an understanding of the three components of each Effort Action and practicing them with improvised movements, divide into eight groups by Effort Action. Continuing to use improvised movements, create a sequence where each group one at a time **enters** from offstage in sixteen quick beats, stops somewhere in the space, and moves **in place** for eight beats, then slowly **lowers** to the floor in eight beats. One group at a time performs. Then together, they all **rise** in sixteen beats, with all continue moving **in place** for sixteen beats. Then all hold still as one group at a time **exits** in eight beats each. All of the movements are performed emphasizing the group's Action. Play Dan Savell, "Driving a Jet." Practice with a dry paintbrush on the floor or table, painting with each of the Effort Actions. Assign a different color of paint for each Action, and using large butcher paper, one student at a time approaches the paper and paints each of the *actions* with its color (e.g., *punch* = black, *float* = blue, *slash* = yellow). Encourage students to fill in the empty spaces with the Actions until the whole paper is full. This is a collaborative work, and students can paint anywhere on the paper in their allotted time. (Note: I thank the brilliant LAUSD Elementary visual arts teacher, Brittany Maddocks, for her partnership in developing this collaborative project.)

THEATRE

Discuss how stories are the basis of all theatre works and how stories can come from anywhere and how they normally consist of a beginning, a middle, and an end (the plot), involving characters and a setting. Practice facial expressions and whole-body movements expressing the nine *Navarasa* moods: *pride, tranquility, sorrow, disgust, love, surprise, anger, joy,* and *fear*.

- **Playwriting.** In three groups, each is given three of the above moods. They create a dance study with a beginning, middle, and end expressing each mood. Play Prem Joshua, "Deccan Queen." After they have performed, groups sit down together and write the story of their dance. Include who the characters are, the setting, and, of course, the events that caused the change of mood. Perform again.

MUSIC

Explore movements of animal characters with rhythm patterns associated with each character.

- ***The First Music.*** See the section "Books about Dance" in chapter 17, "Inspiration." There are eleven characters. In that many small groups, each creates a repeating, rhythmic movement for their character, which follows the rhythm described, plus a traveling movement. Play Bobby McFerrin, "Circlesong Seven."

PE

This is similar to the second- and fourth-grade PE lessons, but with added complexity. After assessing the outdoor playground equipment at the school, sort the equipment pieces out by area and function, such as hanging, climbing balancing, swinging, etc. Then map out a CIRCUIT route connecting them. Discuss the equipment in class and list movements that are normally done on them and what muscle groups are being exercised while using them.

- ***Circuit Dance.*** Divide into groups by piece of equipment, and each group creates a dance phrase that can work the intended muscle groups in two ways on the equipment and then travel to the next area. All groups will teach their phrases to the other groups, and all will practice and perform them in a rotation, where one group does their movements on their equipment with the previous group. Then they alone travel to the next piece of equipment and join the next group. So there will always be two groups performing on the equipment and one group traveling alone. Play Mass Ensemble, "Chaos Nebula."

Sixth Grade

<u>SCIENCE</u>

Discuss the four systems of our earth—the GEOSPHERE (rocks, dirt), HYDROSPHERE (water, ice), ATMOSPHERE (air, wind), and BIOSPHERE (living things)—and how they all blend with one another. Make a chart matching the four systems in six possible ways (geo/hydro, geo/atmo, geo/bio, hydro/atmo, hydro/bio, and atmo/bio), listing some examples of things that exist in both spheres. For example, air and water together make clouds, living things and earth together make plants, water and living things together make fishes.

- ***Blending the Four Geosystems.*** Choose one item from each matched pair of systems, and the whole group maps out a sequence of the six items that makes logical sense. The whole group also creates a movement motif for each of the four systems that all smaller groups will use as part of their phrases. Then divide into six groups, and each creates a dance phrase that expresses their item. Play Mass Ensemble, "Hawk's Gaze" or "Chaos Nebula." Then each group's phrase must include the two system motifs that join to create their item plus their phrase in the middle.

<u>MATH</u>

Discuss and demonstrate in partners the four types of *planar symmetry*: **reflection** (opposite facing, mirroring), **rotational** (opposite facing, same hands, right or left, moving), **translation** (shadowing, facing the same direction with the same hands moving), and **glide** (facing the same direction, opposite hands moving).

- ***Planar Symmetries.*** After practicing the four types of symmetry above, the same partners create and set movements in each type, with at least one in place and one traveling movement in each type of symmetry. Then put pairs together to finish studies, including all four types. Play Prem Joshua, "Return of the Mystics." Then each pair gets sixteen quick beats to perform each of the *planar symmetries*.

LANGUAGE ARTS

Read and discuss the story of Orpheus and Euridice. Practice in-place and traveling movements emphasizing the eight Effort Actions. If available, show any video of Isadora Duncan's *Dance of the Furies* and identify the Effort Actions seen in the dance.

- **Orpheus and Euridice.** Divide into four groups (each group is responsible for two of the eight events in the story, matched with Effort Actions below). Play Gluck, *Orpheo ed Euridice,* "Dance of the Furies." Then create three-part phrases expressing the events in the story, using the Effort Actions as follows:
  1. Happy, love, musical, beautiful, **FLOAT**
  2. Bite of the snake and death, **PUNCH**
  3. Courage or quest, **FLICK**
  4. Frightening journey through the Furies, **SLASH**
  5. Success, don't look back, **GLIDE**
  6. Looking back, **DAB**
  7. The Furies take her back, **PRESS**
  8. Pursued by the Furies, punished, tormented, **WRING**

SOCIAL STUDIES

Show four different illustrations of ancient Egypt and at least one of dancer Lester Horton and briefly describe each. Next, teach short phrase of five movements in Horton-style: **Egyptian walks** (straight legs, slide the flat foot forward as the opposite arm twists forward, arms in square shape, framing head), **primitive squat-hinge** (parallel feet; deep bend with the arms forward, palms facing each other; bend body forward; release and swing up to standing; circle arms and lean back into hinge; low quarter turn; repeat), **strike-hop** (skip up, dip down with the body parallel to the floor, arms straight and down at sides, one leg lifted with the knee bent, repeat on the same side), **lunge walks** (step right foot forward into a deep forward lunge with the arms straight forward, palms facing each other, step left, cross in front of the right with a torso twist and the left elbow in toward the right knee, repeat on the same side), **leg swings with slide** (swing one leg and the opposite arm to side and across the body three times, step on it and slide to that side, repeat with the other leg). Point out similarities between the movements and images seen in Egyptian art.

- *Series of Three Shapes.* Divide into four groups by Egyptian illustration, and each group creates a group shape that represents what they see in their picture. Use the following sequence to alternate group shapes with Horton movements, which all will perform. Play Mass Ensemble, "Green Box."
  1. Horton movement 1
  2. Egyptian group shape A
  3. Horton movement 2
  4. Egyptian group shape B
  5. Horton movement 3
  6. Egyptian group shape C
  7. Horton movement 4
  8. Egyptian group shape D
  9. Horton movement 5

VISUAL ARTS

Go on a brief scavenger hunt, and each student collects one interesting object from around the room or nearby outside. Make sure the objects are large enough for an audience to see if held in a dancer's hand. Discuss three ways to use the objects in making dances: (1) **Imitate** the object and move like it moves and make a still shape that looks like it. (2). **Partner** the object by dancing with it and making a still shape with it. (3) **Use** the object as a tool in some way. (4) **Pass** the object in creative ways to another person. Divide into groups of four to five students, and each brings their object to the group. They put the objects together to create an original sculpture of their found objects.

- **Found Object Sculpture.** Practice and set movements for each of the four ways to dance with the objects, beginning and ending in the sculpture. Play Vivaldi, "Danza Pastorale."

THEATRE

Practice facial expressions and whole-body movements expressing the nine *Navarasa* moods: *pride, tranquility, sorrow, disgust, love, surprise, anger, joy,* and *fear.*

- **Conflict Resolved.** Divide into eight groups. Each gets a mood other than *joy*, which will be used by all as the "resolution" of the conflict. Groups are paired with another mood group, and the movements they set should be directed at the other group. The whole dance will proceed in the style of taking turns, where one group does a movement with their mood and the other group responds with a movement expressing their mood to create a type of conflicting conversation. Go back and forth three times with three different movements to develop the scenario. Then the whole group creates a phrase together that resolves the conflict by expressing *joy*. Play Michael Wall, "AS 6 (5 77)." Dancers respond quickly with the beats in the music.

MUSIC

Practice the element of *space* concepts of *size* and *focus* by practicing in-place and traveling movements, small and large, and with multiple and single focus.

- **Background and Solo.** Play Billie Holiday, "*But Not for Me.*" Divide into four groups (by solo instruments: *piano, guitar, sax,* and *trumpet*), and each creates a "background" movement—repetitive movements that are small and with multiple focus and easily done in unison (swaying together, moving in and out of a circle, slow-motion walk, etc.). They also create a "solo" phrase, where the movements are large in size and the dancers' focus is strong and direct and changes every eight beats. All groups perform their background movements until it is their turn to solo as cued by the music. In the song, there are solos as follows: *voice* twice, *piano*, *guitar*, *sax*, *trumpet*, *voice* twice. The whole group creates a solo phrase, which all will perform during the vocal parts at the beginning and at the end.

<u>PE</u>

Practice movements that work each of the ten muscle groups: PECTORALS/chest; DELTOIDS/shoulders; BICEPS, TRICEPS, ABDOMINALS/stomach; OBLIQUES/sides of the torso; GLUTEALS/ buttocks; QUADRICEPS/front thighs; HAMSTRINGS/back of thighs; and GASTROCNEMII/calves. Also, practice whole-body movements at all four levels in space: *low*, *middle*, *high*, and *airborne*.

- **Muscle Groups.** Divide into five groups, assigning each group two of the above muscle groups. Each group creates a dance that includes two different movements, working each of their two muscle groups, and the four movements must be done at each of the four levels. Emphasize that the movements should go together to form a dance rather than be a series of exercises. Play Mickey Hart, "Island Groove."

PART VI
Experiencing and Responding

The impact of your own and others' work

Chapter 23

Participation
Perspectives from inside a dance and receiving feedback from others

There are really only two ways to participate in dance, either as (1) a dancer from INSIDE a dance or (2) an observer from OUTSIDE a dance. As a dance teacher, your job includes doing both. When you are modeling or demonstrating, you are inside; and of course, when the students are performing, you are on the outside, watching them from a well-informed front-row seat!

This chapter focuses on the important perspective of experiencing dance firsthand as a dancer, going through the process, from creating to performing. There are four points that I think are important to discuss from the perspective of INSIDE a dance:

Self-assessment. Focusing first on their own performance provides your students with an opportunity to take responsibility for their own learning, entering the realm of metacognition and considering their place in the greater experience of performing a dance. At the moment a dance is performed in a single dance class, there may not be much time for self-reflection. So this part might be best implemented in journal-writing activities afterward, when students have a quiet moment to think about their own performance. The downside to this is that when some time goes by, the feelings and impressions might not be as fresh or vivid.

Receiving feedback. Getting a sense of what others perceive helps students compare their own impressions with those of outside observers and draw broader conclusions regarding their own work. Most of us are highly influenced by what others think about us, and how that information is presented is pivotal. It can lift our spirits and give our self-esteem a big boost, or it can be a blow to our feelings of self-worth (more on that in chapter 24, "Observation"). However your students may feel about the impressions of others, it is best to encourage them to be gracious in accepting feedback and remind them not to take any criticism too personally.

Making adjustments. After considering their own performance and hearing the impressions of others, dance students can analyze that information. Then they can either ignore it or think of some changes and implement them to their work if they have the opportunity to perform it again. I have found giving students the opportunity to improve their performance to be extremely valuable. I see the way students light up and appear to feel so much better after having a more successful performance experience. This is the big lesson from the performing arts that can apply to most other aspects of life—the great value of practice or rehearsal. I recommend planning enough time for dances to be revised and performed again if possible.

Defending choices. If students are faced with questioning or criticism from others about their performance, they can do one of two things: (1) make adjustments (as stated above) if they think the points the observers have made are valid OR (2) decide to not make any changes and respond by explaining the reason behind the choices they made in their dance. Since the observers were not inside the performance, they may not know the reasoning behind the choices made, which is not their fault. So this is an opportunity for the creators of the dance to educate them about their process.

Below and on the following pages are some examples of prompts and questions appropriate to each grade level for focusing on and responding to **PARTICIPATION** in a dance:

Prekindergarten
Draw a picture of yourself doing a movement from your dance. What was the experience of performing your dance like? Can you demonstrate your favorite part of the dance? What does it make you think of? What parts of your body did you use to perform those movements?

Kindergarten
Draw a picture and write a word to describe the best part of your dance. What discoveries did you make performing your dance? What was your favorite part of the dance? What was going through your mind when you were dancing? What was the hardest part of the dance?

<table>
<tr><td>First Grade</td></tr>
<tr><td>

Describe your favorite part of your dance and why you liked it.
What movements did you experiment with to create your dance?
What did you learn from performing this dance?
Would you like to perform this dance again?
What would you change about your dance if you were going to perform it again?

</td></tr>
</table>

<table>
<tr><td>Second Grade</td></tr>
<tr><td>

Write and draw about the meaning or the purpose of your dance.
What elements of dance did you use to produce your dance?
What was the most important part of the dance?
What changes would you make to improve the dance?
What did you imagine while you were dancing?

</td></tr>
</table>

<table>
<tr><td>Third Grade</td></tr>
<tr><td>

Write and draw about how the movements of your dance expressed its meaning.
What new or original movements did you invent to create your dance?
How did you use the elements of dance to make the dance interesting?
How did performing this dance make you feel?
What would you change to make the movements more meaningful?

</td></tr>
</table>

Fourth Grade

Describe the purpose or artistic intent of your dance.
How did the movements of your dance develop into the final product?
In what way was this dance meaningful to you?
In what ways do you think the dance achieved its goal? In what ways do you think it did not achieve its goal?
What worked? What didn't work?

Fifth Grade

Describe the process of creating the dance you just performed.
What choreographic tools did you use to construct your dance?
What images were you trying to create in your dance?
How well did your dance communicate its meaning?
How would you expand on your dance if you could?

Sixth Grade

Describe the most effective and least effective movements in your dance.
How did blending various elements of dance reinforce your artistic intent?
What is the theme of your dance?
What does your dance need to more deeply express its meaning?
Do you have any new realizations after creating and performing your dance?

Chapter 24

Observation
Perspectives from outside a dance and developing a critical eye and an opinion

Watching dance as an OUTSIDE observer can be a fun, educational, and inspiring experience; and it is much different from seeing it from the INSIDE. As choreographers, we always want to know what our work looks like from the outside; and when we are in it, it is difficult to gain that perspective. Of course, using mirrors and video recordings can be helpful, and many dancers/choreographers use them as essential tools when unable to step outside and observe.

As dance teachers in schools or community program settings, we might not have mirrors or video recording devices that can provide that perspective, enabling our students to watch themselves. But that is not the end of the world by any means. Building in ways for students to observe one another in a dance they are also a part of can be done either by dividing into smaller groups and taking turns performing a large group work or by taking the time to have individual students step out and watch their group as a choreographer would.

Informal performances give your students an immediate audience. And it is also a golden opportunity for them to learn the difference between watching a live performance versus one on TV. They will need to be reminded that they are not there to simply lie back and be entertained. They are active participants in the performance and have a job to do as observers. They will need to be reminded of proper behavior at a live performance and that being in the same space as the dancers means they can't talk to one another, get up and move around, or interact with the performers—all of which they have the freedom to do at home while watching TV. Also, applauding at the end of a live performance is how we show gratitude and respect for the gift of a dance we have just received!

There are three points that I think are important to focus on when helping your students learn to make an informed and educated OUTSIDE observation of dance:

Developing a critical eye. What makes a dance good? The dancer's skill and expression, visual presentation, production elements, accompaniment, and artistic intent are some things observers can look for to answer that question. Young dance students won't likely know what to look for when observing a dance since they are so tuned into watching movies and videos for the purpose of sensory stimulation. Watching a performance with an eye for certain other characteristics will likely be a new experience for them. It is crucial to front-load information on what to look for whenever your students are getting ready to be an audience.

Developing and expressing an opinion. Sharing impressions out loud is extremely helpful, especially if you, as the teacher, model how to do it. Having your students listen to one another express their opinions is extremely valuable as well. They will provide you with insights into their understanding of the concepts you are teaching and what caught their attention the most. When facilitating a discussion of observations after a performance, I have found it useful to respond to the students' observations with probing questions, such as "Why did you like that part?" or "Could you tell me more about that idea?" Another way of making their observations relevant is by making connections to their lives or other things they are learning.

Providing feedback. When asking students to make comments on a dance performance they have seen, reminders to keep the comments positive are helpful. Reminders about what they were supposed to be watching for might be needed as well. Another obstacle I have run into is the attention of the performers when the audience is making comments on their work. Often, I find myself needing to remind the dancers to listen to the feedback about the performance they just gave. They seem to need to decompress and redirect their focus after the intensity of performing, so allowing the performers to first briefly express their impressions from inside the dance can help them to then focus on the outside perspective. Also, when commenting on what they observed, students will often mention their classmates by name. There are two ways of looking at that: Yes, if the feedback is positive, it can be an emotional boost to the recipient. But if it is negative, we don't want the opposite to happen. If the observers are asked to not mention dancers by name, there is a missed opportunity for that emotional boost, but the feedback tends to be more focused on the dance. How you frame the examples you give of making comments, of course, depends on your class and their needs.

Beginning on the following page are some suggestions for both front-loading **before** your students observe a dance and commenting **after**. When asking for comments, especially from younger dance observers, it is important to ask students to share their thoughts in complete sentences rather than single words. This requires them to think about what they saw more comprehensively.

Prekindergarten

Before:
Watch for who is doing their best.
Watch for one example of . . . (the dance concept being taught).

After:
Demonstrate the best movement you saw in the dance.
Tell us what the movement reminded you of.

Kindergarten

Before:
Look for the most interesting movements in the dance.
Watch for the best example of . . . (the dance concept being taught).

After:
Describe the best part of the dance and why you liked it.
Tell us what you imagined while watching the dance.

First Grade

Before:
Look for what you think the movements are supposed to look like.
Watch for how . . . (the dance concept being taught) was visible in the dance.

After:
Describe how the dancers showed . . . (the dance concept being taught).
Tell us what you think they could have done differently.

Second Grade

Before:
Look for two of . . . (the dance concepts being taught) happening at the same time.
Watch for where . . . (the dance concept being taught) was the most clear.

After:
Describe the best example in the dance of how . . . (the dance concept being taught) was demonstrated.
Tell us what would have made . . . (the dance concept being taught) clearer.

<table>
<tr><td align="center">Third Grade</td></tr>
<tr><td>

Before:
Look at the dance as a whole rather than at individual dancers.
Look for examples of as many elements of dance as you can see in the dance.

After:
Think of and share some words and phrases that describe what you saw in the dance.
Give the dancers a suggestion as to how all the elements of dance could be clearer.

</td></tr>
</table>

<table>
<tr><td align="center">Fourth Grade</td></tr>
<tr><td>

Before:
Watch for examples of how the dance and dancers express their intent.
Look for the original and unique way in which the dancers showed . . . (the dance concept being taught).

After:
Offer a suggestion to the dancers of another way . . . (the dance concept being taught) could have been expressed in their dance. Justify your opinion.

</td></tr>
</table>

Fifth Grade

Before:
Try to determine how the dancers came up with the ideas they express in their dance.
Watch for examples of original ideas in the dance.

After:
Offer a suggestion as to how their artistic intent could have been developed further.
Identify and summarize the most impactful moments of the dance.

Sixth Grade

Before:
Watch for the strongest and weakest parts of the dance.
Look for an emerging theme in the dance.

After:
Describe what makes the strong parts strong and how the weaker parts could be improved upon.
Describe how the intent or meaning of the dance relates to what is important to you in your life.

PART VII
Appendices

Resources and further information

Appendix A
A Quick Reference Guide to the California Arts Standards (CAS) for Dance

Here are some key points that may be helpful in understanding how the California Arts Standards for Dance are organized:

- The CAS are broken down into four **ARTISTIC PROCESSES** that are the same *across all art forms and all grades.* (The music is somewhat different from the other four art forms in the upper elementary and secondary grades). Those *artistic processes* are as follows:

    Creating

    Performing, Presenting, or Producing (for dance, the Process is Performing)

    Responding

    Connecting

- There are eleven **ANCHOR STANDARDS**, divided between the *four artistic processes*, that are also the same *across all art forms and all grades*. Because of that, they are nonspecific in nature so as to be appropriate for all arts disciplines.

- For **dance,** there is one **ENDURING UNDERSTANDING**, one **ESSENTIAL QUESTION**, and one **PROCESS COMPONENT** (that is a single word) for each of the *eleven anchor standards*. All of these are *specific to dance* and stretch *across all grades*.

- The ANCHOR STANDARDS with their accompanying PROCESS COMPONENTS are further broken down into **SUBCOMPONENTS** labeled with lowercase letters *a, b,* or *c,* creating the twenty-one actual **STANDARDS**. These are *specific to dance* and stretch *across all grades* (with the exception of standard 3.b, which starts at grade 7).

To access the complete California Arts Standards for Public Schools 2019, go to the following:

https://www.cde.ca.gov

In the search box, type in ***arts standards***. Then click on the link labeled
California Arts Standards – Content Standards.

In the organizational chart on the next page, there are some italicized words (provided by Karen Hahne, January 2019) in the right column, following the "Process Components." These words indicate the focus or intent of the standard, which is NOT articulated in the wording of the standard itself.

ARTISTIC PROCESSES	PROCESS COMPONENTS (by Anchor Standard)	FOCUS of the STANDARD (by subcomponent)
Creating	Anchor Standard 1. **EXPLORE**	1.a. **EXPLORE** *Inspiration* 1.b. **EXPLORE** *Variations*
	Anchor Standard 2. **PLAN**	2.a. **PLAN** *Choreographic Choices* 2.b. **PLAN** *Artistic Intent*
	Anchor Standard 3. **REVISE**	3.a. **REVISE** *and Refine* 3.b. **REVISE** *and Document**
Performing	Anchor Standard 4. **EXPRESS**	4.a. **EXPRESS** *Space* 4.b. **EXPRESS** *Time* 4.c. **EXPRESS** *Energy*
	Anchor Standard 5. **EMBODY**	5.a. **EMBODY** *Technique* 5.b. **EMBODY** *Health and Safety* 5.c. **EMBODY** *Self-Awareness*
	Anchor Standard 6. **PRESENT**	6.a. **PRESENT** *Onstage* 6.b. **PRESENT** *Production Elements*

	Anchor Standard 7. **ANALYZE**	7.a. **ANALYZE** *Patterns* 7.b. **ANALYZE** *Characteristics*
Responding	Anchor Standard 8. **INTERPRET**	8.a. **INTERPRET** *Meaning*
	Anchor Standard 9. **CRITIQUE**	9.a. **CRITIQUE** *and Evaluate*
Connecting	Anchor Standard 10. **SYNTHESIZE**	10.a. **SYNTHESIZE** *Personal Experience* 10.b. **SYNTHESIZE** *Inquiry*
	Anchor Standard 11. **RELATE**	11.a. **RELATE** *History and Culture*

*This standard applies only from grade 7 through high school, advanced.

Appendix B

The BrainDance

Anne Green Gilbert's BrainDance is a cornerstone of my teaching practice. It is applicable in so many aspects of dance arts learning and can be adapted to fit multiple concepts. It is an eight-step structure that is fluid, yet solid in science and function. At the beginning of all of my classes, at every age/grade level, I do what I call an *opening ritual*, which follows these same steps (see the section "Warm-Up" in chapter 8, "Class Structure"). And please refer to the following website for more information on the BrainDance and the Creative Dance Center:

creativedance.org

Here is the poster I show to explain the eight steps of the BrainDance:

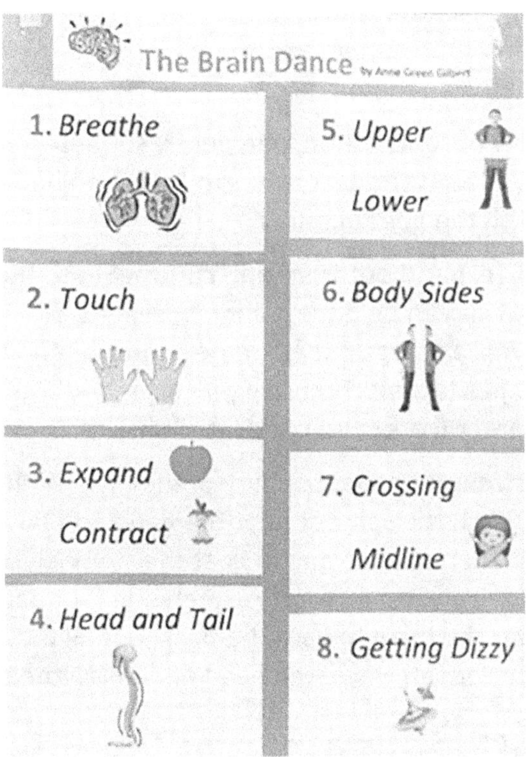

And on the following page is an outline of the movements I generally use to teach the BrainDance as a discrete lesson or as a warm-up for classes of students with special needs who might not be able to follow a choreographed warm-up. Also, see appendix G, "Handouts," for an information sheet that could be shared with teachers, parents, or other professional staff who might be interested.

BrainDance
Created by Anne Green Gilbert

Music: *The Art and Heart of Drum Circle* by Christine Stevens, "Funk Groove," OR any music you like that is long enough. Counting is not essential.

BREATH (oxygen saturation): While breathing steadily and evenly, perform different movements with each inhale and exhale, with a brief pause between them.

TACTILE (sense of touch): Rub, pat, gently squeeze, or tickle all body parts. Use the various touches to "play" on body as if it were a drum set with the beat of music.

CORE/DISTAL (expand out from and contract in to the center of the body): This can be done standing, seated, or lying down. Stretch the arms and legs out from the center of body into various expanded shapes (distal). Then the pull arms and legs inward toward the center (core) into contracted shapes.

HEAD/TAIL (strengthening of spine): Standing with the hands on the knees, arch the spine so that the head and tail are both extending up. Then reverse and look at the stomach so that the head and tail are curved forward. Stretch one foot back and reach both arms over the head toward the back foot. Flip over and touch that foot, then repeat. Move the head and tail to the sides and in circles.

UPPER/LOWER BODY (dual focus): Imagine a horizontal line at the waist. Move only the upper half of the body, while the lower half is frozen in any shape. Then switch and move only the lower half while the upper half is frozen.

BODY SIDE (separating brain hemispheres): Imagine a vertical line down the center of the body (midline). One side is frozen, while the other side moves (the same arm and leg). Then switch. Also, open and close the same side of the arm and leg like a book.

CROSS LATERAL (integrating hemispheres): Touch opposite-side body parts, starting at the head and working your way down to the feet. Then come back up. Do various crossing movements, slapping the feet in the front and back, jumps, or stretches.

VESTIBULAR (getting dizzy): Spin without stopping long enough to get dizzy. Then stop and balance on one foot without falling. Repeat in the other direction, balancing on the other foot. Do whole-body swings (including the head). Reach and focus up. Then slowly melt down to the floor.

After melting to the floor, ask the students to rest there in whatever shape they are in and not move while guiding them through the following visualization, which repeats the above steps:

- Concentrate on breathing and feel the chest rise and fall.
- Notice all the parts of the body that are touching the floor.
- Imagine the center of the body as a candle flame and notice which parts of the body are farthest away from that light.
- Visualize the curve of the spine in the position it is currently in.
- Visualize the position of the upper body and of the lower body.
- Visualize the position of the right side of the body as well as its left side.
- Notice if any parts of the body are crossing over to the other side.
- Close the eyes and imagine spinning extremely fast, then stopping, and everything is completely clear.

Ways to use the BrainDance structure by grade level:

PRE-K to KINDERGARTEN: *Watch One Another.* Divide in half and perform, alternating sections, for one another. Switch parts and repeat. You could add an entrance and exit if desired.

FIRST GRADE: *Element of SPACE.* Divide into six groups. all do first and last sections. Emphasize the following spatial concepts with the steps of the dance: *touch*/pathways, *expand-contract*/size, *head and tail*/curved and straight, *upper-lower*/in-place and traveling, *body sides*/focus, *crossing midline*/levels.

SECOND GRADE: *Partners in Timing.* Get into pairs, and the whole group sets a sequence of movements as follows:

    Breath – At the SAME TIME as a partner

    Tactile – TAKING TURNS, touching each other's body parts, which move when touched

    Core/Distal – Expand at the SAME TIME and contract TAKING TURNS

    Head/Tail – Facing each other, take the hands and pull away, stretching each other's spines at the SAME TIME. Then one turns around, and TAKING TURNS, the partner helps them stretch their spine from the back by taking both hands as they arch forward. Then switch.

    Upper/Lower – Face each other and mirror each other's upper body movements. Then one shadows the other doing lower body movements, both at the SAME TIME.

    Body Side – Stand side by side and hold each other up as both opposite sides move at the SAME TIME. Then turn around to move to both other sides.

    Cross Lateral – Do traveling movements with the legs and arms crossing, TAKING TURNS moving away, and returning to the original space.

    Getting Dizzy – Hold both hands and circle around each other quickly at the SAME TIME. Then stop and hold on, making sure the other person doesn't fall. Repeat in the opposite direction.

THIRD GRADE: *Energy Qualities.* Divide into six groups (all will do the first and last steps of the BrainDance). Then match each of the middle six steps with the six energy qualities, either randomly selected or chosen by the group. Each group creates a phrase of three movements emphasizing both their step of the BrainDance and their energy quality.

FOURTH GRADE: *Transitions.* Make four groups, and each is assigned two consecutive sections of the BrainDance. Each group sets a combination of movements for each of their sections AND creates a transition between them that is the main emphasis of the study.

FIFTH GRADE: *Effort Actions.* Divide into four or eight groups. Each group will be assigned either one or two steps of the BrainDance and either one or two of the eight Effort Actions. Each group creates a phrase with a complete beginning, middle, and end expressing their step(s), which also emphasizes their Effort Action.

SIXTH GRADE: *Variations.* The whole class creates a four-part phrase to go with the first (breathing) section of the BrainDance. Seven groups create a variation on the same phrase for each of the remaining parts, emphasizing the essence of each part. Refine for the performance.

Appendix C

Element of Energy Deconstruction

Energy is the most subtle and mystifying of the elements of dance. But even young dancers can understand and embody its concepts. Here are the organizational structures I use to help students better understand this most exciting element:

FORCE/TEMPO MATRIX:

In its extreme form, *force* can either be *tense* or *relaxed*; and likewise, *tempo* can either be *fast* or *slow*. (Of course, a music teacher would disagree and rightly so, saying there are more specific tempi than just two. But for the purpose of this organizational structure, only two extremes are needed.) For students in **grades 1–2**, I have found this matrix grid to be useful in breaking down and illustrating how two or more elements of dance can overlap and blend with each other.

	TENSE Force	**RELAXED** Force
FAST Tempo	Burst	Rebound

<table>
<tr>
<td>SLOW
Tempo</td>
<td>Press
</td>
<td>Float
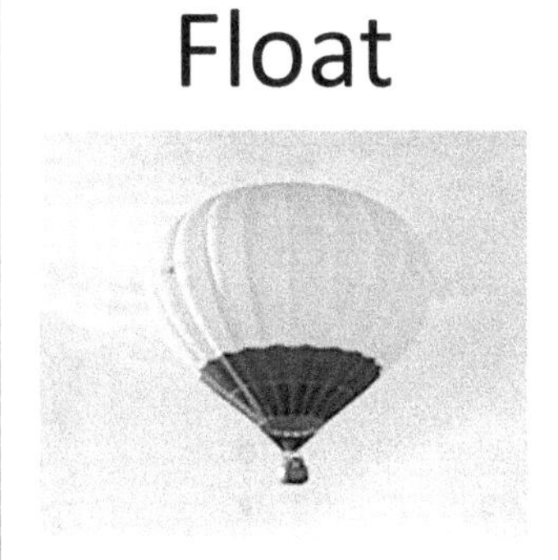</td>
</tr>
</table>

ENERGY QUALITIES:

The following six qualities of movement, developed by Margaret H'Doubler (1889–1982), are a varied and thorough collection of energy use, blending the effects of flow, timing, and weight. I use these with students in **grades 3–4** and find that they are quite able to understand their differences and embody them. The word *quality* means that which is special about something, such as a characteristic or value, and these six are indeed quite unique and special. Below is a brief description of what each quality emphasizes, along with some illustrations. The large picture in each group is for general illustration purposes, and the pictures below it can be for lessons involving wildlife.

Sustained

A continuous, even, and equal release of energy at any speed, with no accent or sudden stop. A seamless flow of motion. The *sustain* pedal on a piano causes the note to be held as the energy level is maintained in a sustained movement.

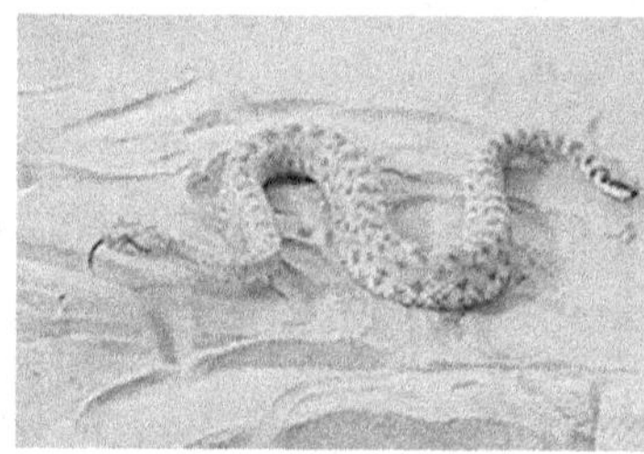

Percussive

Interrupted energy applied quickly with sudden force, then abruptly stopped. A dancer's movements are staccato-like, as in broken pieces, or like the beat of a drum or other *percussion* instruments.

Vibratory

Continuously interrupted energy applied in brief, extremely fast, small movements in quick succession. It is a building up of pressure that causes rapid shaking, as in a pinched pipe. A *vibration* can involve quivering, trembling, or even thrashing.

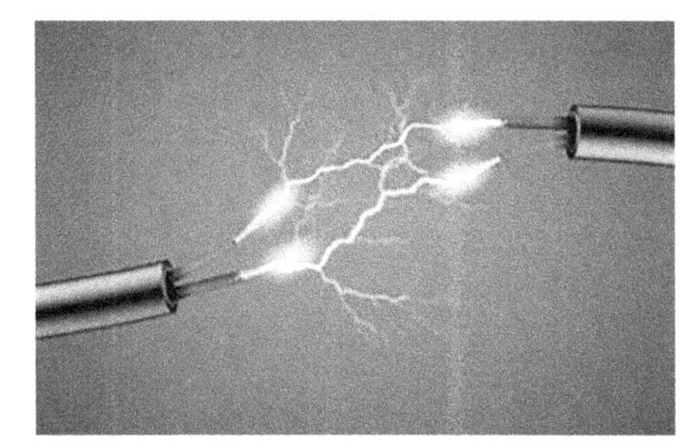

Suspended

This quality uses energy to lift, and continue lifting, a movement in an upward trajectory to experience a moment of weightlessness. The dancer appears to linger or hover at the peak of a movement before being pulled down by gravity. *Suspenders* hold pants up.

Collapse

A release of tension or a feeling of energy being drained out of the body, which produces a noticeable drop. A giving in to gravity as in falling, crumbling, or deflating. An opossum *collapses* when playing dead.

Swinging

Energy applied at the beginning of a movement, released when gravity takes over, then pushed up again by momentum. Resembles the pendulum of a clock, monkeys moving through the branches of trees, or elephants *swinging* their heads and trunks.

Effort Actions:

Effort means "a vigorous and determined attempt," and **Action** is "the process of doing something to achieve an aim." These two words together are what Rudolf Laban (1879–1958)* used to describe the structure he devised to create the sensation or feel that movements have, for both dancers and actors. In this structure, the effort that drives a given action dictates HOW that action is carried out, which, in performance, can also express who we are and what we are thinking and feeling. As performing artists, these are essential skills.

These Actions, broken down in the table below, can be somewhat complex. But I find that my older elementary age students in **grades 5–6** can understand the concepts and differentiate between all eight of them. Laban attached a verb to each of the eight Effort Actions (down the left column), each of which is a unique combination of extremes in three elements of dance:
- ENERGY/Force – either tense or relaxed
- SPACE/Focus – either direct or indirect
- TIME/Timing – either sudden or gradual

Action	Force (Energy)	Focus (Space)	Timing (Time)
FLOAT	Relaxed	Indirect	Gradual
PUNCH	Tense	Direct	Sudden
FLICK	Relaxed	Indirect	Sudden
WRING	Tense	Indirect	Gradual
GLIDE	Relaxed	Direct	Gradual
SLASH	Tense	Indirect	Sudden
DAB	Relaxed	Direct	Sudden
PRESS	Tense	Direct	Gradual

*Rudolf Laban was Austro-Hungarian and known as a pioneering dance artist, choreographer, and dance theorist. He was also known as a Nazi sympathizer, so as brilliant as his artistic work was, we do not need to admire him as a person.

Here are the illustrations I use for the eight Effort Actions:

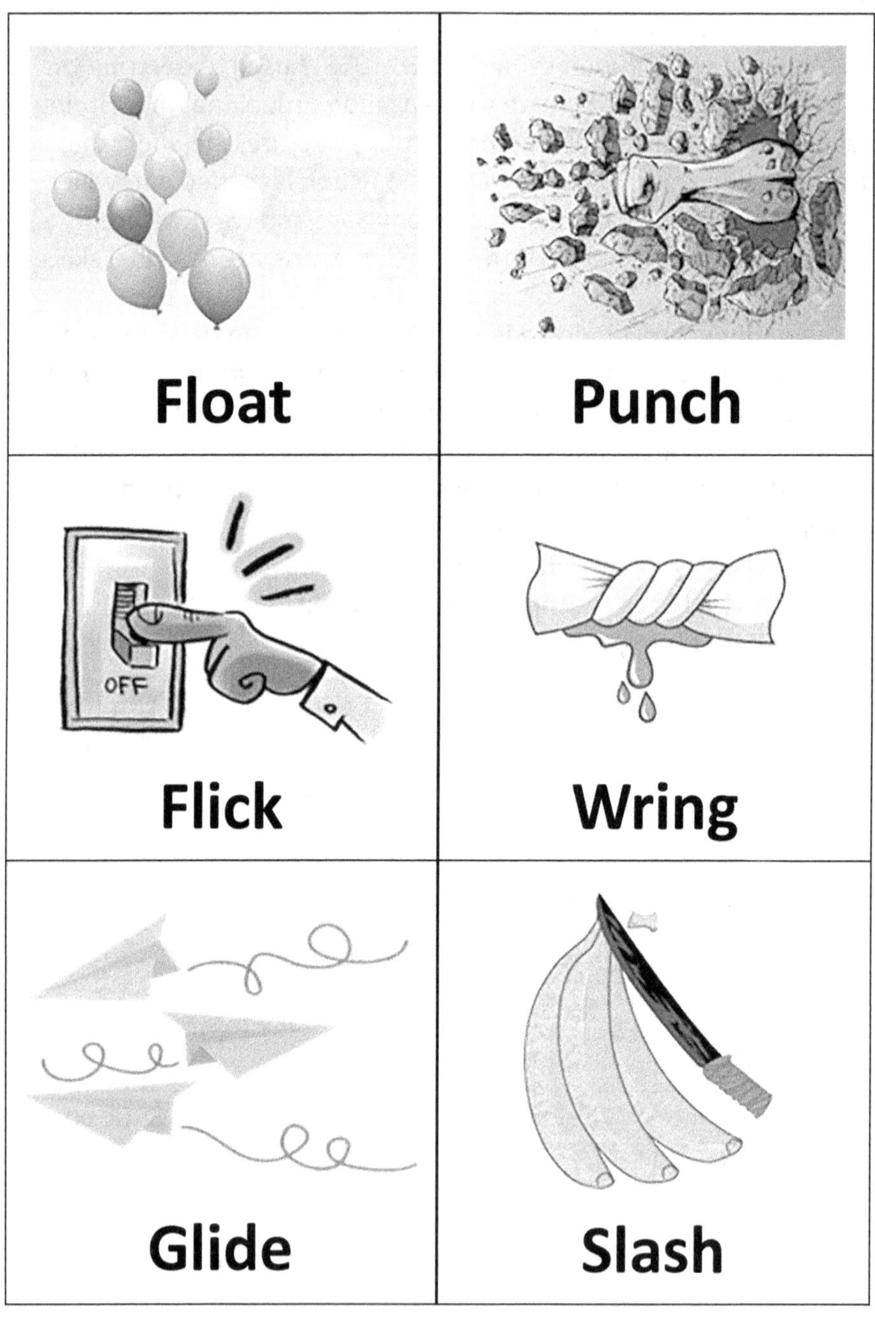

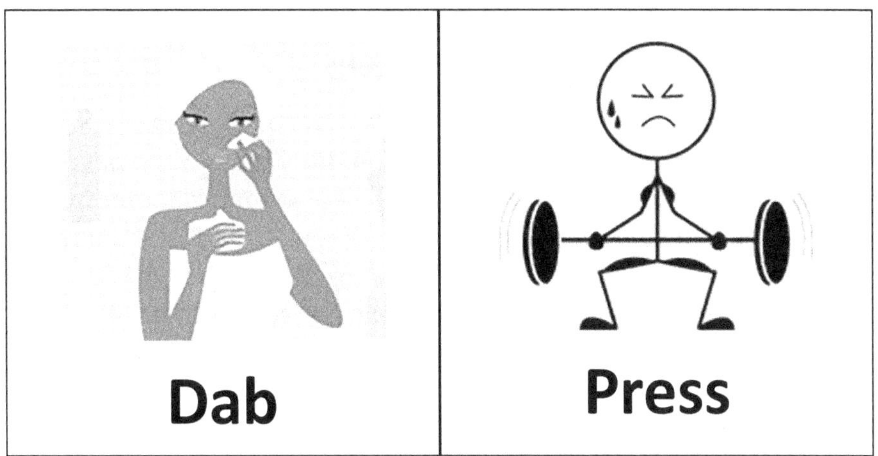
Dab
Press

Appendix D

World Dances

This section is long, but only the size of a grain of sand on the Sahara that is the universe of dance from around our world. In the pages that follow, sixty-seven dances are listed in alphabetical order by name of the dance or dance style, which I have used successfully with elementary students. Also included are the following: the country or region of origin, the grade level range for which I think it is appropriate, the music used, the dance skills needed, a brief story or background of the dance, and the basic choreography. Some also include nontraditional variations for creative exploration.

Quite honestly, teaching world dances is one of my favorite aspects of *dance arts* to share with kids. They always seem to enjoy the dances because (1) there is usually an interesting story or purpose to them, which make them accessible to untrained dancers, and (2) whether they like it or not, they are learning a lot about different people around the world, even though they just think they are doing a fun dance!

It is helpful to have access to a world map to show the students both where they are and from where the dance they are learning originates. Below is an example of a map that would serve that purpose, as long as it is large enough for everyone to see. With middle to upper elementary grades, I often ask if they know where the country or region of the dance they are learning is located on the map. Then I have volunteers come up and point to where they think it is. Sometimes it takes several students trying before someone actually finds the correct location, but it is a fun "process of elimination" group activity that can be done fairly quickly, expanding the activity into a geography lesson!

Enjoy the journey. Ciao, bellas!

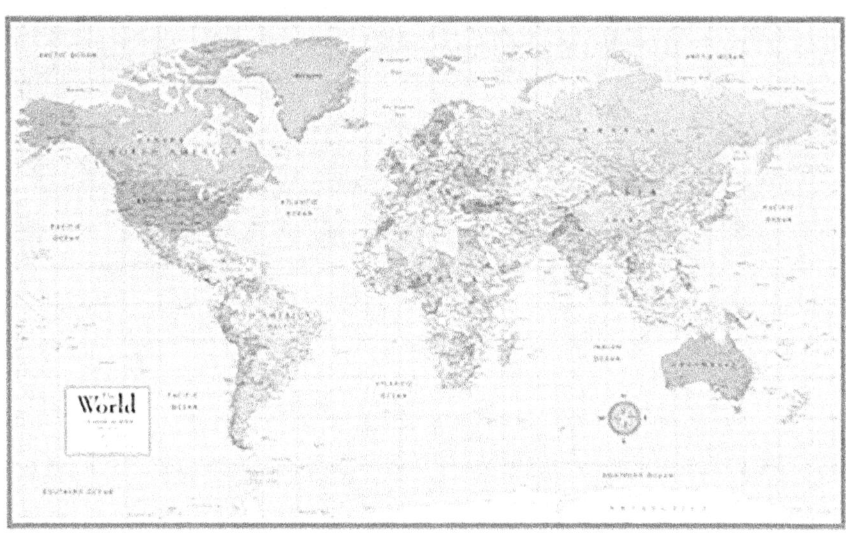
The World

Contents of This Appendix

1. ADZE-EE – Ghana
Second to Third Grade
Music: none
Skills needed: tense and relaxed force, playing a character, chanting

This is a changing-partner dance and/or a game of elimination. Generally, children feel lazy waking up from sweet sleep. They sometimes pretend to have body aches and act out being in pain. Adze-ee is one of many short musicodramatic wake-up activities parents and adults use in getting children ready for a task. Vocalizations in the chant imitate or should express feelings of pain, drowsiness, and complaining. Parents and adults sing this chant to encourage children to dramatize their feelings and "unwillingness," and by so doing, they are energized and motivated for the task ahead. On their own, children use this as a game as they tease one another and play roles as adults or parents.

Adze-ee (pronounced *Ah-jay*) translates to "ouch." The second word is *Adze-oh* (pronounced *Ah-joh*) and is a variation on the same word.

All dancers play both parts. The chant and movements go as follows:
Child: "Adze-ee!" Facing partner, do a little hop and extend heel out to R side with arms opening, R out and down and L out and up (RELAXED), **"Adze-oh!"** Repeat to L side, **"Adze-ee!"** Repeat to R side
Parent: "Shoo shoo shoo!" Quickly run in place and shake both fists forward (TENSE)
Repeat all above.

Parent: (nonvocal) Three quick claps, three quick stomps (TENSE)
Child: "Hey!" Jump a little bit backward, with arms stretching out and up (RELAXED)
In three quick beats, run to find a new partner as fast as possible.

If they do not find a partner in time to start the chant again, they are out and must kneel down where they are. Repeat the chant with the movements and find a new partner each time. Those who are "out" can move around on the floor to interfere with the dancers who are still in, and when there is only one pair or two pairs left or when the participants are tired of it, the dance could end. This could be done in concentric circles, and either the inside or outside circle moves to change partners without elimination.

2. ALUNELUL – Romania
Third to Sixth Grade

Music: Gemini (Sandor and Laszlo Slomovits), "Alunelul"
Skills needed: rhythm patterns, counting, weight shift, force,
connected formations, unison timing

This is a dance performed in rural areas to celebrate the harvest and crushing of the hazelnut. *Alunelul* means "little hazelnut." It is very lively and energetic and involves changing direction right and left and shifting weight quickly. The body is held upright, and the foot stomps are on the heel and are very forceful, as cracking the hard shell of a hazelnut. The pattern is a repeating structure as follows:

Five counts + two stomps – four times
Three counts + one stomp – four times
One count + one stomp – two times, one count + two stomps – one time
Repeat one-count pattern.

The movements are sideward leaps, cross steps, and stomps in place, changing directions with each repetition.

Fives to R: Leap - cross - leap - cross - leap - stomp-stomp (with heel)
Repeat to L
Repeat to R
Repeat to L

Threes to R: Leap - cross - leap - stomp
Repeat to L
Repeat to R
Repeat to L

**Ones starting R: Leap - stomp, leap - stomp, leap - stomp-stomp
Alternate L - R - L - R - L - R**

The upper bodies of dancers should be either holding hands or with the arms around the shoulders, touching the elbows. This can be danced in straight lines or circles.

Nontraditional variation: Replace the two movements (leap and stomp) with any other two movements and attempt to make the pattern work with quicker and quicker direction changes. OR think of different crops we grow and harvest and create movements expressing what that might look like.

3. APPALACHIAN BIG CIRCLE DANCE – Colonial USA
Kindergarten to Sixth Grade
Music: Marian Rose, "Barn Dance"
Skills needed: formations, partnering, call-response

This is a social dance from the Appalachian Mountain region of the United States. It originated from English country dances but changed to fit the eighteenth- to nineteenth-century rural lifestyle of the region. Certain steps and movements have names describing everyday activities. It can be performed with partners or without. If dancing with partners, stand next to the partner in the circle at the beginning of the dance. If not doing the partner section, practice moving from a large circle to smaller circles ahead of time.

One person with a clear voice is the designated "caller," who cues the dancers for each section of the dance as labeled below. Dancers begin in one large circle, holding hands. (Choose from the movements below to fit the grade level.)

Large circle section:
- *"Circle to the Left and Right."* All holding hands, walk, skip, or slide sixteen counts to L and to R, alternating with the following:
- *"Into the Middle and Back."* Four counts moving inward, four counts back out, repeat.
- *"Wind Up the Yarn."* Circle breaks at one point, and "leader" leads everyone in a spiral pathway into the center of the circle. At center, leader turns and leads back out of the spiral as all follow and form one large circle again.
- *"Eye of the Needle."** Last two people in circle form a bridge. Leader goes under, followed by remainder of circle, one by one, still holding hands. Then all form one large circle again.

Small circle section:
- *"Circle Left and Right."* Walk, skip, or slide eight counts in one direction, then eight counts to other direction.
- *Three-Person "Dive for the Oyster, Dive for the Pearl."* One person ducks under hands of other two, then backs out again. Each person in circle takes a turn. All step into middle and back for fourth phrase of music. Repeat with "diver" dropping one person's hand and going behind other person, causing them to turn under their own arm.
- *Four-Person "Dive for the Oyster, Dive for the Pearl."* One couple ducks under another couple's hands, then backs out again. Other couple repeats. First couple ducks under again and drops partner's hand and splits, forcing other couple to turn under their own arms. Re-form circle, and other couple repeats.
- *"Birdie in a Cage / Birdie Fly Away."* One person goes to center of circle and turns one direction as circle skips or walks the other direction. Circle stops. Then center person quickly ducks out, turns, and rejoins circle in eight counts. Repeat with another person in the center.
- *"Form a Star."* All place R hand into center, with palms touching. All walk forward for eight counts, change hands, and repeat to L for eight counts

Partner section:
- *"Promenade."* Couples hold each other's L and R hands and walk side by side around in one large circle.
- *"Wring Out the Dishrag."* From promenade hand position, lift joined hands. Then outside person walks around partner, continually facing them; turns around self; and ends up in original place in eight counts. Repeat with inside partner moving.
- *"Queen's/King's Highway."* Outside partners turn and move clockwise, and inside partners move counterclockwise around circle until they meet each other again.

- *"Weaving."* Facing partner, take R hands and pass each other. Then extend L hand to next person and pass each other. Continue until returning to original partner.
- *"London Bridge."** Lead couple forms a bridge, and each pair in circle ducks under and adds on, forming a large bridge across the center of the circle. When all have gone, lead couple goes under as well. In two parallel lines, all take hands with persons next to them rather than their partner, then open up into one large circle again for the ending. Only two couples will still be next to their partner in the circle.

Ending section:
Form one large circle again.

- *"Circle Left and Right."* Walk, skip, or slide sixteen counts in one direction, then sixteen counts to the other direction.
- *"Into the Middle and Back."* Four counts moving inward, four counts back out, repeat.
- *"End and Bow."* Dancers drop hands as music ends, spin, and bow as follows: Men drop to one knee with arms lifted. Women place hands out to sides, as if lifting a full skirt, and "curtsy" by bending legs with one toe behind the other foot.

* *Eye of the Needle* and *London Bridge* are the same: one is for a single line, and the other is for partners. It is not necessary to do both.

4. ARIRANG – Korea
Pre-K to Second Grade
Music: Sally's Music Circle, "Arirang"
Skills needed: tempo, timing, objects, formations, emotions

This song and dance is about six hundred years old and originates from the mountain villages of Korea. It is about experiencing and overcoming hard times and transforming despair into hope, and it is helpful in self-consoling. The Korean people were once occupied by Japan before there were two Koreas, which was a very difficult time in their history. Since that time, this song has become almost a Korean national anthem.

The words to the song are translated as follows:
> *You are going over Arirang hill. My love, you are leaving me.*
> *Your feet will tire before you go ten miles.*
> *Just as there are many stars in the clear sky, there are also many dreams in our hearts.*
> *There, over there, the mountain where even in the middle of wintry days, flowers bloom.*

As the music begins, the dancers are seated on the floor with their feet tucked under their bottom with their knees together, pantomiming working with their hands in the fields, such as cutting, gathering, and placing harvest in baskets. Each dancer has two small fans, and they are placed on the floor, one next to each knee, flat side in toward knee. Movements are slow, and the music is in 3/4 (triplet) time.

Sixteen triplets:
- Working movements, eight triplets
- Lift fan on R side high and fan self with it, looking up, two triplets
- Lift fan on L side and repeat, moving fan in R hand behind back, two triplets
- Stand by placing one foot flat, then the other and bow with fans behind back, four triplets

Pause in the music.

With voice:
- **Stretches.** Stretch R fan up as knees bend, straighten, and switch fans. Repeat four times.
- **Rainbow.** Bring both fans, slightly separated, from R to L in an arc, two triplets
- **Circle around self.** With corner of L fan touching chest and pointing forward with R fan flat behind back, make small quick running steps in a clockwise circle around self, two triplets
- **Burst.** Stop and face front. Cross fans in front of legs and open them overhead, twisting them as they open at sides, two triplets
- **Follow the leader.** In groups of five to six people with a designated leader, place fans in same position as for "circle around self," and all follow leader into one circle.

Pause in the music – circles re-form into lines with quick steps.

- **Dragon.** Fans are held horizontal in front of chest. Person on far R side of each line leads. All follow, moving fans in a wave motion up and down, with timing just a bit off to make it look like a serpent. Repeat two to four times, four triplets
- **Stretches.** Same as above, but with every other person taking small steps forward and back to stagger the line, four triplets
- **Rainbow.** Repeat above, two triplets
- **Circle around self.** Repeat above, two triplets
- **Rainbow.** Repeat above, two triplets
- **Burst.** Repeat above, two triplets, and finish with fans crossed in front of chest, fluttering

There is no bow at the end. Rather, the head is held high to express hopefulness.

5. BAHAY KUBO – Philippines
Second to Fourth Grade
Music: Bulilit Singers, "Bahay Kubo"
Skills needed: triplet step, objects, partners, formations, directions

Known as the "Philippine medicinal plant song," Bahay Kubo expresses the gratitude of the Filipino people who are able to live off the vegetation growing around their homes. The lyrics list many vegetables in the native language of the Philippines (Tagalog), and the title translates to "small cube-shaped house." The movements of the dance represent carrying baskets of food to market and sharing it with family and friends.

The song is in a 3/4 time signature as are many songs from the Philippines, and the movements follow that pattern. Dancers enter from the side in lines of four to six, with boys and girls alternating places in line. The girls carry baskets of vegetables on one hip, and the boys wear straw hats with their hands on their hips. The dance is in four parts, each consisting of a total of sixteen phrases of three quick beats.

Part 1: Heels-up step. In three beats, step together with heels up. Repeat sixteen times while traveling across stage and turning as needed to avoid exiting on other side. Finish in lines stretching across stage – **sixteen**

Part 2: Lunge stretches. Slide R foot out to forward R diagonal and lift basket or hat high in same direction. Repeat to L. Repeat to R. Then spin in place – **eight**. Girls place basket on the floor. Boys place hat back on head and, with a partner, circle a basket with the above **heels-up step – eight**

Part 3: Cross brushes. With hands on hips, face front, standing next to partner (and behind basket on the floor). Step on L foot and brush R foot across L leg, lifting knee. Repeat on R foot. Repeat six more times – **eight**. Travel to L with same step, but take two sideways steps between brushes three times. Then stop. Repeat to R three times. Then stop – **eight**

Part 4: Square step. Partners stand with R shoulders together, facing opposite directions. Then both do the **heels-up step** forward four times to R, passing each other sideways four times, backward four times, and to L four times, ending up next to partner again, but with L shoulders together.

Ending: Girl picks up basket, spins, and stretches it toward boy, who takes off hat, puts it over his heart, and touches basket with his other hand. They exit the space as they entered, alternating girl-boy, with either a traveling triplet step or step-together-pause.

6. BALLET – France
First to Sixth Grade
Music: various musical selections by Michael Wall or classical piano
Skills needed: ballet technique and terminology, formations,
traveling/in-place, elevation

Ballet originated in France in the courts of King Louis XIV. The king's preference for the look of turned-out legs and high carriage of the upper body and arms was the beginning of this style of dance, which has grown and evolved and is still very popular and well known all over the world. Ballet exercises and technique are the basis of any professional dance training program.

Ballet terminology is in French, and names of movements describe what the movements do or what they look like. Methods of ballet training have developed in Russia and Italy as well as France. Basic ballet classes have a sequence of exercises and movement practice as follows:

Barre:
- Plié (leg bends)
- Tendu (leg and foot stretches)
- Port de bras (placement of the arms)
- Rond de jambe (circles of the legs)
- Battement (high kicks)

Center:
- Adagio combination (stretching and balancing movements performed slowly)
- Petit allegro combination (quick jumps)
- Grand allegro combination (large and fast movements)
- Reverence (cooldown and bows)

Tchaikovsky's *The Nutcracker Suite*, like many classical music works, is divided into short sections that work well with ballet choreography for children. Below are some examples of movements that students can learn and perform by grade level:

- **Russian** (first grade), turnout, jeté, tour, sauté, battement, glissade, grand/petit allegro, grand plié
- **March** (second grade), tendu, rond de jambe, jeté, glissade, arabesque, tour, dégagé, chassé
- **Chinese** (third grade), tour, sauté, arabesque, bourrée, battement, jeté, châiné turns
- **Reed Pipes** (fourth grade), tour, sauté (hop or jump), changement, sous-sous, jeté
- **Spanish** (fifth grade), tour, port de bras, sauté (step-hop), jeté, tour jeté
- **Coda** (sixth grade), jeté, glissade, arabesque, tour jeté, châiné turns, sauté arabesque, pirouette

7. BELE KAWE – Western Africa / Caribbean
Pre-K to Fourth Grade
Music: Gemini Sandor and Laszlo Slomovits, *Rhythmically Moving*, vol. 3, "Bele Kawe"
Skills needed: emotions, formations, directions

This dance is about two girls who might have their eyes on the same boy, and no one ever knows who is watching whom. The movements are shy at first, as if sneaking around to see what's going on. Then their bodies become more upright, indicating that they realize what is going on, and finally become big and protective to scare the rival away.

The dance is done in two concentric circles with the boys on the inside, facing out, and the girls on the outside, facing in. In the first part, the dancers all move forward and pass each other. Then they move backward, pass each other again, and return to their places. Then both circles move to the R - L - R - L, traveling in opposite directions. The music cycles five ties, plus eight additional beats at the end.

Part 1: Moving forward and passing each other
Sixteen beats - Girls have hands down, lifting their "skirts." Boys have hands behind back, with palms away from back. All are leaning forward slightly and have knees bent. Then take very small steps or step-together-steps forward eight times, looking around at each other (interested).

Part 2: Moving backward and passing each other
Sixteen beats - All take quick alternating steps back with front heel touching in front. Push both hands away from chest, with palms facing forward and elbows bent and lifted. Upper body twists side to

side with steps eight times, moving backward back to original places (surprised).

Part 3: Three-step spins
Sixteen beats - With legs wide, knees bent, and arms out to sides and with elbows slightly bent and palms out to sides, do a three-step turn to R (circles travel opposite each other). Then all either clap on fourth beat, lift onto one foot with both arms reaching up to that side, and say "Hah!" or stop and shimmy shoulders (or alternate these) (angry).

Finish with all facing into center with feet apart, knees bent, and hands on knees on final beat.

For younger students: Form one circle, facing inward, in boy-girl order. Put parts 1 and 2 above together. Girls and boys take turns moving into and out of center of common circle. For part 3, all travel together around circle with three steps and clap hands above head and kick one leg to side, alternating inside and outside legs. **OR** circles slide to sides without turning and clap above head and kick, changing direction.

Nontraditional variation: Group generates examples of things that make them feel interested, surprised, and angry. Then create movements that travel forward, backward, and sideways.

8. BHANGRA – India
Fifth to Sixth Grade
Music: Prem Joshua, "Saki"
Skills needed: formations, levels, directions, rhythm, energy, timing

Movements represent hard work in planting and harvesting crops. This dance is traditionally performed by men only. Emphasis is on percussive energy and upper body strength.

Dancers can begin onstage in one or more lines, facing forward. They are behind one another with the arms waving in various shapes and levels, resembling a being with multiple arms.

On cue in the music, dancers disperse from the line to travel across from side to side in lines moving in opposite directions with **seed-throwing** movements (body bent forward, knees bent, walk with beat, one hand gnarled behind back, other hand lightly flicking wrist as if tossing seeds) and **earth-packing** movements (upright with bent knees; walk with beat, alternating high and low steps; hands horizontal at sides with shoulders bouncing). All move in lines as if moving up and down rows of crops. When all lines reach the side, turn around and travel back doing the other movement.

On strong downbeat in the music, all face front with the hands on the knees into a wide second position, with the arms bent and out at sides and the palms facing up. Perform slow slides with shoulders shrugging, as if **carrying** a heavy load. Move into concentric circles.

With the outside circle first, do slow **scoop** movements into the center, low to high, with a **head jiggle**. Then the inside circle follows. Then the outer circle reverses to face out, then the inner circle, without head jiggle.

Pivot-spin backward. Get into a wide second position with **earth-patting** hands, shoulders shrugging. Change direction and repeat.

With one hand behind head and the other out and up and the shoulders shrugged, in **slow walks**, circles move in opposite directions. Arms swing down to change direction. Exit to sides with same walk.

Three-part section: (All follow the change in the music.)
- **Damakas** (sharp **digging** movements), alternating with **water sprinkles** (toe touches to side, arms to side in over-the-top curve). Either back and forth or quarter turns to four directions.
- **Windmill**, traveling spins with arms circling vertically. Lines cross one another.
- **Grapevine**, step side, cross in front, twisting upper body away from front foot, and repeat crossing behind. Then stomp front, stomp side, stomp back. Then jump and switch feet. Repeat four times.

End by bringing back previous movements, then crossing the stage in groups. All place arms above head in an X shape. Arms circle face, maintaining X shape, then turn inside out by raising elbows and lowering and extending hands forward, keeping them crossed with backs of hands together. Then bring both hands to chin, with palms facing up and elbows out to sides at ear level. Lower body and twist with knees slightly bent as the music fades.

Nontraditional variation: Identify the main industry in the local community. Create six to seven movements that represent those activities and replace the movements above.

9. BOBOOBO – Ghana
Fifth to Sixth Grade
Music: *Ghana: Rhythms of the People*, "Boboobo"
Skills needed: pathways, formations, objects

Boboobo is the most popular social music and dance of the central and northern Ewe of Ghana and Togo. It emerged from Kpando, a town in the Volta Region of Ghana during the independence struggle between 1947 and 1957; and it has expanded to all Ewe-speaking territories in Ghana, Togo, and Benin. Boboobo is derived from an older circular dance called Konkoma. White handkerchiefs held in each hand by the dancers symbolize victory, freedom (from colonial rule and domination), joy, and happiness. Among Ewes and many ethnic groups in the region, the color white symbolizes success, victory, joy, peace, and happiness.

The dance travels in a counterclockwise circle after dancers enter in straight lines.

Movement 1, eight beats: *Double step* forward on R with body low and R arm curved down (1–2). Repeat L (3–4). Repeat R (5–6). Jump slightly backward, throwing arms up two times (7–8). Use this movement as entrance in slow beginning of music. Two lines of dancers enter from opposite diagonals, along a straight pathway. They pass each other and form two circles. At change in music, all jump wide, arms out to sides. Run in place four beats into next movement, facing R, then turning to L, then back to front.

Movement 2, four beats: With one hand on hip, ***pivot*** on same foot as other foot touches three times with arm extended and chest pumping in and out. Step together on fourth beat and repeat changing sides. All move around in circles until drum break, then go into scattered formation. Do movement eight times. Then spin with both hands up (twelve counts in music).

Movement 3, two beats repeating: *Hand roll* quickly. With body forward, heel touches in front with leg straight and other leg bent. Head turns away from heel. Switch on every beat, with hands rolling continuously. Then move into small circles. Continue hand rolling and lower slowly down to knees, with toes tucked under, sitting on heels. Quickly roll two handkerchiefs like a vertical helicopter blade, swaying with beat side to side. Shoulders shimmy. Lean back, with handkerchiefs rising, still spinning fast. Come up to one knee, then to a standing position into next movement.

Movement 4, four beats: Step forward on R. Arms *cross swing* in front of body. Step on L, arms open. Step back on R. Arms swing in opposition (L front, R back). Step on L. Arms swing again (R front, L back). Travel around and through each other in short lines out of small circles and into parallel lines.

Ending: Do L-R fan jumps. Then with legs in bent wide second position, lift body with elbows bent and palms forward on last beat of music. Or exit with 4 as music fades.

Nontraditional variation: Brainstorm ideas of things we are proud of and wish to celebrate. Then create movements expressing those things.

10. BOLLYWOOD – India
Fourth to Sixth Grade

Music: Jazzy B, "Bhangra" or Labh Janjua & Panjabi MC,
"Mundian To Bach Ke"
Skills needed: Sequence construction, timing, enter/exit, formations

Bollywood dance originates from India's thriving film industry, which began in the late twentieth century. The name is a combination of Hollywood and the letter *B*, from the city of Bombay (now known as Mumbai). This type of show dance is used in big production numbers in many Indian films. It is performed by both men and women.

1. **Shoulder bounce.** Quickly bounce shoulders. Step with flat feet and knees bent on a slower beat in music. Slowly raise arms to sides until above shoulders in a V shape. Slowly lower again. Movement can travel or stay in place.

2. **Limp step with *come here* and *light bulbs*.** Travel to side, lifting one knee and placing it down again with a strong downward accent, repeating on the same side. *Come here* is a sharp bend in both elbows, reaching across body and down, pulling hands toward face. To do *light bulbs*, place one arm across chest and the other out to side with elbow bent, hands twisting, as if screwing in light bulbs.

3. **Y-spin.** Cross one foot in front of the other to begin rapid spin. Arms come in, up, then out into Y position. Stop by wrapping arms around waist. Then repeat to the other direction.

4. **Four-point turn.** Step to side with R foot, hip, and both hands sliding parallel to the floor. Push off and rotate body quarter

turn to L, bringing hands in. Repeat four times until facing front again. Repeat with R foot and turning to L.

5. **Slides with head shift.** With legs apart, bend both knees and place hands on knees. Slide to R twice. Quickly lift body, and arms frame head with elbows bent. Head shifts side to side as following foot drags in to meet other foot, and both are straight. Repeat four times, alternating sides.

6. **Motorcycle.** Scoot with legs wide apart, slightly leaning back. Place arms in front at a diagonal, with wrists twisting, as if revving a motorcycle throttle.

7. **Twist-cross steps.** With upper body facing forward and lower body twisted to the L, quickly step-cross on R foot with L crossing behind. Arms are straight and extended in front, moving together opposite the upper body twist. Take several quick steps forward. Then turn 180 degrees and travel forward toward the back with L foot stepping and R foot crossing.

Dancers can choose a sequence of the above movements to create a phrase, take turns entering and performing each movement, or perform them in a sequence as a line dance that changes directions or in and out of circles or crossing parallel lines.

11. BRIDGE OF ATHLONE – Ireland
Fourth to Sixth Grade
Music: The Chieftains, "Ferny Hill"
Skills needed: formations, spatial relationships, emotions

The dance mainly stays in two lines (men's and women's), facing each other and holding hands at sides. The purpose of the dance is for boys and girls to first meet each other. Next, they pass by each other as if they aren't interested, then take a stroll to get to know each other, and finally decide they don't like each other and try to get away by hiding under the bridge.

The dancers carry their bodies straight and lifted and begin in lines opposite each other, holding hands loosely at sides.

Meet: R foot lifts and crosses in front of L knee. Then kick, stomp R - L - R, repeat L. Travel forward to meet the other line with short step-together-steps, alternating sides. Repeat cross-kick step in place, facing partner in opposite line. Then do same step-together-steps backward back to lines.

Pass: Same traveling step as above (without kick step first). Instead of stopping and moving backward, hands discreetly drop. Then lines pass through each other and continue to opposite side, where they turn and take hands again to repeat whole sequence above. All end up where they started.

Stroll: "Top" couple holds inside hands, then dances down the aisle between the lines with same traveling step as above. Both spin under held hands, switch hands, and repeat, moving back up to the top spot. Then "cast off," leading their lines to the "bottom" of the aisle.

Bridge: Top couple touches palms together to form the bridge, and the remaining couples pass under, hand in hand. First couple through moves up to the top position and starts the bridge at that end. All couples follow and complete the bridge between the two ends. Of the couple that started the bridge at the bottom spot, man travels down the length of line outside the bridge while woman passes under bridge. Then repeat with woman on outside and man under the bridge. As they are crossing the bridge the second time, the other couples spin under both hands as the couple passes, separating and moving backward to form two lines again. Now there is a new top couple.

Repeat all until all couples have been the top couple. Music fits only two full cycles of the dance. Start over as needed to allow all couples to be top couple.

12. CAIMARUSA – Colombia
Pre-K to First Grade
Music: Marian Rose, "Caimarusa"
Skills needed: directions, formations

The story goes that Caimarusa was a young girl who left her village in Colombia. When she returned, the villagers were so happy to see her that they had a party for her and did this dance to show her how much they missed her, with each person dancing their own individual welcome to her. Surprisingly, the figure of this dance is common in the Anglo and European traditions, and it is not known how it reached South America. Maybe Caimarusa, in her travels, learned this form of dance and brought it back to the village.

Dancers form two straight lines of no more than six people on each side, facing each other, with partners opposite.

Vocal part, sixteen beats:
"Top" couple dances any way they like down the center of two lines. Taking hands is optional. This is where dancers can show off and be individual, or pairs can set movements they do together.

La-la-las, thirty-two beats:
Same couple forms a bridge at bottom of two lines, and the couple now at the top of the lines cast off and circle around to go under the bridge and return to where they started.

New top couple repeats above during the next vocal part, and other dancers repeat the casting off to re-form the lines.

Music cycles through six times.

Nontraditional variation: Brainstorm ideas of where the student might go if they were to travel away from home and what they would bring back with them. Create movements that represent those ideas and perform them within the same formations and framework as above instead of any movement coming down between the two lines.

13. CANOE DANCE – Native American, Sappony
First to Third Grade

Music: Sanna Longden, *Dances of the 7 Continents*, no. 1,
"Canoe Dance"
Skills needed: zigzag pathway, spatial relationships

The Sappony people lived in the area now known as Virginia and North Carolina. The tribe disappeared from historic record in the late 1700s, but other groups have claimed ancestry to them and have preserved this dance. The tribe inhabited the East Coast near the ocean and also traveled on rivers by canoe. This dance is likely a way to help children learn how to safely travel in a canoe, which involves moving together from side to side, staying in line, and not crashing into other canoes.

In a line of about four to six people with the front person being the one who "steers," groups travel in a zigzag, changing directions, passing other canoes, and turning.

Dancers are touching both elbows of the person in front of them.
- **Powwow step** (step-touch) three times to same side. Stop moving forward on a diagonal. All elbows move out to same side on step. Repeat to other side and keep going, changing sides eight times.
- **Change places** when "canoe" pauses. Front person crouches down into a very small ball as next person in line assumes the front. Then all step forward together over the crouching person until the line has passed over. That person now stands and is in the back.

Repeat the sequence as many times as there are dancers in each "canoe" so everyone gets a chance to be in front. Start the song over if needed.

14. CHE CHE KULE – Ghana
Pre-K to First Grade
Music: Iya & the Kuumba Kids, "Kye, Kye Koolay"
Skills needed: body parts, call-response, tempo

This song and dance originates from the Ghanaian Fanti tribe and is commonly learned by schoolchildren. The words "rhyme" in how parts of the previous line are carried to the next line in the song.

It is a **call-response** dance, where one person is the designated leader and does their own movement and then the group repeats it. Leaders can do their own version of either touching or moving the following body parts with the lines of the song as follows:

Che Che Kule
(Head)

Che Che Kofi Sa
(Shoulders)

Kofi Sa Langa
(Hips)

Kaka Shi Langa
(Knees)

Kum Aden Nde, Kum Aden Nde, Kum Aden Nde, Hey!
(Feet)

The music cycles through the song three times, getting a little faster each time. Choose five leaders, one for each body part, before beginning. Then each leader creates a movement done with their body part. Play the whole song for each set of leaders and repeat the song as many times as necessary to give each dancer a chance to be a leader.

Nontraditional variation: Discuss other topics besides body parts, for which five subcategories can be listed. Create movements for each and perform within the same structure as above.

15. CHICKEN DANCE – Switzerland
Pre-K to Second Grade
Music: choose from the many versions of "Chicken Dance" that exist
Skills needed: body parts/whole, in-place/traveling, animal movements

This dance originated in the '50s and was created by a Swiss accordion player. It was first called the Bird Dance. But when asked to perform it in costume, only a chicken suit could be found at the time—and it was known as the Chicken Dance since then. It is a fun dance at parties because no matter how great of a dancer you are, everyone looks silly doing this dance.

Three gestures imitate movements of birds/chicken, followed by four quick claps. Usually in the slower part of the music, partners link elbows and circle around each other, skipping.

Basic movements on quicker part of music:
- Hands "bite" four times, imitating bird's beaks
- Elbows "flap" four times like wings
- Bottom shakes like tail feathers
- Clap four times

Repeat sequence four times.

Options for slower part of music:
1. Partners link elbows or join hands and circle around each other (traditional)
   OR
2. Travel around space, imitating either bird or chicken, walking or flying movements

Nontraditional variation: Choose other animals and create movements they would do. Use the pattern of three different quick body part movements, with four quick claps repeated four times, then a slower traveling movement that shows how the selected animal moves through space with their whole body. This variation does not require partnering.

16. CHINESE FRIENDSHIP DANCE – China
First to Second Grade

Music: Henry "Buzz" Glass, *Dances around the World* (LP), "Chinese Friendship Dance"
Skills needed: focus, spatial relationships, partnering

This is a dance that shows many fun things that friends can do together. It can either be a one-partner dance or a changing-partner dance with every chorus. Start with partners about four steps away, facing each other, scattered around in the space.

Play piano intro for eight beats.
Chorus (on three beats of sticks tapping): Look for a friend
- Hold R hand horizontally over eyes as if looking off in the distance, twisting torso and holding L hand behind back. Switch hands and repeat, finally focusing on partner.
- Make four walking steps to partner, leaning back with a slow heel-ball-toe steps.

Trick section 1 (on triangle ding): Skip AROUND with elbows linked
- With R elbows linked, L arm bends at elbows with fingers toward head in an angular shape.
- Repeat with L elbows linked, changing directions.
- Wave goodbye with one tap of sticks with a sweeping arm movement with both arms (like a windshield wiper) and walk backward away from partner.

Repeat **chorus** section on the sound of the three rhythm sticks, either with same partner or searching for a new one.

Trick section 2 (on triangle ding): Jump NEXT TO each other
- Facing partner, both jump forward on a diagonal so that R shoulders are next to each other, with arms in a V position. Jump diagonally backward so they are face-to-face again,

with arms changing to a W position. Repeat four times, alternating sides on forward jumps.
- Wave goodbye with one beat of sticks and walk backward.

Repeat **chorus** section on the sound of the three rhythm sticks.

Trick section 3 (on triangle ding): Lunge AWAY and TOGETHER
- Hold R hands with partner while standing face-to-face like during a handshake. Then both step out to the L side, stretching L arm out straight and focus beyond fingers.
- Pull back to center to face partner, bringing feet together, and change hands. Repeat four times.
- Wave goodbye with one beat of sticks and walk backward.

Repeat **chorus** section on the sound of the three rhythm sticks.

Trick section 4 (on triangle ding): Umbrella OVER/UNDER
- One bends down and stretches both hands toward partner's legs and the other curves body and arms over like an umbrella protecting their friend from the rain. Then switch places four times.
- Wave goodbye with one beat of sticks and walk backward.

Bow to partner with palms together at end of music.

Nontraditional variation: Discuss and list things the students like to do with their friends. Create movements representing those ideas, making sure there is a spatial relationship between the two friends where they rely on each other.

17. CUMBIA – Colombia
Fourth to Sixth Grade
Music: Unknown artist, "La Pollera Colorda"
Skills needed: rhythm, partnering

Cumbia is a music genre popular throughout Latin America. It originated along Colombia's Caribbean coast and in Panama, creating a musical and cultural fusion that includes native Colombians and Panamanians, in addition to the influence of the African slaves brought over during colonial times.

It began as a courtship dance practiced among the African population and mixed with European and African instruments and musical styles.

The dance can be done alone or with a partner. There is a quick four-beat musical pattern.

If dancing alone, begin with feet together, arms relaxed at sides, and elbows slightly bent.
- **Step back** with R foot. **Step in place** with L foot. **Step back together** with R. **Pause** and slightly pivot body direction to L on fourth beat. Repeat pattern to L side and continue alternating. Arms are held relaxed at sides with elbows bent, and hands move inward in rotating circles three times. Then pause with pause in steps, then continue. Same hand as foot moves.

If dancing with a partner, begin face-to-face with feet together, holding both hands with elbows relaxed and slightly bent.
- **Step back** on opposite feet opening to same side with one hand held side by side, then back to facing each other. Then open to other side, changing held h ands and only holding one hand at a time. Could also slip hand behind partner's back when side by side or alternate with holding hand and placing hand behind back.

18. D'HAMMERSCHMIEDSGSELLN –
Germany
(duh-ham-mair-shmeets-guh-sehln)
Third to Fifth Grade
Music: Christy Lane, "D'Hammerschmiedsgselln"
Skills needed: timing, rhythm, levels, force

The name of the dance translates to "professional blacksmith" and is traditionally performed only by men in Bavaria, so the hand slapping might be very forceful. It is a form of *schuhplattle* dance, part of a dance tradition where men beat rhythms by slapping thighs, shoe soles, and hands (similar to gumboot dance from South Africa). *Plattle* means slapping in German.

In pairs, then in groups of four standing in a circle, partners face each other. The music is a very quick, in a 3/4 time signature, and the slapping movements are very fast. The music cycles through three times from the beginning to end of the song. Part A remains the same; and parts B, C, and D can change.

Part A: *Plattle.* Six-count pattern that repeats eight times. Each movement below takes one beat.
- Clap both hands on your own thighs.
- Clap both hands on your own stomach.
- Clap both hands together.
- Clap your partner's R hand with yours.
- Clap your partner's L hand with yours.
- Clap both of your partner's hands with both of yours.

On the last two counts, all stop their movements and assume positions for part B.

Part B: Single pairs. Hold both hands twisted across chest. Slowly gallop. Change direction and join another pair at end of musical phrase.

Repeat Part A. Variation on Part A: Joining another pair, all facing inward, do the *plattle* movements in canon to avoid hitting hands with the other pair. Or both pairs do them in unison, but change levels each time from middle to high.

Part C: Two pairs together. After doing *plattle* in **canon timing**, all four hold hands or shoulders in a circle and slowly step-hop (skip), lifting knee in **unison**, then change direction.

Repeat Part A.

Part D: Same two pairs together place R hands into center. Then either place them on top of each other or hold wrists in a square shape and do a quick triplet step or slow step-together, then change direction. Girls place outside hand on hip and boys as if holding suspenders with elbow up.

Finish with feet together and hands held and lifted in the circle on last beat of music.

19. EL JUEGO CHIRIMBOLO – Ecuador
Pre-K to First Grade
Music: Sanna Longden, *Dances of the 7 Continents*, no. 1, "El Juego Chirimbolo"
Skills needed: timing, partnering, body parts, tempo

This song and dance is used to help children learn their body parts. Dancers can sing along with the song.

Dancers are in pairs and face each other, holding both hands to begin.

With the lyrics of the song, both **slide** together to side two times, then spin under both arms at the same time and release hands. As lyrics describe body parts, do the following:
- Touch one **foot** to partner's (*piés*), then the other.
- Touch one **hand** to partner's (*manos*) with palms flat, then the other.
- Touch one **elbow** to partner's (*codos*), then the other.

Repeat slides and spin.

Repeat touches above.

Repeat slides and spin again, then release. Jump back and sing "Hey!"

Music repeats at faster tempo.

Nontraditional variation adding other body parts:
- Touch one **shoulder** to partner's (*hombro*), then the other.
- Touch one **knee** to partner's (*rodilla*), then the other.
- Touch one **hip** to partner's (*cadera*), then touch heads (*cabeza*).

Nontraditional variation adding slow tempo: Sing and dance only the original version without the music very slowly. Then dance it with the music, moderate and fast.

Nontraditional variation sitting down: Partners or trios sit facing one another, crisscrossed on the floor or in chairs, with palms touching and fingers laced. Alternate pushing/pulling hands forward and backward. Then trace a circle together. Let go of hands and touch feet, hands, and elbows. Repeat two times and roll onto back and back up at end.

Nontraditional variation in small groups: Form groups of three or more, and all take hands, moving in and out instead of spinning. All touch body parts in the center with all fellow group members.

20. FAN DANCE – China
Kindergarten to Second Grade
Music: David Byrne, main title theme from *The Last Emperor*
Skills needed: smooth, sharp, and vibratory flow; objects

Many Asian countries have fan dances as part of their culture and heritage. This example represents those that originate from China. Traditional Chinese fan dance has been a part of China's heritage for over two thousand years. It is used to help pass down stories and traditions of Chinese culture and also serves as entertainment, featuring detailed and graceful movements (civilian type). Fans are used as props to assist in the telling of a story or to enhance the beauty of the movement. Also, Chinese fan dancing serves as physical exercise as well as an exercise in discipline for its participants using coordinated group movements emphasizing a more rigid and authoritative style (military type). The origins of the fan dance are rooted in the Han dynasty, which was the first in China to value and preserve the arts. Even today, many Chinese fan dancers learn the craft as part of their school curriculum.

To make a pair of fans, simply cut a paper plate or a circle of thin cardboard in half to make two semicircles. Decorate them with different colors on opposite sides. Each dancer holds two fans between their thumb and bent index finger in the middle of the straight edge. Dancers can either begin onstage or enter with tiny steps on balls of feet, holding one fan in front of their face with the head tipped slightly down and the other fan behind the back like a peacock tail.

Part A: Civilian style (vibratory and smooth flow):
- Seated on heels with fans resting on knees and with thumbs forward, both fans begin fluttering (vibratory). Lift L fan up to side, then R, both straight down in front of chest. Cross arms and flip fans. Then lean to R, then to L, still fluttering.

- Step up onto one foot, sweeping (smooth) both fans to same side. Step onto other foot. Repeat sweep to that side, then once more to the first side. Bend knees and place fans on knees with fingers forward.
- Extend arms and one leg opposite each other on a diagonal (smooth). Then lift knee of extended leg. While balancing, slowly twist, bringing fans to opposite side of body from lifted knee. Then touch crossed-over toe to floor and stretch fans further to other side of body, lifting them slightly. Then up on toes, spin like a windmill, bringing both fans back to knees in front.
- Repeat diagonal-cross-touch-spin to opposite side.

Part B: Military style (sharp flow):
- Do chopping movements with four steps in place, feet apart, and both fans together toward low diagonal on same sides as steps.
- Lunge to side quickly (sharp) and "draw a bow" by pulling one elbow back. Quickly change arm position two times, returning to first position. Then quickly face front, crossing arms and fans in front of chest with feet slightly apart.
- Repeat to other side and lower back down to sitting on knees.

Repeat parts A and B.

Part C: Both styles (smooth and sharp):
- Step out to R and circle same-side fan above head while holding other fan in front of stomach (smooth). Repeat on other side.
- With knees bent and feet together and fans in front of knees, quickly flip fans as feet pivot on toes to twist in the opposite direction as fans flip eight times (sharp).
- Repeat both of above, getting lower with last four flips.

Repeat parts A and B and finish in bow and arrow position as the music ends.

21. FOUR-SIDED DANCES – Spain, Mexico, USA/Texas, South Africa
Fourth to Sixth Grade

Music: Los del Rio, "Macarena," Grupo Rasado, "Payaso del Rodeo,"
Brooks & Dunn, "Boot Scootin' Boogie," Miriam Makeba, "Pata Pata"
Skills needed: directions, formations, rhythm

These dances are commonly done at parties and other social gatherings to encourage a sense of unity since all dancers are doing the same movements in the same direction at the same time. And also, because they change direction, there is no "front" or stagelike presentation involved. Since the spectators are likely to be watching from all sides, the dances face each direction with a repeating rhythm and movements that include a ninety-degree turn. This way, all viewers will get an equal view.

Macarena, Spain
Stretch one hand forward with palm down, then other hand. Flip first hand up, then other hand. Touch opposite shoulder, then other shoulder. Touch back of same side of head, then other side. Cross hand and touch opposite hip, then other hip. Touch same side of back, then other side. Hold hands on back and do a big hip circle. Then jump a quarter turn. Repeat four times until facing front again. Could go other direction or repeat either double time or half time. Whole dance takes sixteen beats.

El Payaso del Rodeo, Mexico
At slower part at beginning of music, dancers stay in place and do one or more of the three following movements: (1) Pivot on L leg as R side of body steps in front, then in back as a lady with a big skirt would swish it forward and backward. (2) Pick up and touch R toe on ground, with hip pushing out to side as R hand points up on the beat. (3) Same toe touch with hip out but pick up an imaginary cowboy hat and place it back on head. When the music

picks up, quickly slide to the R. Then quickly slide back to the L, then backward. Then touch L heel forward. Then change feet and touch R heel forward. Quarter turn to L as next set begins. Repeating part of dance takes eight beats.

Texas Line Dance, Texas/USA
Dancers form two-way lines (forward/backward AND side to side) because dance changes directions by quarter turns and travels, so dancers must be in line front to back and side to side. Basic step: Step sideways R. Cross behind with L. Step out again on R. Touch L. Repeat going to L. Step forward on R. Touch L. Step back L. Touch R. Step forward on R. Brush ball of L foot forward. Lift L knee as if kicking the dirt with a cowboy boot and quarter turn to R. This basic step also goes with "No Rompas Mas." Whole pattern takes sixteen beats.

Pata Pata, South Africa
See Pata Pata instructions later in this appendix. Whole pattern takes sixteen beats.

Nontraditional variation: Groups of students can create their own version of a dance that changes directions following the pattern of any of the above examples.

22. GUMBOOT DANCE – South Africa
Third to Sixth Grade
Music: Ladysmith Black Mambazo, "Diamonds on the
Soles of Her Shoes"
Skills needed: rhythm, beat, sound, formations

This dance style originated with the gold mining industry in South
Africa during the time of British rule. It represents how the gold
miners communicated with one another through rhythm in the
mines. Because of the cruel expectation by the British bosses that
the miners not converse with one another while they were in the
dark doing a dangerous job, the miners created various rhythmic
sound patterns by slapping and stomping the rubber boots they
wore, which were their way of sending messages to one another via
a form of code.

Students should imagine they are wearing rubber boots that go up
to the knee and keep their knees slightly bent and their upper body
leaning forward so the hands can quickly reach the boots to allow
for quick stepping and slapping. Rhythmic precision among dancers
is important in this dance form. Also, there are no set movements.
Rather, the dancers create various original patterns of sounds and
movements to fit the situation.

Practice quick boot slapping and stepping skills with some of the
following movements:
- **Marching** steps on the beat, in-place/traveling. Continue
  stepping in place for all of the following patterns.
- **Single slap** on outside of one boot with same-side hand, then
  add the second boot. Continue stepping on the beat.
- **Double slaps** twice as fast on outside, then inside of same
  boot, using both hands on both boots. Continue stepping on
  the beat.

- **Marching/pointing** steps, in-place/traveling. Do four steps with both hands pointing up, then four steps with both hands pointing down.

Below are examples of phrases that miners might have needed to communicate with one another and movement patterns that might represent them:

- **"Are you OK?"** – Do three steps in place and jump-slap boots together.
- **"I am fine."** – Slap outside of one leg, then the other. Then jump, crossing feet. Then jump open.
- **"I found something!"** – Do over/under claps three times on same leg. Bend deep and jump, slapping both legs. Repeat on other leg.
- **"I need help."** – Forming a triangle around body, slap opposite leg behind standing leg. Slap outside of same leg with opposite hand. Slap inside of same leg with first hand, all quick, then two quick steps.
- **"Time for lunch."** – Step to side, cross, step-hop with quick double slap on lifted leg. Repeat on the other side.

Nontraditional variation: Students can brainstorm ideas of what they wish to communicate in the form of simple phrases and create a rhythmic movement patterns for each phrase. Also, create a response. Put phrases together to create a conversation.

23. GUSTAV'S SKOAL – Sweden
Third to Fourth Grade
Music: Sanna Longden, *Dances of the 7 Continents*, no. 1,
"Gustav's Skoal"
Skills needed: spatial relationships, timing, force

The story is that all the people are honoring one of the six King Gustavs of Sweden, most likely Gustav V, who reigned from 1907 to 1950. *Skoal* means "cheers" or "to your health" as one would raise a glass in a toast. Dancers should use exaggerated facial expressions and change the force in their bodies to express the two different groups of people represented in the dance: (1) the people of the king's court, who exhibit tense force, and (2) the peasants, who move with relaxed force.

Dancers are in groups of eight (four pairs), forming a square. They stand NEXT TO their partner, facing inward. Additional dancers called "lurkers" travel AROUND the outside. Since few groups of dancers divide evenly into eights, this dance conveniently provides a fun role for the extras.

Part A, Courtly (tense), thirty-two beats:
With great pride, serious faces, chests and heads high, opposite pairs dance four steps into center TOWARD each other, raising one fist and shouting "Skoal!" Then go back to place. Remaining pairs repeat. Then both sets of pairs repeat above.

Part B, Peasant (relaxed), thirty-two beats:
Playfully, lively, humorous, and smiling, first two pairs stay NEXT TO each other on outside of square and form a bridge with only one hand each CONNECTED and with the other hand on hip to form a "window." Remaining pairs split from their partner and dance UNDER the bridge closest to them, quickly peek back THROUGH the

windows, then return to their original partner and skip AROUND each other with elbows linked. Meanwhile, the "lurkers" are sneaking AROUND the outside with bodies lowered, waiting for a chance to steal a partner and do so when the couples come under the bridges. Those left out become new lurkers. Next time through, opposite couples form bridges.

Music cycles through five times.

24. HERE COMES SALLY – American South
Pre-K to First Grade
Music: Sanna Longden, *Dances of the 7 Continents*, no. 1,
"Here Comes Sally"
Skills needed: directions, formations, timing

This dance has its roots in African American culture of the Deep South. It is a famous party dance and is the origin of the Stroll, a popular slow-moving dance where participants have the opportunity to show off their best moves to a captive audience while moving down the "alley."

Start in two lines facing each other, and one person from each line gets eight beats to travel down the space between the lines known as the "alley."

With lyrics:
First dancer makes their way down the alley, doing improvisational movement with the music as they show off their best or favorite moves. Others in the line move up as five individual dancers from alternating sides take their turns. Or five pairs of dancers could take turns going down together.

Musical break:
On change in the music, all stop and do the following foot pattern following the lyrics of the song:
- With knees bent, one toe touches front-back-side-together-side. Shift weight and repeat with other foot.

End of song:
Dancers remaining in lines dance backward to fill in the empty space left by the five dancers or couples that just traveled down. On last note of song, all stop and raise shaking hands to signal the end of the dance. Song can be played several times to allow all dancers to have a turn.

25. HIGHLIFE – Western Africa
Fourth to Sixth Grade
Music: Christy Lane, "Rhythms of the Highlife"
Skills needed: rhythm, stamina, formations, rondo form

This started out as a spiritual dance, but over time, it has become a popular dance for parties or social gatherings of celebration. The dance celebrates everyday life—in this case, food preparation.

"Chorus" or part A movements: Step together forward, reaching upward toward sky. Step together back, lowering body slightly forward toward earth. Elbows are up behind back. Acknowledge the sky and earth for giving us everything we need.

Dance follows a rondo form as follows:
- **A:** *Thank you, sky. Thank you, earth.*
- **B: Stirring the pot,** wide stance, shifting weight side to side, one arm forming a large round shape like a soup pot, the other circling in it as if stirring.
- **A:** *Thank you, sky. Thank you, earth.*
- **C: Spice,** palms together like prayer hands on one shoulder, flick wrists twice, change sides, and repeat, lowering and coming up again, pivoting on balls of parallel feet
- **A:** *Thank you, sky. Thank you, earth.*
- **D: Chicken,** wide feet, hands either on lower back with palms out or out to sides with elbows and knees bent, chest pump in and out
- **A:** *Thank you, sky. Thank you, earth.*
- **E: Scared chicken,** either bouncing and spinning with feet wide, fists at chest, elbows out, chest pumping, or quick jumps with arms up and shoulders bouncing, knees in
- **A:** *Thank you, sky. Thank you, earth.*

- **F: Sharing,** feet together with knees bent and hands in front of chest, touch one heel to side as same hand twists open to same side with chest pushing forward, repeat to other side
- **A: *Thank you, sky. Thank you, earth.***

When music speeds up at end, run in place. Then finish in wide stance with elbows bent out to sides as "tiger" with clawed hands or "warrior" with hands flat on last beat.

Nontraditional variation: Using the rondo form and keeping part A the same, dancers can choose activities from selected topics from their everyday lives that are not celebrated and create five different movements that express various aspects of the chosen topic. Smaller groups can each have their own topic.

26. HOE ANA – Tahiti / Rarotonga Islands
First to Second Grade

Music: Sanna Longden, *Dances of the 7 Continents*, no. 1, "Hoe Ana"
Skills needed: focus, formations, tempo

Hoe Ana was originally a Rarotongan folk song from the islands west of Tahiti, also called the Cook Islands. The Tahitians have claimed and performed it, so there is some confusion about the origin. The dance is an action dance with hand gestures descriptive of the text. It tells of the days when Polynesian people migrated from island to island, paddling on and on to reach a legendary place just over the horizon.

Dancers are seated on their knees in lines front to back, as if in long canoes. This could be done in classrooms with students sitting on tables, with feet resting on chairs, or in single-file lines of chairs.

Part 1
- **Waves:** R arm curves overhead from the side like a wave, hand rippling two times. Focus on hand. Repeat on L.
- **Rock canoe:** Lean gently side to side four times, with arms straight down at sides and with hands flat, as if on edge of canoe rail. Focus forward.
- **Repeat both of above.**
- **Swirl the water:** On R side, put one hand over the other with both palms down, moving in small circles. Focus down on hands. Repeat on L side, circling in opposite direction.
- **Search for land:** Both hands over brow, twisting and looking R, L, R, L. Focus far off in the distance.
- **Sun and moon:** With fists closed at chest and elbows up, open L hand up and out with palm open, representing the sun. Then return. Open R hand up and out with hand fisted, representing the moon. Focus on hands.

- **Four winds:** Starting with R, stretch both hands and arms up and out four times, tracing an arc overhead, representing four directions. Focus on hands.

Part 2
- **Paddle:** Position hands as if holding an imaginary paddle and take two slow strokes on R side, then two on L side. Focus forward.
- **Rock canoe:** Same as in part 1.
- **Swirl the water:** Same as in part 1.
- **Land to me:** Stretch arms forward with palms up. Focus forward in the distance. Slowly curl arms in toward chest, with focus following hands. Repeat.

Part 3 (faster)
- **Quick paddle:** Same as in part 2, but much faster, with two paddles on R, then L, R, L. Focus forward and lean body forward with determination as if in a race to paddle to shore.
- **Stars in the sky:** Fingers of both hands flick open, alternating quickly and randomly all around above head. Focus follows hands.
- **Dive in the water:** Both hands overhead as if diving into water. Hands and body scoop down and back up and clap two times.
- **Repeat above three parts:** Only one hand clap on second time diving In the water.

Nontraditional variation: Explore ways of doing the movements with the whole body and traveling. Also, since the idea of the dance is traveling to find a new home, brainstorm various places the students would like to live and how they might travel to get there. Choose four locations and create movements expressing those locations and the ways to get there.

27. HOKEY POKEY – England and USA
Pre-K to Kindergarten
Music: any instrumental version of the song "Hokey Pokey"
Skills needed: body parts, formations

This is a very popular song and dance done by children of all ages. The song originated in the '40s in Britain by the name of Cokey Cokey. In America, it was revised and called Hokey Pokey and first became very popular in ski clubs in Sun Valley, Idaho.

Dancers can also sing the song, and it is fun to do at parties because it is silly and fun for everyone.

The dance is done in a circle, and dancers stay in place. Explain that a circle has two sides: an IN side and an OUT side. Each body part is first put in, then taken out.

This version is slightly different from the traditional in that it includes more body parts than just the right and left hands, elbows, feet, etc. Start with both hands and sing while following the words with movements:

"We put our hands in. We take our hands out. We put our hands in, and we shake 'em all about."

"We do the Hokey Pokey, and we turn ourselves around" Turning around self and move hands all around body, facing center of circle again.

"That's what it's all about!" Clap two times in the break before the next verse.

Repeat with different body parts as follows:
- Elbows
- Shoulders
- Head
- Stomach
- Hips
- Knees
- Feet
- Whole self

On "turn ourselves around," keep moving whatever body part was just put in and taken out and clap that body part on "that's what it's all about." On the whole-self part, jump into the circle and back out.

28. HORA – Israel
Fourth to Sixth Grade

Music: any version of "Hava Nagila" (instrumental versions are best)
Skills needed: formations, directions, spatial relationships, pathways

This is a social dance to celebrate Hanukkah or other occasions (such as weddings). Originally from Romania, it migrated to Israel and became more widely associated with Israeli culture. Traditionally, men and women would not touch each other but rather hold a handkerchief between their hands to stay connected. Groups of men might dance with their arms around each other's shoulders.

The basic step is done in eight beats in lines, holding uplifted hands with elbows slightly bent and body relaxed. The lines travel sideways, and the pattern repeats at least four times:

- **In-place:** Step-hop onto one foot. Kick other leg across while landing from hop. Repeat on other side.
- **Traveling:** Step out to side. Cross in front. Step out to same side. Cross behind (grapevine).
- Repeat above pattern.

When music changes, dancers change from sideways motion to forward and backward:

- **Jump-run pattern:** Do two slow and three quick jumps in place, then three slow running steps forward. Then jump, saying "Hey!" Then do four slow running steps backward. Repeat all.

FIRST FORMATION AND ENTRANCE: **Straight** lines dance basic step (above) into space from both sides and pass each other. When music changes, do jump-run pattern (above), moving forward and backward. Then without letting go of hands, take slow running steps into new formation.

SECOND FORMATION: In one large, several small, or concentric **circles**, face inward. Basic step is done in a circle and can change direction after four repetitions if desired. Jump-run pattern can move in toward and out from center of the circle. Do slow running steps into third and final formation.

THIRD FORMATION: Each line has one leader at an end, and that person leads them around the space doing basic step in a **curved**, **wavy**, or **spiraling** pathway. When music changes, do same jump-run pattern as above. But rather than changing to forward and backward motion, continue along the sideways pathway following the leader. Leaders could each lead their lines into a group **semicircle** formation, and on last beat of music, all lift arms with hands still joined and shout "HEY!"

29. IRISH BATTLE REEL – Ireland
Third to Fourth Grade
Music: Gemini (Sandor and Laszlo Slomovits), "Brian Boru"
Skills needed: formations, directions, force, timing

This traditional Irish dance is primarily done with bodies held upright and lifted with head high, a fairly high level of tension in the body. Arms are mostly down at sides, elbows straight, hands held in a loose fist, and shoulders squared. Intricate and quick footwork is also a feature of this style of dance, and this version is simplified to be done by student dancers.

This dance reflects a battle, as Ireland has fought many in its history defending its territory from invaders. It is in three basic parts:

ADVANCE – STANCE – RETREAT

Divide group in half. Then form two straight lines of dancers side by side, moving toward each other from opposite sides of the space in unison, meeting face-to-face.

ADVANCE
- Run forward quickly for six beats and skip in place two times. Repeat four times, ending up face-to-face with opposite line.

STANCE
- In relevé, do a grapevine step with both lines moving to the R, apart from each other for six beats, and bend on count 6. Spin with R arm stretching up, as if pointing a sword upward. Repeat to same side, then twice to the L. Dancers should look each other in the eye as they pass and have facial expressions that are meant to intimidate their opponent.

RETREAT

- Skip backward four beats. Brush back foot forward, as if kicking dirt at the opponents, and step in place with three quick steps. Then repeat kick and steps with other foot. Repeat.

Nontraditional variation: Brainstorm scenarios from students' lives that cause them to argue or fight with each other. Groups create movements that reflect three aspects of the identified conflict and replace the three movements of the traditional dance performed to the same music.

30. ITIK-ITIK – Philippines
Kindergarten to Second Grade
Music: Juan Silos Jr. & Rondalla, "Itik-Itik"
Skills needed: pathways, formations, spatial relationships, focus

An *itik* is a kind of a duck found in the Philippines. The story goes that a very popular and famous dancer was asked to perform at an event, and on the way to the performance, she observed some ducks and enjoyed the way they moved. The dancer decided that rather than perform what she had planned, she would perform a dance mimicking the movements of the ducks, and the audience loved it so much it became a popular social and folkloric dance.

The music is a quick triplet, and the four main movements of the dance are as follows:

1. **Wing stretching.** Traveling and stepping on each beat. Touch heel forward with straight leg and other leg slightly bent. Then take two small steps (heel-step-step). Body is bent slightly forward with a straight back. Lift opposite hand than heel that touches and lower same arm, both wrists broken. Then switch arms, focus following hand that is high.
2. **Flapping.** In-place or traveling. Fisted hands with knuckles together in front of chest, elbows lift and knees bend on count 1. As head tips to side, straighten legs and lower elbows, bringing head back up to straight. Repeat, with head tips alternating sides on each first count.
3. **Cleaning.** In-place or traveling. Hop three times quickly on each beat of the triplet on the same foot, lifting other foot to the back. Hands on hips and same hand as lifted foot reaches up and flips in the air high above head. Focus on hands. Change feet and hands with every triplet.
4. **Swimming.** Traveling. Slide sideways four times with backs of hands coming together at leading hip. Hands separate and palms flip up. Quickly circle back to same hip. Repeat to the other side.

Finish sitting down with feet tucked under in "sitting duck" position (wings back, leaning forward slightly, head up).

Kindergarten version – emphasis on PATHWAYS
1. **Wing stretching** follows a CURVED pathway, with dancers moving in small individual circles
2. **Flapping** with head tipping, following a ZIGZAG pathway
3. **Cleaning** movement with hops traveling in a WAVY pathway
4. **Swimming** to the side in a STRAIGHT pathway

First-grade version – emphasis on FORMATIONS
1. **Wing stretching** partners enter from opposite sides and travel to meet in a PAIRS formation
2. **Flapping** taking smalls steps to form LINES across with other pairs joining
3. **Cleaning** with hops into one large CIRCLE, traveling around
4. **Swimming** either all or every other dancer slides inward toward center of circle into a CLUSTER formation and back out, and either repeat all or other dancers take a turn

Second-grade version – emphasis on SPATIAL RELATIONSHIPS
Wing stretching in trios enter together—one IN FRONT, one in the middle, and one BEHIND
1. **Flapping** standing NEXT TO each other, outside dancers take turns moving BETWEEN the other two, continuing until the music changes
2. **Cleaning** with hops, with one partner staying in place and the other two traveling AROUND them, then switch who is in the middle two times
3. **Swimming** with partners traveling in opposite directions, moving AWAY from each other, then the other way, moving TOWARD each other again, and repeat

31. JAMBO BWANA – Kenya
Kindergarten to First Grade
Music: Lovewhip, "Jambo Bwana"
Skills needed: directions, patterns, translating words to movement

"Jambo Bwana" is a very popular song written in 1979 in response to band members observing visitors to resorts in the city of Mombasa on the east African coast of Kenya. The visitors were attempting to learn and converse in the local language, which is Swahili.

The dance can consist of movement patterns that all do together during the lyrics of the song, and different movement patterns can be created following the solo instrument sections that express the phrases sung. Here is an example of choreography that all dancers can do together:

- **Sixteen beats, intro:** skip in place or skip to enter
- **Sixteen beats:** hold still with both hands up (1–4), hands down (5–8), turn to face L side with both arms stretched forward (to side, 9–16)
- **Sixteen beats:** still facing side, lean back onto back foot, and R arm swings down and back and to front, repeat quickly (1–16)
- **Sixteen beats:** face front and step-hop on alternating feet with arms swinging forward and backward four times (1–8), tip side to side with alternating feet kicking slightly to the side, and circle arms down, out, and up (9–16)
- **Sixteen beats:** repeat last pattern above

Create three different repetitive patterns of movements following the solo instruments, each expressing the phrases in the lyrics as follows:

"How are you?" (*habari gani*) – drums, sixteen beats
"Very fine" (*mzuri sana*) – flute, sixteen beats
"No worries" (*hakuna matata*) – guitar, sixteen beats

Repeat above choreography with lyrics in the song. Then create three more patterns expressing the following phrases, sixteen beats each, during the trombone solo:

"Visitors are welcome" (*wageni mwakaribishwa*)
"Beautiful country" (*nchi ya maajabo*)
"Peaceful country" (*nchi yenye amani*)

On last **eight beats** in music, repeat the first eight beats of choreography, which all dancers do together. Then finish with hands on hips and feet apart, facing forward on last beat in music.

32. LA MARIPOSA – Bolívia
Pre-K to Kindergarten
Music: Colibri, "La Mariposa" (The Butterfly)
Skills needed: tempo, pathways, levels

This is a song sung by children in Bolívia to celebrate the beauty of the butterflies that hatch in the springtime (which is, of course, autumn for us).

Dancers are spread around the stage, down low in a curled-up shape representing being inside a chrysalis, balancing on toes. On shaking sound at beginning of the music, all dancers quickly stretch and shake to represent the butterflies emerging.

With lyrics: All dancers "fly" around the stage in a curving pathway that constantly changes directions, moving high and low very quickly (as butterflies do). The movement is a quick run with tiny steps, arms stretched out to sides and slightly back, body bent slightly forward, and hands shaking.

First chorus: Clap hands three times. Stomp feet three times. Slowly spin in place with arms outstretched like wings. Repeat.

Panpipe: With a partner or in trios, hold both hands and gallop around each other.

Second chorus: Same as first chorus or could clap partner's hands.

"Ly ly ly": Tag game, with two to three selected students acting as "taggers," who quickly run to touch all other dancers' shoulders, which allows them to take flight. While waiting to be tagged, all other dancers slowly bend down low and lift up to standing while lowering and raising straight arms like wings. As music fades, all fly out off to one side.

Nontraditional variation: Brainstorm and select other animals and explore how they awaken or develop, then travel around.

33. LA RASPA – Mexico
Pre-K to Second Grade
Music: Gemini (Sandor and Laszlo Slomovits), "La Raspa"
Skills needed: force, formations, directions, spatial relationships

La Raspa originated in Veracruz, Mexico, and it is a dance often performed during celebrations and at dance schools. The "Mexican hat dance" is a combination of two tunes: "Jarabe Tapatio" and "La Raspa." *La raspa*, or a "rasp," is a tool with a rough side used as a file, which is represented by the sliding and scuffing movements of the feet.

Dancers begin facing a partner with both hands held, and all pairs are arranged in a large circle
1. Slide R feet forward and L backward at the same time three times. Then pause, making sure not to kick each other's toes. Repeat this eight times. Release hands and skip around partner with R elbows linked for eight slow beats. Then switch to L elbows for eight more beats.
2. In one large circle, standing next to partner, girls have hands on hips, and boys have both hands behind back. Either do same foot sliding movement or change to a hop and touch one heel to floor in front of self. Repeat switching feet three times and pause. Repeat this pattern eight times. All in circle take hands and gallop around together.
3. Partners face each other, still in a circle formation. One person slides into center of circle while other slides away from center (partners slide away from each other) two times and do two quick claps. Repeat and slide back together, facing each other. Repeat again away from each other, then back together again. Apart/together pattern should be repeated four times. With partners, one goes onto one knee as partner skips around them. Then switch places and repeat.

To end the dance, all could go down onto one knee and lift both arms up high on last beat of music.

A more complex variation of part 1 could be a *saludo* step, where partners face each other a few steps apart and step toward each other three steps, then clap-clap. Then they do three steps backward away from each other and clap-clap. Repeat four times. Partners place their R hands together with palms flat (high five position), and both do the *seguidillo* step around each other (quick step on L, brush R heel, step on R, repeat seven times, and clap on 8). Change direction and repeat.

34. LIMBO – Trinidad
Second to Third Grade
Music: any version of "Limbo Rock"
Skills needed: levels, formations, abdominal strength, objects

Often considered a Hawaiian dance, the limbo, in fact, originated in Trinidad in the Caribbean. It uses a horizontal stick to challenge dancers to dip down low, leaning back, and emerge on the other side. The dipping and emerging motion may represent life triumphing over death. It may also represent how the people went down into the slave ships—some emerged, some didn't—and how the limited space in the ships was meant for packing, not for standing and not for comfort.

As an introduction, before the lowering under the limbo stick challenge and to get the group excited, dancers carry and pass small sticks that represent torches.

Half of group start in a circle with large spaces between them, squatting down and facing outward with "fire" sticks placed in front of them.
- Wiggle standing up slowly
- Hip pops with hand flicks above head on beat
- All move to R, "kicking dirt" behind them with quick leap-steps and leading hand palm up and flat
- Repeat to L
- Wiggle down to knees, then pick up stick and hold overhead

Other half of group enter and travel to a partner in the circle.
- Slow run around outside of circle and end up behind partner inside circle
- Take stick from partner's head, and with a big sweeping motion, move stick over their head four times, changing stick from hand to hand

- Other partner stands and takes stick as other partner lowers, and repeat above movement

Partners separate from each other and travel to lines on opposite sides, dropping sticks in a pile or a basket on the way. Take a slow run to get into place for limbo lines.

Two people are designated pole holders and could rotate after others have had a turn going under. Hold stick a bit lower each time to provide a greater challenge bending back. This could be done by either (1) holding one stick and two at a time go under or (2) holding two sticks in a V shape and one person at a time goes under each stick.

35. LOS CONCHEROS – Aztec, Mexico
Fourth to Sixth Grade
Music: Cusco, "Montezuma"
Skills needed: formations, weight-sharing, objects, force, timing

The *concheros* are a group of people in Mexico who link ancient Aztec culture with modern beliefs. They dance to the pre-Hispanic gods and the Catholic god with the same devotion they have had for centuries. They are called *concheros* because they blow on a large conch shell to signal the beginning of their ceremonies.

Formations of dancers are very important in this style of dance. Traditionally, a drummer is in the center of the space; and dancers dance around him/her in various formations, some representing the four compass points, the "corners of the earth," or the "four winds." The drummer keeps a quick-over-moderate and steady beat throughout the dance. Dancers hold a single maraca in their right hand, close to the chest, with the elbow out to side, and shake it to the beat of the drum. This is a powerful dance, and bodies are mostly tense and tight through the movements.

*Beginning in an **X** formation*
- **Stomping and leaning.** Dancers are on one knee facing inward toward the center of the formation. Stomp forward foot four times, then lean body forward and back up, shaking maraca. On last lean coming up, push with front foot to come up to standing.
- **Rotating:** Three quick steps in place with feet slightly apart. Jump, crossing feet with R in front and uncross feet to turn in place ninety degrees to the L. Repeat three more times to complete a 3/4 turn and pause for four quick beats.

Travel to + formation with dancers farthest away from drummer taking large steps, while dancers closer to the center take smaller steps. Whole group moves in a counterclockwise direction, maintaining the formation, and finishes almost where they started

- **Run-stomps:** Five quick runs traveling and two stomps in place. Repeat six times and pause in place.

In + formation, person on outside of each line goes first in canon timing.

- **Scoot-runs:** One at a time, scoot forward two times. Run backward three in quick steps. Next person scoots while previous person runs back.

Travel to formation with outside person leading the line. Travel to outside of formation. Turn to face in to center of space. Turn the next corner and form a line along one side of space.

- **Slide-swings:** All slide to their R with L hand held into side with elbow bent. Other arm swings maraca down and out with slides.

Travel to partners from opposite line

- **Jogs:** Partners from opposite sides take a small run toward each other at center, forming a line of partners across the space.
- **Knee-link hops:** Partners hold each other's L shoulder with their hands while still holding maraca in R. Wrap L legs around each other's legs from the outside and hop around each other in one complete rotation.
- **Lunge away:** Unwrap legs and place feet down close together. Hands pull away from shoulders down to wrists while partners lunge away from each other, circling and shaking maracas out, up, and in to chest. Pull each other back in to standing, let go, and jog backward back to previous side of square formation.
- **Other two sides of the formation repeat the same as above.**

Travel to two large concentric circles with first two lines from section above going first to form inner circle, moving counterclockwise, and second two lines forming outer circle, moving clockwise.

- **Run-stomps:** Same as previously done, five quick runs followed by two stomps in place.

For ending, in concentric circles

- **Jog-spins:** Inner circle jogs closer together to center of circle (if a drummer is there, surround them closely). Spin to L in place while jogging. Then outer circle repeats the same.
- **Ending:** All stop spinning and jogging, facing inward. Then cross R foot in front of L. Do a half-turn to face outward. Lower to knees with knees apart and lift both arms in a V shape, shaking maraca and looking up as music fades.

36. LOS MACHETES – Mexico
First to Third Grade
Music: Mariachi Vargas de Tecalitlán, "Los Machetes"
Skills needed: beat, formations, objects

This dance originates from the south-central Mexican state of Jalisco, where men dance with steel machetes (broad-bladed knives), which they use as weapons or as tools for cutting sugarcane or clearing brush.

For the purpose of this dance, rhythm sticks are used since machetes would obviously be too dangerous and because they make a nice sound when tapped together. Practice tapping sticks together on the beat before learning movements.

Dancers hold a stick in each hand to represent the machetes. Typical placement is with R stick over R shoulder and L stick behind back, pointed upward. Dance is in partners, who begin on opposite sides.

1. **Walk in** to scattered formation, with sticks tapping on the beat. One partner entering first in sixteen beats, followed by the other who stands next to them in sixteen beats.
2. **Over-under** knee striking sticks, alternating knees two times. Strike sticks once in front, once behind back. Then three times fast in front. Repeat four times. Partners are standing next to each other, facing front.
3. **Lasso** partner on R. Circle R stick overhead and slide three times to R, followed by a single stomp with L foot. Partner follows with same movement. Second partner repeats to the L, and first partner follows.
4. **Walk around** each other striking R sticks with partner's up high for sixteen beats. Change direction and repeat for sixteen beats. Stick in L hand should be behind back, pointing up.

5. **Over-under with partner,** variation on number 2 above, with partners facing each other. Hit R stick against each other on three quick beats, then L, R, L.

6. **Slash/jump,** both partners strike sticks on beat for eight beats as one partner lowers to knees. Low person slashes both sticks across close to floor two times, as standing partner jumps over the moving sticks with their sticks high. Low person then stands and repeats pattern with the other person lowering.

7. **Walk** striking own sticks on the beats to change formation into one large circle.

8. **Tap floor/shuffle sideways,** all face in toward center of circle and gallop to R, with knees bent, tapping the floor with ends of sticks four times. Then stop in place and tap once in front, once under R leg, in front, under L leg. Repeat traveling to L and repeat both directions again.

9. **Circle lasso,** same as number 3 above, with every other person sliding in to center of circle. Then the remaining people do the same, then back out again.

10. **Walk in a circle,** travel walking in one circle, tapping sticks together and staying on the beat. Music speeds up, so tapping and steps do too. End on one knee and lift both sticks up, facing out from center of circle on last three beats.

37. LOS VIEJITOS – Mexico
Second to Fourth Grade

Music: Mariachi Nuevo de Tecalitlán, "La Danza de Los Viejitos"
Skills needed: character movement, objects, energy qualities,
formations

La Danza de los Viejitos is traditionally performed by men called *danzantes*, or "dancers." It pays respect to the wisdom of elders, who also communicate with spirits, cure the sick, learn from the past, and predict the future. In part, it is also a humorous imitation of the Spanish men known as the conquistadores. The costume consists of white pants and a white long-sleeved shirt under a colorful sarape, a large straw hat with long ribbons or lace hanging down both sides, and a cane or walking stick approximately twenty-four inches long. They can also wear a mask with an elderly man's face painted on it. Most of the time, the body position is bent forward, with one or both hands on a walking stick, knees slightly bent, and head down, imitating the movements and body position of an elderly person.

Dancers begin in four lines in the corners of the stage and are on one knee with both hands leaning on a stick in front of them.

1. On **eight strums,** dancers stand up on wobbly legs.
2. On **quick music,** dancers travel onstage in lines with slow leg lifts in place to R, then to L, then quick little steps traveling forward. Repeat eight times.
3. On **eight strums,** face the audience and shake cane at them four times. Jump with half-turn and repeat shaking cane four times to the sky (communicate with spirits).
4. On **quick music,** hop in place and spin while hitting the opposite lifted foot with the cane on the beat twenty-four times. Then change feet and change direction eight times (curing the sick).

5. On **eight strums,** one at a time, extend cane to person behind with R hand as that person takes it with their L hand. First person holds their cane with both hands behind back.

6. On **quick music,** travel to get into two large circles, with a wide-leg, semiquick waddle, with bodies bent forward. First person takes the stick of the last person in the line to close the circle. Continue traveling in circle (learning about the past/predicting the future). All fall to floor out of chain as music changes.

7. On **eight strums,** dancers struggle to stand up again and face a partner.

8. On **quick music,** dancers strike each other's canes as if sword fighting (imitating Conquistadores) four times on the beat. Then touch cane to floor and spin around it with bent backs and both hands on top of stick. Repeat both three times.

9. On **eight strums,** all gradually turn to face audience, bent over cane with both hands on it, wagging head from side to side.

10. On **quick music,** all spin around canes for eight beats very quickly, then fall down as music ends.

38. LOTT IST TODT – Germany
Kindergarten to First Grade
Music: Marian Rose, "Lott Ist Todt"
Skills needed: emotions, formations, directions

This dance tells a story that is both comical and serious, in which the community shows great grief over the death of a wealthy loved one, Lottie. They become afraid upon seeing her dead body at the funeral, and they quickly recover when they learn she has left them all her money. The traditional version of the dance expresses the emotions **sad**, **fearful**, and **happy**.

Begin in a circle. With the slow music, the dancers lift their arms and slowly and **SADLY** waddle, moving in to the center of the circle as if grief stricken. Then they see the body of Lottie in the center and are **FEARFUL**. Then with the fast music, they pull hands into shoulders and run backward to the large circle again. Repeat.

With the continuing upbeat music, all take hands and skip around the circle **HAPPILY**. Or partners in the circle hold both hands and skip around each other.

Music cycles through four times.

Nontraditional variation: Two other variations are (1) "Dad is mad," to express the emotions **fearful** and **angry**, and (2) "Muck is yuck," to express the emotions **disgusted** and **interested**. (See below.)

Dad is mad:
In a circle but facing outward, slowly creep backward into the center, as if **fearful** of Dad, who is mad. Then quickly tiptoe and run forward with faster music, as if even more fearful and trying to get away. Repeat.

On the upbeat music part, dancers stand and place fists on hips and stomp around in the circle as if they ARE the **angry** dad. Or partners have fists on hips and stomp around each other.

Muck is yuck:
In a circle, dancers slowly trudge into the center of the circle, dragging their feet and bodies, **disgusted**, as if walking through mud. On faster music, quickly move backward, frantically wiping face, arms, and legs, trying to wipe off the muck. Repeat.

On the upbeat music, dancers turn to the person to their R. Now that the muck is removed, they see the beautiful person in front of them and follow them, trying to touch them with great **interest**. Or partners circle around each other, following and reaching out, trying

to touch the back of their partner.

39. MAMBO – Cuba
Fifth to Sixth Grade
Music: Havana Mambo, "Cuban Mambo"
Skills needed: weight sharing, rhythm

This style is a blend of New Orleans jazz and Latin American and African rhythms. It is named after an extremely poisonous snake whose venom is said to cause convulsions and hysteria, hence the wild nature of some of the movements. The music and dance styles are influenced by voodoo beliefs, as in being possessed by some evil spirit. The music and dance are both extremely upbeat and festive. It is traditionally a partner dance with men and women, and it is slightly flirtatious and playful in nature. As with many Latin dances, the body is relaxed, with swaying movement in the hips and shoulders.

One partner (the girl) starts from one side of the floor space, and the other partner (the boy) starts from the other.

A: Entrance/traveling movement. Girls do slow touch-steps, and boys simply do a slow walk. Girls enter first, moving toward the boys. They do a touch-pivot turn one and a half times around to face the direction they came from. Then the boys enter, following the girls. They travel to meet their partners and stand face-to-face, facing sideways.

B: Forward/backward. Couples stay generally in place. One steps forward with R leg as the other steps backward with L. They both step back on the back foot, then step with feet together, then pause for one beat. Repeat with the other feet moving forward. This repeats three times. Then partners take hands on one side (L holding R) and swing arms downward twice and into a spin under their lifted and still-joined hands.

C: Snake bite. With R hands held, the R foot is the anchor and doesn't move. Both partners step forward on the L, whipping their upper body and L arm forward leaning into but not touching their partner. Then step back and open the arm and upper body, reaching away from their partner. Repeat this four times.

D: Slides in a square. Partners release hands, and both slide to the R, facing each other, then do quarter turn to the R and slide L back-to-back. Then do a quarter turn to the R and slide R again, facing each other. Then do one more quarter turn to R and slide L back-to-back, tracing the outline of a square with each slide.

E: Wiggle/strut. One partner (the girl) does a quick whole-body wiggle in place as the other partner (the boy) walks with large steps in a small circle around her, as if to protect her from harm.

F: Final shape. Take hands on same side and do swing and spin under them as in part B above. Then both open to face front with both hands up.

40. MAYIM – Israel
Third to Fourth Grade

Music: Gemini Sandor and Laszlo Slomovits, *Rhythmically Moving*,
vol. 5, "Mayim"
Skills needed: energy qualities, rhythm, formations

The word *mayim* in Hebrew means "water," a valuable thing in the dry climate of Israel. This dance celebrates various forms of water.

Begin in one circle, **holding hands**.

Part 1:
- Do a grapevine step, moving clockwise, with arms moving in a smooth, sustained wavy motion, representing **waves** on bodies of water for sixteen counts.

Part 2:
- Walk quickly forward, taking four steps into center of circle, starting low. Then raise arms above head on count 4 to represent water **splashing**. Then walk backward out of the circle with four steps, lowering arms for eight counts. On four steps moving inward, quickly repeat the word *mayim* four times.
- Repeat above for eight counts.

Part 3:
- Drop hands and stay in place. Then with hands touching, move both arms up, forward, and down to represent a **waterfall**. Do so two times quickly on musical bridge for four counts.

Part 4:
- Hop on R foot eight times while spinning and tapping L foot forward and side to push. Arms are in a diagonal with outside arm higher, representing a **whirlpool**.
- Repeat, hopping on L foot and spinning to L.

Music repeats five times.

Nontraditional variation: Discuss what is of great importance to the community, like water is to the Israelis, and create four movements that express that idea. OR create three smaller groups, each of which gets one of the other three earth elements: *earth*, *fire*, or *air*. They create their own version of *mayim* that represents their element, following the same four-part structure above. Either variation should include a repeated word that is quickly chanted as in part 2 above.

Energy quality matches:

Water – Sustained
Air – Suspended
Earth – Collapse

Fire – Percussive

41. MERENGUE – Dominican Republic
Second to Fourth Grade
Music: Kevin MacLeod, "Notanico Merengue"
Skills needed: rhythm, partnering, formations, spatial relationships

This is a social dance with partners that is somewhat flirtatious. Rhythm and music are a combination of African and Caribbean influences. The dance may have been originated by a man with a bad leg, which would explain the dragging motion in the basic step. Freedom of movement in the hips and shoulders is very important in this dance, as is moving with and feeling the subtle beat of the music. This dance is done in partners.

- ■ **Basic step:** Step out to side, drag other foot in, and step together. Hips, shoulders, and arms swing with step and drag. (**Slide/Swing**)
- ■ **Square step:** Step to either side, cross other leg in front, step back, open back.

One partner enters, followed by the other, in pairs in a scattered formation.

- **Twist and lean** in opposite directions, with one person in front and the other behind, both looking at each other. Then lean to the other sides. Repeat four times.
- **Palms together** above heads after front person turns to face partner. Knees and hips shake as hands separate and trace a large circle moving down.
- **Square step** facing each other and going apart to the sides and back together.
- **Basic step with spins** with both hands held, both do basic step with drag in the same direction for six beats, and one person spins under both arms. Repeat. Then other person spins and travels back the other direction. Both spin under

arms, and repeat, both spinning.

- **Basic step away** with both facing front again, in opposite directions three times, followed by three quick claps. Repeat, then repeat two more times, moving back toward each other.
- **Do-si-do** around each other, walking with shoulders shaking. Repeat in the other direction.

Use these movement patterns to create student choreography. Or it could be a changing-partner dance, where partners use the basic step to leave their partner and find a new one.

42. MUSICAL THEATRE – USA
Second to Sixth Grade

Music: any movie or theatrical soundtrack (e.g., *The Lion King*, *Cats*, *Annie*, or *West Side Story*)

Skills needed: integration with theatre and music, performance

Musical theatre is an art form that combines music, theatre, and dance to tell a story. It originated in the United States as we know it today, but ancient Greek theatre involved music and movement to tell stories as well.

Teach a dance sequence from any selected musical and discuss the story that the dance tells. Some good examples are the following:
- ***WEST SIDE STORY*** ("Dance at the Gym")
- ***ANNIE*** ("It's the Hard-Knock Life")
- ***CATS*** ("Prologue")
- ***THE LION KING*** ("Circle of Life")
- ***JOSEPH AND THE AMAZING TECHNICOLOR DREAMCOAT*** ("Joseph's Coat")

Nontraditional variation: To create your own piece of musical theatre, follow these steps:
1. Outline a story.
2. Create dance movements and/or write songs that express highlights of the story.
3. Practice and memorize the sequence of movements and/or songs.
4. Set to music of your choice.
5. Refine and perform.

43. NATIVE ALASKAN – Southeast Alaska / Canada

Second to Fourth Grade
Music: play a steady beat on a handheld drum
Skills needed: force/energy qualities, formations, directions, beat

The Native peoples of southeast Alaska and western British Columbia include several tribes, all of whom travel to different areas, depending on the seasons, either on foot or in hollowed-out wooden canoes. In the fjords of the Pacific Northwest, mountains meet the ocean, so the people historically would travel along well-known trails to fish in the summertime and trap in the winter. They would travel from island to island by boat to visit one another and celebrate with a potlatch for a special occasion.

TRAIL CHANT – Tsimshian

This dance celebrates the tradition of traveling through the woods during the change in seasons. Dancers should travel across space on a diagonal. Men and women take turns moving and singing the same song. The women sing it with light and gentle voices, and the men sing with strong and loud voices. Men surround the women and stay low with aggressive slashing movements to scare away any hostile invaders. A single drum plays a steady beat.

Women sing one time while standing still in one or two lines.

WOMEN: *Hoo whey, wee huh, hoo whey, wee huh*
Hoo whey - hoo whey - wee huh!

Men sing two times while moving out in front of women, doing low slashing, chopping, clearing movements. Then pause and scout with eyes. Movements are with **BURST**, **SHARP**, or **PERCUSSIVE** energy.

MEN: *Hoo <u>whey!</u> Wee huh! Hoo <u>whey!</u> Wee huh*
Hoo <u>whey</u> – hoo <u>whey</u> – wee huh!

Women sing same song as above two times while doing small side steps on tiptoes with heads held high, hands on hips, and elbows out to show clan crest on back of button blanket. Do half-turn after first phrase and continue in the same direction. Lines should move through the middle of the group of men, who step out of the way to let the women pass. Movements are with **FLOAT**, **LIGHT**, or **SUSPENDED** energy.

Repeat as many times as needed to get to destination. To celebrate arrival, all stomp feet quickly rather than clapping hands while drum beats faster than for the dance.

CANOE SONG – Tlingit

This dance represents traveling by canoe when the clans get together for a potlatch. Men and women together form several lines of six to ten people front to back and move forward, as if in a canoe. A single drum plays a steady beat. The lines of canoes can travel straight across space.

With bodies slightly bent forward and arms extended forward and to one side of body, do a pulling motion, as if paddling, while stepping one foot forward and dragging the back foot to meet it. Repeat on same foot and with arms on the same side two times. Then switch to other side, with other foot leading. These movement have **PRESS**, **HEAVY**, or **SUSTAINED** energy.

ALL SING: *Whey, whey, ee-ah-eh; whey, whey, ee-ah-eh*

All stand up straight, stop moving forward, and hold arms overhead with palms together to represent their paddle. Quickly sway side to side, imagining the light shining off the wet paddles, signaling the people onshore of their arrival. Movements are done with **REBOUND**, **SMOOTH**, or **VIBRATORY** energy.

ALL SING: Ohhhh – oh-oh-oh-oh-oh-oh-ohhhhhh, ee-ah-eh, ee-ah-eh

Repeat phrase as many times as needed to reach destination.

44. OBWISANA – Ghana
First to Second Grade
Music: *Music Together: Family Favorites*, "Obwisana"
Skills needed: rhythm, timing, objects

In Ghana, children sing and play this stone-passing game, which helps teach cooperation and accuracy by requiring a high level of both, which are highly prized in Ghanaian culture. The lyrics loosely translated are as follows:

>*Obwisana sa nana* (the rock has crushed my hand, Grandma)
>*Obwisana sa* (the rock has crushed my hand)

Participants can make the game more complex by tapping two stones together, adding other movements, speeding up, or changing directions, and all the time keeping time with the beat and rhythm of the song. For classroom purposes, use beanbags instead of stones.

The entire dance/song is performed in a circle of five to eight people, keeping in mind that all participants are equal and there is no leader. A possible progression is as follows:

- **No stone:** Pat knees two times. Clap (slow). Start by doing this all together. Then one person at a time takes turns around the circle, keeping the beat.
- **Single stone, seated:** One person at a time passes the stone, placing it on the floor in front of the next person, first with only one hand, then changing hands, faster than above.
- **One stone, each person seated:** All pass at the same time using only one hand to pick up and pass. Then change hands, then overhead, then behind back. Toss to self and catch. Place on head and take off with other hand to pass, etc.
- **Single stone, standing:** Change hands. Pass overhead. Toss and catch under leg, behind back with spin, etc.

- **One stone, each person standing:** Change hands (passing and receiving at the same time). Add movements between passing, or for advanced groups, toss and catch to pass.

Once students are able to do all of the above rhythm patterns, they can begin to create their own unique ways of passing the stone, adding in different elements (such as passing under legs or behind back or adding jumps, spins, or other movements).

45. ORIXÁS – Brazil
Fifth to Sixth Grade
Music: selections from Ouroba, *Cantos Sagrados do Candomblé*
(songs titled after names of orixás)
Skills needed: Effort Actions

There are over four hundred orixás, who are recognized as deities in the current religious practice of Candomblé, which translates to mean "dance in honor of the gods." Each represents a certain aspect of our world. Candomblé is practiced mainly in Brazil by the descendants of African slaves brought there by the Portuguese. It is a blend of African, indigenous South American, and European influences. Santeria is the Cuban version of the same religious practice. Both share the belief that the sacred relationship between nature's elements and human beings should be honored and respected, and a parallel can be seen between the Catholic saints and orixás—each of which resides in and rules a specific place in the natural world and provides a spiritual link between the earth and the heavens.

Dancers, both men and women, wear large hoop skirts, headdresses, and have bare arms and shoulders (possibly imitating European dress), adorned with paint and strings of shells. After becoming familiar with the eight Effort Actions, students can divide into groups and create a phrase of three to four movements that express the different aspect of each orixá's character. Descriptions matched with the Effort Actions are as follows:

OXUM, Float (the goddess of beauty, can be found in the rivers and waterfalls)
- Delicate as a stream among rocks
- Powerful as great waterfalls
- Strokes hands, looks at fingernails, strokes hair
- Admires herself in a mirror she holds

IANSAN (Oya), Punch (the goddess of the winds, is courageous and powerful)
- Fans the fires
- Creates storms
- Stirs the air into wind
- Creates sparks to start fires

OXUMARE, Flick (the god of rainbows and serpents; is mysterious, intelligent, and artistic; connection between the earth and skies; sees the future)
- Is a connection between earth and sky
- Sees the future
- Controls snakes and other serpents
- Creates rainbows

OMOLU, Wring (the god of illness and disease, resides under the earth, is feared, protects the world from disease)
- Creates sickness
- Cures disease
- Carries the illness of the world on his shoulders
- Experiences great pain and suffering

IEMANJA, Glide (the queen of the oceans; is calm, nurturing, and sincere; will help anybody with no exception)
- Controls the waves
- Lifts and lowers the tides
- Creates whirlpools
- Protects the fishermen and returns them safely to her shores

OGUM, Slash (the warrior god; a blacksmith; is athletic; represents civilization, progress, iron, weapons, and strength)
- Makes and wields weapons
- Is hardworking
- Will fight aggressively
- Is fearless and never defeated

OXOSSI, Dab (the hunter god in the forests, protector of animals and those who live by hunting, intolerant of unnecessary killing, never misses, is stealthy)
- Rides a horse in pursuit of prey
- Stalks and searches
- Maintains strong and direct focus
- Is a provider

OXALA, Press (the god of the force of creation, elderly, wearing long robes, uses a walking stick)
- Is the creator of all life
- Creates air and gives us the ability to breathe
- Is a traveler, walking slowly from place to place
- Forms and moves in circles to represent life cycles

Nontraditional variation: Dancers can brainstorm ideas for their own "orixás," things that are important to them, and create three to four different movements that express the spirit that might live in that thing.

46. OXENDANS – Sweden
Fourth to Sixth Grade
Music: Sanna Longden, *Dances of the 7 Continents*, no. 1,
"OxDansen"
Skills needed: emotions, balance, partnering, timing, tempo

This dance represents a humorous mock fight between two people. It supposedly originated at a college in Karlstad, Sweden, where it was used by sophomores to initiate freshmen, called *oxen*, who had to do the dance without smiling.

Before the music starts, pairs of oxen march in side by side, with stomping feet and fisted hands on hips. When all are present, partners turn and face each other with heels together and toes apart. Dancers may scowl and snarl at each other. Movements start with movements at slow tempo, then fast for each section.

CHORUS: Facing each other at close proximity, dancers slide sideways away from each other and stomp trailing foot twice, opening arms with fisted hands up and out to sides, as if flexing muscles. Then slide back together with hands in front of chest, elbows out, and stomp once with other foot. Repeat, with each partner sliding the opposite way. **Repeat chorus after each of the following:**
- **SALUTATION.** Both partners place L foot forward for balance. One bows forward as other leans back, slowly at first, then double time. Hands are still on hips, and faces are close together.
- **TREADING ON TOES.** Both jump and land with R feet forward, hands on hips. Repeat, changing legs. Repeat, then repeat double time.
- **BUMPING ELBOWS.** Both stand with hands on hips and elbows out. Jump quarter turn to L and bump R elbows. Switch and bump L elbows. Repeat, then repeat double time.

- **PUNCHING STOMACHS.** With L hands on partner's R shoulder, one "punches" as the other contracts back center. Then reverse. Repeat. Then repeat double time.
- **SLAPPING FACES.** One "slaps" as the other turns away and claps hands for sound effect. Switch and repeat. Then repeat double time.
- **KICKING BACKSIDES.** One turns back to partner as other pulls foot back and "kicks." Switch and repeat. On fast part, both kick simultaneously and move in a circle, trying to kick each other's backsides.

FINALE: After last CHORUS, partners make like they are going to fight again but turn away and drop down to the floor onto hands, as if exhausted. Then they get up, help each other up, almost fight again, but shake hands and walk off with arms around each other, as if helping each other walk.

47. PATA PATA – South Africa
Fourth to Sixth Grade
Music: Miriam Makeba, "Pata Pata"
Skills needed: directions, relaxed force / dab

This is a very well-known social dance in South Africa. The literal translation is "touch touch," which describes the delicate movements of the toes and feet on the floor. This dance changes direction with each repetition of the pattern. In the United States, Western line dancing was modeled after this dance.

For all movements, the center of gravity is low with knees slightly bent.

Basic Pata Pata steps:
- Step out and lightly touch R toe to R. Return to place. Repeat with L toe.
- Pivot on heels, turning toes out. Pivot on balls of feet, turning heels out. Reverse, turning heels back in and turning toes back in.
- Lift R knee up. Touch same toe to R. Bring knee up again. Place feet together. Repeat with L knee and foot, but rather than placing the feet back together, lift knee up with more force into a hop and turn ninety degrees in the air, lifting both arms up while in the air. Then land on two feet.

A low pony step with swinging arms could travel dancers to different formations or to exit.

Additional in-place movement: Quick touches on own body with both hands together, zigzagging quickly down and up from shoulders to knees. You could add partners touching each other's face, shoulder, elbow, and knee between cycles of the pattern, changing directions.

48. PEOPLETON STICK DANCE – England/Wales

Kindergarten to Second Grade
Music: Marian Rose, "Pop Goes the Weasel"
Skills needed: objects, timing, formations

This dance may be pre-Christian, originating from the Welsh-English border counties. It is a dance to welcome in the spring. It is very festive and playful.

Traditionally, the dance is done in a square dance formation of eight people, where partners are across from each other and neighbors are next to each other. This simplified version of the dance starts in at least two lines, where every two people are facing each other. Each dancer holds one stick in their right hand. The music cycles through eight times, so dancers can either perform all of the figures below or choose four and repeat them.

- **FIGURE A: Lines, in place.** Partners stand next to each other and tap each other's sticks—four times high, four times low, four times high, then one more tap up high on "pop." Then jump and spin all the way around to face same partner. Repeat. If there is an odd number of people, dancers on the end of the line do movements with invisible partner.
- **FIGURE B: Two lines pass.** Both lines turn to face front. Back line skips forward to pass in front and circle around the front line, tapping their sticks as they pass. Then return to their original place and face backward. Line that stays in place holds sticks in front of body with two hands so passing dancers can tap it as they skip by. Then front line does the same, all facing the other direction, skipping around the back line, and returning to their original place.
- **FIGURE C: Pairs.** Facing partner again in line, all hold their own stick over their R shoulder and place L hand on hip.

Gallop around each other. Then stop and hit each other's sticks on "pop." Then turn and repeat in the other direction.

- **FIGURE D: Small circles.** Form several small circles of four to five people, one of whom is in the middle of the circle. Outer circle holds sticks and slides sideways as middle person bends down, holding stick with both hands low. On "pop," outer three stop. Then middle person jumps up and stretches stick overhead, holding it with both hands. Repeat with same person in the middle.
- **FIGURE E: Form a star in small circles.** Person in the middle joins the circle, and all walk forward with sticks touching each other in center of circle and opposite arm stretching up to opposite diagonal. Hit sticks on floor on "pop." Repeat.
- **FIGURE F: Large circle.** All skip together to form one large circle, holding sticks in front of body horizontally with both hands. All stop and jump and spin on "pop," lifting stick above head on jump. Repeat.
- **FIGURE G: Stick solos.** Facing partner, one does their own original stick dance for their partner. Partner kneels and holds their stick in two hands so partner can tap it on "pop." Then switch, and other partner performs their own stick dance and hits partner on "pop."
- **FIGURE A: Repeat first pattern of the dance, with partner.**

All bow to partners as music ends.

49. PROSPECTOR'S DANCE – USA/California
Third to Fifth Grade
Music: Smoky Mountain Strings, "Oh Susanna"
Skills needed: formations, rhythm, partnering

This dance is similar to the Virginia reel and American square dancing, except without the linear formations. Dancers have partners who begin and end across the floor from each other and meet somewhere in the middle of the space, scattered with other pairs. Single dancers are in groups on either side of the floor, scattered, and facing their partner across the way. During the gold rush era, there weren't many women. So dancers could all be dressed as men, and men partner with each other. There is no male-female characterization.

There are **six parts** to the dance, all of which repeat. Two groups of dancers begin on opposite sides of the space, but not in an orderly line:

1. **Bows.** Take three steps forward and bow to partner at a distance on count 4, then four steps backward, and repeat.

2. **Side Steps.** Both groups of dancers move to their R. Step-together-step-together and clap on count 4. Repeat to L, and repeat both.

3. **Elbow Link Skip.** Skip toward partner across the room. Link elbows and skip around each other. Then switch elbows and directions.

4. **Bridge and Boot Kick.** Partners hold R arms over their own heads and grasp R wrists. Walk around each other, stepping L-R. Kick L boots together with a hop. Repeat four times.

5. **Do-Si-Do.** Facing partner, step on the beat and walk forward, passing each other's R shoulder. Without turning around, walk sideways to R, then walk backward and pass each other's L shoulder. Then repeat. Arms are folded in front of chest, and elbows rock side to side on the beat.

6. **Move Backward.** Skip backward away from partner to opposite sides of floor. Place hands on knees and rest before repeating the whole dance.

50. QASHQAI SCARF DANCE – Iran
First to Third grade
Music: Prem Joshua, "Moghul Gardens"
Skills needed: pathways, formations, objects, levels, flow, and weight

The Qashqai tribes inhabit southern Iran and are seminomadic herders of sheep and goats. Dances of the Qashqai often utilize scarves and are characterized by spinning movements. The scarves can represent the wind blowing through the tents, which serve as the Qashqais' homes. Each dancer holds a colorful scarf in each hand.

Begin with four groups onstage in lines behind a designated leader in four corner areas. First group begins immediately with music; and one group at a time, following the musical phrases, does one of the four movements as follows, ending up in the corner where they began:

- *Wind* movement, circling stage in a large **curve**, RUN with both arms up high, representing how the wind blows through the mountains and valleys (**light** weight)
- *Caravan* movement, SLIDE sideways in a **straight** pathway with both arms bending at the elbows and dropping together toward leading leg, representing the effort with which the people travel (**heavy** weight)
- *Rabbit* movement, JUMP in a **zigzag** pathway with arms up, waving scarves side to side, representing the rabbit's ears (**sharp** flow)
- *Snake* movement, with a quick WALK in a **wavy** pathway with both arms stretched in front of body and hands together, representing the serpent's tongue (**smooth** flow)

For the movements listed below, dancers make sweeping arm movements while traveling and turning with tiny quick steps.

Between each of the movements, dancers do a movement referred to as **SPIN and DROP**. They stop traveling and hold scarves down, then spin moving arms out to the side and overhead. Then they stop spinning, drop and touch the floor, then move scarves rapidly up and down in front of body, as if playing a drum, while rising to standing.

All do SPIN and DROP after the above opening movements in groups.

All of the movements below travel with the same basic traveling step, which can be either a simple run with small steps or a quick step-touch-step, alternating sides, depending on skill level. Generally, the feet move quickly, and the arm and upper body movements are slower.

1. ***Tree Swaying.*** With arms held straight up and parallel to each other, sway upper body while quickly flicking both wrists, tossing scarves side to side. Dancers move in **curved** pathways in a **small circles** formation. All SPIN and DROP.

2. ***Herding.*** Hold one scarf down at side and the other over the shoulder and down back. Quickly switch arms so that other scarf touches back of shoulder as a herder might touch their flock to guide them. Following a leader from each small circle, form **lines** and travel across floor in **straight** pathways. All SPIN and DROP.

3. ***Sharing Love.*** With elbows bent and held in at sides, cross arms in front of waist and then open both arms to sides with elbows in. Dancers leave lines into a **scattered** formation and travel all around the space in their own **wavy** pathway, passing and looking at each other. All SPIN and DROP.

4. ***Sweeper.*** With both elbows bent and scarves hanging down back, swing body and both scarves down. Then come up and bend arms at elbow and toss both scarves back over

shoulders, traveling into and around one large **circle** along a **curved** pathway. All SPIN and DROP.

5.   *Windshield Wipers.* Arms alternate bending and straightening side to side, positioning the straight arm out to side and the bent arm so that the scarf falls behind the neck. Travel into the middle of the circle, forming a **cluster**, and back along a **zigzag** pathway. All SPIN and DROP in one large circle again.

End the dance by kneeling on both knees and sitting on heels. Then all throw and release both scarves into center of circle and lower upper body down into Muslim prayer position.

51. SANSA KROMA – Akan/Ghana
Third to Sixth Grade
Music: Alexander L'Estrange, "Sansa Kroma"
Skills needed: rhythm, timing, objects

This Akan/Ghanaian game/song is very much like another one called Obwisana, which is also intended to encourage cooperation and precision, highly valued in Ghanaian culture. The words of the song are loosely translated as follows:

Sansa kroma   (the hawk is high in the sky)
Nee nay woh (voice inflection goes up)   (orphans, be careful)
Che che coco mah   (she will snatch you up!)

Sansa kroma
Nee nay woh (voice inflection goes down)
Che che coco mah

In the music, the above double phrases repeat six times, followed by a break. Then that pattern repeats three more times. The song ends abruptly. It is intended to be a warning song for children not to play outside alone. This game/song is more complex than Obwisana, and participants begin with two sticks each. Traditionally, stones are used. But for classroom purposes, sticks work well and are useful when students create their own rhythmic patterns with passing objects. The whole dance is done seated in circle groups of five to seven.

Warm-up: pick up and pass both sticks on every beat

Add tap: tap sticks two times, pass, slow tempo (two passes per stanza, an action on every other beat)

Add clap: one clap, pick up, two very quick taps, pass, repeat (two passes per stanza, clap on "san" and on "woh")

Once students are able to do the above three variations, they can create their own rhythm patterns and variations on passing the sticks, standing, and moving their whole bodies and adding other movements (such as spins, jumps, lunges). They can change levels as well. They can also alter the phrasing of their pattern by slowing down or speeding up different actions.

> **Add six solos:** In the song, there is a break where the singers sing "sansa kromaaaaa," followed by a pause (which repeats six times), in which individual dancers can do a short solo movement of their own creation.

52. SANTA LUCIA – Sweden/Italy
First to Third Grade
Music: Peppino D'Agostino, "Santa Lucia"
Skills needed: formations, objects, six-beat counting, partnering

Scandinavians, especially Swedes, have special feelings toward light due to the long dark winters. Santa Lucia is the patron saint of the harvest, light, and life. She originally came from Italy and helped the people of the north make it through the dark winters with her generosity and goodwill, sharing food and lighting candles. This dance is traditionally performed around December 13, which, by the lunar calendar, is the longest night of the year. Lucia, in a white costume and crowned with candles, walks around serving coffee, bread, and cookies to the people.

Music plays for about one minute before the dancers begin. Listen for two mandolin trills, and immediately after the second is when the dancers start their procession. They carry baskets or trays of food in front of them with both hands. Music is counted in sets of six quick beats. Dancers enter with procession step from aisles or sides of stage and travel toward center of stage area and form one or two semicircles, facing audience.

Procession step: Take three steps forward on counts 1-2-3, with feet together. Stay in place with knees bent. Twist and "share" their baskets with people nearby on 4-5-6. Repeat, alternating sides on the twist and share.

When music pauses, dancers lift baskets or trays overhead, then spin and place trays on floor. Then quickly walk out onto stage to face their partner.
- Two 6s – Facing partners, one person bows, then the other.
- Two 6s – With R palms touching partner's, walk smoothly

around each other, ending up on the side they started from.

- Four 6s – "Handshaking," L hands clasp below Rs. Then Rs clasp below Ls. Then Ls below. Then Rs below (knees bending to lower bodies). Then coming back up with Rs above. Then Ls, then Rs, then Ls. Release both hands, and partners exit to opposite sides with a quick walk.
- Four 6s – Group on one side enters galloping in a line and curves inward to center and forms a cluster with hands lifted together, making fingers "flicker" to indicate one bright candle.
- Four 6s – Other group enters galloping in a line and forms a circle around the cluster and goes down on one knee.
- Two 6s – Cluster group brings hands down into the middle of their cluster. Keep R hands in the middle and sweep L arms up. Open bodies out from the center of circle in three beats, then back in to center in three beats. Repeat two more times, and on last inward motion, bodies turn into center of circle. Then all lower down to crouching position with fingertips on floor.
- One 6 – Outer group stands lifting arms to sides, then up. Then move inward, covering the cluster with their arms.
- One 6 – Cluster group rises and reaches arms up, then walks quickly backward between the outer group as they stand straight. New outer group takes hands surrounding the new inner group, forming two concentric circles, all facing inward.
- Six 6s – Inner and outer circles gallop sideways in opposite directions, holding hands.
- Four 6s – All slow to a stop and separate. Then walk back to baskets, spin while lifting them, and stop, facing front in semicircle formation.

Exit – Repeat opening walk/share sequence (procession step), traveling out of space the way they came in as music ends.

53. SASHA – Ukraine
First to Third Grade
Music: Marian Rose, "Sasha!"
Skills needed: timing, changing partners

This is a changing-partner dance expressing the search for one's best friend by the name of Sasha, which can be either a boy's or a girl's name. It requires precise timing and coordination on clapping their partner's hands on the beat and the finding of a new partner with the changes in the music.

Practice the chant, which repeats at the beginning of each cycle of the dance, which is as follows: ***Sasha! Sasha! Ras dva tri!*** "Ras dva tri" is counting to three in Ukrainian (also in Russian and Polish). Dance begins in partners, facing each other, scattered around the space.

Partners clap each other's hands as follows:

RRR, LLL, both both both (their own) knees knees knees

Repeat.

Partners link R elbows and **skip** around each other for eight beats. Then switch elbows and skip for seven more beats, releasing elbows. Then jump up with arms up and say "Hey!"

With hands up high, partners separate, and individuals walk around the room in search of a new Sasha. They keep searching until the music changes back to the beginning, and by then, they must be face-to-face with a new partner. If they find a new partner before the music changes, they continue walking in place and lower arms.

That way, dancers still looking for a partner can look for someone who has their hands up.

Repeat the whole dance. Music cycles through six times.

At end of music, stand next to last partner and put arms around each other's shoulders. Extend outside arms up and out on last big beat of music.

54. SCHUHPLATTLE – Germany/Bavaria
Fourth to Sixth Grade
Music: Herzbuben Chor & Orchester, "Schuhplattler-Jodler"
Skills needed: rhythm

This form of dance comes from the region of central to southeastern Germany known as Bavaria. It originates in the days of the clans in medieval times in Europe, about one thousand years ago. The movements express work activities using tools, benches, or tables, creating various complex rhythm patterns on the body. It was originally performed only by men in their attempt to impress the women with their strength and rhythmic skills. The word *schuhplattle* means "foot board," describing the emphasis on stomping of feet, likely on wooden floors, tables, or benches.

Most rhythmic patterns are in a 3/4 time signature, with a movement or sound of some kind on every beat of the triplet.

Part A: (thirty-two triplets) Begin seated on a stool or bench.
- Stomp both feet on floor three times.
- Slap both thighs three times.
- Stand and slap R foot with L hand in front. Slap L foot with R hand behind.
- Kick L foot to side. Step in place two times.
- Skip to L side of stool and around to face it.
- Spin and lift R leg over stool and sit facing front again.

Repeat above four times, alternating sides.

Part B: (sixteen triplets) Begin seated again, facing front.
- With legs together, lean back and tap feet on floor three times. Open legs, lean forward, and tap seat of stool with both hands three times.

Repeat above three times.

- Tap both thighs three times and stand and clap once.
- Quickly step to R. Cross L. Step on stool with L. Tap L knee two times (six quick beats). Repeat to L side. Repeat to R side again. Then either step over stool or spin to sit facing front again.

Dance fits music in the following sequence:

A - B - A - B - B - A - B

55. SECOND LINE – USA / New Orleans
Kindergarten to Third Grade
Music: upbeat New Orleans–style jazz with brass (such as
"Ballin' the Jack")
Skills needed: pathways, force

The second line is a tradition from New Orleans that follows the funeral procession. While the first line is on the way to the cemetery (where the music is more somber), the second line is leaving the cemetery to celebrate the life of the deceased. A line is formed by the musicians playing upbeat music and all the nearby people joining in. Some of the movements are a mixture of an evolved version of the African bamboula dance with Native American influences regarding costumes and chants.

Colors worn will often be coordinated. Women might carry umbrellas, and men might wave handkerchiefs. Sashes will be worn, and brass instruments will be played as part of the procession. Musicians will precede the rest of the dancers. Dancers travel in procession and move with the music.

Some movements include the following:
- Fast feet in "wild abandon," while the upper body is relatively still
- Jumping and reaching up
- Twisting down low and back up
- Sideways step-cross, slow, strut-type walk
- Wide legs, bouncing and shaking the knees in and out very fast
- Running in place around self with arms out low like wings, tilted
- Lower body twist, slapping one thigh very fast

Dancers could move in lines and in and out of circles, changing directions as desired. They could also throw gifts, such as Mardi Gras beads, out to spectators.

56. SEVEN JUMPS – Denmark
First to Second Grade
Music: Shenanigans, "Seven Jumps"
Skills needed: body parts, formations, levels

This very popular Danish folk dance was developed to help children learn body parts. During the held-note sections of the music, a different body part is either lifted or touches the ground. Also, it is a memory dance as the sequence builds with each repetition. The "jumps" refer to how the dancers have to suddenly jump up to travel in the circle again.

In one large or two or three small circles, dancers face inward, and all hold hands. On rhythmic section of the music, all gallop or jog around circle in one direction for sixteen beats or change direction after eight beats.

On held notes in music, dancers stop traveling and add on one of the following with each repetition of the musical pattern:

Traditional (with hands held):
1. Lift one foot
2. Lift other foot
3. One knee on floor
4. Both knees on floor
5. One elbow on floor (release hands)
6. Both elbows on floor
7. Touch head on floor (could be held in hands)
8. Touch stomach on floor (lie down)

Nontraditional variations:
- Touch own body parts
- Body parts into center of circle
- Connect different body parts to a partner
- Make different shapes emphasizing each body part
- Focus a different way each time in a different shape

57. SHOEMAKER'S DANCE – Denmark
Kindergarten to First Grade
Music: Gemini Sandor and Laszlo Slomovits, *Rhythmically Moving*, vol. 3, "Little Shoemaker"
Skills needed: formations, spatial relationships, partnering

This is a simple repeating-pattern dance done with a partner to show work activities, specifically those of a shoemaker, and finally showing off the finished product.

Begin facing partner and follow cues in music to change movements.

1. **Winding Thread:** Rolling fist quickly, lean toward and away from partner one time, two beats forward, two beats backward.
2. **Pulling Thread:** Both elbows pull back with strong motion and knees bending two times.
3. **Nailing:** Thump fists together three times quickly.

Repeat all three parts above.

4. **Skipping:** With both hands held and twisting bodies slightly away from each other, skip forward circling around each other.

With same partner, repeat the first three parts. Then instead of skipping with them, go on to part 5:

5. **Showing the Shoe:** Walk with heel-toe steps, with one hand on hip and the other hand lifted with palm up, as if displaying their shoe. Travel to a new partner.

Repeat whole thing from the beginning. Music cycles through ten times, so each dancer will have five partners. At end of the tenth cycle, show shoe to the audience. Finish with one shoe forward and upper body bowing with both arms down framing the shoe.

Nontraditional variation: Brainstorm ideas of other things people can make with their hands and create three movements that can be done facing a partner expressing those activities. Then show off what they have made.

58. SUGARCANE HARVEST – Colombia
Third to Fifth Grade
Music: Gemini (Sandor and Laszlo Slomovits), "Carnavalito"
Skills needed: formations, tempo, force, pathways

This dance represents the movements of harvesting sugarcane. Dancers hold a stick in their right hand to represent a machete, which is used for chopping the thick stalks of the sugarcanes. The movements are relaxed and slow to represent the hot climate and the fatigue of the workers.

Begin offstage on both sides in four lines. Enter traveling in curved pathways. Movements change with changes in music.

Music cycles through three times.

Chopping step: Repeat eight times, traveling
Step R. Touch L toe behind. Step R. Repeat stepping L and alternating. Stick (machete) in R hand is slowly swung down from out at R side to across body to L (cross when stepping L and out when stepping on R). L arm is relaxed at side of body. Lines pass each other. Then each follows a leader into either one large or four small circles.

Digging step pattern: Repeat eight times, traveling
Same step as above, with both hands holding stick. "Dig" down, and when stepping on L, "throw" over L shoulder as if shoveling. Then repeat dig and "throw" over R shoulder.

Cleaning pattern: Repeat two times, in-place (facing outward when in circle)
Sixteen beats: slow jab downward with stick (1–2). R foot steps forward. Then pull back (3–4) and bring R foot back. Repeat (5–6 and

7–8) faster. Next, hold stick horizontally in two hands and "smash" four times on knees and on the beat (9–12). Then in R hand only, swing stick in a circle two times (13–14). Then do one big forceful "chop" with R arm moving downward on a diagonal across body.

Repeat all of above three times. As music ends, bring R foot back onto knee and hold stick horizontally overhead, facing out from center of circle.

Nontraditional variation: Brainstorm ideas of other outdoor work or physical labor activities that can be done with a tool that the stick could represent. Then create three different movements that express aspects of those activities, including how the movements would change depending on the weather.

59. SWING DANCE – USA
Third to Sixth Grade

Music: Christy Lane, "Sing, Sing, Sing" or Buddy Bregman Big Band,
"It Don't Mean a Thing If It Ain't Got That Swing"
Skills needed: weight / swinging energy, partnering, counterbalance

A partner dance style accompanied by a musical genre also known as swing from the big band era of the '40s and '50s in the US. The dance involves male/female partners, where there is a tremendous amount of physical contact in weight sharing and shifting, pulling/ pushing, balancing, and using momentum. Both dancers keep a low center of gravity with their weight mostly on the balls of their feet with a light bounce, knees and hips slightly bent, and arms extended out from the body to enable fast-paced stepping, turning, and shifting weight. The basic step is in a six-beat pattern.

Partners begin face-to-face with both hands held in a loose fingerhold ("leaders" have palms up, while "followers" have palms down), with elbows slightly bent. Partners can trade parts to get the chance to both lead and follow.

Basic step: SIMPLE: Shift weight to follower's R and leader's L for two beats. Shift weight to opposite side for two beats. Step and shift weight back onto one foot (follower's R and leader's L). QUICK: Step-touch to side, then other side. Then step-step back.

Send out: With basic step (SIMPLE or QUICK), follower opens out, with one hand held, then comes back.

Single turn: Using either basic step, follower spins inward under held hands, then takes both hands, facing each other.

Double turn: Do single turn. Then follower shifts weight and reverses to return to place.

Change places: Facing each other slightly off-center, do basic step, starting with outside foot. Then pull closer together. Then quickly switch places and push out, still holding both hands. Alternate this with next movement (sugar push).

Sugar push: Holding both hands, leader is primarily doing the pushing and pulling but could be more balanced. They push away with basic step, then pull back in with same.

Behind the head: With both hands held, both lift arms and put one hand behind their heads and walk or do basic step around each other.

Duck walk: Either in close position or side by side holding hands, a traveling step where they step forward on heel. Back toe comes in, and repeat on the same foot. Hips move forward with back foot.

Yo-yo: Facing each other with one hand held, follower steps away from leader, then spins in to leader, ending up back to front, then out again with basic step.

Chicken head: Partners face each other, holding both hands, and push apart and then pull together with heads going past each other, alternating sides.

Kicks and lie back (more advanced): Holding both hands, do four step-kicks traveling around each other. Then follower lifts one hand overhead and flips onto back horizontally as leader supports her/ him around waist. Follower kicks two times from the knees in laid-back position. As leader kicks two times to side in place, follower flips back up to standing. Then they cross kick outside each other's legs two times and switch.

One of the most exciting things about swing dancing is to just freestyle with your partner. It's all about pushing, pulling, and sharing and shifting weight. If you have a partner with whom you can do this well, try to make up some of your own swing moves!

60. TANGO – Argentina
Kindergarten to First Grade / Second to Fourth Grade

Music: Denise Gagne, "Turkey Tango," or Gotan Project, "Santa Maria (Del Buen Ayre)"
Skills needed: partnering, directions, smooth/sharp flow, force, focus

The tango is the most popular dance from Argentina. It developed in the late nineteenth century in working-class neighborhoods of both Buenos Aires, Argentina, and Montevideo, Uruguay, and was practiced by Uruguayan and Argentine dancers, musicians, and immigrant laborers. African and European immigrants would dance in public; and for this reason, tango is a fusion of European (Spanish and Italian), African, and gaucho styles. It is traditionally a very sensuous and seductive dance originating from the fact that most of the immigrants in that part of the Americas were men, and they were attempting to attract any of the few women in the neighborhood nightclubs. It became famous all over the world around the early twentieth century and is a main staple of ballroom dance repertoire.

"Turkey Tango" (for kindergarten to first grade): The song lyrics (if using the vocal version) can be used to help students learn the movements, and additional movements and verses can be created to replace these. After a four-beat intro:

Chorus: *Any turkey can tango, any turkey can dance*
Any turkey can tango, if they have the chance

Movements: In partners facing each other, one with their back to the audience, lead arms straight, with hand held, trailing arms bent and touching elbows. Focus toward the leading hands. Travel toward stage left, taking seven slow, smooth, tense steps. Then suddenly/sharply change direction and arm position on count 8. Repeat to stage right. Then person with back to audience spins open to L.

Verse: *Any turkey can **tap tap tap*** (both knees bent, feet apart, tap one toe three times)
*Any turkey can **clap clap clap*** (hands up and to one side of head)
*Any turkey can **snap snap snap*** (flinging alternating hands up)
Any turkey can tango (resume partner position face-to-face, switching places)

Repeat above chorus.

Verse: *Any turkey can **spin around*** (not touching partner, with R arm up)
*Any turkey can **touch the ground*** (R foot out and bend to touch floor)
*Any turkey can **strut through town*** (stand facing L, three quick steps in place)
Any turkey can tango (return to partner)

Repeat above chorus and repeat last line (one spins under the other's arm, then the other spins). Then repeat last line again slower (then walk quickly around each other). Then big finish (both open out to face front with one hand held at the end)!

"Santa Maria (Del Buen Ayre)" (for second to fourth grade): The song has a moderate to slow tempo and a slow-slow-quick-quick-slow rhythmic pattern. Choreography can be created using the following tango steps:

- **Basic step:** Walk five steps in eight counts, following a slow-slow-quick-quick-slow pattern, which will result in the feet alternating sides every eight counts. When stepping, keep both knees bent (African influence) and push with the back foot to propel forward and drag top of back toes.
- **Basic step with partner:** Same pattern as above, but facing each other. Holding either both hands or one, one person walks backward as other walks forward with same-side legs moving together.
- **Ocho:** Either with a partner or alone, cross R in front of L. Bring L to meet R and swivel a quarter turn to L, keeping

knees bent and shoulders, hips, and knees together. Then cross L in front of R, and repeat on the other side, tracing a figure eight on the floor, with elbows lifted, palms facing in, and keeping arms steady. Twist rest of the body. With a partner, intersperse the Ochos with above walks and only one person does the Ocho at a time.

- **Lunge:** With partners facing each other or one slightly behind the other, both slide same-side foot out to side into a deep lunge for three slow beats and hold. Then quickly come back up to straight. Repeat the other side. Or could lunge away from each other, holding on to one hand stretched out, and pull each other back together.
- **Circle each other:** One partner stays in place as the other walks around him/her with R hands held above head. Could go into a dip when circle is complete if the person who circles brings feet together, ducks under their own R hand, turns away from partner, but closer. Standing partner lunges with R leg, places hand behind partner's back, and takes weight. Then circling partner leans back and extends one leg.
- **Toe circles:** Either facing partner or standing next to them, both bend the knees low and draw circles on the floor with same-side toes two times slowly. Then quickly kick foot and quarter turn to same side as toe that was circling.

These are just a few simple tango steps, all of which should be done with exaggerated emotions and drama. Choreography can be created using any of the above steps, simplifying or complicating as appropriate for the group.

61. TARANTELLA – Italy
Second to Third Grade
Music: Christy Lane, "Tarantella"
Skills needed: formations, pathways, objects

This is a Gypsy dance that represents how a person might react upon seeing a tarantula spider. In an attempt to both get away from and scare off the frightful arachnid, the movements have quick bursting energy, shaking of tambourines, and hopping off the ground. All dancers hold one tambourine that **always stays in their right hand**, and it should have colorful (green, white, and red) ribbons streaming from it.

Dancers begin onstage in a scattered formation, standing with feet slightly apart, hands fisted on hips, and a tambourine held in the R hand. Note: tambourines can be made out of paper plates stapled together with a few beans or popcorn kernels inside.

After eight quick beats of intro:
- **Sixteen beats:** Cross, cross, open, open four times, with tambourine tracing an arc overhead from L to R on second and fourth (curved pathway).
- **Sixteen beats:** Hop on L foot eight times, with R foot touching floor heel-toe four times. Then switch legs and repeat, simultaneously pumping tambourine overhead up and down (straight pathway).
- **Sixteen beats:** Hit self with tambourine on L shoulder-R hip-L knee-R hip-L shoulder-R shoulder. Then beat it overhead with L hand two times. Do tarantella step (step-together-step) four times, moving forward (zigzag pathway).
- **Sixteen beats:** Repeat above, but do tarantella step backward.
- **Thirty-two beats:** With a partner, one on knee doing tambourine hits on their own shoulder and hip, while the

other does tarantella step around them for sixteen beats. Then switch parts and repeat (curved pathway). **OR** in groups of four, in a line front to back, all on knee doing shoulder hits, except back person, who weaves forward with tarantella step and kneels in front. Then next back person stands and does the same (wavy pathway).

- **Thirty-two beats:** Form a star with tambourines touching in center. All do tarantella step (or walk) around the circle for sixteen beats. Switch direction and have L hands in center of circle and tambourines out and up while going around for sixteen beats.

Music cycles through three times. At end, all kneel down onto R knee, place L hand on L hip, and dramatically stretch tambourine up on last beat in the music!

Nontraditional variation: Brainstorm other things that are frightening to the students other than spiders. Create movements that represent both how they would respond if the thing was present and how they would attempt to get rid of it.

62. TOKYO DONTAKU – Japan
First to Second Grade
Music: Sanna Longden, *Folk Dance Music for Kids and Teachers*, vol. 1, "Tokyo Dontaku"
Skills needed: size, focus, formations, objects

The name of the dance translates to mean "a day off in Tokyo." The movements represent some things a person might do enjoying a day off outdoors in the lovely city of Tokyo. As with many Japanese dances, the movements are very small and precise, with a lot of attention to detail. Steps are small and do not travel very far, representing the tight kimonos that are traditionally worn.

The movement pattern repeats and can travel around in a circle, following a leader who takes any path they like, or individuals can follow their own path.

Begin after sixteen beats pass in the music. Pattern cycles through four times, plus first movement again at end, which can finish in a hands-together bow facing audience.
- **Eight Beats: Open the door.** Forward slow step-clap two times. Backward quick step-step-brush/swing hands out and back together. Forward slow step-together-clap. Repeat.
- **Two Beats: Boat ride.** Step-touch and "paddle" with both flat hands to one side, then the other side. Only one beat each side.
- **Two Beats: Shading.** Shade eyes from sun (one hand with palm facing back next to side of face and other hand forward with arms straight and wrist flexed, palm forward). Hands switch quickly three times. Take three steps.
- **Two Beats: Walk in the woods.** Step and balance on one foot and make the shape of a wide round "tree" with fingers touching overhead. Lean slightly toward balancing leg. Other foot touching ankle. Repeat with other leg.

- **Two Beats: Clean up.** Stay in place with feet together and knees slightly bent with three quick wrist flicks under other elbow to represent "brushing the sleeves" of the kimono to clean the dirt off.

Tokyo Dontaku with fans. Each dancer has two small fans held between thumb and all four fingers. On ***Open the door***, instead of step-clap, step forward holding both fans overlapping in front of face. Then do brush down with backward step as usual. No change on ***Paddle*** step. No change on ***Shading*** step. On ***Walk in the woods***, no change in movement but hold fans with tips together overhead to form a point of empty space between fans. No change on ***Clean up***.

Nontraditional variation: Students can brainstorm ideas of outdoor activities they like to do in their community. Then create five movements that represent those things, the first of which represents opening the kind of doors they have.

63. TROIKA – Russia
Second to Fourth Grade
Music: Kauriga Balalaika Ensemble, "Troika"
Skills needed: formations, spatial relationships, grouping

This is an old and very popular Russian folk dance. The word *troika* means three-horse team. The dance is traditionally performed in groups of three dancers (two women and one man), and the movements represent the quick-moving prancing of horses pulling a carriage or sled.

The trios hold hands side by side (next to each other), to begin with arms in the W position. Trios could make a wheel formation, and all travel forward (in front of and behind another trio). Center person in each trio can rotate to next group forward, or trios can stay together and travel around space on their own.

Part 1: Traveling
- **Sixteen beats** - Run traveling with feet coming up high under body (kicking self in the bottom) and head held high, like a prancing pony.

Part 2: Under-arm spins
- **8 + 8 beats** - Do in-place runs while outer person in each trio goes under two arms of other two in group, followed by center person. Then both return to their places, then inner person, followed by center person, who repeats the same.

Part 3: Circling, stomping
- **12 + 4, 12 + 4 beats** - Trio forms a small circle facing in, and hands are on each other's shoulders. Cross step (around) to L first for twelve beats. Then stomp or do small kicks four times. Then repeat to R. If desired, center person rotates to next group, or trio stays intact and opens up to side-by-side position with hands held again, with one of the side people now in the center. Music cycles through six times.

64. VIRGINIA REEL – Colonial USA
First to Third Grade
Music: Christy Lane, "American Folk Dance Medley"
Skills needed: formations, directions, size

This dance became popular from about the mid-1800s in what is now the eastern part of the United States. It copied English court dances, but in a country, barnyard-type setting. It is danced at parties or other social gatherings. The movements are bouncy, upbeat, lively, and big!

This is a "contra" dance, where men and women are partners in separate lines facing each other. Most forward man and woman are the "lead couple." Lines should be four paces apart.

- **Bow:** All couples take three steps toward partner. Do a small **bow** on count 4, then four steps back, and repeat.
- **Elbow Skip:** Come together skipping. Link R elbows and skip around each other for eight beats. Then change direction and skip back to lines.
- **Do-Si-Do:** Walk forward and around partner without turning around. Men with arms crossed at chest, and women hold skirts or have hands on hips. Then repeat. First time pass R shoulders, second time pass L shoulders.
- **Sachee:** Lead couple holds both hands and slides down the middle to other end of the line. All others clap as they go by.
- **The Reel:** Lead couple does **elbow skip** with each other, with R elbows. Then separate and do the same with next person in line of the opposite gender with L elbows. Then back together. Then with each person up the line, alternating with a turn with each other.
- **Cast Off:** Back at the top, lead couple splits and leads their line away from center and moves to other end of line with all in their line following them.

- **Bridge:** At the other end, lead couple places palms together up high, and each couple goes under the bridge. The first couple through go to the top position to be the next lead couple. All others following form a longer bridge. Lead couple does not go through the bridge.
- **Push Away:** Gently push partner's hands and take four steps backward to separate into two lines. Repeat whole dance with a new lead couple.

End the dance with women first, then men. Do a big hitch-kick. Men bend down on one knee with hands on front knee, and women stand with hands on hips, both looking at each other.

Nontraditional variation: The traditional version is danced with a happy and uplifted feeling throughout, and the same structure can be used to express other **emotions** as well. In the eight movements described above, four other emotions could be matched with them (e.g., *bows*/fearful, *elbow skip*/disgusted, *do-si-do*/angry, *sachee*/sad, *reel*/fearful, *cast off*/disgusted, *bridge*/angry, and *push away*/sad).

65. WALTZ – Colonial USA, Northern Mexico, Austria
Third to Sixth Grade
Music: see each version below.
Skills needed: triplet step, formations, timing, spatial relationships

There are many waltzes around the world, and one thing that defines them is the 3/4 or triplet time signature. Practice the triplet step in place, traveling around the room, and adding various movements (such as spins) prior to learning any of the dances below.

BINGO Waltz: Marian Rose, "Red Rose Waltz"

Irish colonists in the eastern US did this country dance but possibly counted 1–5 or spelled another five-letter word of their choice instead of *BINGO*. Partners constantly change but begin in a circle of pairs, with women and men alternating.

Part 1: All hold hands and move into center and out again with "balance step." Then girls spin under arm of the boy to their L and end up in the space between the two boys to L. This is called a "rollaway" or "throw the girl away." Repeat this pattern four times, so all will likely have new partner.

Part 2: New partners face each other, holding both hands, and do two slides into the center and back out. Then repeat.

Part 3: Grand R and L, where dancers face opposite directions around the circumference of the circle and walk forward, passing each other with a handshake, also spelling out the letters to *BINGO* with every new hand hold. On *O*, say "OOOOOHHHHHH!" as the new partners either spin under each other's arms or high-five.

Music cycles through three times.

El Vals de los Paños: Asche & Spencer, "Carriage Ride"

This is known as the "waltz of the handkerchiefs." It was popular between 1750 and 1850 with the colonial people of the Pacific coast and New Mexico who were influenced by the Spanish and Austrian rulers of Mexico.

Dancers form trios joined together by holding four handkerchiefs or scarves between them. Arms are held in W position. A wheel is formed by an even number of trios, every other trio facing the opposite way and traveling opposite directions. If there are extra people, groups of four will work.

GREETING: On first sixteen measures of music, trios move toward one another with a triplet step (down-up-up) for two measures. Then stop, nod, and bow slightly (eye contact and flirting are OK). Then do the triplet step backward for two measures. Stop and nod to partners in their own trio. Repeat.

UNDER THE ARCHES: Outside person in each trio dances under an arch formed by the other two in their trio. Middle person follows and spins. Inside person does the same, and middle person spins again.

PASSING: Trios move forward again toward the other trio. Both outside people let go of handkerchiefs connected to middle person as they pass the other trio. Retake handkerchiefs again to continue once they are past the others. Then stop on eighth measure and swing arms and handkerchiefs down. Then proceed to the next trio they meet and repeat passing with each oncoming trio.

SWINGING/SPINNING: In place, trios swing arms back, then forward. Then middle person lifts arms and swirls scarves in opposite directions as connected dancers spin under scarf. Repeat spinning the opposite way so the scarves don't get twisted.

Nontraditional variation: Trios can create new movements following a triplet step while remaining connected by handkerchiefs.

Viennese Waltz: Johann Strauss II, *Le Beau Danube* (Grand Waltz)

This type of waltz is slightly faster than other waltzes, and there is a distinct down-up-up in the footwork with the triplet rhythm, causing dancers to take a larger step on count 1 and smaller steps on counts 2–3. It is all about counterbalancing with your partner while moving, and feeling your partner's weight shift is essential.

ONE HAND HELD: Partners face each other, holding R hands up high. **One triplet** step partners move together, **two triplet** step apart, **three triplet** step together again, and **four triplet** apart and change places. Repeat all. Then one partner does triplet step in place as the other spins under the arm, also doing triplet step. Switch parts and repeat.

FORWARD/BACKWARD: Partners face each other with both hands held in front with space between bodies. Posture is raised, with upper body leaning back slightly with elbows high. Leader steps forward as follower steps backward on same-side leg, taking a small step that brings feet together. Step on first foot again. Repeat going the opposite direction. Repeat eight times, traveling straight forward and backward.

TURNING: Same basic step as above, but leader turns forward and to L as follower turns backward to L. Repeat eight times, traveling in a curved pathway, spinning. Repeat eight times.

OPEN APART: Keeping one hand held, push apart with other palms. Step open and extend outer arms. Step back in to face each other. Repeat, opening other direction. Next triplet, one wraps the other into them, then unwraps. Then switch. Repeat.

66. WAVES OF TORY – Ireland
Fourth to Sixth Grade
Music: Sanna Longden, *Dances of the 7 Continents*, no. 1,
"Waves of Tory"
Skills needed: formations, spatial relationships

Tory is an island off the coast of Donegal with rough seas and high waves. This is one of a group of figure or set dances known as ceilidh (KAY-lee) dances, often done at Irish dance parties by the same name. The music has a dramatic feeling to express the ferocity of the sea on the west coast of Ireland.

The formation is two straight lines of about six to twelve people in each. Partners are next to each other in the lines. It is best to have an even number of couples because they join other couples to make groups of four that will later form "whirlpools" and face other groups of 4 in the over/under section.

Part A, sixteen beats, *Waves crashing*:
Dancers in lines join hands and step with a bouncy walk or skip (or a very quick step-together-step) toward each other, lifting all hands when they get close to the other line in four beats. Then walk backward, lowering hands. Then repeat.

Part B, sixteen beats, *Whirlpools*:
Groups of four form a R-hand star, all touching R hands together, turning clockwise for eight beats. Then reverse and form a L-hand star for eight more beats. Return to lines on opposite sides.

Repeat parts **A and B, thirty-two beats**.

Part C, thirty-two beats, *Waves sweep out to sea*:
Dancers turn and stand next to their partners and take R-R and L-L hands. Designate one lead couple. Then all "promenade," following

leading couple around the space once, ending up back in original places in lines on opposite sides.

Part D, forty-eight beats, *Big waves* (over and under):
Couples take inside hands, and every other couple faces forward, and all others face backward. All walk forward as couples facing forward raise hands and form an arch as couples facing backward duck under. Then all switch as they continue to move forward, each couple going up and down. When a couple reaches the end of the line, they turn around and go the other direction. Continue until all are back in original places.

Bow to partner at the end.

67. YANKO RIBBON DANCE – China
Pre-K to Third Grade
Music: Christy Lane, "Bu Bu Jiao"
Skills needed: objects, pathways, traveling and in-place, formations

Ribbon dances were originally intended to entertain royalty because of their color and beauty. They then became dances to celebrate harvest. Dancers hold one stick with a long colorful ribbon attached. Most of the time, the hand not holding the ribbon is behind the back.

Dancers can begin with a "flower" made of the ribbon and hold it in front of face and peek out from behind, hide again, peek again, hide again. Or trios can hold them together like a bouquet, then throw flower forward, causing the whole ribbon to extend.

These four main movements can be repeated up to eight times before changing to the next:
- The **PEACH**: Bend and stretch low to high (up to balls of feet), with ribbon going up and down, forming a curve like the side of a peach. Can add a jump with a half-turn.
- The **RAINBOW**: Touching the floor with stick on one side, trace an arc all the way up and over body to the other side on the floor. Spread feet apart and lunging out to side, then together when ribbon touches the floor.
- The **FIGURE EIGHT**: Or circles, standing in place, tracing that path in front of body.
- The **SNAKE**: Turn to face side and move backward with ribbon dragging slowly on the floor in a wavy pathway.

Dancers or groups can create many other movements using the ribbon sticks, such as the following:
- SPIN in place, with ribbon making a wavy pathway around body

- JUMP traveling around space, making big circles with ribbon, one circle per jump
- SLIDE sideways, with ribbon making big circles across body
- SKIP around space, with ribbon making an arc overhead
- SWING in place, with ribbon making a large "smile" shape in front of body

Nontraditional variation: Patterns can be created where groups could enter with an original traveling movement, change to an in-place movement, change to a different in-place movement, and exit with the same traveling movement. Also, dancers could be grouped by ribbon color to perform various movements one group at a time. Different formations could be used, as well as partnering.

World Dances by Grade Level

The following lists include all of the dances from appendix D, "World Dances," and are organized here by what I have found to be successful at each elementary grade level. You will notice all of the dances are listed more than once, simply because there is a range of ages for whom the dances are appropriate. The dances are also listed here in alphabetical order.

Prekindergarten	Kindergarten	First
Arirang	Appalachian Big Circle	Appalachian Big Circle
Bele Kawe	Arirang	Arirang
Caimarusa	Bele Kawe	Ballet
Che Che Kule	Caimarusa	Bele Kawe
Chicken Dance	Che Che Kule	Caimarusa
El Juego Chirimbolo	Chicken Dance	Canoe Dance
Here Comes Sally	El Juego Chirimbolo	Che Che Kule
Hokey Pokey	Fan Dance	Chicken Dance
La Mariposa	Here Comes Sally	Chinese Friendship Dance
La Raspa	Hokey Pokey	El Juego Chirimbolo
Peopleton Stick Dance	Itik-Itik	Fan Dance
Qashqai Scarf Dance	Jambo Bwana	Here Comes Sally
Yanko Ribbon Dance	La Mariposa	Hoe Ana
	La Raspa	Itik-Itik
	Lott Ist Todt	Jambo Bwana
	Peopleton Stick Dance	La Raspa
	Qashqai Scarf Dance	Los Machetes
	Second Line	Lott Ist Todt
	Shoemaker's Dance	Obwisana
	Tango	Peopleton Stick Dance
	Yanko Ribbon Dance	Qashqai Scarf Dance
		Santa Lucia
		Sasha
		Second Line
		Seven Jumps
		Shoemaker's Dance
		Tango
		Tokyo Dontaku
		Virginia Reel
		Yanko Ribbon Dance

Second	Third	Fourth
Adze-ee	Adze-ee	Alunelul
Appalachian Big Circle	Alunelul	Appalachian Big Circle
Arirang	Appalachian Big Circle	Bahay Kubo
Bahay Kubo	Bahay Kubo	Ballet
Ballet	Ballet	Bele Kawe
Bele Kawe	Bele Kawe	Bollywood
Canoe Dance	Canoe Dance	Bridge of Athlone
Chicken Dance	D'Hammerschmiedsgselln	Cumbia
Chinese Friendship	Gumboot Dance	D'Hammerschmiedsgselln
Dance	Gustav's Skoal	Four-Sided Dances
Fan Dance	Irish Battle Reel	Gumboot Dance
Hoe Ana	Limbo	Gustav's Skoal
Itik-Itik	Los Machetes	Highlife
La Raspa	Los Viejitos	Hora
Limbo	Mayim	Irish Battle Reel
Los Machetes	Merengue	Limbo
Los Viejitos	Musical Theatre	Los Concheros
Merengue	Native Alaskan	Los Viejitos
Musical Theatre	Prospector's Dance	Mayim
Native Alaskan	Qashqai Scarf Dance	Merengue
Obwisana	Sansa Kroma	Musical Theatre
Peopleton Stick Dance	Santa Lucia	Native Alaskan
Qashqai Scarf Dance	Sasha	Oxendans
Santa Lucia	Second Line	Pata Pata
Sasha	Sugarcane Harvest	Prospector's Dance
Second Line	Swing Dance	Sansa Kroma
Seven Jumps	Tango	Schuhplattle
Tango	Tarantella	Sugarcane Harvest
Tarantella	Troika	Swing Dance
Tokyo Dontaku	Virginia Reel	Tango
Troika	Waltz	Waltz
Virginia Reel	Yanko Ribbon Dance	Waves of Tory
Yanko Ribbon Dance		

Fifth	Sixth
Alunelul	Alunelul
Appalachian Big Circle	Appalachian Big Circle
Ballet	Ballet
Bhangra	Bhangra
Boboobo	Boboobo
Bollywood	Bollywood
Bridge of Athlone	Bridge of Athlone
Cumbia	Cumbia
D'Hammerschmiedsgselln	Four-Sided Dances
Four-Sided Dances	Gumboot
Gumboot Dance	Highlife
Highlife	Hora
Hora	Limbo
Limbo	Los Concheros
Los Concheros	Mambo
Mambo	Musical Theatre
Musical Theatre	Orixás
Orixás	Oxendans
Oxendans	Pata Pata
Pata Pata	Sansa Kroma
Prospector's Dance	Schuhplattle
Sansa Kroma	Swing Dance
Schuhplattle	Waltz
Sugarcane Harvest	Waves of Tory
Swing Dance	
Waltz	
Waves of Tory	

Appendix F
Stories

Below and on the following pages is a list of several stories and the appropriate grade levels that I have found work well for students. They are both enjoyable and provide learning opportunities around various personal and moral issues. Of course, the literary world is vast and varied, and school libraries or the children's section of any public library can provide a universe of material to choose from. Refer back to chapter 17, "Inspiration," for more details on ways to create dance works based on literature.

Here are just a very few stories, along with possible action words that tell them and suggestions for musical accompaniment:

Pre-K to Kindergarten: *The Farmyard Cat* by Christine Anello
Music: *Rhythmically Moving* series, vol. 4, "Sneaky Snake"

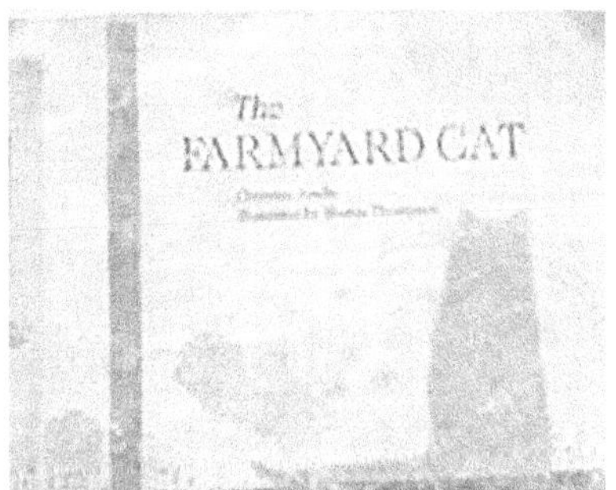

- HIDING
- FALLING
- CHASING
- SMASHING
- CHASING
- STOPPING
- SPLASHING
- WAVING

Pre-K to Kindergarten: *You Be You* by Linda Kranz
Music: Eric Chappelle, *Music for Creative Dance: Contrast and Continuum*, vol. 2, "Whales"

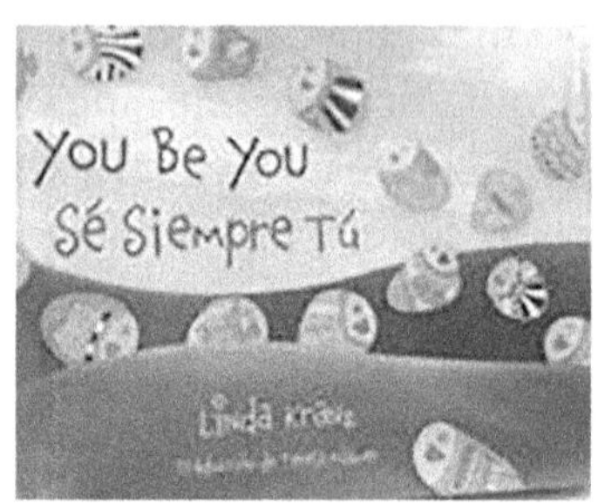

- Left/Right
- Circle/Line
- Up/Down
- Quiet/Loud
- Colorful/Plain
- Different/Same
- Big/Tiny
- Smooth/Spiny
- High/Low
- Together/Alone

Kindergarten to First Grade: *The Little Red Hen* by Paul Galdone
Music: *Dances around the World*, "Nixie Dances"

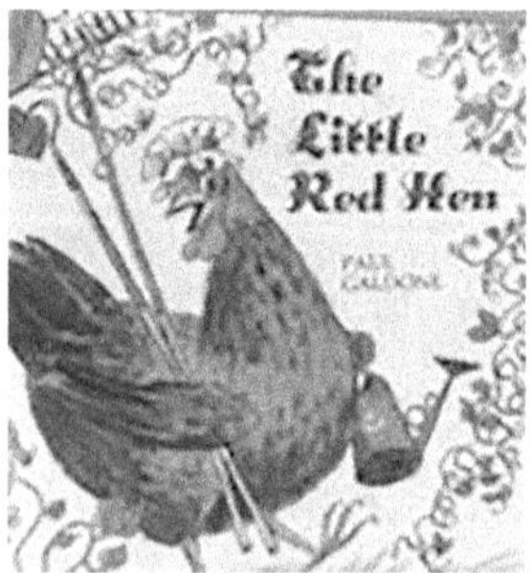

- WORKING – SLEEPING
- GROWING – SLEEPING

- CUTTING – SLEEPING
- CARRYING – SLEEPING
- BAKING – SMELLING
- OFFERING – SMELLING
- REFUSING – SMELLING
- WORKING

Kindergarten to First Grade: *The Little Old Lady Who Was Not Afraid of Anything* by Linda Williams
Music: Angelo Badalamenti, "Audrey's Dance"

- WALKING
- CLOMPING
- WIGGLING
- SHAKING
- CLAPPING/NODDING
- SCARING
- RUNNING
- COOPERATING
- SCARING

First to Second Grade: *Swimmy* by Leo Lionni
Music: Eric Chappelle, *Music for Creative Dance: Contrast and Continuum*, vol. 4, "Amphibious"

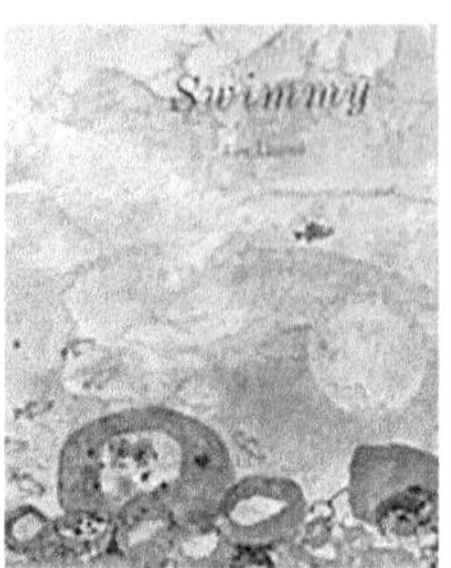

- SWIMMING
- DARTING
- SWALLOWING/ESCAPING
- FLOATING, CHUGGING, PULLING, GROWING, STRETCHING, SWAYING
- HIDING
- CONNECTING
- CHASING

Second to Third Grade: *Officer Buckle and Gloria* by Peggy Rathmann
Music: Eric Chappelle, *Music for Creative Dance: Contrast and Continuum*, vol. 1, "Jammin' on the Porch"

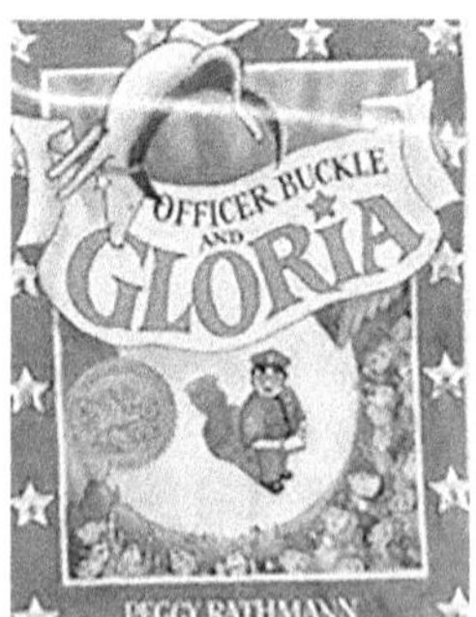

- FALLING
- SNORING

- INJURING
- OBEYING
- UPSTAGING
- OBEYING
- UPSTAGING
- CHEERING
- DISAPPOINTING
- SNORING
- SPLATTERING
- PARTNERING

Third to Fourth Grade: *The Legend of the Bluebonnet*, retold and illustrated by Tomie dePaola
Music: Michel Cusson, "The Wolf and the Bear"

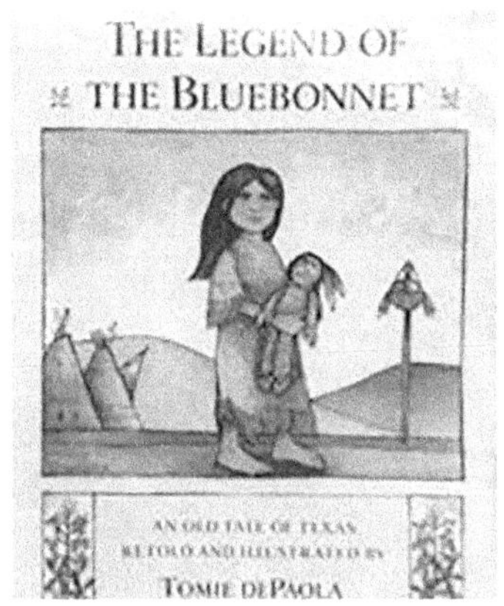

- DYING
- DANCING
- SACRIFICING
- SCATTERING
- BLOOMING
- RAINING
- RENEWING

Fourth to Fifth Grade: *The Spider Weaver* by Margaret Musgrove
Music: Bobby McFerrin, "Circlesong Seven"

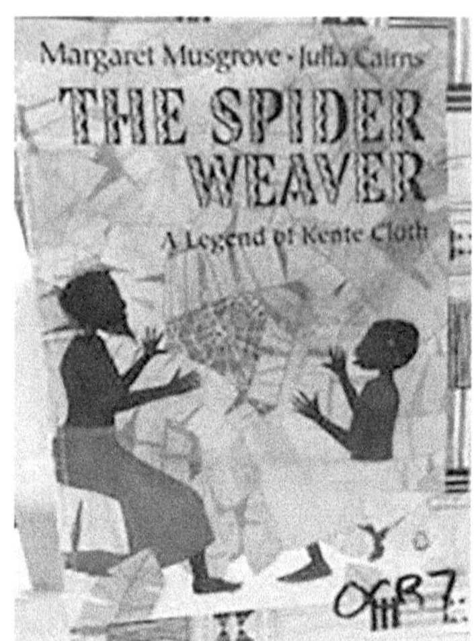

- WEAVING
- AMAZING
- COLLAPSING
- TROUBLING
- SEARCHING
- AMAZING
- TEACHING
- CELEBRATING
- WEAVING
- SPREADING

Fifth to Sixth Grade: *Coyote and the Magic Words* by Phyllis Root
Music: William Presland, "Spirit Flight"

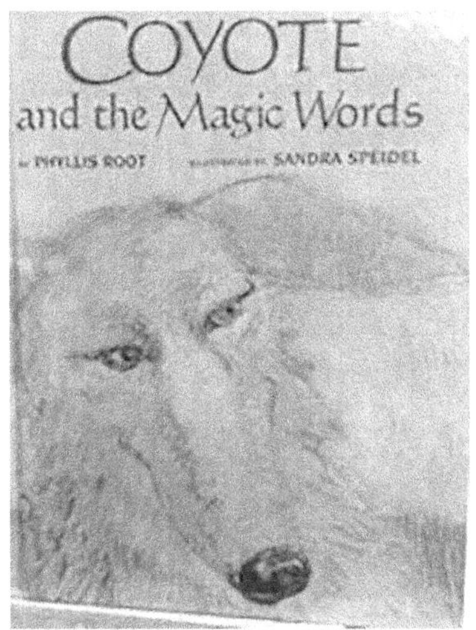

- CREATING
- SAYING
- PROVOKING
- ARGUING
- ARGUING
- LAUGHING
- TREMBLING
- COMPLAINING
- SLINKING
- REMOVING
- WORKING
- STORYTELLING
- HOWLING

Appendix G

Handouts

Most of the general population, it seems, doesn't have the same depth of knowledge that *dance arts* educators have; and providing some supplemental information can help. The documents included here are examples of what I have handed out to general education teachers and other interested parties at various points in our dance class sessions. They are fairly brief, written in less-than-academic form, and are listed here in a logical order that they might be shared. I hope this is helpful.

Introduction Letter to Classroom Teachers (two pages)

Karen Hahne
LAUSD elementary dance teacher
(310) 227-6165
kmh8785@lausd.net

Welcome to dance class!

Dear friend,

I am delighted to be working with you and your students this year and look forward to an exciting session of dance classes together! I sincerely hope this note finds you well, rested, and ready for a journey through the world of Dance Arts. Since health and safety are our highest priorities, there are a few precautions we will take to ensure dance can be experienced fully. Dance classes need to be held indoors and involve, at times, strenuous physical exercise

---

and occasional physical contact. A personal space bubble should be maintained by all dancers most of the time when in class, and we will be guided by local public health guidelines regarding the use of masks and hand sanitizer. Also, everyone should be dressed appropriately (as they would be for school), making sure shoelaces are tied, clothing is neither too big nor too small to allow freedom of movement, and shorts or leggings are worn under skirts.

Below are my overarching **beliefs** and **goals** for elementary dance students and will be infused throughout all lessons. They are as follows:

DANCE involves the body, the mind, and the heart working in harmony with one another to create an experience that strengthens and expands the capabilities of all three.

CREATIVITY is generating an original thought or idea, influenced but not dictated by outside sources and personal experience and by using skill and craft, transforming that idea into something that can be shared with others. What all artists do!

Goals for the body
- Alignment of the spine, legs, arms, and neck
- Increased strength, stamina, and flexibility
- Correct and safe execution of movements
- Coordination and precision
- Experience new ways of moving the *whole* body
- Injury prevention

Goals for the mind
- Concentration, focus, and self-control
- Organization of sensory input (auditory, visual, kinesthetic, proprioceptive, tactile)
- Awareness of time, counting, and rhythm

- Perception of space, distance, and shape
- Understanding of the laws of physics (motion, momentum, gravity, and force)
- Originality and craftsmanship in dance composition
- Making connections to prior knowledge

Goals for the heart
- Engagement and interest
- Connection of inner feelings to self-expression
- Experiencing improvement and success
- Moving with confidence
- Discovering new abilities and talents

Here are some guidelines for success in dance classes:
- **All students participate.** If there is a reason that some students are unable to participate in dance, I will defer to you for guidance. Additional expectations are that all students maintain a positive attitude and stay safe.
- **Your participation.** Seeing you engage in dance class makes a powerful impression on your students. I encourage you to participate in any way you feel comfortable, such as moving along with your students, encouraging and assisting them in their movements, and interjecting connections to other concepts they are learning.
- **Follow-up assignments.** I can provide additional activities to be completed on the students' time or your own time if you like. This may consist of writing/drawing assignments, viewing videos, or activities in preparation for the next class. I understand if your schedule doesn't allow for time to complete these, so please don't worry if you can't fit it in. The last thing I wish to do is to add stress.

Warm regards and many thanks. See you in class!

—Karen Hahne

A Guide to Grading in DANCE (two pages)

A Guide to Grading in DANCE

You will have many opportunities to observe and evaluate your students in our dance classes, even starting from the first lesson—from the warm-up routine, through movement skills practice, and in informal performances held frequently throughout our class sessions.

The following are the most general and universal abilities to look for in dance:
- **Memorized the dance pattern, phrase, or study**
- **Started and stopped on cue and moved with the music**
- **Performed all movements correctly and safely**
- **Was engaged in activity and danced with expression**

It is my opinion that each of these holds equal weight, and their abilities in each category can be evaluated on any numeric scale you choose and then averaged to calculate their grade. On the back of this page is a blank chart you might find useful in keeping track of your students' performance in dance.

Beyond the above four criteria, others that are more specific to each lesson will be presented. So if any of the above is not observed or applicable, other criteria could be used, such as the ability to follow a clear pathway in space, demonstrating the use of correct timing with other dancers, or clearly showing various energy qualities in movements. There is a blank column on the far right of the chart for this purpose.

If you prefer to evaluate your students' PROGRESS in dance, you can use the warm-up dance, which will remain consistent throughout the lessons, and simply observe them at the beginning of our sessions and again at the end. Or having students self-evaluate could be done through writing, at the beginning and again at the end of the session.

Using video is very helpful also, as you may need to watch a performance more than once to observe every student and/or multiple criteria.

STUDENT'S NAME	Memorized the dance	Moved on cue, with music	Movements done correctly	Engaged, showed expression	

The BrainDance by Anne Green Gilbert (one page)

created by Anne Green Gilbert

Music: *The Art and Heart of Drum Circle* by Christine Stevens, "Funk Groove" OR any music you like that is long enough. Counting is not essential.

BREATHE (Oxygen saturation): Do steady and even breathing. Body does different movements with each inhale and exhale, with a brief pause between them.

TOUCH (Tactile sense): Rub, pat, gently squeeze, or scratch all body parts. Use the various touches to "play along" on body with rhythm of music.

EXPAND/CONTRACT (Core/distal moving in to and out from the center of body): Standing, seated, or lying down, stretch arms and legs out from center of body into various expanded shapes (distal). Then pull arms and legs inward toward center (core) into contracted shapes.

HEAD/TAIL (Central nervous system strengthening): Arch spine so that head and tail are both stretching up. Then reverse the curve so head and tail are curved forward and look at stomach. Stretch both arms overhead toward one foot in back. Flip over and touch that foot. Then repeat. Move head and tail to sides and in circles.

UPPER/LOWER BODY (Dual focus): Imagine a horizontal line at the waist. Move only the upper half of body, while the lower half is frozen in any shape. Then switch and move only the lower half, while the upper half is frozen.

BODY SIDES (Separating brain hemispheres): Imagine a vertical line down the center of the body (midline). One side is still, while the other side moves (same arm and leg). Then switch. Also, open and close same-side arm and leg like a book.

CROSSING MIDLINE (Integrating hemispheres): Touch opposite side body parts, starting at head and working your way down to feet. Then come back up. Do various crossing movements, slapping feet in front and back, jumps, or stretches.

GETTING DIZZY (Vestibular system challenge): Spin without stopping long enough to get dizzy. Then stop and balance on one foot. Repeat in the other direction, balancing on the other foot. Whole body swings. Reach up, then slowly melt.

Twenty Body Movements (one page)

20 Body Movements

Walk	Stretch	Jump
Twist	Bounce	Slide
Skip	Shake	Swing
Hop	Spin	Gallop
Crawl	Run	Leap
Wiggle	Waddle	Bend
Sway	Scoot	

Alphabet Dance (one page)

Alphabet Dance

Music: Carl Orff, *Orff-Schulwerk*, vol. 2, "Tranquillo"

(Begin lying down as if sleeping)

- - - - - - Four-count introduction in music - - - - - -

A . . . Awake

B . . . Bounce

C . . . Curve

D . . . Dig

E . . . Expand

F . . . Fall

- - - - - - - - Change in music - - - - - - - -

G . . . Grow

H . . . High

I . . . Imagine you can fly

J . . . Jump down to the ground

K . . . Kick your

L . . . Legs all around

M . . . Monster moves

N . . . Near a friend

O . . . Over the rainbow

P . . . Punch the air

Q . . . Quickly

R . . . Run

S . . . Stop

- - - - - - - - Pause in music - - - - - - - -

T . . . Twist

U . . . Upside down

V . . . Vibrate

W . . . Walk and wave

X . . . X marks the spot

Y . . . Yawn

Z . . . Zigzag, z z z z z z z

(End lying down as if sleeping)

Spanish Alphabet Dance (one page)
(Not a translation of the English alphabet dance)
Danza de Alfabeto Español
Musica: *Flamenco Guitar*, "Canción de la Luna"

A (ah) . . . ¡Atención! (*attention*, stand up quickly)

B (be) . . . Brinca (*jump* in place)

C (ce) . . . Camina y Corre (*walk and run*, traveling)

Ch (che) . . . Cha Cha Cha (quick steps forward and backward with hips moving)

D (de) . . . Doble (*bend* at any joint)

E (eh) . . . Estire (*stretch* in all directions)

F (efe) . . . Forma Fuerte (*strong shape*, holding still)

G (ge) . . . Gira (*spin* in place)

H (ache) . . . Hombros (*shoulders*)

I (ee) . . . Izquierdos (*left*)

J (jota) . . . Juntos (*together*, touching another's left shoulder)

K (ka) . . . Karate (*karate*, pantomime)

L (ele) . . . Lento (*slow*, any movement)

LL (elle) . . . Lluvia (*rain*, hands and wiggly fingers moving down to floor)

M (eme) . . . ¡Movemientos Monstruosos! (*enormous movements*)

N (ene) . . . Natación (*swimming* with arms, standing or lying)

Ñ (eñe) . . . Ñoñería (*silliness*, funny faces and movements)

O (oh) . . . Ondulado (*wavy*, body movements)

P (pe) . . . Pesado (*heavy*, stomping)

Q (cu) . . . ¡Quietos! (*still*, frozen)

R (ere) . . . Retuerce (*twist*, at center of body or arms or legs)

RR (erre) . . . aRRiba (*up*, with arms)

S (ese) . . . Sientense Suave (*sit softly* down to floor)

T (te) . . . Toca tu Tobillo (*touch your ankle*)

U (oo) . . . Unidos (*united*, all hands in, in groups)

V (ve) . . . Volando (*leaping/flying*, traveling)

W (doble oo) . . . W con los brazos (*W* position with arms)

X (equis) . . . Xilofonista (*xylophone player*, pantomime)

Y (i griega) . . . ¡Yo! (*me*! point at self proudly)

Z (zeta) . . . Zancada (*stride* offstage)

Poetic Forms (five pages, by grade span)

Accents and Syllables – Kindergarten to First Grade

Choose a concept or idea. Then choose five words with varying numbers of syllables and arrange them with the single-syllable word last.

The following is based on "community helpers," written by a first-grade class:

CONSTRUCTION WORKERS   ***FIREFIGHTERS***

NURSES   ***BUS DRIVERS***

COPS

This is based on "school," written by a first-grade class:

TEACHERS   ***LESSON***

ATTENDANCE   ***AUDITORIUM***

LEARN

Explore and set movements that represent each of the words emphasizing the accent of the word with the strongest part of the movement.

I Wish . . . – First to Second Grade

This is composed of four lines that all start with the words "I wish . . ." Students can use their own ideas about what they wish for. Try to steer them away from emphasis on material possessions or acquisition. The last words in the second and fourth lines should rhyme.

Examples:

I wish the sky would stay red all day
I wish I could touch a cloud
I wish the stars would shine in the morning
I wish the music was loud

I wish the cars would never crash
I wish the road was straight
I wish I could travel to outer space
I wish there was no hate

Cinquain – Second to Third Grade

This is a descriptive poem in five lines, using mostly single words. Choose a topic and write a poem structured as follows:

NOUN

ADJECTIVE   **ADJECTIVE**

VERB   **VERB**   **VERB**

Four- to five-word sentence quoting subject and expressing emotion with a different but related NOUN

Here is an example of a cinquain written by a second-grade class on the topic of Santa Claus:

SANTA

JOLLY   *UNUSUAL*

JUMPS   *LAUGHS*   *FLIES*

"I CAUGHT YOU BEING GOOD"

CHRISTMAS

Explore and set movements that represent each of the words. Then remind students to use their <u>whole bodies</u> rather than just facial expressions or everyday gestures.

If/Then/So – Third to Fourth Grade

This is a three-line structure following a progression of describing a possibly unlikely situation and what might result from it.

Examples:

If I were a light bulb
Then I would glow hot
So people could read in bed at night

If the world was a cube
Then there would be sharp corners
So the oceans would be waterfalls

If cats were the size of mice
Then they could hide better
So dogs would not see them

If it were summer all year long
Then we could go to the beach every day
So school would be at the beach

Haiku – Third to Fourth Grade

This is a Japanese form of poetry with a line structure as follows:

First line: five syllables

Second line: seven syllables

Third line: five syllables

Choose any topic and write a haiku. Then explore movements that express images in the poem. The following haikus were written by third- and fourth-grade students:

The pounding rain comes
Drip, drop, drip, it is raining
The lake is shiny

I saw snow today
I am seeing white round snow
Today is Christmas

Red slimy lava
Lava dripping everywhere
Volcanoes explode!

Turtles are greenish
Turtles, turtles have big shells
Slowly turtles walk

Clouds look smooth like silk
Clouds look really nice in white
They float really slow

Leaves falling down deep
Crunchy, those leaves are so loud
It's a windy day

Apples are yummy
They grow on trees and smell good
Apples are the best

Dance is so awesome
We do different kinds of moves
We do exercise

Bears stand on two feet
Humans are afraid of bears
Bears eat from rivers

Dogs are brown or white
There are different kinds of breeds
They can protect you

I am so hungry
I want to eat right now please
Thank you for the food

My mom is the best
She is helpful and nice too
I love my mommy

<u>Here, There, and Everywhere</u> – Fourth to Fifth Grade

This poem structure includes adjectives and verbs, and writers can fill in the blanks. Also, the topic can be changed to other characters or nouns, such as *teachers, athletes, officers, mothers, horses, trees, clouds*, etc.

Here is the structure of the poem:

> ***Dancers here, dancers there, dancers, dancers everywhere***
> ***<u>(adjective)</u> dancers <u>(verb)</u>,***
> ***<u>(different adjective)</u> dancers <u>(different verb)</u>,***
> ***Dancers here, dancers there, dancers, dancers everywhere***

The adjective and verb spaces could be filled in with words selected by students, such as *smart/crawl, quiet/watch, beautiful/leap, crazy/strut, happy/play, shiny/twist*, or *bumpy/grow*.

Students create a dance phrase that includes three movements to represent the repeating two lines at the beginning and end of the poem. To include the element of space, dancers should create a movement that focuses on themselves and/or stays in place for **HERE**, a movement that focuses on a single object away from themselves, and/or travels to another place for **THERE**, and finally a movement that has multiple focus and/or travels all around the space for **EVERYWHERE**. Of course, students create movements to express the two different adjective/verb lines as well.

A dance to this poem structure could be performed to any music, but a good choice would be "Here, There and Everywhere" by the Beatles or the instrumental version of the same song by David Benoit.

Other examples:

> ***Trees here, trees there, trees, trees everywhere***
> ***Bumpy trees squish***
> ***Orange trees creep***
> ***Trees here, trees there, trees, trees everywhere***

> ***Cars here, cars there, cars, cars everywhere***
> ***Slow cars bounce***
> ***Black cars swim***
> ***Cars here, cars there, cars, cars everywhere***

> ***Teachers here, teachers there, teachers, teachers everywhere***
> ***Happy teachers grow***
> ***Spotted teachers twist***
> ***Teachers here, teachers there, teachers, teachers everywhere***

Five Senses Poem – Fifth to Sixth Grade

Connections to: **Language arts** (metaphor, simile)
Dance (movement interpretation)
Science (sensory perception)

Choose any topic, and in seven lines, describe your topic as follows:
1. ***Color . . .*** describe the color(s) of your topic
2. ***Feels like . . .*** (tactile sense)
3. ***Sounds like . . .*** (auditory sense)
4. ***Tastes like . . .*** (gustatory sense)
5. ***Smells like . . .*** (olfactory sense)
6. ***Looks like . . .*** (visual sense)
7. ***Makes me feel like . . .*** (emotional response)

Dancers can create a phrase of movement for each line of their poem. Remember to use **whole-body movements**. It is easy to use facial expressions or everyday gestures, but these are literal

interpretations rather than artistic. Using the whole body in creative and unexpected ways is what sets dance apart from pantomime.
Any music can be used to accentuate these dance studies. Try to find music that fits the topic and feeling of the poem.

EXAMPLES:

War is brown
It feels wet and cold
It sounds like thunder
It tastes like bitter grapes
It smells like yesterday's garbage
It looks like ancient ruins
It makes me feel like crying

Television is blue
It feels crackly
It sounds like laughter
It tastes like plastic
It smells like burning dust
It looks like flashes of light
It makes me feel annoyed

Wind is invisible
It feels like a push against my skin
It sounds like a faraway monster growling
It tastes like it's alive
It smells like the earth
It looks like everything that can move does
It makes me feel excited

Lemons are bright yellow
They feel cool and bumpy
They sound like a thud when they hit the ground
They taste sour
They smell fresh and clean
They look like little yellow footballs
They make me feel refreshed

Appendix H

Good Lessons in Limited Space

If you find yourself required to teach in a less-than-optimal space, rather than cancelling dance classes, here are some lessons that I have found to work well in either a classroom with desks or a space that is cleared of furniture but is too small for regular dance instruction. Of course, showing videos to students is an excellent alternative to getting up and moving themselves. But you can only do that for so many lessons before it becomes a dance appreciation class, which is also good, but not the point of this appendix.

This is my all-time favorite classroom lesson, and I call it **desktop choreography**. It can be done with any elementary grade level, from first through sixth, and is entirely done with students seated at desks in a classroom. This lesson helps students learn how to count and follow a beat in music while counting, create original movements, memorize a sequence, collaborate on a dance phrase within a small group, and perform their work for others. Some music I have used for this lesson are Eric Chappelle, *Music for Creative Dance: Contrast and Continuum*, vol. 2, "Caribbean Leaps" (four counts) and Dan Savell, "Driving a Jet" (eight counts).

After arranging students into small groups (which might already be done if you are in their classroom and they have assigned table groups), begin by playing the music you have selected and assist the students in listening carefully to the repeating patterns (rhythm) in the music and counting the musical phrases. Then the teacher demonstrates various upper body movements that change every time count 1 is repeated. Encourage your students to create the most interesting and creative movements they can and to avoid movements that are too simple, such as clapping for eight beats or tapping the table. Each member of each group must create an original movement that lasts the designated number of beats and teach it to the other members of their group. They decide on an order of the movements, practice, and perform together, taking turns with the other groups.

Other lesson structures that are good for limited spaces are the use of **poetic forms**, **stories**, and other lessons that involve written stimuli (see chapter 17, "Inspiration"). Part of the assignment can be for the students to write their own poems or stories and create movements that reflect images in their writing. Also, lessons that are integrated with other subjects can work the same way (see chapter 22, "Integrating Content Areas"). When your space is limited, focus on the nonmovement part of the project.

Below are references to various lessons described in previous chapters. So rather than repeat them here, please refer back to the sections indicated.

For younger elementary students:
My Hands. See chapter 11, "Element of Body," section "Body Parts/ Isolations."
Touch of Life. See chapter 11, "Element of Body," section "Body Parts/Isolations."
Movements and Shapes. See chapter 11, "Element of Body," section "Shape."
Grow and Wilt. See chapter 12, "Element of Space," section "Levels."
Clap and Move. See chapter 13, "Element of Time," section "Beat."
Mirror. See chapter 14, "Element of Energy," section "Flow."
Move and Stop. See chapter 18, "Choreographic Tools," Prekindergarten, Design Tool – Stillness. Use only in-place movements.
Echo Dance. See chapter 18, "Choreographic Tools," Kindergarten, Design Tool – Echoing
Che Che Kule. See appendix D, "World Dances."

For middle elementary students:
In-Place and Traveling. See chapter 11, "Element of Body," section "Shape." Only do the in-place part.
Echo Dance. See chapter 12, "Element of Space," section "Levels."

This is not to be confused with the echo dance for younger students. However, it does use the same music.

Two-Movement Combination. See chapter 13, "Element of Time," section "Timing." Use in-place movements.

Melt and Grow. See chapter 14, "Element of Energy," section "Force."

Chairs. See chapter 15, "Element of Relationship," section "Spatial Relationships." Perform in a classroom, where each student has a chair.

Gumboot Dance. See appendix D, "World Dances."

Hoe Ana. See appendix D, "World Dances."

Obwisana. See appendix D, "World Dances."

Tokyo Dontaku. See appendix D, "World Dances." Place emphasis on small size movements.

For upper elementary students:

Body Pinball. See chapter 11, "Element of Body," section "Body Parts/Isolations," Body Pinball.

Positive and Negative Space. See chapter 11, "Element of Body," section "Shape."

Symmetry/Asymmetry. See chapter 11, "Element of Body," section "Shape."

Body Percussion. See chapter 13, "Element of Time," section "Beat."

Three Kinds of Timing. See chapter 13, "Element of Time," section "Timing."

Stick and Milk. See chapter 14, "Element of Energy," section "Force." Use in-place movements.

Paintbrushes. See chapter 14, "Element of Energy," section "Effort Actions." Use soft dry paintbrushes, one for every two students.

Shapes in Transition. See chapter 18, "Choreographic Tools," Fourth Grade, Transition

Four-Sided Dances. See appendix D, "World Dances," Macarena and Pata Pata only.

Sansa Kroma. See appendix D, "World Dances."

About the Author

Karen Hahne has been teaching dance since 1985 in a wide range of venues to all ages and ability levels. Her dance background is primarily in modern dance with strong jazz, ballet, and musical theatre influences. Karen studied with Tandy Beal in Santa Cruz, California, at the Martha Graham School of Contemporary Dance and the Nikolais/Louis Dance Lab in New York City, as well as with the Francisco Martinez Dancetheatre and Charles Edmondson in Los Angeles.

From 2004 to 2022, Karen was an itinerant elementary dance educator with the Los Angeles Unified School District; and during that time, in 2018, she was a member of the Standards Advisory Committee for the California Arts Standards for Dance. She also held the positions of dance department chair for the 2009–2010 school year and was vice chair of the United Teachers Los Angeles–Elementary Dance Teachers chapter from 2019 to 2022. Prior to working for LAUSD, Karen lived and worked in Ketchikan, Alaska, as an early intervention educator, dance artist in residence for preschool through high school, and studio dance teacher. She also produced, directed, choreographed, and performed in multiple dance and theatre productions; was cofounder of the annual Gigglefeet Dance Festival, which began in 1995; and was honored as "Volunteer of the Year" by the Ketchikan Area Arts and Humanities Council for the year 2000.

Karen received her bachelor of education degree from the University of Alaska Southeast and has held a California-Clear Multiple-Subject Teaching Credential with a Subject Matter Authorization in dance and a Single-Subject Teaching Credential in PE. Karen also has expertise in working with students with special needs and welcomes learners of all abilities in dance.